CONSUMER GUIDE®

1987 CARS

Contents

Introduction

Since the domestic car companies had to resort to low-rate financing and cash rebates to clear out a glut of 1986 models, you would think that would make price increases unlikely on the 1987 models. Not so. With few exceptions, the 1987 models are more expensive than last year's. A fully-equipped Chevrolet Nova, for example, is priced nearly $1500 higher than a year ago, while base prices on the Dodge Caravan/Plymouth Voyager minivans are $700-1000 higher, and those vehicles have not been substantially changed.

However, most increases on domestic models are modest compared to what's going on with the imports. Base price on the popular Honda Accord LX sedan is nearly $1900 higher than a year ago and the Toyota Cressida's base price is more than $3000 higher. Most European cars are considerably more expensive than a year ago as well. The foreign manufacturers have raised their prices to try to make up for the decline in the value of the U.S. dollar in the past year. A year ago, every dollar that the Japanese car companies made in the U.S. was worth 240 yen. At this writing, a dollar is worth only 160 yen. European currencies have been affected similarly, so they too have been hurt by the fall of the dollar.

The result has been drastic price increases over the past year on most foreign cars. This situation has no doubt encouraged the domestic companies to increase their prices, so cars in general, not just imports, are more expensive.

This means that more than ever it pays to be a careful shopper who has the right information to get the best available deal on a new car. The auto editors of CONSUMER GUIDE® magazine have compiled roundups of the changes on more than 100 of the 1987 models, with the latest prices and specifications, to start you on the road to finding the right car at the right price. Prices, of course, are subject to change by the manufacturers. Numerical ratings in 20 categories are presented in chart form at the back of this book. The ratings are based on the auto editors' experiences with the 1987 models and tests of similar models from previous years.

Acura Integra

Acura Integra 3-door

Introduced just last spring, Integra will be carried over for 1987 virtually unchanged. Integra is available as a 3-or 5-door hatchback and serves as the lower-priced half of the Acura program, American Honda's new division. Integra stresses sporty qualities instead of luxury, the domain of the higher-priced Legend sedan. Power is from a double overhead cam 1.6-liter 4-cylinder engine with four valves per cylinder, available with either a 5-speed manual or 4-speed overdrive automatic transmission. The Integra 3-door looks, feels and performs so much like other Hondas that at times we think of it as a 4-seat CRX, a hatchback Prelude or a sportier Accord. Despite Integra's similarity to Honda's U.S. models, we still find it has a distinct, likeable personality of its own. The high-revving 1.6-liter engine (best enjoyed with manual transmission) has an eager nature and produces spirited acceleration, once you get it above 4000 rpm. Below that, there's just not enough torque for brisk acceleration, a problem more apparent with automatic transmission. Front seat room is adequate for most adults, though the wheelarches intrude on foot room, and the rear seat in the 3-door is short of head and leg room. With split, folding rear seatbacks, both Integra body styles offer good cargo-carrying flexibility. It can be argued that Integra is just another sporty Honda, but there's nothing wrong with having another good car on the market.

Specifications

	3-door sedan	5-door sedan
Wheelbase, in.	96.5	99.2
Overall length, in.	168.5	171.3
Overall width, in.	65.6	65.6
Overall height, in.	53.0	53.0
Front track, in.	55.9	55.9
Rear track, in.	56.5	56.5
Curb weight, lbs.	2326	2390
Cargo vol., cu. ft.	16.0	16.0
Fuel capacity, gal.	13.2	13.2
Seating capacity	5	5
Front headroom, in.	37.5	37.5
Front shoulder room, in.	NA	NA
Front legroom, max., in.	40.7	40.7
Rear headroom, in.	35.8	36.3
Rear shoulder room, in.	NA	NA
Rear legroom, min., in.	33.3	33.9

Body/Chassis

Drivetrain layout: transverse front engine/front-wheel drive. **Front suspension:** MacPherson struts, torsion bars, stabilizer bar. **Rear suspension:** beam axle, panhard rod, trailing links, stabilizer bar. **Steering:** rack and pinion, power assisted, 3.6 turns lock-to-lock. **Turn diameter, ft.:** 31.5/32.1. **Front brakes:** 9.5-in. discs. **Rear brakes:** 9.4-in. discs. **Construction:** unit.

Powertrains

	dohc I-4
Displacement, l/cu. in.	1.6/97
Compression ratio	9.3:1
Fuel delivery	PFI
Net bhp @ rpm	113@ 6250
Net torque @ rpm	99@ 5500
Availability	S
Final drive ratios	
5-speed OD manual	4.21:1
4-speed OD automatic	4.21:1

KEY: bbl = barrel (carburetor); **bhp** = brake horsepower; **torque** = pounds/feet; **Cal.** = California only; **TBI** = throttle body (single-point) fuel injection; **PFI** = port (multi-point) fuel injection; **MFI** = mechanical fuel injection; **ohv** = overhead valve; **ohc** = overhead cam; **dohc** = double overhead cam; **I** = inline engine; **V** = V engine; **flat**

= horizontally opposed engine; **D** = diesel; **T** = turbocharged; **OD** = overdrive transmission; **S** = standard; **O** = optional.

PRICES

ACURA INTEGRA	Retail Price	Dealer Invoice	Low Price
RS 3-door coupe, 5-speed	$9859	—	—
RS 3-door coupe, automatic	10389	—	—
RS 5-door sedan, 5-speed	10559	—	—
RS 5-door sedan, automatic	11089	—	—
LS 3-door coupe, 5-speed	10359	—	—
LS 3-door coupe, automatic	11889	—	—
LS 5-door sedan, 5-speed	12159	—	—
LS 5-door sedan, automatic	12689	—	—
Destination charge	255	255	255

Dealer invoice and low price not available at time of publication.

STANDARD EQUIPMENT (included in above prices):

RS: 1.6-liter (97-cid) PFI 16-valve 4-cylinder engine, 5-speed manual or 4-speed automatic transmission as above, power steering, power 4-wheel disc brakes, front air dam, front mud guards, wraparound bodyside molding, dual remote mirrors, tinted glass, rear defogger and wiper/washer, side window demisters, remote hatch and fuel filler releases, center console, front door map pockets, lockable glovebox, right visor mirror, cigar lighter, cargo area light, rear armrest storage area, cargo tiedown straps, cargo area cover, reclining front bucket seats, split folding rear seatback, 7-ounce cut-pile carpeting including cargo area and lower door panels, adjustable steering column, digital quartz clock, tachometer, intermittent wipers, P195/60R14 Michelin MXV tires. **LS 3-door** adds: alloy wheels, removable sunroof, cassette storage in console, 14-ounce carpeting, cruise control, AM/FM ST ET cassette with graphic equalizer. **LS 5-door** deletes sunroof and adds power windows and door locks.

OPTIONS are available as dealer-installed accessories; prices may vary.

Acura Legend

American Honda's rival for upscale European sedans will be available with leather upholstery and a power driver's seat for 1987. Leather upholstery and the 4-way power driver's seat are part of a new luxury option package that also includes heated outside mirrors and dual illuminated visor vanity mirrors. The luxury option package adds

Acura Legend

$1800 to Legend's base price. All 1986 Legends came with a standard power moonroof, but buyers can save $650 and gain some front head room this year by ordering a Legend without the moonroof. The front-drive Legend sedan was launched last March as the most expensive Japanese sedan sold in the U.S. Legend's basic design and 2.5-liter V-6 engine will also be used in the new Sterling 825 sedan, to be built in England by the Rover Group in a joint venture with Honda and marketed in the U.S. starting in January. Our conclusions are that this is a very good sedan that could just as easily wear a Honda badge instead of Acura. Some of the interior trim and dashboard controls look like they were lifted from the Accord LXi. The main differences are that the Legend is roomier inside than the Accord and powered by a larger, more powerful engine. Legend's V-6 makes expensive sounds and has the refinement of a BMW engine. The ride is supple and well-controlled and Legend shows impressive handling and road grip. Is it worth $20,000? We think it is, especially compared to some of its European rivals that offer less performance and comfort. Shop around; Legends are selling for well under suggested retail price in our neck of the woods.

SPECIFICATIONS

	4-door sedan
Wheelbase, in.	108.6
Overall length, in.	189.4
Overall width, in.	68.3
Overall height, in.	54.7

	4-door sedan
Front track, in.	59.0
Rear track, in.	57.5
Curb weight, lbs.	3077
Cargo vol., cu. ft.	NA
Fuel capacity, gal.	18.0
Seating capacity	5
Front headroom, in.	37.2
Front shoulder room, in.	55.8
Front legroom, max., in.	42.3
Rear headroom, in.	36.1
Rear shoulder room, in.	55.4
Rear legroom, min., in.	34.2

Body/Chassis

Drivetrain layout: transverse front engine/front-wheel drive. **Front suspension:** upper and lower control arms, coil springs, stabilizer bar. **Rear suspension:** MacPherson struts, trailing links, coil springs, stabilizer bar. **Steering:** rack and pinion, power assisted, 3.5 turns lock-to-lock. **Turn diameter, ft.:** 36.1. **Front brakes:** 10.3-in. discs. **Rear brakes:** 10.2-in. discs. **Construction:** unit.

Powertrains

	ohc V-6[1]
Displacement, l/cu. in.	2.5/152
Compression ratio	9.0:1
Fuel delivery	PFI
Net bhp @ rpm	151@ 5800
Net torque @ rpm	154@ 4500
Availability	S

1. Four valves per cylinder

Final drive ratios

5-speed OD manual	4.20:1
4-speed OD automatic	4.20:1

KEY: bbl = barrel (carburetor); **bhp** =brake horsepower; **torque** = pounds/feet; **Cal.** = California only; **TBI** = throttle body (single-point) fuel injection; **PFI** = port (multi-point) fuel injection; **MFI** = mechanical fuel injection; **ohv** = overhead valve; **ohc** = overhead cam; **dohc** = double overhead cam; **I** = inline engine; **V** = V engine; **flat** = horizontally opposed engine; **D** = diesel; **T** = turbocharged; **OD** = overdrive transmission; **S** = standard; **O** = optional.

PRICES

ACURA LEGEND	Retail Price	Dealer Invoice	Low Price
4-door sedan, 5-speed	$19898	—	—

Prices are accurate at time of printing; subject to manufacturer's change.

	Retail Price	Dealer Invoice	Low Price
4-door sedan, automatic	20523	—	—
4-door sedan, 5-speed, sunroof	20548	—	—
4-door sedan, automatic, sunroof	21173	—	—
4-door sedan, 5-speed, Luxury Pkg	22348	—	—
4-door sedan, automatic, Luxury Pkg . . .	22973	. —	—
Destination charge	255	255	255

Dealer invoice and low price not available at time of publication.

STANDARD EQUIPMENT (included in above prices):

2.5-liter (152-cid) PFI 24-valve V-6 engine, 5-speed manual or 4-speed automatic transmission as above, power steering, power brakes, power windows and door locks, air conditioning with rheostatic fan control, halogen headlamps, fog lamps, front mud guards, wraparound bodyside moldings, bronze tinted glass, height-adjustable steering column, lockable remote trunk release, remote fuel filler door release, 20-ounce cut-pile carpeting including trunk and lower door panels, front door storage pockets, right visor mirror, side window demisters, rear defogger with timer, front seatback storage pockets, rear passenger assist grips, door courtesy lights, trunk light, front and rear cigar lighters, reclining front bucket seats with moquette upholstery, fold-down rear center armrest, cruise control, AM/FM ST ET cassette with graphic equalizer and diversity antenna system, digital quartz clock, tachometer, variable intermittent wipers, 195/60R14 tires on aluminum wheels. **Luxury Package** adds: leather upholstery, 4-way power driver's seat, heated outside mirrors, lighted visor mirrors.

OPTIONS are available as dealer-installed accessories; prices may vary.

Audi 4000/Coupe GT

The 4000 sedan and similar Coupe GT carry on this year with minor exterior changes and mechanical updates. The sedan is available as the 4-cylinder/front-drive 4000S or the 5-cylinder/4-wheel-drive 4000CS Quattro, while the Coupe is sold only with the 5-cylinder engine and front-wheel drive. A restyled 4000 sedan that bears a strong resemblance to the aerodynamic 5000 line debuted in Europe this fall, but won't be introduced in the U.S. as a 1987 model. The new 4000 may arrive late next spring as an early '88. The 5-cylinder engine standard in the 4000CS Quattro and Coupe GT will get a horsepower boost (to 130)

Audi 4000S

before the end of the model year. Balanced, well-rounded performance and a functional design make the 4000 sedans and Coupe GT enjoyable to drive and practical to own. All three models have competent, entertaining road manners, though the 4000CS Quattro takes top honors with its permanent, full-time 4-wheel-drive system that makes it a fine choice as an all-season sport sedan. The 5-cylinder engine in the Quattro and Coupe provides better low-end flexibility and more sprightly acceleration than the 1.8-liter Volkswagen 4-cylinder engine used in the 4000S. The sedans have ample room for four adults and, surprisingly, so does the Coupe, rather unusual for a sporty 2-door. The 4000 and Coupe GT used to be reasonably priced, but the decline in the value of the U.S. dollar has helped raise prices of European cars considerably. Audi's generous warranties (3 years/50,000 miles on the whole car and six years on rust for 1986 models) are some compensation for the high prices.

Specifications

	2-door coupe	4-door sedan
Wheelbase, in.	99.8	99.8
Overall length, in.	177.0	176.6
Overall width, in.	66.3	66.2
Overall height, in.	53.1	53.8
Front track, in.	55.1	55.1
Rear track, in.	55.9	55.9
Curb weight, lbs.	2507	2337[1]

	2-door coupe	4-door sedan
Cargo vol., cu. ft.	11.2	12.8
Fuel capacity, gal.	15.8	15.8[2]
Seating capacity	4	5
Front headroom, in.	38.1	37.0
Front shoulder room, in.	53.5	49.2
Front legroom, max., in.	39.9	42.0
Rear headroom, in.	36.9	34.2
Rear shoulder room, in.	53.1	54.6
Rear legroom, min., in.	33.5	35.2

1. 2824 lbs., Quattro   2. 18.5 gal., Quattro

Body/Chassis

Drivetrain layout: longitudinal front engine/front-wheel drive (4wd, Quattro). **Front suspension:** MacPherson struts, lower control arms, coil springs, stabilizer bar. **Rear suspension:** torsion beam axle, Panhard rod, coil springs, stabilizer bar. **Steering:** rack-and-pinion, power assisted, 3.4 turns lock-to-lock. **Turn diameter, ft.:** 34.0. **Front brakes:** 9.4-in. discs. **Rear brakes:** 7.9-in. drums. **Construction:** unit.

Powertrains	ohc I-4	ohc I-5
Displacement, l/cu. in.	1.8/109	2.2/136
Compression ratio	10.0:1	8.5:1
Fuel delivery	PFI	PFI
Net bhp @ rpm	102@ 5500	110@ 5500
Net torque @ rpm	111@ 3250	122@ 2500
Availability	S	S

Final drive ratios

5-speed OD manual	4.11.1	4.90:1
3-speed automatic	3.42:1	3.08:1

KEY: bbl = barrel (carburetor); **bhp** =brake horsepower; **torque** = pounds/feet; **Cal.** = California only; **TBI** = throttle body (single-point) fuel injection; **PFI** = port (multi-point) fuel injection; **MFI** = mechanical fuel injection; **ohv** = overhead valve; **ohc** = overhead cam; **dohc** = double overhead cam; **I** = inline engine; **V** = V engine; **flat** = horizontally opposed engine; **D** = diesel; **T** = turbocharged; **OD** = overdrive transmission; **S** = standard; **O** = optional.

PRICES

AUDI 4000	Retail Price	Dealer Invoice	Low Price
S 4-door sedan	$15875	—	—
CS Quattro 4-door sedan	19850	—	—

Prices are accurate at time of printing; subject to manufacturer's change.

Dealer invoice, low price and destination charge not available at time of publication.

STANDARD EQUIPMENT (included in above prices):

S: 1.8-liter (109-cid) PFI 4-cylinder engine, 5-speed manual transmission, power steering, power brakes, power mirrors, air conditioning, power windows and door locks, right visor mirror, rear defogger, tinted glass, wide bodyside moldings, front door map pockets, choice of cloth or leatherette upholstery, full carpeting, tachometer, coolant temperature, oil pressure and voltage gauges, halogen headlamps, glovebox and luggage compartment lights, intermittent wipers, rear center armrest, rear headrests, cruise control, driver's seat height adjustment, 175/70R13 SBR tires on alloy wheels. **CS Quattro** adds: 2.2-liter (136-cid) 5-cylinder engine, close-ratio 5-speed manual transmission, four-wheel drive, four-wheel disc brakes, sport seats, decklid spoiler, AM/FM ST ET cassette, 195/60R14 SBR tires on 6-inch-wide alloy wheels (175/70R14 all-season tires available at no cost).

OPTIONAL EQUIPMENT:

3-speed automatic transmission, S	500	—	—
California compliance equipment	85	—	—
Full leather interior, Quattro	1025	—	—
Clearcoat metallic paint	355	—	—
Sport seats, S	275	—	—
Power tilt & slide sunroof	750	—	—
Trip computer, Quattro	225	—	—
Heatable front seats	195	—	—
AM/FM ST ET cassette, S	420	—	—

AUDI COUPE GT

2-door coupe	$17580	—	—

Dealer invoice, low price and destination charge not available at time of publication.

STANDARD EQUIPMENT (included in above prices):

2.2-liter (136-cid) 5-cylinder PFI engine, 5-speed manual transmission, power steering, power brakes, air conditioning, power windows, wide bodyside moldings, tinted glass, heated power mirrors, sport front reclining bucket seats, driver's seat heigh adjustment, rear headrests, leather-wrapped steering wheel and shift knob, full carpeting, front door map pockets, lighted right visor mirror, center console, trip odometer, clock, full instrumentation (tachometer, coolant temperature, oil pressure and voltage gauges), halogen headlamps, courtesy lights, intermittent wipers, cruise control, rear defogger, 185/60HR14 tires on alloy wheels.

Prices are accurate at time of printing; subject to manufacturer's change.

OPTIONAL EQUIPMENT:

	Retail Price	Dealer Invoice	Low Price
3-speed automatic transmission	500	—	—
California compliance equipment	85	—	—
Clearcoat metallic paint	355	—	—
Leather interior	1025	—	—
Rear wiper/washer	250	—	—
Manual tilt/removable sunroof	535	—	—
Heatable front seats	195	—	—
Power door locks	215	—	—
AM/FM ST ET cassette	420	—	—
Power signal amplifier antenna	95	—	—

Audi 5000

Audi 5000CS Turbo Quattro 4-door

The base 5-cylinder engine in the 5000 series will get 20 more horsepower, boosting the total to 130, though the more powerful engine won't arrive until later in the model year. Anti-lock brakes, standard on the 4-wheel-drive Quattro models and optional on the front-drive 5000CS Turbo sedan last year, are available on the base 5000S sedan and wagon for '87. All 5000 models with automatic transmission will be equipped with Automatic Shift Lock, an electro-mechanical device that prevents the transmission from being shifted from Park to Reverse or Drive unless the brake pedal is depressed. Automatic Shift Lock is being installed in the wake of allegations by safety groups that 5000 models with automatic transmission suffer from sudden acceleration that has caused deaths and injuries. Audi denies that the cars suffer from a technical defect, but the company is voluntarily recalling all 1978-86 5000 models to have the Automatic Shift Lock installed free of charge. The sudden-acceleration complaints against Audi are being investigated by the National Highway Traffic Safety Administration. Audi sales dropped off towards the end of 1986 from the publicity surrounding the sudden-acceleration complaints. We have been highly impressed with the performance of the current 5000 generation and gave last year's Turbo Quattro sedan especially high marks for its combination of performance, luxury, reassuring safety features and abundant convenience features. All models are covered by generous warranties and with 2-sided galvanized steel used on all body panels, there's little need to worry about rust.

Specifications	4-door sedan	5-door wagon
Wheelbase, in.	105.8	105.8
Overall length, in.	192.7	192.7
Overall width, in.	71.4	71.4
Overall height, in.	54.7	55.7
Front track, in.	57.8	57.8
Rear track, in.	57.8	57.8
Curb weight, lbs.	2844[1]	2954[2]
Cargo vol., cu. ft.	16.8	38.5
Fuel capacity, gal.	21.1	21.1
Seating capacity	5	5
Front headroom, in.	37.5	37.5
Front shoulder room, in.	NA	NA
Front legroom, max., in.	NA	NA
Rear headroom, in.	36.5	36.5
Rear shoulder room, in.	NA	NA
Rear legroom, min., in.	NA	NA

1. 3342 lbs., Quattro   2. 3437 lbs., Quattro

Body/Chassis

Drivetrain layout: longitudinal front engine/front-wheel drive (4wd, Quattro). **Front suspension:** MacPherson struts, lower control arms, coil springs, stabilizer bar. **Rear suspension:** torsion-crank beam axle with integral stabilizer bar, Panhard rod, coil springs, Quattro: independent; trapezoidal lower control arms. **Steering:** rack and pinion, power assisted, 3.5 turns lock-to-lock. **Turn diameter, ft.:** 34.2. **Front brakes:** 10.2-in. discs (11.0-in., Quattro). **Rear brakes:** 9.4-in. discs. **Construction:** unit.

Powertrains	ohc I-5	ohc I-5T
Displacement, l/cu. in.	2.2/136	2.2/136
Compression ratio	8.5:1	7.8:1
Fuel delivery	PFI	PFI
Net bhp @ rpm	110@ 5500	158@ 5500
Net torque @ rpm	122@ 3000	166@ 3000
Availability	S	S[1]

1. Turbo models only

Final drive ratios

5-speed OD manual	4.11:1	3.89:1
3-speed automatic	3.46:1	3.25:1

KEY: bbl = barrel (carburetor); **bhp** = brake horsepower; **torque** = pounds/feet; **Cal.** = California only; **TBI** = throttle body (single-point) fuel injection; **PFI** = port (multi-point) fuel injection; **MFI** = mechanical fuel injection; **ohv** = overhead valve; **ohc** = overhead cam; **dohc** = double overhead cam; **I** = inline engine; **V** = V engine; **flat** = horizontally opposed engine; **D** = diesel; **T** = turbocharged; **OD** = overdrive transmission; **S** = standard; **O** = optional.

PRICES

AUDI 5000	Retail Price	Dealer Invoice	Low Price
S 4-door sedan	$20060	—	—
S 5-door wagon	21390	—	—
CS Turbo 4-door sedan	26640	—	—
CS Turbo Quattro 4-door sedan	31215	—	—
CS Turbo Quattro 5-door wagon	32555	—	—

Dealer invoice, low price and destination charge not available at time of publication.

STANDARD EQUIPMENT (included in above prices):

S: 2.2-liter (136-cid) 5-cylinder PFI engine, 5-speed manual transmission, power steering, power four-wheel disc brakes, automatic air conditioning, power windows and door locks, power mirrors, rear defogger, rear wiper/washer (wagon), folding center armrest, passenger assist handles, computerized auto-check system, full carpeting including trunk/cargo area, cigar lighters, digital clock, coat hooks, center console, tachometer, coolant temperature gauge, heatable power mirrors, tinted glass, halogen headlamps, rear seat heat ducts, lamps for luggage compartment, ashtray, engine compartment and glovebox, locking fuel filler and glovebox doors, front seatback map pockets, lighted visor mirrors, wide bodyside moldings, radio prep with power antenna and rear headphone jacks, velour front seats with driver's height adjustment, leather shift knob, intermittent wipers, P185/70R14 tires on alloy wheels. **CS Turbo** adds: turbocharged engine, 3-speed automatic transmission, padded front center armrest with cassette storage, digital

Prices are accurate at time of printing; subject to manufacturer's change.

CONSUMER GUIDE®

clock with stopwatch, coin holder, full-length center console, digital boost pressure gauge, courtesy lights with delay, metallic paint, AM/FM ST ET cassette, eight-way power seats with driver's side memory, ski sack, leather-wrapped sport steering wheel, power tilt & slide sunroof, trip computer, 205/60HR15 SBR tires. **CS Turbo Quattro** adds: four-wheel drive, 5-speed manual transmission, anti-lock braking system, 10-speaker sound system, Alcantara/leather interior; full leather interior is available at no cost.

OPTIONAL EQUIPMENT:

3-speed automatic transmission, S	500	—	—
California compliance equipment	85	—	—
Perforated leatherette interior, S wagon	95	—	—
Full leather interior, S	1185	—	—
Clearcoat metallic paint, S	400	—	—
Pearlescent paint, Quattro	400	—	—
Heatable front seats w/temp control, S	195	—	—
Heatable front & rear seats, Quattro	350	—	—
Power seats w/driver's side memory, Turbo	750	—	—
Roof rails, wagons	200	—	—
Ski sack, Turbo	95	—	—
Power tilt & slide sunroof, S	1055	—	—
Trip computer, S	225	—	—
Anti-lock braking system, S & Turbo	1075	—	—
AM/FM ST ET cassette, S	420	—	—
7J × 15 forged alloy wheels, Quattro	250	—	—

BMW 3-Series

BMW will add three new models to its 3-Series next spring: a full convertible, a high-performance M3 model and a 4-wheel-drive sedan that will compete with the Audi 4000 Quattro and other 4WD passenger cars. The M3 2-door will have a dual-cam, 16-valve 2.3-liter 4-cylinder engine rated at close to 200 horsepower, making it a direct rival for the Mercedes-Benz 190E 2.3-16. The M3 is already available in Europe, as is the 4WD model (called 325iX in Germany); the convertible is not yet out. Until those new models arrive next spring, the smaller BMWs will be carried over with minor equipment changes and new exterior colors. The base 325 is available as a 2-door or 4-door, the sporty 325es comes only as a 2-door and the luxury 325e only as a 4-door. The 2.7-liter "eta" 6-cylinder engine became standard in the entry-level BMW series last year,

BMW 325es

as did anti-lock brakes. The carryover 3-Series models differ in interior trim and in the 325es sport model's firmer suspension, sport seats, spoilers and limited-slip differential. The standard 2.7-liter 6-cylinder engine develops lots of torque at low engine speeds, making it well-suited for use with automatic transmission. There isn't much head or leg room in the rear seat of the compact 3-Series sedans and the rear doorways are narrow on the 4-door, so try one on for size before you buy. BMW prides itself on sound engineering and quality equipment (the entire car is warranted for 3 years/36,000 miles), so there's nothing here that isn't functional. The result is a fully equipped car that offers plenty of driving enjoyment, but at a pretty steep price.

Specifications

	2-door sedan	4-door sedan
Wheelbase, in.	101.2	101.2
Overall length, in.	176.8	176.8
Overall width, in.	64.8	64.8
Overall height, in.	54.3	54.3
Front track, in.	55.4	55.4
Rear track, in.	55.7	55.7
Curb weight, lbs.	2710	2765
Cargo vol., cu. ft.	14.3	14.3
Fuel capacity, gal.	14.5	14.5
Seating capacity	5	5
Front headroom, in.	37.7	37.7
Front shoulder room, in.	52.0	52.0

Prices are accurate at time of printing; subject to manufacturer's change.

CONSUMER GUIDE®

	2-door sedan	4-door sedan
Front legroom, max., in.	NA	NA
Rear headroom, in.	36.4	36.4
Rear shoulder room, in.	52.4	52.4
Rear legroom, min, in.	NA	NA

BODY/CHASSIS

Drivetrain layout: longitudinal front engine/rear-wheel drive. **Front suspension:** MacPherson struts, lower control arms, coil springs, stabilizer bar. **Rear suspension:** independent, semi-trailing arms, coil springs, stabilizer bar. **Steering:** rack and pinion, variable power assist, 3.9 turns lock-to-lock. **Turn diameter, ft.:** 32.2. **Front brakes:** 10.2-in. discs. **Rear brakes:** 10.2-in. discs. **Construction:** unit.

Powertrains	ohc I-6
Displacement, l/cu. in.	2.7/164
Compression ratio	9.0:1
Fuel delivery	PFI
Net bhp @ rpm	121@ 4250
Net torque @ rpm	170@ 3250
Availability	S

Final drive ratios

5-speed OD manual	2.79:1
4-speed OD automatic	2.79:1

KEY: bbl = barrel (carburetor); **bhp** = brake horsepower; **torque** = pounds/feet; **Cal.** = California only; **TBI** = throttle body (single-point) fuel injection; **PFI** = port (multipoint) fuel injection; **MFI** = mechanical fuel injection; **ohv** = overhead valve; **ohc** = overhead cam; **dohc** = double overhead cam; **I** = inline engine; **V** = V engine; **flat** = horizontally opposed engine; **D** = diesel; **T** = turbocharged; **OD** = overdrive transmission; **S** = standard; **O** = optional.

PRICES

BMW 3-SERIES	Retail Price	Dealer Invoice	Low Price
325 2-door sedan	$21475	$17610	$21275
325 4-door sedan	22015	18055	21815
325e 4-door sedan	25150	20625	24950
325es 2-door sedan	24370	19985	24170
Destination charge	295	295	295

These models sell at or above retail in many locations.

Prices are accurate at time of printing; subject to manufacturer's change.

STANDARD EQUIPMENT (included in above prices):

325: 2.7-liter (164-cid) PFI 6-cylinder engine, 5-speed manual transmission, power steering, power 4-wheel disc brakes, anti-lock braking system, halogen fog lights, power outside mirrors, central locking, power windows, air conditioning, cloth or leatherette upholstery , AM/FM ST ET cassette with anti-theft feature, two-way manual sunroof, Active Check Control monitoring system, 195/65R14H tires on alloy wheels. **325e** adds: leather upholstery, leather steering wheel and shift knob, adjustable rear seat head restraints, rear seat folding center armrest, cruise control, Onboard Computer, power sunroof. **325es** adds: front spoiler with integrated fog lights, rear spoiler, sport suspension, sport seats, limited-slip differential, M-Technic steering wheel, map reading lights.

OPTIONAL EQUIPMENT:

4-speed automatic transmission	595	495	565
Leather upholstery, 325es	850	720	810
Uprated sound system (NA 325)	225	185	215
Limited-slip differential, 325 & 325es . . .	370	320	350

BMW 5-, 6- and 7-Series

BMW 635CSi

A new 7-Series sedan is coming to the U.S. next spring, probably with electronic suspension adjustments and anti-wheelspin controls. The new sedan's styling is a refinement of the current 7-Series styling, retaining BMW's traditional kidney-shaped grille and round headlamps, though the frontal area has been compacted for better aerodynamics. The new model will be called 735i and will be powered by a revised version of the present 3.4-liter in-line 6-cylinder engine, rated at about 208 horsepower (26 more than present). Next year, a V-12-powered model called 750i is scheduled to debut in Europe and is expected to eventually be offered in the U.S. Until next spring, the present 7-Series sedans will be carried over in 735i and L7 trim. The 5-Series sedans and the 635CSi coupe will be carried over with minor equipment revisions, except that the 524td turbodiesel model has been dropped and a 535is sedan has been added. The 535is is mechanically identical to the 535i, but gains sport seats, front air dam, rear spoiler and other trim items. The 635CSi's "sport seats" have been replaced by "luxury seats" and a second air conditioning unit for the rear seat is now standard. All the bigger, costlier Bimmers come with standard anti-lock brakes, BMW's thorough engineering, competent road manners and high-quality materials, plus the top-line L7 sedan comes with a driver-side air bag. The bigger BMWs get outrageously expensive, but you're getting top quality and good warranties for your money.

Specifications

	528e/ 535i 4-door sedan	635CSi 2-door coupe	735i 4-door sedan
Wheelbase, in.	103.3	103.5	110.0
Overall length, in.	189.0	193.8	197.4
Overall width, in.	66.0	67.9	70.9
Overall height, in.	55.7	53.7	56.3
Front track, in.	56.3	56.3	59.1
Rear track, in.	57.5	57.5	59.7
Curb weight, lbs.	3075	3380	3585
Cargo vol., cu. ft.	16.2	14.6	17.0
Fuel capacity, gal.	16.6	16.6	22.5
Seating capacity	5	4	5
Front headroom, in.	36.7	37.7	37.1
Front shoulder room, in.	54.3	55.4	57.7
Front legroom, max., in.	40.9	41.7	42.1
Rear headroom, in.	36.0	35.7	36.1
Rear shoulder room, in.	53.9	54.1	57.2
Rear legroom, min, in.	34.8	29.9	35.2

Body/Chassis

Drivetrain layout: longitudinal front engine/rear-wheel drive.
Front suspension: MacPherson struts, lower lateral links, coil springs, stabilizer bar. **Rear suspension:** independent, semi-

trailing arms, coil springs, stabilizer bar. **Steering:** recirculating ball, power assisted, 3.5 turns lock-to-lock. **Turn diameter, ft.:** 5-series: 32.8; 635CSi: 33.1; 735i: 34.8. **Front brakes:** 11.2-in. discs (11.0-in. 735i). **Rear brakes:** 11.2-in. discs (11.0-in. 735i). **Construction:** unit.

Powertrains	ohc I-6	ohc I-6
Displacement, l/cu. in.	2.7/164	3.4/209
Compression ratio	9.0:1	8.0:1
Fuel delivery	PFI	PFI
Net bhp @ rpm	121 @ 4250	182 @ 5400
Net torque @ rpm	170 @ 3250	214 @ 4000
Availability	S[1]	S[23]

1. 528e only   2. others

Final drive ratios

5-speed OD manual	2.93:1	3.45:1
4-speed OD automatic	2.93:1	3.45:1

KEY: bbl = barrel (carburetor); **bhp** = brake horsepower; **torque** = pounds/feet; **Cal.** = California only; **TBI** = throttle body (single-point) fuel injection; **PFI** = port (multipoint) fuel injection; **MFI** = mechanical fuel injection; **ohv** = overhead valve; **ohc** = overhead cam; **dohc** = double overhead cam; **I** = inline engine; **V** = V engine; **flat** = horizontally opposed engine; **D** = diesel; **T** = turbocharged; **OD** = overdrive transmission; **S** = standard; **O** = optional.

PRICES

BMW 5-, 6-, & 7 SERIES	Retail Price	Dealer Invoice	Low Price
528e 4-door sedan	$28330	$22945	$28130
535i 4-door sedan	33600	NA	NA
535is 4-door sedan	35200	NA	NA
635CSi 2-door coupe	46965	37570	46765
735i 4-door sedan	42475	33980	42275
L7 4-door sedan	46675	37340	46475
Destination charge	295	295	295

These models sell at or above retail in many locations. Add $650 Gas Guzzler Tax on 635CSi, $850 on 7-Series.

STANDARD EQUIPMENT (included in above prices):

528e 2.7-liter (164-cid) PFI 6-cylinder "eta" engine, 5-speed manual transmission, power 4-wheel disc brakes with anti-lock system, power steering, power windows and central locking, air conditioning, velour carpeting, digital clock, cruise control, rear defogger, halogen headlights and fog lamps, service interval and fuel economy indicators, trip computer, time-delay courtesy lights, engine compartment and trunk lights, dual heated power mirrors,

Prices are accurate at time of printing; subject to manufacturer's change.

lighted glovebox, AM/FM ST ET cassette with anti-theft feature, power antenna, 8-way front seats with choice of cloth or leatherette upholstery, folding front and rear center armrests, telescopic steering column, power sunroof, tachometer, coolant temperature gauge, trip odometer, electronic driver information system, toolkit, tinted glass with upper windshield band, heated driver's door lock, lockable glovebox, 195/70R14 tires on alloy wheels. **535i** adds: 3.4-liter (209-cid) 6-cylinder engine, leather upholstery, leather sport steering wheel, 200/60VR390 TRX tires. **535is** adds: sport suspension, ten-way power sport seats, front air dam with integrated halogen fog lamps, rear spoiler. **635CSi** adds to 535i: memory power driver's seat, passenger assist grips, premium sound system with EQ, roll-up rear window sunshade, door map pockets, 220/55VR390 TRX tires on forged alloy wheels. **735i** adds: 4-speed automatic transmission, rear reading lights, Kingwood interior trim, 205/70VR14 tires on alloy wheels. **L7** adds: supplemental restraint system, upgraded all-leather interior, heated front seats, 225/55VR390 Michelin TRX tires on forged alloy wheels.

OPTIONAL EQUIPMENT:

4-speed automatic transmission	595	495	565
635CSi	795	650	755
5-speed manual transmission, 735i (credit) .	(795)	(650)	(650)
Leather upholstery, 528e	1090	980	1035
Heated driver's seat, 735i	200	160	190
Limited-slip differential	390	340	270
220/55VR390 TRX tires w/wheels, 735i . .	850	650	810

Buick Century/ Oldsmobile Cutlass Ciera

Century and Cutlass Ciera are part of GM's A-body quartet of front-drive intermediates that includes the Chevrolet Celebrity and Pontiac 6000 (see separate entries). Century and Ciera are similar in content and price, plus both are available with a 3.8-liter V-6 not offered in Celebrity or 6000. Like its corporate cousins, Century and Ciera adopt this year's new Generation II 2.5-liter 4-cylinder engine as standard, with horsepower up by six. The optional 2.8-liter V-6 also returns as a Generation II, with fuel injection and 13 more horsepower than last year's carbureted 2.8. Model designations and option packages have been rearranged on both Century and Ciera. The Century T Type sedan and Gran Sport coupe vanish for '87 in favor of "T package" and Exterior Sport Package option groups. Olds-

Buick Century Limited 4-door

mobile has added a plusher, pricier Brougham wagon, while the extra-cost ES package has been dropped. Century and Ciera are roomy, pleasant intermediates that suddenly looked much older when the Ford Taurus and Mercury Sable debuted last year (GM's A-bodies arrived for 1982). Olds has tried to spruce up Ciera's styling with the S and SL coupes, introduced last spring sporting shorter, more rounded roof treatment to replace the squared style still used on the other A-body coupes. Despite this year's improvements, the base 4-cylinder engine lacks the power to move these cars at anything more than an adequate pace and is a poor choice for the station wagon. We recommend the optional V-6 engines instead, with the 3.8 having enough power to make most drivers forget about the V-8 engines of the past.

Specifications	2-door coupe	4-door sedan	5-door wagon
Wheelbase, in.	104.9	104.9	104.9
Overall length, in.	189.1	189.1	191.2
Overall width, in.	69.4	69.4	69.4
Overall height, in.	53.7	53.7	54.2
Front track, in.	58.7	58.7	58.7
Rear track, in.	56.8	56.8	56.8
Curb weight, lbs.	2707	2753	2919
Cargo vol., cu. ft.	16.2	16.2	74.4
Fuel capacity, gal.	15.7	15.7	15.7
Seating capacity	6	6	6
Front headroom, in.	38.6	38.6	38.6
Front shoulder room, in.	56.2	56.2	56.2

	2-door coupe	4-door sedan	5-door wagon
Front legroom, max., in.	42.1	42.1	42.1
Rear headroom, in.	37.9	38.0	38.9
Rear shoulder room, in.	57.0	56.2	56.2
Rear legroom, min., in.	36.1	35.9	34.8

Body/Chassis

Drivetrain layout: transverse front engine/front-wheel drive. **Front suspension:** MacPherson struts, lower control arms, stabilizer bar. **Rear suspension:** beam twist axle with integral stabilizer bar, trailing arms, Panhard rod, coil springs. **Steering:** rack and pinion, power assisted, 3.1 turns lock-to-lock. **Turn diameter, ft.:** 38.5. **Front brakes:** 9.3-in. discs. **Rear brakes:** 8.9-in. drums. **Construction:** unit.

Powertrains	ohv I-4	ohv V-6	ohv V-6
Displacement, l/cu. in.	2.5/151	2.8/173	3.8/231
Compression ratio	9.0:1	8.9:1	8.5:1
Fuel delivery	TBI	PFI	PFI
Net bhp @ rpm	98 @ 4800	125 @ 4800	150 @ 4400
Net torque @ rpm	135 @ 3200	160 @ 3600	200 @ 2000
Availability	S	O	O
Final drive ratios			
3-speed automatic	2.84:1	2.84:1	
4-speed OD automatic		3.33:1	2.84:1

KEY: **bbl** = barrel (carburetor); **bhp** = brake horsepower; **torque** = pounds/feet; **Cal.** = California only; **TBI** = throttle body (single-point) fuel injection; **PFI** = port (multipoint) fuel injection; **MFI** = mechanical fuel injection; **ohv** = overhead valve; **ohc** = overhead cam; **dohc** = double overhead cam; **I** = inline engine; **V** = V engine; **flat** = horizontally opposed engine; **D** = diesel; **T** = turbocharged; **OD** = overdrive transmission; **S** = standard; **O** = optional.

PRICES

BUICK CENTURY	Retail Price	Dealer Invoice	Low Price
Custom 4-door sedan	$10989	$9484	$10220
Custom 2-door coupe	10844	9358	10085
Custom 5-door wagon	11478	9906	10675
Limited 4-door sedan	11593	10005	10780
Limited 2-door coupe	11397	9836	10600
Estate 5-door wagon	11998	10354	11160
Destination charge	414	414	414

Prices are accurate at time of printing; subject to manufacturer's change.

STANDARD EQUIPMENT (included in above prices):

Custom: 2.5-liter (151-cid) TBI 4-cylinder engine, 3-speed automatic transmission, power steering, power brakes, bumper guards and rub strips, cut-pile carpeting, side window defoggers, halogen headlamps, map lights, instrument panel courtesy lights, glovebox, ashtray, engine compartment and trunk lights, lockable glovebox, cloth notchback bench seats, AM radio, headlamps-on chime, deluxe wheel covers, P185/75R14 all-season SBR tires. **Wagon** adds: load floor carpet and storage compartment, split folding rear seatback, two-way tailgate. **Limited** adds: windsplit moldings, wide rocker panel moldings, 55/45 notchback cloth seat, upgraded steering wheel.

OPTIONAL EQUIPMENT:

Engines			
2.8-liter (173-cid) V-6	610	519	560
3.8-liter (231-cid) V-6 (4-speed auto trans req.)	745	633	685
4-speed automatic transmission	175	149	161
Air conditioning	775	659	715
Tailgate air deflector, wagon	37	31	34
3.18 axle ratio (2.8 V-6 req.; NA wgn.)	NC	NC	NC
Heavy-duty battery	26	22	24
Center console w/shift lever	85	72	78
Heavy-duty cooling system			
w/air conditioning	40	34	37
w/o air conditioning	70	60	64
Cruise control	175	149	161
Electric rear-window defroster	145	123	133
Power door locks			
Coupes	145	123	133
Sedans, wagons	195	166	179
Tinted glass, full	120	102	110
Engine block heater	18	15	17
Digital electronic instruments	225	191	207
Temp gauge, voltmeter & trip odo	48	41	44
Above w/tachometer (3.8 V-6 req.)	126	107	116
California emissions system	99	84	91
Front door courtesy & warning lights, Ltd & Estate	44	37	40
Front seat reading lamps	24	20	22
Twilight Sentinel	57	48	52
Left remote mirror	25	21	23
Dual remote mirrors	61	52	56
Dual power mirrors	139	118	128
Decklid luggage rack	115	98	106
Floormats			
Front	17	14	16

Prices are accurate at time of printing; subject to manufacturer's change.

	Retail Price	Dealer Invoice	Low Price
Rear	12	10	11
Front w/inserts	25	21	23
Rear w/inserts	20	17	18
Lighted right visor mirror	58	49	53
Bodyside moldings	60	51	55
Wide rocker panel moldings, Custom	65	55	60
Windsplit moldings, Custom	22	19	20
Designer's accent paint	205	174	189
Special color (solid)	200	170	184
Sound systems			
AM/FM stereo ET	168	143	155
AM/FM stereo ET cassette	354	301	325
AM & FM stereo ET cassette w/graphic EQ	504	428	465
AM delete (credit)	(56)	(48)	(48)
Roof rack, wagons	115	98	106
Seat recliner, passenger only	45	38	41
Seat recliners, dual	90	77	83
6-way power seat (driver)	240	204	220
Third seat, wagons	215	183	198
Sport steering wheel	50	43	46
Tilt steering wheel	125	106	115
Lockable storage compartment, wagons	44	37	40
Flip-open glass sunroof	350	298	322
Heavy-duty suspension, F40	27	23	25
Gran touring suspension, F41 (NA wagon)	27	23	25
Landau vinyl top, coupes	200	170	184
Heavily padded, coupes	640	544	590
Full vinyl top, sedans	175	149	161
55/45 front seat, Custom	133	113	122
Bucket seats, Custom	97	82	89
45/45 leather & vinyl seat, Ltd	295	251	270
Trunk covering, Custom	47	40	43
Limited	25	21	23
Swing-out rear quarter vent windows, wagon	75	64	69
Remote decklid or liftgate release	50	43	46
Power windows			
Coupes	210	179	193
Sedans, wagons	285	242	260
Intermittent wipers	55	47	51
Rear window wiper/washer, wagons	125	106	115
Woodgrain bodyside applique, wagons	350	298	322
Exterior sport pkg., Custom sedan	100	85	92
Limited sedan	40	34	37
T pkg. (NA wgn)	568	483	525

Leather-wrapped steering wheel, Gran Touring suspenion, P215/60R14 Eagle GT tires on aluminum wheels.

Prices are accurate at time of printing; subject to manufacturer's change.

OLDSMOBILE CUTLASS CIERA

	Retail Price	Dealer Invoice	Low Price
4-door sedan, S 2-door coupe	$10940	$9441	$10010
Cruiser 5-door wagon	11433	9867	10460
Brougham 4-door sedan, SL 2-door coupe	11747	10138	10750
Brougham Cruiser 5-door wagon	12095	10438	11065
Destination charge	414	414	414

STANDARD EQUIPMENT (included in above prices):

Base and S: 2.5-liter (151-cid) TBI 4-cylinder engine, 3-speed automatic transmission, power steering, power brakes, front and rear ashtrays, cigar lighter, cut-pile carpeting, carpeted lower door panels, side window demisters, headlamps-on reminder, velour bench seat with center armrest, AM radio, deluxe wheel discs, P185/75R14 all-season SBR tires. **SL and Brougham** add: 55/45 front seat with individual controls, composite halogen headlamps, Convenience Group (underhood and trunk lights, right visor mirror, chime tones), knit velour upholstery, dual reading lamps.

OPTIONAL EQUIPMENT:

2.8-liter (173-cid) PFI V-6	610	519	560
3.8-liter (231-cid) PFI V-6	745	633	685
4-speed auto trans (2.8 or 3.8 req.)	175	149	161
Power seats (each)	240	204	220
55/45 front seat, base	133	113	122
Rear-facing third seat, wagons	215	183	198
Sport reclining bucket seats, base & S	147	125	135
55/45 front seat, SL & Brougham (credit)	(25)	(21)	(21)
Reclining seatbacks (each)	45	38	41
Power door locks, 2-doors	145	123	133
4-doors	195	166	175
Wagons	245	208	225
Power trunklid or tailgate release	50	43	46
Locking stowage compartments, wagon	44	37	40
Tinted glass	120	102	110
Power windows, 2-doors	210	179	193
4-doors, wagons	285	242	260
Rear shelf storage compartment, 2-doors	25	21	23
Lower bodyside moldings, base & S	126	107	116
Woodgrain exterior appliques, wagons	350	298	320
Bodyside moldings	60	51	55
Intermittent wipers	55	47	51
Full vinyl roof, 4-doors	175	149	161
Rear wiper/washer, wagons	125	106	115
Rear defogger	145	123	133
Air deflector, wagons	40	34	37
Air conditioning	775	659	715
Exterior opera lamps	102	87	94
Dual reading lamps, base & S	30	26	28

Prices are accurate at time of printing; subject to manufacturer's change.

CONSUMER GUIDE®

Remote left mirror	23	20	21
Left remote & right manual mirrors	61	52	56
Console with floorshift	110	94	101
Two-tone paint	200	170	184
Firm ride & handling pkg.	30	26	28
Touring car ride & handling pkg.	439	373	405
Automatic leveling system	175	149	161
Cruise control	175	149	161
Leather-wrapped steering wheel, base	90	77	83
SL, Brougham	54	46	50
Locking fuel filler cap	10	9	9
Tilt steering column	125	106	115
Super Stock wheels	99	84	91
Aluminum wheels	199	169	183
Locking wire wheel covers	199	169	183
Convenience Group, S & base sedan	51	43	47
Base wagon	44	37	44
Halogen headlamps, base & S	15	13	14
Heavy-duty battery	26	22	24
Delete AM radio (credit)	(56)	(48)	(48)
AM/FM ST ET	207	176	190
AM/FM ST ET cassette	354	301	325
AM/FM ST ET w/cassette & EQ	504	428	465
Rallye instruments	142	121	131
Digital trip monitor	90	77	83
Electronic instrument panel	225	191	205
Power antenna	70	60	64
Heavy-duty cooling, w/A/C	40	34	37
w/o A/C	70	60	64
Roof or decklid luggage rack	115	98	106
Custom leather seating	364	309	335
GT Pkg., base & S	3060	2601	2815

3.8-liter V-6, 4-speed automatic transmission, touring car ride and handling suspension, blackout exterior treatment, front air dam, fog lamps, left remote and right manual mirrors, full-length console with shift lever, contour reclining bucket seats, tachometer, trip odometer, coolant temperature, oil pressure and voltage gauges, P215/60R14 all-season tires on alloy wheels.

California emissions pkg.	99	84	91
Interior Comfort Group, SL & Brougham	544	462	500
Base & S, w/GT Pkg.	499	424	460

Buick Electra/ Oldsmobile Ninety-Eight

Buick's and Oldsmobile's flagship front-drive cars get revised model lineups for '87 and fresh front-end styling.

Prices are accurate at time of printing; subject to manufacturer's change.

Buick Electra Park Avenue 4-door

The Electra line loses the Limited coupe, leaving Limited and sporty T Type sedans and the posh Park Avenue coupe and sedan. Oldsmobile lifts a page from last year's Cadillac catalog and issues a more sporting edition of the Ninety-Eight called Touring Sedan. The base Ninety-Eight coupe is dropped, leaving a base sedan and Brougham coupe and sedan. Both Electra and Ninety-Eight now have flush-mount composite headlamps with combined tungsten-halogen high/low beams, while Buick offers a new quartz-drive analog gauge cluster as an alternative to the standard digital electronic display. On the mechanical front, the 3.8-liter V-6 standard in all models gets low-friction roller valve lifters and other internal changes to increase horsepower by 10 to 150. A late-'86 option expected to be in better supply this year is GM's anti-lock brake system (ABS), developed with the Alfred Teves company of Germany. The front-drive Electra and Ninety-Eight debuted in 1984 and last year were joined by the Buick LeSabre and Olds Delta 88, both built from the same basic design. Most but not all that you get on the Electra and Ninety-Eight also is available on the cheaper LeSabre and Delta 88, including the 3.8-liter V-6 engine and, on LeSabre, the optional ABS, which we highly recommend despite its high price. GM calls these "full-size" cars, but we view them as roomy 4-seaters, though they can hold up to six people with some squeezing. The trunk, however, is hard pressed to hold luggage for even four people, so that's one area where they aren't full-size. The price tags certainly haven't been downsized, but Electra's and Ninety-Eight's warranties cover major powertrain, suspension and electrical components for up to 36,000 miles and body rust for up to 100,000 miles, so you're getting more than plush upholstery for your money.

Specifications

	2-door coupe	4-door sedan
Wheelbase, in.	110.8	110.8
Overall length, in.	197.0	197.0
Overall width, in.	72.1	72.1
Overall height, in.	54.3	54.3
Front track, in.	60.3	60.3
Rear track, in.	59.8	59.8
Curb weight, lbs.	3269	3274
Cargo vol., cu. ft.	16.4	16.4
Fuel capacity, gal.	18.0	18.0
Seating capacity	6	6
Front headroom, in.	39.3	39.3
Front shoulder room, in.	58.9	58.9
Front legroom, max., in.	42.4	42.4
Rear headroom, in.	38.2	38.2
Rear shoulder room, in.	57.6	58.8
Rear legroom, min., in.	41.5	41.5

Body/Chassis

Drivetrain layout: Transverse front engine/front-wheel drive. **Front suspension:** MacPherson struts, lower control arms, barrel springs, stabilizer bar. **Rear suspension:** independent struts, coil springs, lower control arms, stabilizer bar, electronic level control. **Steering:** rack and pinion, power assisted, 3.1 turns lock-to-lock. **Turn diameter, ft.:** 39.7. **Front brakes:** 10.0-in. discs. **Rear brakes:** 8.9-in. drums. **Construction:** unit.

Powertrains

	ohv V-6
Displacement, l/cu. in.	3.8/231
Compression ratio	8.5:1
Fuel delivery	PFI
Net bhp @ rpm	150 @ 4400
Net torque @ rpm	200 @ 2000
Availability	S
Final drive ratios	
4-speed OD automatic	2.73:1

KEY: bbl = barrel (carburetor); **bhp** = brake horsepower; **torque** = pounds/feet; **Cal.** = California only; **TBI** = throttle body (single-point) fuel injection; **PFI** = port (multi-point) fuel injection; **MFI** = mechanical fuel injection; **ohv** = overhead valve; **ohc** = overhead cam; **dohc** = double overhead cam; **I** = inline engine; **V** = V engine; **flat**

Prices are accurate at time of printing; subject to manufacturer's change.

= horizontally opposed engine; **D** = diesel; **T** = turbocharged; **OD** = overdrive transmission; **S** = standard; **O** = optional.

PRICES

BUICK ELECTRA	Retail Price	Dealer Invoice	Low Price
4-door sedan	$16902	$14586	$15720
T Type 4-door sedan	18224	15727	16950
Park Avenue 4-door sedan	18769	16198	17455
Park Avenue 2-door coupe	18577	16032	17275
Destination charge	500	500	500

STANDARD EQUIPMENT (included in above prices):

3.8-liter (231-cid) V-6 engine, 4-speed automatic transmission, automatic climate control, electronic level control, six-way power driver's seat, side window defoggers, trip odometer, remote fuel filler door release, courtesy lights, headlights-on reminder, velour upholstery, AM/FM ST ET, power windows, P205/75R14 all-season steel-belted radial tires. **T Type** adds: uprated suspension, sport steering wheel. **Park Avenue** adds to base equipment: tilt steering column, AM/FM ST ET, power door locks, power decklid release front reading lights, cruise control, luxury cloth or leather upholstery.

OPTIONAL EQUIPMENT:

Automatic climate control air conditioning .	165	140	152
2.97 axle ratio, T Type	NC	NC	NC
2.53 axle ratio, base & Park Ave.	NC	NC	NC
Heavy-duty battery	26	22	24
Anti-lock braking system	925	726	850
Heavy-duty engine & transmission cooling .	40	34	37
Cruise control, base & T Type	175	149	161
Rear defogger	145	123	133
Power door locks, base & T Type	195	166	179
Automatic power door locks, base & T Type .	285	242	260
Park Ave.	90	77	83
Four-note horn	28	24	26
Engine block heater	18	15	17
Low washer fluid indicator	16	14	15
Low fuel indicator	16	14	15
Tach, temp, oil pressure & voltage gauges .	126	107	116
Electronic instruments (NA T Type; int. wipers & tilt steering req.)	315	268	290
Keyless entry system (NA T Type; power locks req.)	185	157	170
Door courtesy & warning lights, base & T Type	70	60	64
Cornering lamps	60	51	55

Prices are accurate at time of printing; subject to manufacturer's change.

Oldsmobile Ninety-Eight Touring Sedan

Illuminated driver's door lock & interior light control	75	64	69
Twilight Sentinel	60	51	55
Front & rear monitor lamps	77	65	71
Rear seat reading lamps, base & T Type	50	43	46
Decklid luggage rack	115	98	106
Front floormats w/inserts, base	25	21	23
Rear floormats w/inserts, base	20	17	18
Trunk mat	15	13	14
Dual remote mirrors, base & T Type	91	77	84
Dual power mirrors w/heated left, base & T Type	126	107	116
Park Ave.	35	30	32
Lighted visor mirror, base & T Type (each)	58	49	53
Automatic day/night mirror	80	68	74
Special exterior color (NA T Type)	200	170	184
w/Firemist paint	210	179	193
AM/FM stereo ET cassette	132	112	121
Above w/AM stereo & graphic EQ	282	240	260
Delco-GM/Bose music system	905	769	835
Delete standard radio (credit)	(275)	(234)	(234)
Concert Sound speakers	70	60	64
Automatic power antenna	70	60	64
Astroroof	1230	1046	1130
Power passenger seat	240	204	220
Memory power driver's seat	178	151	164
Power recliner, each side	145	123	133
Tilt steering col., base & T Type	125	106	115
Tilt & telescope, base	185	157	170
Park Ave.	60	51	55
Cassette tape storage, T Type	25	21	23

Prices are accurate at time of printing; subject to manufacturer's change.

	Retail Price	Dealer Invoice	Low Price
Heavy-duty suspension (exc. T Type) ...	27	23	25
Gran Touring suspension (std. T Type) ..	27	23	25
Theft deterrent system	159	135	146
Heavily padded full vinyl top (NA T Type) .	260	221	240
55/45 leather & vinyl front seat, Park Ave..	425	361	390
45/45 leather & vinyl front seat, T Type ..	325	276	300
Deluxe trunk trim	53	45	49
Power trunklid pulldown	80	68	74
Power trunk release, base & T Type	50	43	46
Aluminum wheels, base	255	217	235
Park Ave....................	220	187	200
Locking wire wheel covers, base	199	169	183
Park Ave....................	164	139	151
Intermittent wipers, base & T Type	55	47	51
T pkg.[1], base	508	432	465
Park Ave....................	407	346	375

Leather-wrapped steering wheel, Gran Touring suspension, 2.97 axle ratio, P215/65R15 Eagle GT tires on aluminum wheels.

Cellular telephone accommodation	215	183	198

OLDSMOBILE NINETY-EIGHT REGENCY

	Retail Price	Dealer Invoice	Low Price
4-door sedan	$17371	$14991	$15980
Brougham 2-door coupe	18388	15869	16915
Brougham 4-door sedan	18388	15869	16915
Destination charge	500	500	500

STANDARD EQUIPMENT (included in above prices):

3.8-liter (231-cid) PFI V-6 engine, 4-speed automatic transmission, power steering, power brakes, power windows and door locks, air conditioning, dual remote mirrors, halogen headlamps, opera lamps, front and rear armrests and cigar lighters, right visor mirror, trip odometer, reading lamp, AM/FM ST ET, 6-way power driver's seat, side window defoggers, tinted glass, padded vinyl landau roof (coupes), P205/75R14 all-season SBR tires. **Brougham** adds: cornering lamps, wire wheel covers w/locks, sail panel reading lamps, automatic climate control, intermittent wipers.

OPTIONAL EQUIPMENT:

Anti-lock braking system	925	786	850
6-way power passenger seat	240	204	220
Power driver's seat w/memory	178	151	164
Automatic power door locks	90	77	83
Reclining seatbacks (each)	90	77	83
Power operated	145	123	133

Prices are accurate at time of printing; subject to manufacturer's change.

Power decklid release	50	43	46
Bodyside moldings, base	60	51	55
Full padded vinyl roof	260	221	240
Intermittent wipers	55	47	51
Astroroof	1230	1046	1130
Rear defogger	145	123	133
Tempmatic air conditioning	125	106	115
Sail panel reading lamps, base	48	41	44
Illuminated entry system	75	64	69
Automatic day/night mirror	80	68	74
Power remote mirrors	65	55	60
Illuminated right visor mirror	51	43	47
Two-tone paint, 4-doors	225	191	205
Touring car ride & handling pkg., base	348	296	320
Brougham	149	127	137
Firm ride & handling pkg.	30	26	28
Engine block heater	18	15	16
Cruise control	175	149	161
Power fuel door release	25	21	23
Tilt steering wheel, base	125	106	115
Tilt & telescope steering wheel, Brougham	60	51	55
Base	185	157	170
Aluminum wheels, base (NC Brougham)	199	169	183
Locking wire wheel covers, base	199	169	183
Puncture-sealing tires	150	128	138
Twilight Sentinel	60	51	55
Cornering lamps	60	51	55
High-capacity battery	26	22	24
AM/FM ST ET delete (credit)	(256)	(218)	(218)
AM/FM ST ET cassette	157	133	144
40-channel CB	290	247	265
Delco-GM/Bose music system	885	752	815
Voice information system	82	70	75
Cellular phone wiring	395	336	365
Cellular phone	2850	2423	2620
Gauge pkg.	66	56	61
Digital trip monitor	90	77	83
Exterior lamp monitors	77	65	71
Electronic instruments	299	254	275
5-wire harness	30	26	28
California emissions pkg.	99	84	91
High-capacity radiator	30	26	28
Glamour metallic paint	210	179	193
Rear bumper guards	24	20	22
Decklid luggage rack	115	98	106
Leather trim	379	322	350
Grande pkg., Brougham	975	829	895
Reminder pkg.	82	70	75

Prices are accurate at time of printing; subject to manufacturer's change.

	Retail Price	Dealer Invoice	Low Price
Interior comfort group	584	496	535
w/Grande pkg.	205	174	189

Buick LeSabre/ Oldsmobile Delta 88

Buick LeSabre 2-door

New last year, the Buick and Oldsmobile versions of the GM front-drive H-body gain composite headlamps, while an anti-lock braking system (ABS) is now optional on the LeSabre (but not on Delta 88). Automatic front seat belts will be standard equipment on the new LeSabre T Type coupe and all Delta 88s to help GM meet the new federal requirement for passive restraints on 10 percent of 1987 models. The same system is found on selected models at other GM divisions; it's a 3-point lap/shoulder belt with the outboard inertia reels on the doors instead of the central roof pillars. Leaving the single inboard buckle fastened allows automatic belt extension and retraction as the door is opened and closed, so that occupants need only slide in under the belt to be properly harnessed. Last year's base 3.0-liter V-6 has been dropped, making a 3.8 V-6 standard and the only engine available. The T Type coupe comes with a complete set of quartz-drive analog instruments standard; the analog gauges are available on other models as a new option. Since LeSabre and Delta 88 are built from the same design as the Electra and Ninety-Eight, they are mechanically the same and have similar interior and trunk

Prices are accurate at time of printing; subject to manufacturer's change.

space, but the higher-priced Electra and Ninety-Eight are plusher and come with more standard equipment. We welcome the addition of anti-lock brakes to LeSabre's options list, since it makes this important safety feature available on lower-cost cars that more motorists can afford. LeSabre and Delta 88 aren't cheap by any means, but they're definitely worth looking at if you're in the market for a roomy family car.

Specifications

	2-door coupe	4-door sedan
Wheelbase, in.	110.8	110.8
Overall length, in.	196.2	196.2
Overall width, in.	72.1	72.1
Overall height, in.	54.7	55.5
Front track, in.	60.3	60.3
Rear track, in.	59.8	59.8
Curb weight, lbs.	3196	3236
Cargo vol., cu. ft.	15.7	16.4
Fuel capacity, gal.	18.0	18.0
Seating capacity	6	6
Front headroom, in.	38.1	38.9
Front shoulder room, in.	59.4	59.1
Front legroom, max., in.	42.4	42.4
Rear headroom, in.	37.6	38.3
Rear shoulder room, in.	57.8	59.5
Rear legroom, min., in.	37.4	38.7

Body/Chassis

Drivetrain layout: transverse front engine/front-wheel drive. **Front suspension:** MacPherson struts, lower control arms, barrel springs, stabilizer bar. **Rear suspension:** independent, struts, coil spring, lower control arms, stabilizer bar. **Steering:** rack and pinion, power assisted, 3.1 turns lock-to-lock. **Turn diameter, ft.:** 39.7. **Front brakes:** 10.0-in. discs. **Rear brakes:** 8.9-in. drums. **Construction:** unit.

Powertrains

	ohv V-6
Displacement, l/cu. in.	3.8/231
Compression ratio	8.5:1
Fuel delivery	PFI
Net bhp @ rpm	150 @ 4400
Net torque @ rpm	200 @ 2000
Availability	S

Final drive ratios

4-speed OD automatic 2.73:1

KEY: bbl = barrel (carburetor); **bhp** = brake horsepower; **torque** = pounds/feet; **Cal.** = California only; **TBI** = throttle body (single-point) fuel injection; **PFI** = port (multi-point) fuel injection; **MFI** = mechanical fuel injection; **ohv** = overhead valve; **ohc** = overhead cam; **dohc** = double overhead cam; **I** = inline engine; **V** = V engine; **flat** = horizontally opposed engine; **D** = diesel; **T** = turbocharged; **OD** = overdrive transmission; **S** = standard; **O** = optional.

PRICES

BUICK LE SABRE	Retail Price	Dealer Invoice	Low Price
4-door sedan	$13438	$11597	$12495
Custom 4-door sedan	13616	11751	12665
Custom 2-door coupe	13616	11751	12665
Limited 4-door sedan	14918	12874	13875
Limited 2-door coupe	14918	12874	13875
Destination charge	475	475	475

STANDARD EQUIPMENT (included in above prices):

3.8-liter (231-cid) PFI V-6 engine, 4-speed automatic transmission, power steering, power brakes, air conditioning, bumper rub strips, full carpeting including trunk, tinted glass, dual-note horn, AM radio, cloth bench seat, headlamps-on warning tone, engine compartment and trunk lights, deluxe wheel covers, P205/75R14 all-season tires. **Custom** adds: notchback front seat, left remote and right manual mirrors. **Limited** adds: rear bumper guards, electroluminescent instrument panel, lower bodyside moldings, 55/45 reclining cloth front seat, upgraded steering wheel.

OPTIONAL EQUIPMENT:

Automatic climate control	165	140	152
2.97 axle ratio	NC	NC	NC
Anti-lock braking system	925	786	850
Heavy-duty battery	26	22	24
Rear bumper guards, base & Custom ...	24	20	22
Heavy-duty engine and transmission cooling	40	34	37
Cruise control	175	149	161
Rear defogger	145	123	133
Power door locks, coupes	145	123	133
Sedans	195	166	179
Engine block heater	18	15	17
Trip odometer	16	14	15
Tachometer, temp., oil press. & voltage gauges w/o console	126	107	116

Prices are accurate at time of printing; subject to manufacturer's change.

CONSUMER GUIDE®

	Retail Price	Dealer Invoice	Low Price
w/console, Custom coupe	142	121	131
Low washer fluid indicator	16	14	15
Low fuel indicator	16	14	15
Electronic instrumentation	315	268	290
Front & rear seat courtesy lights	54	46	50
Door courtesy lights, Limited	44	37	40
Decklid luggage rack	115	98	106
Left remote & right manual mirrors, base .	36	31	33
Dual power mirrors, base	127	108	117
Custom, Limited	91	77	84
Lighted passenger visor mirror	58	49	53
Lower bodyside moldings, base & Custom .	60	51	55
Sound systems			
AM/FM stereo ET	232	197	215
AM/FM stereo ET cassette	354	301	325
AM/FM stereo ET cassette w/graphic EQ .	504	428	465
Delco-GM/Bose music system	1127	958	1035
AM delete (credit)	(56)	(48)	(48)
Concert Sound speakers	85	72	78
Power antenna	70	60	64
Vista Vent removable sunroof	350	298	325
6-way power seats (each side)	240	204	220
Manual recliners, Custom (each side) ...	75	64	69
Power passenger seatback recliner, Custom	145	123	133
Limited	70	60	64
Tilt steering wheel	125	106	115
Sport steering wheel	50	43	46
Cassette tape storage, Custom	25	21	23
Heavy-duty suspension, F40	27	23	25
Gran Touring suspension, F41	27	23	25
Full vinyl top, sedans	200	170	184
55/45 front seat, Custom	133	113	122
45/45 seat (incl. console); Custom coupe .	258	219	235
Trunk trim	53	45	49
Power trunk release	50	43	46
Aluminum wheels, 14"	255	217	235
15"	285	242	260
Locking wire wheel covers	199	169	183
Power windows, 2-doors	210	179	193
4-doors	285	242	260
Intermittent wipers	55	47	51
T pkg.	508	432	465
Leather-wrapped steering wheel, 2.97 axle ratio, P215/65R15 tires on aluminum wheels.			
T Type pkg., Custom coupe	1975	1679	1815
T pkg. plus front air dam, rear spoiler, tri-color taillamps, operating console, dual exhaust outlets; black bodyside moldings, exterior blackout treatment, AM/FM stereo ET w/cassette & graphic EQ, gauge package, tilt steering column, intermittent wipers, 45/45 front seat.			

Prices are accurate at time of printing; subject to manufacturer's change.

OLDSMOBILE DELTA 88 ROYALE

	Retail Price	Dealer Invoice	Low Price
2-door coupe	$13639	$11770	$12480
4-door sedan	13639	11770	12480
Brougham 2-door coupe	14536	12545	13300
Brougham 4-door sedan	14536	12545	13300
Destination charge	475	475	475

STANDARD EQUIPMENT (included in above prices):

3.0-liter (181-cid) PFI V-6 engine, 4-speed automatic transmission, power steering, power brakes, air conditioning, full cut-pile carpeting, cigar lighter, side window defoggers, carpeted lower door panels, tinted glass, halogen headlamps, headlamps-on warning, left remote mirror, AM radio, custom bench seat with center armrests, P205/75R14 all-season tires. **Brougham** adds: Convenience Group (lamps, right visor mirror and chime tones), 55/45 divided front seat with individual controls.

OPTIONAL EQUIPMENT:

6-way power seats, each side	240	204	220
55/45 front seat, Royale	133	113	122
Reclining seatbacks, each	70	60	64
Power door locks, 2-doors	145	123	133
4-doors	195	166	179
Power windows, 2-doors	210	179	193
4-doors	285	242	260
Power decklid release	50	43	46
Deluxe luggage compartment trim	53	45	49
Intermittent wipers	55	47	52
Full vinyl roof, 4-doors	200	170	184
Rear defogger	145	123	133
Tempmatic air conditioning	125	106	115
Front header courtesy & reading lamps	54	46	50
Exterior opera lamps	102	87	94
Interior illumination package	75	64	69
Automatic day/night mirror	80	68	74
Dual power remote mirrors	116	99	107
Left remote & right manual mirror	39	33	36
Illuminated passenger visor mirror	51	43	47
Dual remote manual mirrors	69	59	63
Custom two-tone paint	225	191	205
Touring car ride & handling pkg. (FE3)	593	504	545
Firm ride & handling pkg. (F41)	30	26	28
Automatic leveling suspension	175	149	161
Engine block heater	18	15	16
Cruise control	175	149	161
Power remote fuel filler release	25	21	23
Tilt steering wheel	125	106	115

Prices are accurate at time of printing; subject to manufacturer's change.

CONSUMER GUIDE®

Aluminum wheels	199	169	183
Locking wire wheel covers	199	169	183
Convenience group, Royale	21	18	19
Cornering lamps	60	51	55
Heavy-duty battery	26	22	24
AM radio delete (credit)	(56)	(48)	(48)
AM/FM ST ET	207	176	190
AM/FM ST ET cassette	354	301	325
AM/FM ST ET w/cassette & EQ	504	438	465
CB	290	247	265
Delco-GM/Bose music system	1082	920	995
Voice information system	82	70	75
Cellular telephone wiring	215	183	198
Gauge cluster	66	56	61
Trip odometer	16	14	15
Digital trip monitor	90	77	83
Exterior lamp monitor	77	65	71
Electronic instrument panel	299	254	275
Power antenna	70	60	64
Tri-band power antenna	110	94	101
California emissions system	99	84	91
Heavy-duty radiator	30	26	28
Decklid luggage rack	115	98	106
Custom leather seating, Brougham	379	322	350
Reminder pkg.	82	70	75
Interior comfort group, Brougham	584	496	535

Buick LeSabre & Electra Estate/ Oldsmobile Custom Cruiser/ Pontiac Safari

Returning mechanically unchanged for '87, this trio of full-size rear-drive station wagons is left over from GM's B-body family of cars. Chevrolet still offers a full line of Caprice coupes, sedans and wagons from the same design, while Buick, Olds and Pontiac only field the wagons. Pontiac's version was called Parisienne last year, but is dubbed Safari this year and it continues on with some notable changes: Air conditioning, tinted glass, AM/FM stereo, dual sport mirrors and white wall tires are now standard,

Buick LeSabre Estate

and heavy-duty cooling is a new option. Safari is powered by a 5.0-liter (305-cubic-inch) Chevrolet V-8, while the Buick Estates and Olds Custom Cruiser use Oldsmobile's 5.0-liter (307-cubic-inch) V-8. All models comes with a 4-speed overdrive automatic transmission. Otherwise, these wagons differ mainly in interior trim and price. Full-size rear-drive wagons such as these still have a big enough following to justify their existence and it's easy to see why when you look at what they offer: Room for six people, more than 87 cubic feet of cargo space and 5000-pound towing capacity. You'll have to look at vans to beat those figures and vans just aren't everyone's idea of happy motoring. The virtues of these full-size wagons come from their size and brawn, but so do their vices. The V-8s work up a heavy thirst hauling around two tons of weight and that will probably doom these vehicles if the price of gasoline goes up again. They can be cumbersome to drive in urban areas because of their boatlike handling, so they're much more at home cruising on the open road, where they can easily tow a boat behind them. We prefer something smaller and more agile, but since station wagons are supposed to be roomy beasts of burden, there are still good reasons for buying one of these.

Specifications

	5-door wagon
Wheelbase, in.	115.9
Overall length, in.	220.5
Overall width, in.	79.3
Overall height, in.	59.3
Front track, in.	62.2

	5-door wagon
Rear track, in.	64.0
Curb weight, lbs.	4160
Cargo vol., cu. ft.	87.9
Fuel capacity, gal.	22.0
Seating capacity	6
Front headroom, in.	39.6
Front shoulder room, in.	60.9
Front legroom, max., in.	42.2
Rear headroom, in.	39.3
Rear shoulder room, in.	60.9
Rear legroom, min., in.	37.8

Body/Chassis

Drivetrain layout: longitudinal front engine/rear-wheel drive. **Front suspension:** unequal-length upper and lower control arms, coil springs, stabilizer bar. **Rear suspension:** rigid axle, four links, coil springs, stabilizer bar. **Steering:** recirculating ball, power assisted, 3.5 turns lock-to-lock. **Turn diameter, ft.:** 39.2. **Front brakes:** 11.9-in. discs. **Rear brakes:** 11.0-in. drums. **Construction:** body on frame.

Powertrains

	ohv V-8
Displacement, l/cu. in.	5.0/307
Compression ratio	8.0:1
Fuel delivery	4 bbl.
Net bhp @ rpm	140 @ 3200
Net torque @ rpm	255 @ 2000
Availability	S
Final drive ratios	
4-speed OD automatic	2.73:1

KEY: bbl = barrel (carburetor); **bhp** = brake horsepower; **torque** = pounds/feet; **Cal.** = California only; **TBI** = throttle body (single-point) fuel injection; **PFI** = port (multipoint) fuel injection; **MFI** = mechanical fuel injection; **ohv** = overhead valve; **ohc** = overhead cam; **dohc** = double overhead cam; **I** = inline engine; **V** = V engine; **flat** = horizontally opposed engine; **D** = diesel; **T** = turbocharged; **OD** = overdrive transmission; **S** = standard; **O** = optional.

PRICES

BUICK LE SABRE & ELECTRA ESTATES	Retail Price	Dealer Invoice	Low Price
LeSabre Estate 5-door wagon	$14724	$12707	$13700
Electra Estate 5-door wagon	17697	15273	16460
Destination charge	500	500	500

Prices are accurate at time of printing; subject to manufacturer's change.

STANDARD EQUIPMENT (included in above prices):

LeSabre Estate: 5.0-liter (307-cid) 4 bbl. V-8 engine, 4-speed automatic transmission, air conditioning, power steering, power brakes, full carpeting, bumper guards, tinted glass, left remote and right manual mirrors, AM radio, cloth or vinyl bench seat, heavy-duty suspension, two-way power tailgate, P225/75R14 all-season tires whitewall tires on styled aluminum wheels. **Electra Estate** adds: quartz digital clock, AM/FM ST ET, roof rack, 55/45 front seat with 2-way power driver's side, tilt steering column, headlamps-on chime, power windows including tailgate, power door locks, belt reveal moldings, door edge guards, remote tailgate lock.

OPTIONAL EQUIPMENT:

Automatic climate control	150	128	138
Air deflector (roof rack req. LeSabre)	40	34	37
Limited slip differential	100	85	92
Heavy-duty battery	26	22	24
Heavy-duty cooling system	40	34	37
Cruise control	175	149	161
Rear defogger	145	123	133
Power door locks, LeSabre	195	166	179
Automatic power door locks, LeSabre	285	242	260
Electra	90	77	83
Engine block heater	18	15	17
Four-note horn	28	24	26
Trip odometer, LeSabre	16	14	15
Lamp and Indicator Group, LeSabre	70	60	64
Electra	86	73	79
Door courtesy & warning lamps	70	60	64
Cornering lamps	60	51	55
Illuminated driver's door lock & interior light control	75	64	69
Twilight Sentinel	60	51	55
Tungsten halogen headlamps	25	21	23
Front monitor lamps	37	31	34
Dual power remote mirrors	91	77	84
Dual manual remote mirrors	49	42	45
Lighted visor mirror, each	58	49	53
Bodyside molding	60	51	55
Belt reveal molding, LeSabre	40	34	37
Door edge guards (incl. w/woodgrain) LeSabre	25	21	23
Wide rocker & lower fender moldings, Electra	65	55	60
Exterior molding package, LeSabre	110	94	101
AM/FM stereo ET, LeSabre	207	176	190
w/cassette, LeSabre	329	280	305
w/cassette, Electra	132	112	121

Prices are accurate at time of printing; subject to manufacturer's change.

	Retail Price	Dealer Invoice	Low Price
Above w/graphic EQ, LeSabre	479	407	440
Electra	282	240	260
CB radio	295	251	270
AM delete, LeSabre (credit)	(56)	(48)	(48)
AM/FM stereo delete, Electra (credit)	(250)	(213)	(213)
Power antenna	70	60	64
Triband power antenna	115	98	106
Roof rack, LeSabre	115	98	106
2-way power driver's seat, LeSabre	60	51	55
6-way power driver's seat, LeSabre	240	204	220
Electra	210	179	193
6-way power passenger seat	240	204	220
6-way power driver & passenger seats			
LeSabre	480	408	440
Electra	450	383	415
Manual seatback recliner, passenger	75	64	69
Electric seatback recliners, each	145	123	133
Third seat	220	187	200
Tilt steering column, LeSabre	125	106	115
Automatic level control suspension	175	149	161
Power remote tailgate lock, LeSabre	60	51	55
Self-sealing tires	150	128	138
55/45 front seat, LeSabre	133	113	122
Power windows, LeSabre	285	242	260
Intermittent wipers	55	47	51
Woodgrain vinyl applique, LeSabre	345	293	315
Woodgrain applique delete (credit), Electra	(320)	(272)	(272)

OLDSMOBILE CUSTOM CRUISER

	Retail Price	Dealer Invoice	Low Price
5-door wagon	$14420	$12444	$13195
Destination charge	475	475	475

STANDARD EQUIPMENT (included in above prices):

5.0-liter (307-cid) 4bbl. V-8, 4-speed automatic transmission, power steering and brakes, power tailgate window, air conditioning, cigar lighter, carpeted lower door panels, full carpeting including cargo area, tinted glass, left remote mirror, AM radio, right visor mirror, chime tones, rear storage compartment lock, 55/45 bench seat with dual controls, P225/75R15 tires.

OPTIONAL EQUIPMENT:

6-way power driver's seat	240	204	220
Passenger side	240	204	220
Rear-facing third seat	220	187	200
Reclining passenger seatback	70	60	64
Power door locks	245	208	225
Power windows	285	242	260

Prices are accurate at time of printing; subject to manufacturer's change.

Oldsmobile Custom Cruiser

	Retail Price	Dealer Invoice	Low Price
Lower bodyside moldings	80	68	74
Woodgrain exterior treatment	315	268	290
Bodyside moldings	60	51	55
Intermittent wipers	55	47	51
Rear defogger	145	123	133
Rear air deflector	40	34	37
Tempmatic air conditioning	55	47	51
Dome & reading lamps	15	12	13
Illuminated entry system	75	64	69
Dual power remote mirrors	116	97	107
Litter container	12	10	11
Illuminated right visor mirror	51	43	47
Automatic leveling control	175	149	161
Limited slip differential	100	85	92
Engine block heater	18	15	16
Cruise control	175	149	161
Locking gas cap	10	9	9
Tilt steering wheel	125	106	115
Locking wire wheel covers	199	169	183
Puncture-sealing tires	150	128	138
Halogen headlights	15	13	14
Cornering lamps	60	51	55
Heavy-duty battery	26	22	24
Digital clock	60	51	55
AM radio delete (credit)	(56)	(48)	(48)
AM/FM ST	86	73	79
AM/FM ST cassette	196	167	180
AM/FM ST ET cassette	317	269	290
Gauge pkg.	66	56	61
Trip odometer	16	14	15
Exterior lamp monitors	77	65	71
Power antenna	70	60	64
5-wire harness	30	26	28

Prices are accurate at time of printing; subject to manufacturer's change

Rear bumper step	25	21	23
California emissions system	99	84	91
High-capacity radiator	30	26	28
Rooftop luggage carrier	115	98	106
Reminder pkg.	82	70	75

PONTIAC SAFARI

5-door wagon	$13959	$12047	$12840
Destination charge	475	475	475

STANDARD EQUIPMENT (included in above prices):

5.0-liter (305-cid) 4 bbl. V-8 engine, 4-speed automatic transmission, power steering and brakes, air conditioning, front and rear ashtrays, cigar lighter, tinted glass, carpeted lower door panels, courtesy lights, lighted front ashtray and glovebox, lockable glovebox, left remote and right manual mirrors, color-keyed bodyside moldings, hood windsplit molding, AM/FM ST ET, notchback bench seat with center armrest, rear-facing third seat, custom wheel covers, P225/75R15 tires.

OPTIONAL EQUIPMENT:

Option Group 1	882	750	810
Power windows & door locks, cruise control, tilt steering wheel, intermittent wipers, lamp group.			
Option Group 2	1309	1113	1205
Group 1 plus power seat, bumper guards, cornering lamps, lighted right visor mirror, cargo area carpet, dual remote mirrors, halogen headlamps.			
Limited-slip differential	100	85	92
HD cooling system	66	56	59
Rear defogger	145	123	133
California emissions pkg.	99	84	91
Rally gauges w/trip odometer	71	58	65

Pontiac Safari
Prices are accurate at time of printing; subject to manufacturer's change.

	Retail Price	Dealer Invoice	Low Price
Roof luggage carrier	155	131	143
AM/FM ST ET cassette	122	104	112
AM/FM ST ET w/cassette & EQ	272	231	250
AM/FM ST ET delete (credit)	(273)	(224)	(224)
Power antenna	70	60	64
55/45 front seat, vinyl or cloth	133	113	122
Reclining passenger seat (55/45 req.) . . .	70	60	64
Super-Lift shock absorbers	64	54	59
7-wire trailer wiring harness	30	26	28
Trailering pkg.	66	56	61
Locking wire wheel covers	214	182	197
Simulated woodgrain siding	345	293	315

Buick Riviera/ Oldsmobile Toronado

Buick Riviera T Type

Buick's and Oldsmobile's personal-luxury coupes were all-new last year and sales of both were dismal. Most of the blame has been placed on the shrunken size of the new models and the similarly bland styling. Here's what's happening for 1987: Horsepower on the 3.8-liter V-6 standard in both models is now rated at 150, up 10, with the addition of roller valve lifters. New Riviera options include a more complex multi-adjustable power driver's seat, a companion manual passenger's version and automatic- dimming rearview mirror. The standard Graphic Control Center (GCC) with touch-sensitive TV-type screen is revamped in response to customer and press feedback. The displays are now called up by pressing small pushbuttons instead of the perimeter of the screen and there are more readouts. At Oldsmobile, the base Toronado has been joined by a sportier offering called Trofeo (pronounced tro-FAY-oh). Its basic ingredients are a more subdued exterior, leather interior with bucket seats, FE3 sport suspension and P215/60R15 Eagle GT performance tires on aluminum wheels. Both Toronados get larger sound and climate system control buttons and a new cellular telephone option. Another new standard Toronado feature is GM's automatic front seat belt system, to be phased in shortly after '87 production starts. Riviera and Toronado have always appealed to big-car fans, so it's easy to see how the current generation comes up short (and light). Too bad, since we find this generation performs much more capably than the previous models, which were clumsy and overweight by comparison. However, in this price range, we still prefer the Lincoln Mark VII LSC.

Specifications	2-door coupe
Wheelbase, in.	108.0
Overall length, in.	187.2
Overall width, in.	71.7
Overall height, in.	53.5
Front track, in.	59.9
Rear track, in.	59.9
Curb weight, lbs.	3307
Cargo vol., cu. ft.	13.9
Fuel capacity, gal.	18.0
Seating capacity	5
Front headroom, in.	37.8
Front shoulder room, in.	57.9
Front legroom, max., in.	42.7
Rear headroom, in.	37.8
Rear shoulder room, in.	57.4
Rear legroom, min., in.	35.7

Body/Chassis

Drivetrain layout: transverse front engine/front-wheel drive. **Front suspension:** struts, barrel-type springs, link-type control arms, stabilizer bar. **Rear suspension:** independent, transverse leaf spring, control arms, electronic level control. **Steering:** rack and pinion, turns lock-to-lock NA. **Turn diameter, ft.:** 38.9. **Front brakes:** discs. **Rear brakes:** discs. **Construction:** unit.

Powertrains

	ohv V-6
Displacement, l/cu. in.	3.8/231
Compression ratio	8.5:1
Fuel delivery	PFI
Net bhp @ rpm	150 @ 4400
Net torque @ rpm	200 @ 2000
Availability	S

Final drive ratios

4-speed OD automatic	2.84:1

KEY: bbl = barrel (carburetor); **bhp** = brake horsepower; **torque** = pounds/feet; **Cal.** = California only; **TBI** = throttle body (single-point) fuel injection; **PFI** = port (multipoint) fuel injection; **MFI** = mechanical fuel injection; **ohv** = overhead valve; **ohc** = overhead cam; **dohc** = double overhead cam; **I** = inline engine; **V** = V engine; **flat** = horizontally opposed engine; **D** = diesel; **T** = turbocharged; **OD** = overdrive transmission; **S** = standard; **O** = optional.

PRICES

BUICK RIVIERA	Retail Price	Dealer Invoice	Low Price
2-door coupe	$20377	$17551	$18545
Destination charge	500	500	500

STANDARD EQUIPMENT (included in above prices):

3.8-liter (231-cid) PFI V-6 engine, four-speed overdrive automatic transmission, automatic climate control air conditioning, power steering, power four-wheel disc brakes, electronic level control, Graphic Control Center with touch-sensitive cathode ray tube, remote fuel filler door and decklid releases, side window defoggers, assist straps, sliding sunscreen extensions on visors, dome and reading lamps, cruise control, tool kit, P205/75R14 tires.

OPTIONAL EQUIPMENT:

T Pkg.	581	494	535
F41 suspension, 2.97 axle ratio, leather-wrapped steering wheel, fast-ratio power steering, P215/60R15 tires on aluminum wheels.			
T Type Pkg.	1844	1567	1695
T Pkg. plus reclining leather and suede power comfort seats, silver accent paint, silver bodyside moldings.			
HD battery	26	22	24
HD engine & trans cooling	40	34	37
Rear defogger	145	123	133
Automatic power door locks	90	77	83
California emissions pkg.	99	84	91

Prices are accurate at time of printing; subject to manufacturer's change

Engine block heater	18	15	17
Four-note horn	28	24	26
Low washer fluid indicator	16	14	15
Rear seat reading lights	50	43	46
Illuminated driver's door lock & interior light control	75	64	69
Twilight Sentinel	60	51	55
Automatic day/night mirror	80	68	74
Power mirrors w/heated left	35	30	32
Lighted visor mirrors, each	58	49	53
Bodyside moldings	60	51	55
Designer's accent paint	190	162	175
Firemist paint, special color	210	179	193
AM & FM ST ET cassette	152	129	140
w/EQ & Concert sound speakers	342	291	315
Delco-GM/Bose music system	925	786	850
Concert Sound speakers	70	60	64
Astroroof	1230	1046	1130
Power passenger seat	240	204	220
Power seatback recliners, each	75	64	69
Leather steering wheel & shift handle	119	101	109
F41 Gran Touring suspension	27	23	25
Theft deterrent system	159	135	146
Trailer towing harness	30	26	28
Leather & suede trim	487	414	450
Performance driver's seat, w/cloth	680	578	625
w/leather & suede	1167	992	1075
Power trunklid pulldown	80	68	74
Locking wire wheel covers	199	169	183
Aluminum wheels	199	169	183

OLDSMOBILE TORONADO

Brougham 2-door coupe	$19938	$17991	$18640
Trofeo 2-door coupe	NA	NA	NA
Destination charge	500	500	500

STANDARD EQUIPMENT (included in above prices):

3.8-liter (231-cid) PFI V-6 engine, 4-speed automatic transmission, power steering, power 4-wheel disc brakes, air conditioning, power windows and door locks, power antenna, front and rear center armrests, passenger assist grips, bumper rub strips, Convenience Group including lamps, visor mirror and chime tones, side window defoggers, cruise control, electronic gauge cluster including tachometer and reminder package, carpeted lower door panels, tinted glass, courtesy lamps, dual remote mirrors, automatic leveling system, AM/FM ST ET, 55/45 front bench seat with dual recliners, 6-way power driver's side and passenger easy-entry feature, tilt steering column, header panel storage unit, intermittent wipers, P205/75R15 tires.

Prices are accurate at time of printing; subject to manufacturer's change

Oldsmobile Toronado Trofeo

OPTIONAL EQUIPMENT:

Power passenger seat	240	204	220
Automatic power door locks	90	77	83
Power recliner	75	64	69
Power trunklid release	50	53	46
Power trunklid pulldown	80	68	74
Bodyside moldings	60	51	55
Astroroof	1230	1046	1130
Rear defogger	145	123	133
Reading lamps	48	41	44
Door lock & interior illumination pkg.	75	64	69
Automatic day/night mirror	80	68	74
Dual power mirrors w/heated left	35	30	32
Console w/floorshift	110	94	101
Right lighted visor mirror	51	43	47
Left lighted visor mirror	58	49	53
Firm ride & handling pkg.	30	26	28
Touring Car ride & handling pkg.	378	321	350
Leather-wrapped steering wheel	54	46	50
Power fuel filler door release	25	21	23
Locking wire wheel covers	199	169	183
Aluminum wheels	254	216	235
Puncture-sealant tires	150	128	138
P215/60R15 tires	74	63	68
Twilight Sentinel	60	51	55
HD battery	26	22	24
Theft deterrent system	159	135	146
AM/FM ST ET cassette	152	129	140
AM/FM ST ET cassette w/Bose speakers	885	752	815
Voice information system	82	70	75
Cellular telephone wiring provision	395	336	365
Cellular telephone	2350	1998	2160
Deluxe cellular telephone	2850	2423	2622
Dimensional Sound speakers	70	60	64
AM/FM ST ET cassette w/EQ	352	299	325
5-wire harness	30	26	28

Prices are accurate at time of printing; subject to manufacturer's change

HD radiator	30	26	28
HD cooling system	40	34	37
Glamour metallic paint	210	179	193
Decklid luggage rack	115	98	106
Custom leather seat trim	384	326	355
California emissions pkg.	99	84	91
Comfort/Value Group	519	441	475

Includes power split bench seat or bucket seats, floormats, leather seat trim.

Buick Skyhawk/ Oldsmobile Firenza

Buick Skyhawk 4-door

Mechanical changes dominate the news for Buick's and Oldsmobile's versions of the front-drive J-body subcompact this year. All four engines available in Skyhawk and Firenza are extensively reengineered. The Chevy-built 2.0-liter overhead-valve engine standard in Skyhawk and Firenza acquires a new single-point fuel injection system, distributor-less Computer Controlled Coil Ignition, larger valves, cast-aluminum cylinder head and aluminum-alloy pistons. For all this, the result is only two more horsepower for a total of 90. The optional Pontiac-supplied overhead-cam four is enlarged to 2.0 liters from 1.8 in both normally aspirated and turbocharged form. The non-turbo version packs 96 horsepower, 12 more than before. The turbo engine (available only in Skyhawk) also gets a larger turbocharger with new water-cooled center bearing for a rated 165 horsepower, 15 more than last year. Exclusive to the Firenza GT is Chevy's more powerful Generation II 2.8-liter injected V-6, also with new cylinder head, bigger valves and distributor-less coil ignition system. The standard transmission for the Firenza GT and turbocharged Skyhawks is this year's new GM-built 5-speed designed by the German company, Getrag. The T Type disappears as a separate Skyhawk model, but its content is distributed among four independent option groups: Exterior and Interior Sport Packages for 2-doors and hatchbacks only, "T" suspension package and Turbo Performance Package for all but wagons. Even with this year's changes, neither of the 4-cylinder engines is a model of refinement or at the head of the class for performance, especially with automatic transmission. However, the optional overhead-cam four now seems to be worth the extra money. The 165-horsepower turbocharged engine turns the Skyhawk into a street racer, while the V-6 gives the Firenza GT impressive performance. Skyhawk and Firenza are built from the same design as the Pontiac Sunbird and the Chevrolet Cavalier and both those cars cost less than Buick's or Olds' versions of the GM J-body.

Specifications

	2-door coupe	3-door coupe	4-door sedan	5-door wagon
Wheelbase, in.	101.2	101.2	101.2	101.2
Overall length, in.	175.3	179.3	181.3	181.7
Overall width, in.	65.0	65.0	65.0	65.0
Overall height, in.	54.0	51.9	54.0	54.4
Front track, in.	55.6	55.6	55.6	55.4
Rear track, in.	55.2	55.2	55.2	55.2
Curb weight, lbs.	2348	2396	2396	2471
Cargo vol., cu. ft.	12.6	36.5	13.5	64.4
Fuel capacity, gal.	13.6	13.6	13.6	13.6
Seating capacity	5	5	5	5
Front headroom, in.	37.7	37.6	38.6	38.3
Front shoulder room, in.	53.7	52.9	53.7	53.7
Front legroom, max., in.	42.2	42.2	42.2	42.2
Rear headroom, in.	36.7	36.4	38.0	38.8
Rear shoulder room, in.	52.6	52.0	53.8	53.8
Rear legroom, min., in.	31.8	31.8	34.3	33.7

Body/Chassis

Drivetrain layout: transverse front engine/front-wheel drive. **Front suspension:** MacPherson struts, lower control arms, coil springs, stabilizer bar. **Rear suspension:** semi-independent, beam axle, trailing arms, coil springs, stabilizer bar on T Type. **Steering:** rack and pinion, 4.0 turns lock-to-lock manual; 2.9

power. **Turn diameter, ft.:** 34.7. **Front brakes:** 9.7-in. discs.
Rear brakes: 7.9-in. drums. **Construction:** unit.

Powertrains

	ohv I-4	ohc I-4	ohc I-4T
Displacement, l/cu. in.	2.0/121	2.0/121	2.0/121
Compression ratio	9.0:1	8.8:1	8.0:1
Fuel delivery	TBI	TBI	PFI
Net bhp @ rpm	90 @ 5600	96 @ 4800	165 @ 5600
Net torque @ rpm	108 @ 3200	118 @ 3600	175 @ 4000
Availability	S	O	O

Final drive ratios

	ohv I-4	ohc I-4	ohc I-4T
4-speed OD manual	3.65:1		
5-speed manual		3.45:1	3.61:1
3-speed automatic	3.18:1	3.18:1	3.18:1

KEY: bbl = barrel (carburetor); **bhp** =brake horsepower; **torque** = pounds/feet; **Cal.** = California only; **TBI** = throttle body (single-point) fuel injection; **PFI** = port (multi-point) fuel injection; **MFI** = mechanical fuel injection; **ohv** = overhead valve; **ohc** = overhead cam; **dohc** = double overhead cam; **I** = inline engine; **V** = V engine; **flat** = horizontally opposed engine; **D** = diesel; **T** = turbocharged; **OD** = overdrive transmission; **S** = standard; **O** = optional.

PRICES

BUICK SKYHAWK	Retail Price	Dealer Invoice	Low Price
Custom 4-door sedan	$8559	$7643	$8080
Custom 2-door coupe	8522	7610	8045
Custom 5-door wagon	9249	8259	8730
Sport 3-door coupe	8965	8006	8465
Limited 4-door sedan	9503	8486	8970
Limited 2-door coupe	9445	8434	8915
Limited 5-door wagon	9841	8788	9290
Destination charge	370	370	370

STANDARD EQUIPMENT (included in above prices):

2.0-liter (121-cid) TBI OHV 4-cylinder engine, 4-speed manual transmission, power brakes, passenger assist strap, cut-pile carpeting, coin holder, full-length console with floorshift, side window defoggers, halogen headlamps, instrument panel courtesy lights, lights for ashtray, glovebox, trunk/cargo area and engine compartment, lockable glovebox, AM radio, dual reclining cloth bucket seats with adjustable headrests, trip odometer, swing-out rear quarter windows (coupes), deluxe wheel covers, P175/80R13 SBR tires. **Sport** adds: front bumper guards, load floor carpeting, concealed headlamps, split folding rear seatback, turbine spoke wheel covers. **Limited** adds to base equipment: acoustic insulation, front seat armrest, fog lamps, coolant temperature, oil pressure and voltage gauges, upgraded steering wheel, easy-entry front passenger seat, upgraded seat trim.

Prices are accurate at time of printing; subject to manufacturer's change.

OPTIONAL EQUIPMENT:

2.0-liter (121-cid) OHC TBI 4-cyl. engine (5-speed or automatic req.)	50	43	46
5-speed manual trans (OHC engine req.)	75	64	69
3-speed auto trans, w/o Turbo Performance pkg.	490	417	450
w/Turbo Performance pkg.	415	353	380
Acoustic pkg., Custom & Sport	36	31	33
Air conditioning	675	574	620
Front center armrest, Custom 2- & 3-doors	45	38	41
Heavy-duty battery	26	22	24
Cruise control	175	149	161
Rear defogger	145	123	133
Power door locks, 2- and 3-doors	145	123	133
4- and 5-doors	195	166	179
Tinted glass	105	89	97
Concealed headlamps, Ltd sedan, Custom & wagons	160	136	147
Engine block heater	18	15	17
Dual horns (std. Ltd)	15	13	14
Headlamps-on indicator	15	13	14
Trip odometer, Custom & Sport	15	13	14
Gauge pkg. (coolant temp., oil pressure, voltage, trip odometer), Custom & Sport	60	51	55
Gauge pkg. w/tachometer, Custom & Sport	138	117	127
Limited	78	66	72
Front seat reading lamps	30	26	28
Decklid luggage rack	115	98	106
Left remote & right manual mirrors	53	45	49
Lighted passenger visor mirror	45	38	41
Designer's accent paint	195	166	179
Lower accent paint, 2- and 3-doors	195	166	179
Heavy-duty radiator, w/A/C	40	34	37
w/o A/C	70	60	64
AM/FM stereo ET	168	143	155
Above w/cassette	354	301	325
Above w/cassette & graphic EQ	504	428	465
AM delete (credit)	(56)	(48)	(48)
Extended range speakers	25	21	23
Power antenna	70	60	64
Removable glass sunroof (NA wagons)	350	298	320
Roof rack, wagons	115	98	106
Easy entry passenger seat, 2- and 3-doors	16	14	15
4-way manual seat adjuster (NA wagons)	35	30	32
Power driver's seat	240	204	220
Cargo security cover, 3- and 5-doors	69	59	63
Rear spoiler, 3-doors	70	60	64
Power steering	225	191	205

Prices are accurate at time of printing; subject to manufacturer's change

Tilt steering col.	125	106	115
Sport steering wheel	50	43	46
Leather steering wheel, w/o Interior Sport or			
Turbo	90	77	83
w/Interior Sport or Turbo	40	34	37
Louvered rear window sunshield, 3-doors .	199	169	183
Gran Touring suspension	27	23	25
Remote trunk or tailgate release	50	43	46
Power windows, 2- and 3-doors	210	179	193
4- and 5-doors	285	242	260
Rear wiper/washer, 3- and 5-doors	125	106	115
Intermittent wipers	55	47	51
T pkg., (NA wagons)	574	488	530

Leather steering wheel, Gran Touring suspension, P205/60R14 tires on aluminum wheels.

Exterior Sport pkg., Custom 2-door	167	142	154
3-doors	197	167	181
Limited 2-door	141	120	130

Blackout moldings, turbo hood, fog lamps.

Interior Sport pkg., Custom 2- and 3-doors .	495	421	455

Black and grey interior, easy-entry passenger seat, sport steering wheel, gauge pkg. including tachometer.

Interior Sport pkg., w/o T pkg. or Turbo			
Custom 2- and 3-doors, Sport	495	421	455
Limited 2-door	368	313	340
Interior Sport pkg., w/Turbo			
Custom 2-door, 3-doors	307	261	282
Limited 2-door	240	204	220
Interior Sport pkg., w/T pkg.			
Custom 2-door, 3-doors	445	378	410
Limited 2-door	318	270	295
Turbo Performance pkg. (NA wagons)			
Custom & 3-doors	1607	1366	1480
Limited	1547	1315	1425

T pkg. plus 2.0-liter turbo engine, turbo hood.

OLDSMOBILE FIRENZA

2-door coupe	$8541	$7627	$8030
S 3-door coupe	8976	8016	8435
4-door sedan	8499	7590	7990
Cruiser 5-door wagon	9146	8167	8595
LC 2-door coupe	9639	8608	9060
GT 3-door	11034	9853	10370
LX 4-door sedan	9407	8400	8845
Destination charge	370	370	370

STANDARD EQUIPMENT (included in above prices):

2.0-liter (121-cid) TBI 4-cylinder engine, 4-speed manual transmission,

Prices are accurate at time of printing; subject to manufacturer's change.

power brakes, carpet, console, side window defoggers, AM radio, reclining front bucket seats, folding rear seat on 3- and 5-door, deluxe wheel discs (sedan and wagon), rally stainless steel wheels (2- and 3-door), swing-out rear quarter windows (2- and 3-door), P175/80R13 tires. **LX** adds: left remote and right manual mirrors, power steering, leather steering wheel. **LC** adds: rally instruments. **GT** adds: 2.8-liter (173-cid) PFI V-6, firm ride and handling suspension, styled aluminum wheels.

OPTIONAL EQUIPMENT:

1.8-liter (121-cid) OHC engine	50	43	46
5-speed manual transmission (std. GT)	75	64	69
3-speed automatic transmission	490	417	450
6-way power driver's seat	240	204	220
Glass sunroof (NA wagon)	350	298	320
4-way manual seat adjuster	35	30	32
Power door locks, 2- & 3-doors	145	123	133
4- & 5-doors	195	166	179
Power trunk or liftgate release	50	43	46
Tinted glass	105	89	97
Power windows, 2- & 3-doors	210	179	193
4- & 5-doors	285	242	260
Bodyside woodgrain, wagon	300	255	275
Bodyside moldings	50	43	46
Intermittent wipers	55	47	51
Rear wiper/washer, 3- & 5-doors	125	106	115
Rear defogger	145	123	133
Air conditioning	675	554	620
Rear window sunshade, 3-doors	199	169	184
Folding front armrest	58	49	53
Left remote & right manual mirrors	53	45	49
Cargo area cover, 3- & 5-doors	69	59	63
Two-tone paint	200	170	184
Firm ride & handling pkg.	30	26	28
FE3 suspension (touring car), exc. wagon	415	353	380
Wagon	457	388	420
Engine block heater	18	15	17
Cruise control	175	149	161
Leather-wrapped steering wheel	90	77	83
Locking fuel door	10	8	9
Tilt steering wheel	125	106	115
Power steering (std. LC, GT, LX)	225	191	205
Aluminum wheels, base sedan & LC	199	169	183
Base 2- & 3-doors, wagon	157	133	144
Locking wire wheel covers, base sedan & LC	199	169	183
Base 2- & 3-doors, wagon	157	133	144
Convenience Group	54	46	50
Halogen headlamps	15	13	14
High-capacity battery	26	22	24

Prices are accurate at time of printing; subject to manufacturer's change

Oldsmobile Firenza GT 3-door

Delete AM radio (credit)	(56)	(48)	(48)
AM/FM ST ET	207	176	190
AM/FM ST ET cassette	354	301	325
Dual horns	15	13	14
Rally instruments (std. LC & GT)	142	121	131
California emissions system	99	84	91
Roof or decklid luggage rack	115	98	106

Buick Skylark & Somerset/ Oldsmobile Calais

These front-drive compacts are built from the same N-body design as the Pontiac Grand Am (see separate entry). Buick calls its sedan version Skylark and its coupe Somerset, while Olds sticks with Calais for both body styles. The standard 2.5-liter 4-cylinder engine has been substantially revised this year, gaining GM's multi-coil ignition system, a higher-flow intake manifold and cylinder head and re-calibrated engine control module. Net horsepower climbs to 98, a gain of six. With the standard 5-speed manual transmission, the engine also gets contra-rotating balance shafts that help smooth out the secondary shaking forces inherent in a large-displacement four. As before, 3-speed automatic is optional and your only choice with the extra-cost 3.0-liter V-6. Federal regulations call for passive restraints on 10 percent of each automaker's 1987 cars, and

Buick Skylark Custom

the Somerset and Calais have been tapped to help meet GM's quota with an automatic front seat belt system. The Somerset T Type disappears as a separate model in favor of independent Exterior Sport and "T" suspension packages. The suspension package is also optional on Skylark. On the Calais, flush-mounted composite headlamps and red/amber taillamps are the major appearance changes. Also new is a GT package for the base sedan to replace last year's ES package. The optional V-6 engine is the way to go with the Skylark/Somerset duo or Calais, despite the improvements to the standard 2.5-liter four. The 2.5 is adequate for cars of this size and weight, but it lacks the V-6's spirited acceleration and brisk passing response. Inside, there's adequate space for four adults, but those in the rear get little leg room. Trunk space is just adequate too, and the rear seatbacks don't fold down for extra cargo room. Overall, these are pleasant, comfortable compacts that become pricey when fully equipped.

Specifications	2-door coupe	4-door sedan
Wheelbase, in.	103.4	103.4
Overall length, in.	180.1	180.1
Overall width, in.	66.6	66.6
Overall height, in.	52.1	52.1
Front track, in.	55.6	55.6
Rear track, in.	55.2	55.2
Curb weight, lbs.	2524	2571
Cargo vol., cu. ft.	13.4	13.4
Fuel capacity, gal.	13.6	13.6

	2-door coupe	4-door sedan
Seating capacity	5	5
Front headroom, in.	37.7	37.7
Front shoulder room, in.	53.7	53.7
Front legroom, max., in.	42.9	42.9
Rear headroom, in.	37.1	37.1
Rear shoulder room, in.	55.4	53.2
Rear legroom, min., in.	34.3	34.3

Body/Chassis

Drivetrain layout: transverse front engine/front-wheel drive. **Front suspension:** MacPherson struts, lower control arms, coil springs, stabilizer bar. **Rear suspension:** semi-independent, beam axle, trailing arms, coil springs, stabilizer bar optional. **Steering:** rack and pinion, power assisted, 2.9 turns lock-to-lock. **Turn diameter, ft.:** 35.4. **Front brakes:** 9.8-in. discs. **Rear brakes:** 7.9-in. drums. **Construction:** unit.

Powertrains	ohv I-4	ohv V-6
Displacement, l/cu. in.	2.5/151	3.0/181
Compression ratio	9.0:1	9.0:1
Fuel delivery	TBI	PFI
Net bhp @ rpm	98 @ 4800	125 @ 4900
Net torque @ rpm	135 @ 3200	150 @ 2400
Availability	S	O

Final drive ratios
5-speed OD manual	3.35:1	
3-speed automatic	2.84:1	2.53:1

KEY: bbl = barrel (carburetor); **bhp** = brake horsepower; **torque** = pounds/feet; **Cal.** = California only; **TBI** = throttle body (single-point) fuel injection; **PFI** = port (multipoint) fuel injection; **MFI** = mechanical fuel injection; **ohv** = overhead valve; **ohc** = overhead cam; **dohc** = double overhead cam; **I** = inline engine; **V** = V engine; **flat** = horizontally opposed engine; **D** = diesel; **T** = turbocharged; **OD** = overdrive transmission; **S** = standard; **O** = optional.

PRICES

BUICK SOMERSET AND SKYLARK	Retail Price	Dealer Invoice	Low Price
Somerset Custom 2-door coupe	$9957	$8892	$9400
Somerset Limited 2-door coupe	11003	9826	10385
Skylark Custom 4-door sedan	9915	8854	9910
Skylark Limited 4-door sedan	11003	9826	10385
Destination charge	370	370	370

Prices are accurate at time of printing; subject to manufacturer's change.

STANDARD EQUIPMENT (included in above prices):

Custom: 2.5-liter (151-cid) 4-cylinder TBI engine, 5-speed manual transmission, power steering, power brakes, front center armrest, bumper rub strips, cut-pile carpeting, tinted glass, halogen headlamps, electronic digital instrumentation including tachometer, voltmeter, oil pressure and coolant temperature gauges, engine compartment and trunk lights, locking glovebox, right manual mirror (Skylark only), right visor mirror, reclining cloth or vinyl bucket seats with easy-entry feature on passenger side (Somerset), headlamps-on warning, P185/80R13 all-season tires. **Limited** adds: left remote and right manual mirrors, rear center armrest, front header and roof rail courtesy lights, special steering wheel, remote fuel door release (Skylark).

OPTIONAL EQUIPMENT:

3.0-liter (181-cid) V-6 (auto trans. req.) . .	660	561	607
3-speed automatic transmission	490	417	450
Air conditioning	675	574	620
Cruise control	175	149	161
Rear defogger	145	123	133
Power door locks, Somerset	145	123	133
Skylark	195	166	179
Remote fuel filler door release, Custom . .	11	9	10
Engine block heater	18	15	17
Front & rear reading & courtesy lights, Limited	40	34	37
Custom	54	46	50
Front courtesy lights, Custom	14	12	13
Decklid luggage rack	115	98	106
Left remote & right manual mirrors, Custom	53	45	49
Dual power remote mirrors, Custom	139	118	128
Limited	86	73	79
Lighted visor mirror	38	32	35
Bodyside molding	50	43	46
Rocker panel moldings, Custom	26	22	24
Wide rocker panel moldings, Custom . . .	76	65	70
Limited	50	43	46
Wheel opening moldings, Custom	30	26	28
Designer's Accent Paint	195	166	179
AM/FM stereo ET	167	142	154
Above w/cassette	314	267	290
Above w/casset & graphic EQ	454	386	420
Delco-GM/Bose music system	1005	854	925
AM ET delete (credit)	(96)	(82)	(82)
Extended range speakers	25	21	23
Concert Sound speakers	125	106	115
Power antenna	70	60	64
Flip-open removable glass sunroof, Limited .	350	298	320
Custom	379	322	350
6-way power driver's seat	240	204	220

Prices are accurate at time of printing; subject to manufacturer's change

Tilt steering column	125	106	115
Sport steering wheel	50	43	46
Leather & vinyl bucket seats, Limited . . .	275	234	255
Trunk trim, Skylark Custom	35	30	32
Power decklid release	50	43	46
Styled aluminum wheels	229	195	210
Locking wire wheel covers	199	169	183
Power windows, Somerset	210	179	193
Skylark	285	242	260
Gran Touring suspension	27	23	25
Intermittent wipers	55	47	51
T pkg.	592	563	545

Leather-wrapped steering wheel, Gran Touring suspension, P215/60R15 tires on aluminum wheels.

Exterior Sport pkg. (blackout trim),			
Skylark Custom	294	250	270
Skylark Limited	238	202	220

OLDSMOBILE CALAIS	Retail Price	Dealer Invoice	Low Price
2-door coupe	$9741	$8699	$9110
Supreme 2-door coupe	10397	9285	9720
4-door sedan	9741	8699	9110
Supreme 4-door sedan	10397	9285	9720
Destination charge	370	370	370

STANDARD EQUIPMENT (included in above prices):

2.5-liter (151-cid) 4-cylinder TBI engine, 5-speed manual transmission, power steering, power brakes, tinted glass, front & rear armrests, full-length console with integral armrest, full cut-pile carpeting, side window defogger, carpeted lower door panels, tungsten halogen headlamps, headlamps-on warning, dual horns, rallye gauge cluster, header panel courtesy lights,

Oldsmobile Calais GT 2-door

Prices are accurate at time of printing; subject to manufacturer's change.

black left outside mirror, bumper and wheel opening moldings, AM radio, contour reclining front bucket seats, trip odometer, P185/80R13 all-season SBR tires. **Supreme** adds: dual outside mirrors, convenience group, lower bodyside moldings, lower door panel storage compartment.

OPTIONAL EQUIPMENT:

3.0-liter (181-cid) V-6 (auto trans req.) . .	660	561	605
3-speed automatic transmission	490	417	450
Power driver's seat	240	204	220
4-way manual seat adjuster	35	30	32
Power door locks, 2-doors	145	123	133
4-doors	195	166	179
Power windows, 2-doors	210	179	193
4-doors	282	242	260
Power trunklid release	50	43	46
Deluxe bodyside moldings, base	50	43	46
Intermittent wipers	55	47	51
Rear defogger	145	123	133
Air conditioning	675	574	620
Front header & reading lamps	24	20	22
Exterior opera lamps, 4-doors	102	87	94
Sail panel/roof rail lamps, base	44	37	40
Supreme	30	26	28
Fold-down center armrest	60	51	55
Left remote & right manual mirrors, base .	53	45	49
Lighted right visor mirror, w/Conv. Grp. . .	38	32	35
Base w/o Conv. Grp.	45	38	41
Dual remote mirrors, Supreme	30	26	28
Two-tone paint	200	170	184
Firm ride & handling pkg.	30	26	28
Touring car ride & handling pkg.	475	404	435
Cruise control	175	149	161
Leather-wrapped steering wheel, base . . .	90	77	83
Supreme	54	46	50
Remote fuel door release	11	9	10
Tilt steering column	125	106	115
Locking wire wheel discs	199	169	183
Super Stock styled wheels	99	84	91
Styled aluminum wheels	199	169	183
Convenience Group, base	35	30	32
Lamps, right visor mirror, chime tones.			
Delete standard radio (credit)	(56)	(48)	(48)
AM/FM ST ET cassette	354	301	325
Power antenna	70	60	64
AM/FM ST ET w/cassette & EQ	504	428	465
Rallye instrument cluster	126	107	116
Digital trip monitor	90	77	83

Prices are accurate at time of printing; subject to manufacturer's change.

Electronic instruments	265	225	245
GT	139	118	128
Extended range rear speakers	25	21	23
High-capacity cooling, w/A/C	40	34	37
w/o A/C	70	60	64
Delete floorshift (credit)	(110)	(94)	(94)
Decklid luggage carrier	115	98	106
Custom leather seating	364	309	335
GT pkg., base	1350	1148	1240

Sport exterior decor, touring car suspension, leather-wrapped steering wheel, rallye instrument cluster, manual 4-way driver's seat.

Sport Appearance Pkg., base	195	166	179
Supreme	150	128	138
California emissions pkg.	99	84	91

Cadillac Allante

Cadillac Allante

Cadillac enters the international ultra-luxury market with its first production 2-seater, intended to rival the Mercedes-Benz 560SL and other sporty prestige cars. Allante is expected to sell for around $50,000 and only about 6000 will be built for the model year. Interior and exterior design are by Pininfarina, the Italian coachbuilder, who will supply Allante bodies from a new facility near Turin to start what Cadillac proudly terms "the world's longest assembly line." Bodies are flown 3300 miles to Detroit, where driveline and underbody components are installed. Allante is a full convertible with integral folding soft top and detachable aluminum hardtop. An all-disc power brake system with Bosch ABS III anti-lock control is standard.

Goodyear's new Eagle VL tires, specially designed for Allante and exclusive to it for '87, are also standard. Powering Allante is Cadillac's aluminum-block 4.1-liter V-8 with several changes, including multi-point instead of single-point fuel injection, roller valve lifters, high-flow cylinder heads and tuned intake manifold. In line with its market mission and flagship status, Allante comes fully equipped. The only option is a cellular telephone, installed in a lockable center console bin for security and featuring the industry's first retractable AM/FM/telephone antenna. Brief drives in early-production Allantes indicate Cadillac and Pininfarina have done their jobs well. Acceleration is smooth, quiet and amply quick, the handling taut and responsive, and the ride firm yet absorbent. Wind buffeting in the fully open mode is well controlled and structural rigidity is among the best of any convertible we've seen. More of a grand touring car than sports car, the Allante is aimed at a very narrow market. The big question is whether its exclusivity and Pininfarina cachet are enough to offset the low-class image of the Cadillac name among the rich and famous, who'd usually rather have a Mercedes.

Specifications

	2-door coupe
Wheelbase, in.	99.4
Overall length, in.	178.6
Overall width, in.	73.4
Overall height, in.	52.2
Front track, in.	60.5
Rear track, in.	60.5
Curb weight, lbs.	3494
Cargo vol., cu. ft.	13.0
Fuel capacity, gal.	22.0
Seating capacity	2
Front headroom, in.	37.2
Front shoulder room, in.	57.7
Front legroom, max., in.	43.1
Rear headroom, in.	—
Rear shoulder room, in.	—
Rear legroom, min., in.	—

Body/Chassis

Drivetrain layout: transverse front engine/front-wheel drive.
Front suspension: MacPherson struts, lateral links, trailing links, coil springs, stabilizer bar. **Rear suspension:** MacPherson

struts, H-control arm, transverse leaf spring. **Steering:** rack and pinion, power assisted, 3.0 turns lock-to-lock. **Turn diameter, ft.:** 38.0. **Front brakes:** 10.25-in. discs w/anti-lock. **Rear brakes:** 10.0-in. discs w/anti-lock. **Construction:** unit.

Powertrains	ohv V-8
Displacement, l/cu. in.	4.1/249
Compression ratio	8.5:1
Fuel delivery	PFI
Net bhp @ rpm	170 @ 4300
Net torque @ rpm	230 @ 3200
Availability	S
Final drive ratios	
4-speed OD automatic	2.95:1

KEY: bbl = barrel (carburetor); **bhp** = brake horsepower; **torque** = pounds/feet; **Cal.** = California only; **TBI** = throttle body (single-point) fuel injection; **PFI** = port (multi-point) fuel injection; **MFI** = mechanical fuel injection; **ohv** = overhead valve; **ohc** = overhead cam; **dohc** = double overhead cam; **I** = inline engine; **V** = V engine; **flat** = horizontally opposed engine; **D** = diesel; **T** = turbocharged; **OD** = overdrive transmission; **S** = standard; **O** = optional.

PRICES

(prices not available at time of publication)

STANDARD EQUIPMENT: 4.1-liter (249-cid) PFI V-8 engine, 4-speed automatic transmission, power steering, power 4-wheel disc brakes with Bosch anti-lock system, removable hardtop, folding convertible top, ten-way power Recaro seats with leather upholstery and driver's side position memory, Delco-GM/Bose Symphony music system, tilt/telescopic steering column, dual power remote mirrors, intermittent wipers, automatic day/night mirror, P225/60VR15 Goodyear Eagle VL tires on aluminum wheels.

OPTIONAL EQUIPMENT: cellular telephone.

Cadillac Brougham

Formerly called Fleetwood Brougham, this is the sole survivor from Cadillac's full-size, rear-drive C-body generation and it sold well again last year, helped by the drop in gasoline prices. Cadillac limits the changes for '87 to new colors and modest trim changes inside and out. The only noteworthy mechanical news is availability of an op-

Cadillac Brougham

tional heavy-duty trailer-towing package rated for 5000 pounds. As before, the extra-cost D'Elegance package offers plusher cabin appointments in the traditional idiom. Oldsmobile's 5.0-liter V-8 and a 4-speed overdrive automatic transmission return unchanged as the one and only drivetrain. This is the kind of car that was Cadillac's bread and butter for years, but doesn't promise much of a future since most Brougham buyers are in their 60s. It's a traditional American luxury car that offers plenty of room, a soft ride and loads of ostentatious luxury surrounded by acres of sheetmetal. However, it lacks the roadability that comes standard with European luxury cars that are attracting increasing numbers of affluent buyers, especially younger ones that Cadillac desperately needs. The Brougham will continue in production as long as fuel prices stay low and demand for this kind of car stays high. It never has been on our list of preferred luxury cars, since we put a higher premium on acceleration, handling and braking than we do on posh furnishings.

Specifications

	4-door sedan
Wheelbase, in.	121.5
Overall length, in.	221.0
Overall width, in.	75.3
Overall height, in.	56.7
Front track, in.	61.7
Rear track, in.	60.7
Curb weight, lbs.	4045
Cargo vol., cu. ft.	19.6
Fuel capacity, gal.	20.7
Seating capacity	6

	4-door sedan
Front headroom, in.	39.0
Front shoulder room, in.	59.4
Front legroom, max., in.	42.0
Rear headroom, in.	38.1
Rear shoulder room, in.	59.4
Rear legroom, min., in.	41.2

Body/Chassis

Drivetrain layout: longitudinal front engine/rear-wheel drive. **Front suspension:** unequal-length upper and lower control arms, coil springs, stabilizer bar. **Rear suspension:** rigid axle, four links, coil springs, electronic level control. **Steering:** recirculating ball, power assisted, 3.2 turns lock-to-lock. **Turn diameter, ft.:** 40.5. **Front brakes:** 11.7-in. discs. **Rear brakes:** 11.0-in. drums. **Construction:** body on frame.

Powertrains

	ohv V-8
Displacement, l/cu. in.	5.0/307
Compression ratio	8.0:1
Fuel delivery	4 bbl.
Net bhp @ rpm	140 @ 3200
Net torque @ rpm	245 @ 2000
Availability	S

Final drive ratios
4-speed OD automatic	2.73:1

KEY: bbl = barrel (carburetor); **bhp** = brake horsepower; **torque** = pounds/feet; **Cal.** = California only; **TBI** = throttle body (single-point) fuel injection; **PFI** = port (multipoint) fuel injection; **MFI** = mechanical fuel injection; **ohv** = overhead valve; **ohc** = overhead cam; **dohc** = double overhead cam; **I** = inline engine; **V** = V engine; **flat** = horizontally opposed engine; **D** = diesel; **T** = turbocharged; **OD** = overdrive transmission; **S** = standard; **O** = optional.

PRICES

CADILLAC BROUGHAM	Retail Price	Dealer Invoice	Low Price
4-door sedan	$22637	$19309	$20715
Destination charge	500	500	500

STANDARD EQUIPMENT (included in above prices):

5.0-liter (307-cid) 4 bbl. V-8 engine, 4-speed automatic transmission, power steering, power brakes, Dual Comfort 55/45 front seats, illuminated entry system, front and rear center armrests, four ash receivers, headlights-on

Prices are accurate at time of printing; subject to manufacturer's change.

warning, front and rear cigar lighters, power windows, power door locks, door pull swing handles, automatic climate control system, front and rear lamp monitors, cornering lights, halogen headlamps, engine compartment and trunk lights, sunshade support and door courtesy lights, glovebox light, carpeted litter receptacle, low fuel level indicator, dual remote mirrors, front seatback pockets, power driver's seat, tinted glass, trip odometer, padded sunvisors, low washer fluid level indicator, AM/FM ST ET with power antenna, full padded vinyl roof, front bumper guards, door sill plates, full carpeting, opera lamps, automatic parking brake release, P215/75R15 all-season SBR tires.

OPTIONAL EQUIPMENT:

Accent striping	65	55	60
Heavy-duty battery	40	34	37
Intermittent wipers	60	50	55
Cruise control	195	164	179
Rear defogger	170	143	156
d'Elegance pkg., w/cloth upholstery	1950	1638	1795
w/leather upholstery	2510	2108	2310

Accent striping, loose-pillow-look upholstery, power passenger seat, power trunklid release, intermittent wipers, adjustable rear seat reading lamps, manual passenger seatback recliner, three roof-mounted assist handles, Dual-Comfort 50/50 front seats, turbine vane wheel discs, deluxe carpet and floormats.

Automatic power door locks	185	155	170
Engine block heater	45	38	41
Remote fuel filler door release	65	55	60
Garage door opener transmitter	140	118	128
Guidematic headlamp control	95	80	87
Heavy-duty ride pkg.	323	271	295
Leather seating area	560	470	515
Electronic level control	203	171	187
Driver's seat position memory	215	181	198
Automatic day/night mirror	80	67	74
Dual illuminated visor mirrors	150	126	138
Power remote mirrors	101	85	93
Firemist paint	240	202	220
AM/FM ST ET cassette	309	260	285
Rear compartment reading lamps	33	28	30
Power recliner, driver's seat	160	134	147
Passenger seat, w/d'Elegance	95	80	87
w/o d'Elegance	410	344	375
Power passenger seat	250	210	230
Security Option Pkg.	400	336	370

Remote fuel filler door release, automatic power door locks, theft deterrent system.

Leather-wrapped steering wheel	115	97	106
Tilt/telescopic steering column	205	172	189
Theft deterrent system	200	168	184
Puncture sealing tires	155	130	143

Prices are accurate at time of printing; subject to manufacturer's change.

Trailering pkg.	912	766	840

Electronic level control, heavy-duty cooling system, battery and shock absorbers, 3.23:1 axle, wiring harness, 25.0-gallon fuel tank.

Trumpet horn	45	38	41
Power trunklid release	50	43	46
Power trunklid release & pulldown			
w/d'Elegance	80	67	74
w/o d'Elegance	130	109	120
Trunk mat	36	30	33
Twilight Sentinel	95	80	87
Locking wire wheel discs, w/d'Elegance . .	320	269	295
w/o d'Elegance	400	336	370
Turbine vane wheel discs	80	67	74
Wire wheels, w/o d'Elegance	940	790	865
w/d'Elegance	860	722	790

Cadillac Cimarron

Cadillac Cimarron

A V-6 engine and last year's D'Oro option package are now standard in the most expensive version of the GM J-body subcompact as Cadillac tries to further separate the Cimarron from its siblings. Cadillac decided shortly before the model year began to drop the 2.0-liter 4-cylinder engine as the standard powerplant for Cimarron. That means the Generation II version of the Chevy-supplied 2.8-liter V-6 is now standard. The V-6 has new aluminum cylinder heads, more extensive use of lightweight materials and GM's distributor-less Computer Controlled Coil Ignition system, plus five more horsepower. Like corresponding Cavaliers that use the same engine, V-6 Cimarrons get a new standard transmission this year, the GM-built 5-speed manual designed by Getrag of Germany. A 3-speed automatic returns at extra cost. Other technical changes include making the Delco-Bilstein suspension package standard and minor brake system modifications aimed at improved pedal feel and reduced effort. Outside, the '87 Cimarron is identified by flush-mount composite headlamps (phased in for the D'Oro package option late last year) in a reshaped front end cap with wraparound side marker lamps. Despite Cadillac's best efforts, the most expensive of GM's five front-drive J-cars remains a slow seller, though Cimarron is finally equipped the way it should have been from the start, including the V-6 engine. You can also get the V-6 in a Cavalier or Oldsmobile Firenza, leaving Cadillac with the same problem of trying to peddle a J-body subcompact that offers little that you can't get for less at another GM division.

Specifications

	4-door sedan
Wheelbase, in.	101.2
Overall length, in.	177.8
Overall width, in.	65.0
Overall height, in.	55.0
Front track, in.	55.4
Rear track, in.	55.2
Curb weight, lbs.	2575
Cargo vol., cu. ft.	12.0
Fuel capacity, gal.	13.6
Seating capacity	5
Front headroom, in.	38.2
Front shoulder room, in.	53.1
Front legroom, max., in.	42.2
Rear headroom, in.	37.6
Rear shoulder room, in.	53.1
Rear legroom, min., in.	34.3

Body/Chassis

Drivetrain layout: transverse front engine/front-wheel drive. **Front suspension:** MacPherson struts, coil springs, stabilizer bar. **Rear suspension:** semi-independent, beam axle, trailing arms, coil springs, stabilizer bar. **Steering:** rack and pinion, power assisted, 2.5 turns lock-to-lock. **Turn diameter, ft.:** 38.8. **Front brakes:** 9.7-in. discs. **Rear brakes:** 7.9-in. drums. **Construction:** unit.

Powertrains

	ohv V-6
Displacement, l/cu. in.	2.8/173
Compression ratio	8.9:1
Fuel delivery	PFI
Net bhp @ rpm	125 @ 4500
Net torque @ rpm	160 @ 3600
Availability	S
Final drive ratios	
5-speed OD manual	3.61:1
3-speed automatic	3.18:1

KEY: bbl = barrel (carburetor); **bhp** = brake horsepower; **torque** = pounds/feet; **Cal.** = California only; **TBI** = throttle body (single-point) fuel injection; **PFI** = port (multi-point) fuel injection; **MFI** = mechanical fuel injection; **ohv** = overhead valve; **ohc** = overhead cam; **dohc** = double overhead cam; **I** = inline engine; **V** = V engine; **flat** = horizontally opposed engine; **D** = diesel; **T** = turbocharged; **OD** = overdrive transmission; **S** = standard; **O** = optional.

PRICES

CADILLAC CIMARRON	Retail Price	Dealer Invoice	Low Price
4-door sedan	$15032	$13424	$13980
Destination charge	370	370	370

STANDARD EQUIPMENT (included in above prices):

2.8-liter (173-cid) PFI V-6 engine, 5-speed manual transmission, Delco-Bilstein suspension, power steering, power brakes, air conditioning, cruise control, power windows and door locks, halogen headlamps, dual power mirrors, leather seating areas, power driver's seat, tilt steering column, power trunklid release, rear defogger, intermittent wipers, front and rear center armrests, three overhead assist handles, headlights-on reminder, front cigar lighter, front floor console with removable storage compartment, coin holder, side window defoggers, engine compartment and trunk lights, ashtray and glovebox lights, instrument panel courtesy lights, dual spot reading lights, low-fuel warning indicator, passenger visor mirror, pockets in front door panels and front seatbacks, reclining front bucket seats, tinted glass, trip odometer, dual padded sun visors, AM/FM ST ET, front and rear bumper guards and rub strips, door sill plates, full carpeting, locking fuel filler door, bodyside, rocker panel and wheel opening moldings, leather-wrapped steering wheel, P195/70R13 SBR all-season tires on alloy wheels.

OPTIONAL EQUIPMENT:

3-speed automatic transmission	415	353	380
Lower body accent molding	450	383	415
Heavy-duty battery	26	22	24

Prices are accurate at time of printing; subject to manufacturer's change.

	Retail Price	Dealer Invoice	Low Price
Cloth upholstery (credit)	(100)	(85)	(85)
Engine block heater	20	17	18
Garage door opener transmitter	165	140	152
Garage door opener retainer	25	21	23
Electronic instrument cluster	238	202	220
Decklid luggage rack	145	123	133
Dual illuminated visor mirrors	105	89	97
Delco-GM/Bose music system	905	769	835
AM & FM ST ET w/cassette & EQ	233	198	215
AM/FM ST ET delete (credit)	(151)	(128)	(128)
Power passenger seat	240	204	220
P205/60R14 tires	104	88	96
Trunk mat	36	31	33
Twilight Sentinel	95	81	87
Vista Vent removable glass sunroof	350	298	320
Aluminum alloy wheels	40	34	37

Cadillac DeVille/ Fleetwood/Sixty Special

Cadillac Fleetwood Sixty Special

In a bid to give its front-drive big car design wider appeal, Cadillac revives the historic Sixty Special nameplate (last seen in 1972) for a stretched version of the Fleetwood D'Elegance sedan. Planned model year production will be only about 2000 units. Wheelbase goes up by five inches to 115.8, all of it added in the back seat area. Standard equipment is expanded to include moveable rear footrests, twin roof-mounted rear vanity mirrors, and the new-for-'86 GM/

Teves anti-lock braking system that's optional on other models (and should be more readily available this year). Returning on the front-drive C-body platform introduced for 1985, the DeVille and Fleetwood wear a mildly re-shaped grille flanked by Euro-style composite headlamps with combined high/low tungsten-halogen beams, plus new rear bumpers and fender caps that add 1.5 inches to overall length. Also new are hydro-elastic instead of solid rubber engine mounts, which Cadillac claims will reduce noise and vibration. The front-drive DeVille/Fleetwood may not be big enough to satisfy some Cadillac buyers, but we find them roomy enough inside, except for trunk space. The 4.1-liter V-8 has sufficient power for a car of this weight, though gas mileage still is nothing to rave about. The availability of anti-lock brakes is a big plus with us, and Cadillac's warranties cover the drivetrain and other major systems for 5 years/50,000 miles and body rust for 5 years/100,000 miles. In all, these Cadillacs strike us as much better choices than the rear-drive Brougham.

Specifications

	2-door coupe	4-door sedan	4-door sedan[1]
Wheelbase, in.	110.8	110.8	115.8
Overall length, in.	196.5	196.5	201.5
Overall width, in.	71.7	71.7	71.7
Overall height, in.	55.0	55.0	55.0
Front track, in.	60.3	60.3	60.3
Rear track, in.	59.8	59.8	59.8
Curb weight, lbs.	3311	3370	NA
Cargo vol., cu. ft.	15.7	15.7	15.7
Fuel capacity, gal.	18.0	18.0	18.0
Seating capacity	6	6	6
Front headroom, in.	39.3	39.3	39.3
Front shoulder room, in.	59.0	59.1	59.1
Front legroom, max., in.	42.4	42.4	42.4
Rear headroom, in.	38.1	38.1	38.1
Rear shoulder room, in.	57.6	58.6	58.6
Rear legroom, min., in.	41.4	41.3	46.3

1. Sixty Special

Body/Chassis

Drivetrain layout: transverse front engine/front-wheel drive. **Front suspension:** MacPherson struts, lower control arms, coil springs, stabilizer bar. **Rear suspension:** independent struts, coil springs, stabilizer bar, electronic level control. **Steering:** rack and pinion, power assisted, 3.4 turns lock-to-lock. **Turn diameter,**

ft.: 41.7. **Front brakes:** 10.25-in. discs. **Rear brakes:** 8.9-in. drums. **Construction:** unit.

Powertrains

	ohv V-8
Displacement, l/cu. in.	4.1/249
Compression ratio	9.0:1
Fuel delivery	TBI
Net bhp @ rpm	130 @ 4200
Net torque @ rpm	200 @ 2200
Availability	S
Final drive ratios	
4-speed OD automatic	2.97:1

KEY: bbl = barrel (carburetor); **bhp** = brake horsepower; **torque** = pounds/feet; **Cal.** = California only; **TBI** = throttle body (single-point) fuel injection; **PFI** = port (multipoint) fuel injection; **MFI** = mechanical fuel injection; **ohv** = overhead valve; **ohc** = overhead cam; **dohc** = double overhead cam; **I** = inline engine; **V** = V engine; **flat** = horizontally opposed engine; **D** = diesel; **T** = turbocharged; **OD** = overdrive transmission; **S** = standard; **O** = optional.

PRICES

CADILLAC DE VILLE	Retail Price	Dealer Invoice	Low Price
2-door Coupe de Ville	$21316	$18183	$19400
4-door Sedan de Ville	21659	18475	20145
Fleetwood d'Elegance 4-door sedan	26104	22266	23755
Fleetwood Sixty Special 4-door sedan ...	34850	29727	31365
Destination charge	500	500	500

STANDARD EQUIPMENT (included in above prices):

4.1-liter (249-cid) fuel-injected V-8 engine, 4-speed automatic transmission, power steering, power brakes, tungsten halogen headlamps, body color protective side molding, six-way power driver seat, manual recliners, power windows, power door locks, side window defogger, electronic climate control system, AM/FM ST ET, remote control door mirrors, sail panel courtesy/reading lights, P205/75R14 all-season SBR tires. **Fleetwood d'Elegance** adds: Dual-Comfort 45/55 front seats, power passenger seat, power trunklid release, dual power mirrors, rear seat reading lamps, digital instrument cluster, formal cabriolet roof, locking wire wheel discs. **Sixty Special** adds: rear passenger footrests, rear overhead console, anti-lock braking system, vinyl top.

OPTIONAL EQUIPMENT:

Accent striping, de Ville	65	55	60
Tri-band antenna	55	46	51

Prices are accurate at time of printing; subject to manufacturer's change.

Option			
Astroroof (NA Sixty Special)	1255	1054	1155
Heavy-duty battery	40	34	37
Anti-lock braking system	925	777	850
Intermittent wipers	60	50	55
Cruise control	195	164	179
Rear defogger & heater mirrors	170	143	156
Touring pkg., de Ville	2880	2419	2650
Uprated suspension, P215/65R15 Eagle GT tires on aluminum wheels.			
Dimming Sentinel	130	109	120
Dual comfort front seats, de Ville	255	214	235
Remote fuel filler door release	65	55	60
Garage door opener transmitter	140	118	129
Illuminated entry system	90	76	83
Digital instrument cluster, de Ville	238	200	220
Leather seating area	525	441	485
Driver's seat position memory	235	197	215
Automatic day/night mirror	80	67	74
Dual illuminated visor mirrors	150	126	138
Dual power mirrors, de Ville	101	85	93
Mobile cellular telephone	2850	2394	2620
Provisions for above	395	332	365
Firemist or Pearlmist paint	240	202	220
Delco-GM/Bose music system	905	760	835
AM & FM ST ET w/cassette & EQ	329	276	305
CB transceiver	278	234	255
Power front seatback recliners, each			
Fleetwood & Sixty Special	95	80	87
de Ville	160	134	147
Formal cabriolet roof, Coupe de Ville	713	599	655
Cambria cloth roof, Coupe de Ville	925	777	850
Vinyl roof delete, Fleetwood (credit)	(374)	(314)	(314)
Power passenger seat, de Ville	250	210	230
Security Option Pkg.	490	312	450
Automatic power door locks, illuminated entry system, remote fuel filler door release, theft deterrent system.			
Leather-wrapped steering wheel, de Ville	115	97	106
Tilt/telescope steering column	205	172	189
Theft deterrent system	200	168	184
Puncture sealing tires	155	130	143
Touring suspension, de Ville	705	592	650
Fleetwood & Sixty Special	270	227	250
Power trunklid release, de Ville	50	43	46
Power trunklid release & pulldown,			
Fleetwood & Sixty Special	80	67	74
de Ville	130	109	120
Twilight Sentinel	95	80	87
Locking wire wheel discs, de Ville	320	269	295
Alloy wheels, de Ville	435	365	400
Fleetwood & Sixty Special	115	97	106

Prices are accurate at time of printing; subject to manufacturer's change.

Cadillac Eldorado/Seville

Cadillac Eldorado

Following last year's redesign, Cadillac's front-drive personal-luxury pair suffered a whopping 60-percent sales drop. Buyer resistance to the new generation's smaller format and generic GM styling are the main reasons. The Eldorado coupe and Seville sedan share the same basic design as the Buick Riviera and Olds Toronado built alongside them, but the Cadillacs are powered by a 4.1-liter V-8, the Buick and Olds by a 3.8-liter V-6. The standard Eldorado/Seville suspension is retuned for greater ride softness, complemented by taller, 75-series 205mm tires (previously 70-series). Other shared changes include major body panels are now marked with vehicle identification numbers to discourage "chop-shop" thieves as part of a federal requirement, locking inertia reels for the rear seatbelts and an easier-to-operate mobile cellular telephone option. Downsizing hasn't been a good idea so far with the Eldorado/Seville, which lost 16 inches and about 350 pounds last year. Both models also lost their distinctive styling that for better or worse set them apart from other cars on the road. Now, they blend in with cheaper, smaller GM models. Looks aside, the new models offer better performance and as much luxury as their predecessors, plus more capable handling and a steadier ride. Too many previous Eldorado and Seville owners apparently measure value in pounds and inches, so the new models haven't measured up. Cadillac has extended warranty coverage to

5 years/50,000 miles while cutting 1987 prices on these cars to try to make them more marketable.

Specifications	2-door coupe	4-door sedan
Wheelbase, in.	108.0	108.0
Overall length, in.	188.2	188.2
Overall width, in.	71.3	70.9
Overall height, in.	53.7	53.7
Front track, in.	59.9	59.9
Rear track, in.	59.9	59.9
Curb weight, lbs.	3360	3419
Cargo vol., cu. ft.	14.1	14.1
Fuel capacity, gal.	18.0	18.0
Seating capacity	5	5
Front headroom, in.	37.8	37.9
Front shoulder room, in.	57.6	57.2
Front legroom, max., in.	42.7	42.7
Rear headroom, in.	37.8	37.9
Rear shoulder room, in.	59.4	57.6
Rear legroom, min., in.	35.7	35.7

Body/Chassis

Drivetrain layout: transverse front engine/front-wheel drive. **Front suspension:** MacPherson struts, coil springs, stabilizer bar. **Rear suspension:** independent, transverse leaf, struts, electronic level control. **Steering:** rack and pinion, power assisted, turns lock-to-lock NA. **Turn diameter, ft.:** 42.2. **Front brakes:** 10.4-in. discs. **Rear brakes:** 10.0-in. discs. **Construction:**

Powertrains	ohv V-8
Displacement, l/cu. in.	4.1/249
Compression ratio	9.0:1
Fuel delivery	TBI
Net bhp @ rpm	130 @ 4200
Net torque @ rpm	200 @ 2200
Availability	S
Final drive ratios	
4-speed OD automatic	2.97:1

KEY: bbl = barrel (carburetor); **bhp** = brake horsepower; **torque** = pounds/feet; **Cal.** = California only; **TBI** = throttle body (single-point) fuel injection; **PFI** = port (multipoint) fuel injection; **MFI** = mechanical fuel injection; **ohv** = overhead valve; **ohc** = overhead cam; **dohc** = double overhead cam; **I** = inline engine; **V** = V engine; **flat** = horizontally opposed engine; **D** = diesel; **T** = turbocharged; **OD** = overdrive transmission; **S** = standard; **O** = optional.

CADILLAC ELDORADO & SEVILLE	Retail Price	Dealer Invoice	Low Price
Eldorado 2-door coupe	$23740	$20250	21365
Seville 4-door sedan	26326	22456	23695
Destination charge	500	500	500

STANDARD EQUIPMENT (included in above prices):

4.1-liter (249-cid) TBI V-8 engine, power steering, power 4-wheel disc brakes, automatic air conditioning, power windows and door locks, retained accessory power system, cruise control, Twilight Sentinel, dual electric remote mirrors, overhead assist handles, reclining cloth and leather bucket seats, digital instrument cluster including tachometer, coolant temperature gauge and voltmeter, low fuel warning light, trip computer, outside thermometer, fold-down center armrest with two storage bins (one locking), rotating cup holder and coin retainer, leather-wrapped steering wheel with tilt and telescope feature, lamp monitors, 6-way power driver's seat, AM/FM stereo ET, translucent visor sunshade extensions, locking glovebox, dual spot/map lights with retainer for garage door opener, symmetrical reversible carpeted floormats, two-tone paint (Seville), P205/75R14 tires on aluminum wheels.

OPTIONAL EQUIPMENT:

Accent molding, Eldorado	75	63	69
Seville	150	126	138
Walnut wood appliques, Eldorado	245	206	225
Astroroof	1255	1054	1155
HD battery	40	34	37
Biarritz Pkg. w/cloth, Eldorado	3095	2600	2845
w/leather	3505	2944	3225

Power front seat recliners and lumbar support adjusters, six-way power passenger seat, front seatback pockets, walnut instrument panel, console and door panel trim, cabriolet padded roof with opera lamps, two-tone paint, closed-in rear window treatment, wire wheel discs, accent molding, deluxe carpet, reversible front and rear floormats.

California emissions pkg.	99	83	91
Rear defogger	170	143	156
Dimming Sentinel	130	109	120
Automatic power door locks	185	155	170
Elegante Pkg. w/cloth, Seville	3595	3020	3305
w/leather	4005	3364	3685

Eldorado Biarritz content plus leather-trimmed headrests, mid-tone paint treatment.

Engine block heater	45	38	41
Remote fuel filler door release	65	55	60
Garage door opener transmitter & retainer .	140	118	129
Illuminated entry system	90	76	83
Automatic day/night mirror	80	67	74

Prices are accurate at time of printing; subject to manufacturer's change.

Lighted visor mirrors	150	126	138
Mobile cellular telephone	2850	2394	2620
Provisions for above	395	332	365
Firemist or Pearlmist paint, primary	190	160	175
Secondary	50	42	46
Two-tone paint, Seville	600	504	550
Delco-GM/Bose music system	905	760	835
AM ST ET & EQ	329	276	305
Power passenger seat recliner	345	290	315
Cabriolet roof, Eldorado	495	416	455
Full cabriolet roof	NA	NA	NA
Power passenger seat	250	210	230
Security Option Pkg.	490	412	460

Remote fuel filler door release, automatic power door locks, theft deterrent system.

Theft deterrent system	200	168	184
Puncture sealing tires	200	168	184
Touring suspension	155	130	143
Locking wire wheel discs	190	160	175

Chevrolet Astro

Chevrolet Astro

Chevy's rear-drive compact van gains greater trailer-towing capacity, plus some other new options. A new towing package increases maximum trailer weight to 6000 pounds on the Astro (also marketed as the GMC Safari), 1000 pounds more than last year and enough to keep Chevy ahead of its rivals in the compact van field. A new "Touring Package" option due at mid-year will include new front bucket seats with velour upholstery and a center bench

Prices are accurate at time of printing; subject to manufacturer's change.

seat with split, reclining seatbacks and adjustable head rests. The right side of the center seat folds forward for easier entry to the rear bench seat. Also due at mid-year is a new air dam with integral 55-watt fog lights. A roof-mounted luggage rack is a new option this year. A 150-horsepower, fuel-injected 4.3-liter V-6 is standard on passenger versions of Astro, optional on cargo versions. A 98-horsepower, injected 2.5-liter 4-cylinder engine is standard on cargo versions. Seating arrangements in passenger models range from four bucket seats to space for eight, using bench seats in the middle and rear, buckets in front. Chevrolet is capitalizing on the Astro's strengths, taking advantage of the rear-drive design to increase towing capacity beyond what the front-drive Dodge Caravan/Plymouth Voyager can handle. The Astro is a far different animal from the carlike Caravan/Voyager, having the ride and feel of a traditional van. If you need a brawny compact van more than a family wagon, this is a good choice (but also check out the Ford Aerostar). If passenger use is your primary need, the Caravan/Voyager is probably a better choice.

Specifications

	5-door van
Wheelbase, in.	111.0
Overall length, in.	176.8
Overall width, in.	77.0
Overall height, in.	71.7
Front track, in.	NA
Rear track, in.	NA
Curb weight, lbs.	3084
Cargo vol., cu. ft.	151.8
Fuel capacity, gal.	17.0[1]
Seating capacity	5[2]
Front headroom, in.	NA
Front shoulder room, in.	NA
Front legroom, max., in.	NA
Rear headroom, in.	NA
Rear shoulder room, in.	NA
Rear legroom, min, in.	NA

1. 27.0-gal. optional   2. 4-, 7- and 8-pass. opt.

Body/Chassis

Drivetrain layout: longitudinal front engine/rear-wheel drive. **Front suspension:** unequal length upper and lower control arms, coil springs, stabilizer bar. **Rear suspension:** rigid axle, variable-

Prices are accurate at time of printing; subject to manufacturer's change.

rate single-leaf springs. **Steering:** recirculating ball, turns lock-to-lock NA. **Turn diameter, ft.:** NA. **Front brakes:** 12.0-in. discs. **Rear brakes:** 9.5-in. drums. **Construction:** unit.

Powertrains

	ohv V-6
Displacement, l/cu. in.	4.3/262
Compression ratio	9.3:1
Fuel delivery	TBI
Net bhp @ rpm	155 @ 4000
Net torque @ rpm	230 @ 2400
Availability	S
Final drive ratios	
5-speed OD manual	3.08:1
4-speed OD automatic	2.73:1

KEY: bbl = barrel (carburetor); **bhp** = brake horsepower; **torque** = pounds/feet; **Cal.** = California only; **TBI** = throttle body (single-point) fuel injection; **PFI** = port (multi-point) fuel injection; **MFI** = mechanical fuel injection; **ohv** = overhead valve; **ohc** = overhead cam; **dohc** = double overhead cam; **I** = inline engine; **V** = V engine; **flat** = horizontally opposed engine; **D** = diesel; **T** = turbocharged; **OD** = overdrive transmission; **S** = standard; **O** = optional.

PRICES

CHEVROLET ASTRO/GMC SAFARI	Retail Price	Dealer Invoice	Low Price
Base 4-door van	$9833	$8781	$9290
CS 4-door van	10314	9210	9745
CL 4-door van	11079	9894	10470
Destination charge	465	465	465

STANDARD EQUIPMENT (included in above prices):

Base: 4.3-liter (262-cid) TBI V-6 engine, 5-speed manual transmission, engine cover storage box, front armrests, swing-out side windows, black rubber floor covering, high-back bucket seats, 5-passenger seating, P195/75R15 all-season SBR tires. **CS** adds: color-keyed rubber floor covering, side window defoggers, inside fuel door release, lighted vanity mirrors, under-floor spare tire carrier. **CL** adds: bumper rub strips, trip odometer, voltmeter, oil pressure and coolant temperature gauges, custom steering wheel, wheel trim rings, auxiliary lighting, cigar lighter, carpet.

OPTIONAL EQUIPMENT:

4-speed automatic transmission	550	468	505
4-passenger seating, base & CS	670	570	615
CL	583	496	535

Prices are accurate at time of printing; subject to manufacturer's change.

	Retail Price	Dealer Invoice	Low Price
7-passenger seating, base & CS	1351	1148	1245
CL	1263	1074	1160
8-passenger seating, base & CS	626	532	575
CL	678	576	625
Seatback recliner & dual armrests	241	205	220
Custom highback bucket seats (cloth or vinyl)			
w/8-pass. seating	158	134	145
w/5-pass. seating	106	90	98
Special two-tone paint (striping included)	251	213	230
Sport two-tone paint	172	146	158
Optional axle ratio	38	32	35
Locking differential	252	214	230
Front air conditioning, base	781	664	720
CS & CL	736	626	675
Front & rear air conditioning, CS & CL	1320	1122	1215
Air dam w/fog lamps	115	98	106
Heavy-duty battery	56	48	52
Deluxe front & rear bumpers, base & CS	128	109	118
CL	76	65	.70
Color-keyed bumpers, base & CS	52	44	48
Increased cargo capacity (4- or 5-pass. seating req.)	334	284	305
Roof carrier	126	107	116
Spare tire carrier, base	22	19	20
Engine oil cooler (HD radiator & trans. cooler req.)	126	107	116
Heavy-duty radiator	56	48	52
w/trans oil cooler, w/o f & r A/C	118	100	109
w/f & r A/C	63	54	58
Cold Climate Pkg., base w/o f&r A/C	150	128	138
Cold Climate Pkg., CS & CL w/f&r A/C	105	89	97
Roof console	83	71	76
Power door locks	211	179	194
Remote fuel filler release	27	23	25
Carpeting, CS	117	99	108
Rubber floor covering, base	45	38	41
Gauge Pkg., base & CS	62	53	57
Complete body glass	128	109	118
Tinted glass, w/o complete body glass	75	64	69
w/complete body glass	104	88	96
Tinted windshield	40	34	37
Deep tinted glass, w/o complete body glass	236	201	215
w/complete body glass	365	310	336
Swing-out rear door glass	59	50	54
Deluxe grille, base & CS	27	23	25

Prices are accurate at time of printing; subject to manufacturer's change.

CONSUMER GUIDE®

	Retail Price	Dealer Invoice	Low Price
Trailer wiring harness	41	35	38
Halogen headlamps	24	20	22
Engine block heater	33	28	30
Rear heater	267	227	245
Deluxe heater	45	38	41
Dome & reading lamps	33	28	30
Cigaret lighter, base & CS	32	27	29
Auxiliary light group, base	149	127	137
CS	128	109	118
Deluxe left & right mirrors	52	44	48
Right side visor mirror, base	50	43	46
CS & CL	43	37	40
Black bodyside moldings, base & CS	59	50	54
Power windows and door locks	411	349	380
Protective interior panels, base	27	23	25
Sound systems			
AM radio	112	104	103
AM/FM stereo ET, base	253	215	235
CS & CL	293	249	270
AM/FM stereo ET cassette, base	434	369	400
CS & CL	474	403	435
Above w/graphic EQ, base	584	496	535
CS & CL	624	530	575
Heavy-duty front & rear shocks	36	31	33
Cruise control	205	174	189
Front stabilizer bar	40	34	37
Power steering	292	248	270
Tilt steering column	121	103	111
Custom steering wheel (std. CL)	28	24	26
Positive stop rear door, base	37	31	34
27-gallon fuel tank	70	60	64
Cargo tiedowns	32	27	29
Deadweight trailer hitch	68	58	63
Trailering Special Equipment, heavy duty			
w/o front & rear AC	555	472	510
w/front & rear AC	498	423	460
Trailering Special Equipment, light duty . .	109	93	100
Bright metal wheel covers, base & CS . . .	42	36	39
Wheel trim rings, base & CS	60	51	55
6.5″ argent rally wheels, base & CS	92	78	85
CL	50	43	46
Cast aluminum 15″ wheels, base & CS . .	316	269	290
CL	274	233	250
Power windows	200	170	184
Intermittent wipers	59	50	54

Prices are accurate at time of printing; subject to manufacturer's change.

Chevrolet Camaro

Chevrolet Camaro IROC-Z

A revised model lineup and new engines highlight the Camaro line for 1987, with the performance-oriented IROC-Z finally getting the 5.7-liter Corvette V-8 that was first promised for the middle of the 1986 model year. A Camaro convertible, the first since 1969, is scheduled to go on sale in January in all price/trim levels. Last year's base 4-cylinder engine and high-output, carbureted V-8 have been dropped. The Camaro line consists of the Sport Coupe, LT (replacing the Berlinetta series), Z28 and IROC-Z. Two engines are available in the Sport Coupe and LT: The standard Generation II 2.8-liter V-6 and the optional 5.0-liter 4-barrel V-8. That V-8 is standard in the Z28, which has the 5.0-liter tuned port injected V-8 as optional (note that this engine is rated at 215 horsepower with the 5-speed, only 190 with automatic). All of these engines are available with a 5-speed manual or 4-speed overdrive automatic. Both 5.0-liter V-8s are also available in the IROC-Z with either transmission, but the 225-horsepower 5.7-liter V-8 is an option exclusive to the IROC-Z, and available only with automatic transmission. Much of Camaro's continued popularity is due to its racy styling and muscle-car performance of the available V-8 engines, which keep getting more powerful as the years go on. If you drive only on glass-smooth roads and never encounter rain or snow, the V-8 powered Camaros can be great. However, where we drive, the Z28 and IROC-Z suspensions are much too stiff, resulting in a jolting, jarring ride, while rain and snow make the wide high-performance tires on these cars slip treacherously. For those who can get by with less performance, a V-6 powered Sport Coupe or LT might be easier to manage.

Specifications

	3-door coupe
Wheelbase, in.	101.0
Overall length, in.	188.0[1]
Overall width, in.	72.8
Overall height, in.	50.0
Front track, in.	60.7
Rear track, in.	61.6
Curb weight, lbs.	3062
Cargo vol., cu. ft.	31.0
Fuel capacity, gal.	15.5
Seating capacity	4
Front headroom, in.	37.0
Front shoulder room, in.	57.5
Front legroom, max., in.	43.0
Rear headroom, in.	35.6
Rear shoulder room, in.	56.3
Rear legroom, min., in.	29.8

1. 192.0 on Z28 and IROC-Z

Body/Chassis

Drivetrain layout: longitudinal front engine/rear-wheel drive. **Front suspension:** modified MacPherson struts, lower control arms, coil springs, stabilizer bar. **Rear suspension:** rigid axle, torque tube, longitudinal control arms, coil springs, Panhard rod, stabilizer bar. **Steering:** recirculating ball, power assisted, 2.5-3.0 turns lock-to-lock. **Turn diameter, ft.:** 36.9. **Front brakes:** 10.5-in. discs. **Rear brakes:** 9.5-in. drums (discs optional). **Construction:** unit.

Powertrains	ohv V-6	ohv V-8	ohv V-8	ohv V-8
Displacement, l/cu. in.	2.8/173	5.0/305	5.0/305	5.7/350
Compression ratio	8.9:1	9.3:1	9.3:1	9.0:1
Fuel delivery	PFI	4 bbl.	PFI	PFI
Net bhp @ rpm	135 @ 4900	165 @ 4400	215[2] @ 4400	225 @ 4400
Net torque @ rpm	160 @ 3900	245 @ 2800	295 @ 3200	330 @ 2800
Availability	S	S[1]	O	O[3]

1. Z28   2. 190 bhp @ 4000 and 295 lb. ft. @ 2800 w/auto trans   3. IROC-Z

Final drive ratios	ohv V-6	ohv V-8	ohv V-8	ohv V-8
5-speed OD manual	3.42:1	3.23:1	3.08:1	
4-speed OD automatic	3.42:1	2.73:1	2.73:1	3.27:1

KEY: bbl = barrel (carburetor); **bhp** = brake horsepower; **torque** = pounds/feet; **Cal.** = California only; **TBI** = throttle body (single-point) fuel injection; **PFI** = port (multipoint) fuel injection; **MFI** = mechanical fuel injection; **ohv** = overhead valve; **ohc** = overhead cam; **dohc** = double overhead cam; **I** = inline engine; **V** = V engine; **flat** = horizontally opposed engine; **D** = diesel; **T** = turbocharged; **OD** = overdrive transmission; **S** = standard; **O** = optional.

PRICES

CHEVROLET CAMARO	Retail Price	Dealer Invoice	Low Price
3-door Sport Coupe	$9995	$8926	$9445
Z28 3-door coupe	12819	11447	12115
Destination charge	414	414	414

STANDARD EQUIPMENT (included in above prices):

2.8-liter (173-cid) PFI V-6 engine, 5-speed manual transmission, power steering, power brakes, center console, full carpeting, bucket seats, sport mirrors, fold-down rear seatback, automatic hatch pulldown, P205/70R14 tires. **Z28** has over base Sport Coupe: 5.0-liter (305-cid) 4 bbl. V-8 engine, handling suspension, dual horns, leather-wrapped steering wheel, full instrumentation, black exterior accents, front air dam, special hood, rear deck spoiler, dual resonators and tailpipes, body color sport mirrors with left remote, courtesy lights, quartz analog clock, P215/65R15 high-performance tires.

OPTIONAL EQUIPMENT:

5.0-liter TPI (PFI) V-8, Z28	745	633	685
5.0-liter 4 bbl. V-8, Sport Coupe	400	340	370
5.7-liter (350-cid) TPI (PFI) V-8, Z28 ...	1045	888	960
4-speed automatic transmission	490	417	450
Air conditioning	775	659	715
Limited slip differential	100	85	92
Performance axle ratio	21	18	19
Heavy-duty battery	26	22	24
4-wheel disc brakes	179	152	165
Engine oil cooler	110	94	101
Locking rear storage cover	80	68	74
Rear defogger	145	123	133
Power door locks	145	123	133
California emissions pkg.	99	84	91
Gauge pkg., Sport Coupe	149	127	137
Tinted glass	120	102	110
Rear window louvers	210	179	193

Prices are accurate at time of printing; subject to manufacturer's change.

	Retail Price	Dealer Invoice	Low Price
Deluxe luggage compartment trim,			
Sport Coupe	164	139	151
Z28	84	71	77
Bodyside moldings	60	51	55
Power antenna	70	60	64
T-top roof	866	736	795
Split folding rear seatback	50	43	46
Rear spoiler, Sport Coupe	69	59	63
Cast aluminum wheels w/locks	215	183	198
Sound systems, Sport Coupe			
AM/FM ST ET cassette	364	309	335
AM/FM ST ET	242	206	225
AM/FM ST ET w/cassette & EQ	514	437	475
Delco-GM/Bose music system	1127	958	1035
AM mono	39	33	36
Sport Coupe Option Pkg. 2	1212	1030	1115

Tinted glass, air conditioning, tilt steering column, AM/FM ST ET.

	Retail Price	Dealer Invoice	Low Price
Sound systems w/Sport Coupe Pkg. 2			
AM/FM ST ET cassette	122	104	112
AM & FM ST ET w/cassette & EQ	272	231	250
Delco-GM/Bose music system	885	752	815
AM/FM ST ET delete (credit)	(298)	(253)	(253)
Sport Coupe Option Pkg. 3	1628	1384	1500

Pkg. 2 plus four floormats, bodyside moldings, intermittent wipers, rear spoiler, cruise control, AM/FM ST ET w/cassette and extended range speakers.

	Retail Price	Dealer Invoice	Low Price
Sport Coupe Option Pkg. 4	2126	1807	1955

Pkg. 3 plus power windows and door locks, power hatch release, cargo cover, halogen headlamps, auxiliary lighting.

	Retail Price	Dealer Invoice	Low Price
Sound systems w/Sport Coupe Option Pkgs. 3 or 4			
AM/FM ST ET w/cassette & EQ	150	128	138
Delco-GM/Bose music system	763	649	700
AM/FM ST ET delete (credit)	(420)	(357)	(357)
LT Option Pkg. 1	1522	1294	1400

Tinted glass, air conditioning, tilt steering column, AM/FM ST ET, full wheel covers, bodyside stripes, custom interior, quiet sound group.

	Retail Price	Dealer Invoice	Low Price
Sound systems w/LT Option Pkg. 1			
AM/FM ET cassette	122	104	112
AM/FM ET w/cassette & EQ	272	231	250
Delco-GM/Bose music system	885	752	815
AM/FM ST ET delete (credit)	(298)	(253)	(253)
LT Option Pkg. 2	1938	1647	1785

Pkg. 1 plus floormats, bodyside moldings, intermittent wipers, rear spoiler, cruise control, AM/FM ST ET cassette w/extended range speakers.

	Retail Price	Dealer Invoice	Low Price
LT Option Pkg. 3	2387	2029	2195

Pkg. 2 plus power windows and door locks, power hatch release, cargo cover, halogen headlamps.

	Retail Price	Dealer Invoice	Low Price
LT Option Pkg. 4	2858	2429	2630

Pkg. 3 plus power seat, interior roof console, automatic day/night mirror, power remote mirrors, halogen fog lamps.

	Retail Price	Dealer Invoice	Low Price
Sound Systems w/LT Option Pkg. 2, 3 or 4			
AM/FM ST ET w/cassette & EQ	150	128	138

Prices are accurate at time of printing; subject to manufacturer's change.

	Retail Price	Dealer Invoice	Low Price
Delco-GM/Bose music system	763	649	700
AM/FM ST ET cassette delete (credit) . .	(420)	(357)	(357)
Sound Systems, Z28			
AM/FM ET cassette	325	276	300
AM/FM stereo ET	203	173	187
AM/FM w/cassette & EQ	475	404	435
Delco-GM/Bose music system	1088	925	1000
Z28 Option Pkg. 2	1999	1699	1839

Sport equipment (unspecified), tinted glass, air conditioning, tilt steering wheel, floormats, body-side moldings, intermittent wipers, cruise control, AM/FM ST ET cassette with extended range speakers.

	Retail Price	Dealer Invoice	Low Price
Z28 Option Pkg. 3, w/o cargo cover	2470	2100	2270
w/cargo cover	2539	2158	2335

Pkg. 2 plus power windows and door locks, power hatch release, auxiliary lighting, halogen headlamps, cargo cover, power mirrors, power seat, automatic day/night mirror, interior roof console, halogen fog lamps.

	Retail Price	Dealer Invoice	Low Price
Sound systems w/Z28 Option Pkg. 2 or 3			
AM/FM ST ET w/cassette & EQ	150	128	138
Delco-GM/Bose music system	763	649	700
AM/FM ET w/cassete, delete (credit) . . .	(381)	(274)	(274)
IROC Option Pkg. 1	669	569	615

Halogen fog lamps, uprated suspension, P245/50VR16 tires on aluminum wheels.

	Retail Price	Dealer Invoice	Low Price
Sound systems w/IROC Pkg. 1			
AM/FM ST ET cassette	325	276	300
AM/FM ST ET	203	173	187
AM/FM ST ET w/cassette & EQ	475	404	435
Delco-GM/Bose music system	1088	925	1000
IROC Option Pkg. 2	2409	2048	2215

Pkg. 1 plus sport equipment (unspecified), tinted glass, air conditioning, tilt steering column, floormats, intermittent wipers, AM/FM ST ET cassette with extended range speakers, power windows and door locks, power hatch release.

	Retail Price	Dealer Invoice	Low Price
Sound systems w/IROC Pkg. 2			
AM/FM ST ET w/cassette & EQ	150	128	138
Delco-GM/Bose music system	763	649	700
AM/FM ST ET cassette, delete (credit) . .	(381)	(274)	(274)

Chevrolet Camaro LT

Prices are accurate at time of printing; subject to manufacturer's change

IROC Option Pkg. 3	3273	2782	3010
w/o cargo cover	3204	2723	2950

Pkg. 2 plus power mirrors, cruise control, bodyside moldings, cargo cover, auxiliary lighting, automatic day/night mirror, power seat, interior roof console, AM & FM ST ET with cassette and equalizer, extended range speakers.

Sound systems w/IROC Pkg. 3			
Delco-GM/Bose music system	613	521	565
AM & FM ST ET w/cassette & EQ, delete (credit)	(531)	(451)	451)

Chevrolet Caprice

Chevrolet Caprice 4-door

New headlamps, roller valve lifters and more models are the changes for 1987 in the Caprice. Introduced in this form for the 1977 model year, the Caprice lineup is the last complete full-size, rear-drive car line at General Motors, with coupe, sedan and wagon models. Buick, Oldsmobile and Pontiac still offer station wagons based on the same design. New aerodynamic composite headlamps combine separate high and low beams in a single unit. The Caprice Classic Brougham added last year has a new higher-priced running mate, the Brougham LS sedan with formal landau-style vinyl roof. A lower-priced, base Caprice wagon has been added. The base 4.3-liter V-6 and optional 5.0-liter (305-cid) Chevrolet V-8 now have roller valve lifters, which Chevy claims will increase both fuel economy and performance. Chevrolet now lists Oldsmobile's 307-cubic-inch V-8 as standard on Caprice wagons. There are still a lot of buyers who equate size and weight with value and safety, and others who need the room only a full-size, rear-drive car can provide. This is a good choice for that type of car, but the Caprice is now pretty much a tossup against the Ford LTD Crown Victoria. With less standard equipment and a standard V-6 engine, the Caprice starts out cheaper than the Crown Vic and gives buyers more options to choose from. Comparably equipped, the two makes are pretty close in price. We would stick with the V-8 because it provides stronger performance with little difference in fuel economy. Cars like this are still hard to beat for passenger and cargo space, plus the Caprice has a pretty good durability record and an impressive injury rating from the insurance industry.

Specifications

	2-door coupe	4-door sedan	5-door wagon
Wheelbase, in.	116.0	116.0	116.0
Overall length, in.	212.8	212.2	215.1
Overall width, in.	75.3	75.4	79.3
Overall height, in.	56.4	56.4	58.2
Front track, in.	61.7	61.7	62.2
Rear track, in.	60.7	60.7	64.1
Curb weight, lbs.	3512	3510	4114
Cargo vol., cu. ft.	20.9	20.9	87.9
Fuel capacity, gal.	24.5	24.5	22.0
Seating capacity	6	6	6[1]
Front headroom, in.	38.5	39.2	39.6
Front shoulder room, in.	60.9	60.9	60.9
Front legroom, max., in.	42.2	42.2	42.2
Rear headroom, in.	38.0	38.0	39.3
Rear shoulder room, in.	58.7	60.9	60.9
Rear legroom, min., in.	38.3	39.1	37.8

1. 8 w/opt. third seat

Body/Chassis

Drivetrain layout: longitudinal front engine/rear-wheel drive. **Front suspension:** unequal-length upper and lower control arms, coil springs, stabilizer bar. **Rear suspension:** rigid axle, four links, coil springs (stabilizer bar optional). **Steering:** recirculating ball, power assisted, 3.2 turns lock-to-lock. **Turn diameter, ft.:** 38.7 (39.7 wagon). **Front brakes:** 11.0-in. discs (11.9-in. wagon). **Rear brakes:** 9.6-in. drums (11.0-in. wagon). **Construction:** body on frame.

Powertrains

	ohv V-6	ohv V-8	ohv V-8
Displacement, l/cu. in.	4.3/262	5.0/305	5.0/307
Compression ratio	9.3:1	9.5:1	8.0:1
Fuel delivery	TBI	4 bbl.	4 bbl.
Net bhp @ rpm	140 @ 4200	170 @ 4400	140 @ 3200

	ohv V-6	ohv V-8	ohv V-8
	225 @	250 @	225 @
Net torque @ rpm	2000	2800	2000
Availability	S	O[1]	S[2]

1. exc. wagon   2. wagon

Final drive ratios

3-speed automatic	2.56:1		
4-speed OD automatic		2.56:1[1]	2.56:1

1. 2.73:1 opt.; std. wagons

KEY: bbl = barrel (carburetor); **bhp** = brake horsepower; **torque** = pounds/feet; **Cal.** = California only; **TBI** = throttle body (single-point) fuel injection; **PFI** = port (multi-point) fuel injection; **MFI** = mechanical fuel injection; **ohv** = overhead valve; **ohc** = overhead cam; **dohc** = double overhead cam; **I** = inline engine; **V** = V engine; **flat** = horizontally opposed engine; **D** = diesel; **T** = turbocharged; **OD** = overdrive transmission; **S** = standard; **O** = optional.

PRICES

CHEVROLET CAPRICE	Retail Price	Dealer Invoice	Low Price
4-door sedan	$10995	$9489	$10390
Classic 2-door coupe	11392	9831	10765
Classic 4-door sedan	11560	9976	10925
Brougham 4-door sedan	12549	10830	11860
Brougham LS 4-door sedan	13805	11914	13045
5-door wagon	11995	10352	11335
Classic 5-door wagon	12586	10862	11895
Destination charge	475	475	475

STANDARD EQUIPMENT (included in above prices):

4.3-liter (262-cid) TBI V-6 engine, 3-speed automatic transmission, power brakes, power steering, carpeting, knit cloth bench seat, cigar lighter, P205/75R15 BSW steel-belted radial tires. **Classic** adds: electric clock, dual horns, wheel opening moldings, Quiet Sound Group, vinyl door pull straps, bright wide lower bodyside moldings, headlamps-on reminder, stand-up hood ornament, carpeted lower door panels. **Brougham** adds: 20-oz carpet, front door courtesy lights, fully vinyl roof, 55/45 cloth front seat with center armrest. **LS** adds: Landau-style vinyl roof, sport mirrors, tinted glass. **Wagon** adds to base equipment: 5.0-liter (307-cid) 4bbl. V-8 engine, 4-speed automatic transmission, P225/75R15 SBR tires.

OPTIONAL EQUIPMENT:

5.0-liter (305-cid) V-8, sedans	440	361	405
4-speed auto trans, sedans	175	149	161
Cloth bench seat, base wagon	28	24	26
Vinyl bench seat, base sedan	28	24	26

Prices are accurate at time of printing; subject to manufacturer's change

	Retail Price	Dealer Invoice	Low Price
Vinyl 50/50 seat, base sedan	225	191	205
Base wagon	195	166	179
Cloth 50/50 seat, base sedan	195	166	179
Base wagon	225	191	205
Classic	195	166	179
Custom two-tone paint	141	120	130
Laundau roof & sport mirrors (std. LS) . .	321	273	295
Full vinyl roof (std. Brougham)	200	170	184
Air conditioning	775	659	715
Rear air deflector, wagons	65	55	60
Limited slip differential	100	85	92
Performance axle ratio	21	18	19
Heavy-duty battery	26	22	24
Bumper rub strips, base	66	56	61
Bumper guards	62	52	57
Roof luggage rack	115	98	106
Heavy-duty cooling, w/o A/C	70	60	64
w/A/C	40	34	37
Rear defogger	145	123	133
Power door locks, 2-doors	145	123	133
4-doors, wagons	195	166	179
California emissions system	99	84	91
Estate equipment	307	261	280
Deluxe load floor carpeting, wagons	89	76	82
Gauge package	64	54	59
Tinted glass	120	102	110
Engine block heater	20	17	18
Cornering lamps	55	47	51
Auxiliary lighting (std. Brougham), base . .	50	43	46
Classic	32	27	29
Deluxe luggage compartment trim	59	50	54
Left remote mirror	23	20	21
Dual remote mirrors, w/o Landau roof . . .	91	77	84
w/Landau roof	30	26	28
Left remote & right manual mirrors, base .	61	52	56
Illuminated passenger visor mirror	50	43	46
Bodyside moldings	60	51	55
Quiet Sound Group, base	66	56	61
Sound systems			
AM/FM ST ET, Classic & Brougham . . .	129	110	119
Base	168	143	155
AM/FM ST ET cassette, Classic & Brougham	290	247	265
Base	329	280	305
Above w/EQ, Classic & Brougham	435	370	400
Classic wagon	400	340	370

Prices are accurate at time of printing; subject to manufacturer's change

Base sedan	474	403	435
Base wagon	439	373	405
AM delete (credit), base	(56)	(48)	(48)
Classic & Brougham	(95)	(81)	(81)
Power antenna	70	60	64
Extended range speakers	35	30	32
Deluxe rear compartment decor, wagons	129	110	119
Power seats (each)	240	204	220
Passenger seat recliner	45	38	41
Cruise control	175	149	161
Tilt steering wheel	125	106	115
Heavy-duty suspension, F40 (std. wagon)	26	22	24
Sport suspension, F41	49	42	45
Inflatable rear shock absorbers	64	54	59
Power tailgate lock	60	51	55
Puncture sealant tires, exc. wagon	125	106	115
Wagon	150	128	138
Remote trunk release	50	43	46
Locking wire wheel covers	199	169	183
Power windows, 2-doors	210	179	193
4-doors, wagons	285	242	260
Intermittent wipers	55	47	51

Chevrolet Cavalier

Chevrolet Cavalier Z24 2-door

Once again there are 13 Cavalier models available from
five body styles and four trim levels, the most in the car
business. In all of them, the powertrains have been upgraded over last year with new Generation II 4- and 6-cy-
linder engines and a 5-speed manual transmission designed by the German firm, Getrag. The base engine for

Prices are accurate at time of printing; subject to manufacturer's change.

most of the front-drive Cavalier lineup is a 2.0-liter four that now has GM's Computer Controlled Coil Ignition (which eliminates the distributor) and is rated at two more horsepower (now up to 90). The Generation II 2.8-liter V-6 standard in the Z24 and optional in the RS convertible is rated at 130 horsepower, 10 more than last year. The new Getrag-designed 5-speed manual transaxle is being built in Muncie, Indiana, and is also used in other GM cars this year with the 2.8 V-6 and a turbocharged 2.0-liter four. Other changes to the Z24 include making 14-inch aluminum wheels standard, the addition of a functional fresh-air induction hood and a less-restrictive exhaust system. Performance has never been one of the base 2.0-liter engine's strong points and this year's Generation II version doesn't promise much improvement with only two more horsepower. Still, it's a fairly economical engine, especially with manual transmission. Leg room is limited in the rear seats of all body styles and the coupe and sedan have modest trunk capacity, yet they are the most popular with buyers. While the extensive Cavalier lineup gives buyers plenty of choices in body styles and equipment, it can cause headaches for consumers trying to comparison shop, since with so many options available (especially on base and CS models) the possibilities are endless. Cavalier is a popular but unexceptional subcompact that should be readily available below suggested retail prices in most areas.

Specifications	2-door coupe	3-door coupe	2-door conv.	4-door sedan	5-door wagon
Wheelbase, in.	101.2	101.2	101.2	101.2	101.2
Overall length, in. . . .	172.4	172.4	172.4	174.3	174.5
Overall width, in.	66.0	66.0	66.0	66.3	66.3
Overall height, in. . . .	50.2	50.2	52.7	52.1	52.8
Front track, in.	55.4	55.4	55.4	55.4	55.4
Rear track, in.	55.2	55.2	55.2	55.2	55.2
Curb weight, lbs.	2300	2359	2519	2345	2401
Cargo vol., cu. ft.	13.2	38.3	10.4	13.6	64.4
Fuel capacity, gal. . . .	13.6	13.6	13.6	13.6	13.6
Seating capacity	5	5	4	5	5
Front headroom, in. . .	37.7	42.2	42.9	38.6	38.3
Front shoulder room, in.	53.7	53.7	53.7	53.7	53.7
Front legroom, max., in.	42.2	42.2	42.9	42.2	42.9
Rear headroom, in. . . .	36.7	36.4	37.4	38.0	38.8
Rear shoulder room, in.	52.6	52.0	38.0	53.7	53.7
Rear legroom, min., in.	31.8	31.6	37.4	34.3	33.7

Body/Chassis

Drivetrain layout: transverse front engine/front-wheel drive. **Front suspension:** MacPherson struts, lower control arms, coil springs, stabilizer bar. **Rear suspension:** beam axle, trailing arms, coil springs (stabilizer bar optional). **Steering:** rack and pinion, 4.0 turns lock-to-lock. **Turn diameter, ft.:** 34.7. **Front brakes:** 9.7-in. discs. **Rear brakes:** 7.9-in. drums. **Construction:** unit.

Powertrains

	ohv I-4	ohv V-6
Displacement, l/cu. in.	2.0/121	2.8/173
Compression ratio	9.0:1	8.9:1
Fuel delivery	TBI	PFI
Net bhp @ rpm	90 @ 5600	130 @ 4500
Net torque @ rpm	108 @ 3200	165 @ 3600
Availability	S	S[1]

1. std. Z24; avail. on RS conv. (125 bhp and 160 lb. ft.)

Final drive ratios

4-speed OD manual	3.65:1	
5-speed OD manual	3.83:1	3.61:1
3-speed automatic	3.18:1	3.18:1

KEY: bbl = barrel (carburetor); **bhp** = brake horsepower; **torque** = pounds/feet; **Cal.** = California only; **TBI** = throttle body (single-point) fuel injection; **PFI** = port (multipoint) fuel injection; **MFI** = mechanical fuel injection; **ohv** = overhead valve; **ohc** = overhead cam; **dohc** = double overhead cam; **I** = inline engine; **V** = V engine; **flat** = horizontally opposed engine; **D** = diesel; **T** = turbocharged; **OD** = overdrive transmission; **S** = standard; **O** = optional.

PRICES

CHEVROLET CAVALIER	Retail Price	Dealer Invoice	Low Price
2-door coupe	$7255	$6696	$6965
4-door sedan	7449	6875	7150
5-door wagon	7615	7029	7310
CS 2-door coupe	7978	7310	7540
CS 4-door sedan	7953	7102	7515
CS 5-door wagon	8140	7270	7690
RS 2-door convertible	13446	12007	12705
RS 2-door coupe	8318	7428	7860
RS 3-door coupe	8520	7608	8050
RS 4-door sedan	8499	7590	8030
RS 5-door wagon	8677	7749	8200
Z24 2-door coupe	9913	8852	9370
Z24 3-door coupe	10115	9033	9560
Destination charge	370	370	370

Prices are accurate at time of printing; subject to manufacturer's change

STANDARD EQUIPMENT (included in above prices):

2.0-liter (121-cid) OHV TBI 4-cylinder engine, 4-speed manual transmission, power brakes, padded armrests, bumper rub strips, carpet, floor console with storage bin, coin holder and rear ashtray, side window defoggers, day/night mirror, vinyl reclining front bucket seats, integral air deflector and tailgate ajar warning light (wagon), P185/80R13 tires. **CS** adds: load floor carpet, bodyside moldings. **RS** adds: power steering, cockpit-style instrument panel, exterior moldings, wheel trim rings, sport suspension, P195/70R13 tires on rally wheels. **Z24** has CS equipment plus: 2.8-liter (173-cid) PFI V-6 engine, 5-speed manual transmission, power steering, blackout exterior treatment, F41 sport suspension, P215/60R14 tires on aluminum wheels.

OPTIONAL EQUIPMENT:

2.8-liter PFI V-6, RS conv.	660	561	605
3-speed automatic transmission	490	417	450
Z24	415	353	380
5-speed manual transmission	75	64	69
Cloth bucket seats, base & CS	28	24	26
Two-tone paint, CS	176	150	162
RS	123	105	113
Air conditioning	675	574	620
Heavy-duty battery	26	22	24
Deluxe seatbelts, base	26	22	24
Roof rack, wagons	115	98	106
Decklid rack, 2- & 4-doors	115	98	106
CL Custom Interior, 3-doors	271	230	250
Wagons	295	251	270
RS & Z24 2-doors	221	188	205
CS & RS 4-doors	245	208	225
Cargo area cover	69	59	63
Rear defogger	145	123	133
Power door locks, 2- and 3-doors	145	123	133
4- & 5-doors	195	166	179
California emissions system	99	84	91
Gauge package	69	59	63
Tinted glass (std. conv.)	105	89	97
Halogen headlamps	25	21	23
Engine block heater	20	17	18
Electronic instrument cluster (std. Z24)	295	251	270
Auxiliary lighting			
All exc. wagons & convertible	52	44	48
Wagon	58	49	53
RS conv.	35	30	32
Left remote & right manual mirrors	53	45	49
Bodyside moldings, base	50	43	45

Prices are accurate at time of printing; subject to manufacturer's change.

Sound systems			
AM radio, base	122	104	112
AM/FM ST ET, base	307	261	280
Others	207	176	190
Above w/cassette, base	429	365	395
Others	329	280	305
Above w/EQ, RS & Z24	479	407	440
AM delete (credit), all exc. base	(56)	(48)	(48)
Fixed-mast antenna w/o factory radio	41	35	38
Power liftgate release	50	43	45
Split folding rear seat (NA 2- & 4-doors) .	50	43	45
Cruise control	175	149	161
Rear spoiler	200	170	184
Power steering, base & CS	225	191	205
Tilt steering column	125	106	115
Removable glass sunroof	350	298	320
Heavy-duty suspension, F40	26	22	24
Sport suspension, F41			
Base & CS exc. wagons	49	42	45
Wagons	44	37	40
Remote trunk/liftgate release	50	43	46
Cast aluminum wheels	212	180	195
Power windows, 2- & 3-doors	210	179	193
4-doors, wagons	285	242	260
Intermittent wipers	55	47	51
Rear wiper/washer, 3-doors & wagons . . .	125	106	115

Chevrolet Celebrity

Chevrolet Celebrity 4-door

Drivetrain improvements are the major changes for Celebrity, but Chevrolet's front-drive intermediate also has new aerodynamic composite headlamps with integral side marker lamps. Celebrity is part of the GM A-body family, sharing its design with the Buick Century, Oldsmobile Cutlass Ciera and Pontiac 6000. Both available engines—a base 2.5-liter 4-cylinder and optional 2.8-liter V-6—have been substantially reworked and dubbed Generation II. The base 4-cylinder engine has a multi-coil ignition system and six more horsepower (to 98). The 2.8-liter V-6 is 35 pounds lighter due to generous use of aluminum, including in the new cylinder heads. Horsepower is up to 125 on the multi-point fuel-injected V-6, the only V-6 available in Celebrity this year. The new Getrag-designed 5-speed is offered as a credit option with the V-6, previously available only with automatic transmission. A 3-speed automatic transmission is standard with either the base 2.5 or optional V-6 and a 4-speed overdrive automatic is optional with the V-6. Even with this year's changes to the base engine, we still recommend the optional V-6, since it too has been improved. The V-6 offers more power, greater refinement and better driveability with automatic transmission, plus it probably will be more durable than the base 4-cylinder engine. We also recommend the Eurosport option, a relatively low-cost suspension and appearance package that changes the Celebrity's handling from ordinary to above average, while firming up the ride for better high-speed stability. All Celebrity buyers will get plenty of room for four adults (up to six in a pinch) and ample trunk space. The Ford Taurus is more stylish, more modern and at least as functional, but the Celebrity is still a pretty good package with the right equipment.

Specifications

	2-door sedan	4-door wagon	5-door sedan
Wheelbase, in.	104.9	104.9	104.9
Overall length, in.	188.3	188.3	190.8
Overall width, in.	69.3	69.3	69.3
Overall height, in.	54.1	54.1	54.3
Front track, in.	58.7	58.7	58.7
Rear track, in.	57.0	57.0	57.0
Curb weight, lbs.	2685	2715	2847
Cargo vol., cu. ft.	16.2	16.2	75.1
Fuel capacity, gal.	15.7	15.7	15.7
Seating capacity	5	5	6
Front headroom, in.	38.6	38.6	38.6
Front shoulder room, in.	55.9	56.2	56.2
Front legroom, max., in.	42.1	42.1	42.1

	2-door sedan	4-door wagon	5-door sedan
Rear headroom, in.	37.9	38.0	38.9
Rear shoulder room, in.	57.0	56.2	56.2
Rear legroom, min., in.	35.8	36.4	35.6

Body/Chassis

Drivetrain layout: transverse front engine/front-wheel drive.
Front suspension: MacPherson struts, lower control arms, coil springs, stabilizer bar. **Rear suspension:** beam twist axle with integral stabilizer bar, trailing arms, Panhard rod, coil springs.
Steering: rack and pinion, power assisted, 3.0 turns lock-to-lock.
Turn diameter, ft.: 36.9. **Front brakes:** 9.7-in. discs (10.2-in. wagons). **Rear brakes:** 8.9-in. drums. **Construction:** unit.

Powertrains	ohv I-4	ohv V-6
Displacement, l/cu. in.	2.5/151	2.8/173
Compression ratio	9.0:1	8.9:1
Fuel delivery	TBI	PFI
Net bhp @ rpm	98 @ 4800	125 @ 4500
Net torque @ rpm	135 @ 3200	160 @ 3600
Availability	S	O

Final drive ratios		
3-speed automatic	2.39:1	2.84:1
4-speed OD automatic		3.06:1

KEY: bbl = barrel (carburetor); **bhp** = brake horsepower; **torque** = pounds/feet; **Cal.** = California only; **TBI** = throttle body (single-point) fuel injection; **PFI** = port (multi-point) fuel injection; **MFI** = mechanical fuel injection; **ohv** = overhead valve; **ohc** = overhead cam; **dohc** = double overhead cam; **I** = inline engine; **V** = V engine; **flat** = horizontally opposed engine; **D** = diesel; **T** = turbocharged; **OD** = overdrive transmission; **S** = standard; **O** = optional.

PRICES

CHEVROLET CELEBRITY	Retail Price	Dealer Invoice	Low Price
2-door coupe	$9995	$8626	$9295
4-door sedan	10265	8859	9545
5-door wagon (2-seat)	10425	8997	9695
5-door wagon (3-seat)	10672	9210	9925
Destination charge	414	414	414

STANDARD EQUIPMENT (included in above prices):

2.5-liter (151-cid) TBI 4-cylinder engine, 3-speed automatic transmission, power brakes, power steering, front bench seat, cloth upholstery, full car-

Prices are accurate at time of printing; subject to manufacturer's change.

peting, AM radio, P185/75R-14 fiberglass-belted radial tires, bodyside moldings, glovebox lamp and lock, day/night mirrors, black left door mirror, dome and instrument panel courtesy lights.

OPTIONAL EQUIPMENT:

2.8-liter (173-cid) V-6	610	519	560
4-speed automatic transmission (V-6 req.)	175	149	161
5-speed manual trans (V-6 req.; credit)	(440)	(374)	(374)
Air conditioning	775	659	715
Rear window air deflector, wagon	40	34	37
Performance axle ratio	21	18	19
Heavy-duty battery	26	22	24
Bumper guards	56	48	52
Roof carrier (wagon) or decklid rack (others)	115	98	106
Center console w/shift lever	110	94	101
Heavy-duty cooling system			
w/air conditioning	40	34	37
w/o air conditioning	70	60	64
Rear defogger	145	123	133
Power door locks			
Coupe	145	123	133
Sedans, wagons	195	166	179
California emissions pkg.	99	84	91
Estate equipment, wagon	325	276	300
Eurosport Package[1]	240	204	220
Gauge Package (incl. trip odometer)	64	54	59
Tinted glass	120	102	110
Engine block heater	20	17	18
Auxiliary lighting			
Coupe	52	44	48
Sedan	64	54	59
2-seat wagon	70	60	64
3-seat wagon	56	48	52
Coupe w/sunroof	28	24	26
Sedan w/sunroof	40	34	37
2-seat wagon w/sunroof	46	39	42
3-seat wagon w/sunroof	32	27	29
Deluxe luggage compartment trim	47	40	43
Left remote mirror	23	20	21
Left remote & right manual mirrors	61	52	56
Dual remote mirrors	91	77	84
Right visor mirror	7	6	6
Illuminated right visor mirror	50	43	46
Exterior molding pkg.	55	47	51
Sound systems			
AM radio	39	33	36
AM/FM ST ET	168	143	155
Above w/cassette	329	280	305

Prices are accurate at time of printing; subject to manufacturer's change.

CONSUMER GUIDE®

Above w/graphic EQ	514	437	475
Extended range speakers	35	30	32
Deluxe rear compartment decor	40	34	37
Power driver's seat	240	204	220
Reclining front seatbacks (each)	45	38	41
Inflatable rear shock absorbers	64	54	59
Cargo area security pkg., wagon	44	37	40
Cruise control	175	149	161
Tilt steering column	125	106	115
Removable glass sunroof	350	298	320
Heavy-duty suspension, F40	26	22	24
Tachometer	90	77	83
Power trunk or liftgate release	50	43	46
Locking wire wheel covers	199	169	183
Cast aluminum wheels, w/o Eurosport	199	169	183
w/Eurosport	143	122	132
Rally wheels	56	48	52
Swing-out rear vent windows, wagon	75	64	69
Swing-out tailgate window, wagon	105	89	97
Power windows, coupe	210	179	193
Sedan & wagon	285	242	260
Intermittent wipers	55	47	51
Rear wiper/washer, wagon	125	106	115

1. Eurosport Package: sport suspension, sport steering wheel, P195/75R14 all season tires, rally wheels, side moldings and rub strips w/specific color treatment and blackout decor.

Chevrolet Chevette/ Pontiac 1000

Chevette is the oldest model in Chevrolet's lineup and the familiar but proven formula—small size, economical engine and affordable price—continues for one more season before the design is retired. The base price has been cut on the 3-door hatchback to $4995, making it the cheapest domestically built car. This rear-drive subcompact is also available as the similar Pontiac 1000; both return with very few changes for 1987. The optional 1.8-liter diesel has been dropped, leaving the 1.6-liter gas four as the only engine, and a Delco low-profile maintenance-free battery is now standard equipment. Most Chevettes are now sold to car rental companies, who use the aged subcompact as their low-price offering. Cramped, rear-drive and gener-

Prices are accurate at time of printing; subject to manufacturer's change.

Chevrolet Chevette 5-door

ally uncomfortable, Chevette is basic, low-cost transportation for the budget-conscious buyer. It does have a few virtues, but nothing that you can't find somewhere else. However, it really is short on interior space compared to modern front-drive subcompacts, has a coal-cart ride, mediocre handling, poor roadholding from its ancient rear-drive chassis and comes with an engine that lacks the performance and refinement now expected in small cars. Chevrolet has sold millions of Chevettes, and many owners have been happy with them. That was yesterday. Today there are just too many better small cars for us to recommend this one, despite the Third World base price of $4995.

Specifications

	3-door sedan	5-door sedan
Wheelbase, in.	94.3	97.3
Overall length, in.	161.9	164.9
Overall width, in.	61.8	61.8
Overall height, in.	52.8	52.8
Front track, in.	51.2	51.2
Rear track, in.	51.2	51.2
Curb weight, lbs.	2078	2137
Cargo vol., cu. ft.	27.1	28.8
Fuel capacity, gal.	12.2	12.2
Seating capacity	4	4
Front headroom, in.	37.8	37.9
Front shoulder room, in.	50.1	49.8
Front legroom, max., in.	41.7	41.7
Rear headroom, in.	37.1	36.9

	3-door sedan	5-door sedan
Rear shoulder room, in.	49.4	49.4
Rear legroom, min., in.	30.6	34.0

Body/Chassis

Drivetrain layout: longitudinal front engine/rear-wheel drive. **Front suspension:** unequal-length upper and lower control arms, coil springs, stabilizer bar. **Rear suspension:** rigid axle, four links, torque tube and track bar, coil springs. **Steering:** rack and pinion, 3.6 turns lock-to-lock manual; 3.0 power. **Turn diameter, ft.:** 30.2. **Front brakes:** 9.7-in. discs. **Rear brakes:** 7.9-in. drums. **Construction:** unit.

Powertrains

	ohc I-4
Displacement, l/cu. in.	1.6/98
Compression ratio	9.0:1
Fuel delivery	2 bbl.
Net bhp @ rpm	65 @ 5600
Net torque @ rpm	80 @ 3200
Availability	S
Final drive ratios	
4-speed manual	3.36:1
5-speed OD manual	3.36:1
3-speed automatic	3.36:1

KEY: bbl = barrel (carburetor); **bhp** =brake horsepower; **torque** = pounds/feet; **Cal.** = California only; **TBI** = throttle body (single-point) fuel injection; **PFI** = port (multi-point) fuel injection; **MFI** = mechanical fuel injection; **ohv** = overhead valve; **ohc** = overhead cam; **dohc** = double overhead cam; **I** = inline engine; **V** = V engine; **flat** = horizontally opposed engine; **D** = diesel; **T** = turbocharged; **OD** = overdrive transmission; **S** = standard; **O** = optional.

PRICES

CHEVROLET CHEVETTE CS	Retail Price	Dealer Invoice	Low Price
3-door sedan	$4995	$4695	$4845
5-door sedan	5495	5165	5330
Destination charge	290	290	290

STANDARD EQUIPMENT (included in above prices):

1.6-liter (98-cid) 4-cylinder engine, four-speed manual transmission, front air dam, bumper guards, cut-pile carpeting, cigar lighter, center console, front door map pockets, day/night mirror, AM radio, reclining front bucket seats, folding rear seat, custom cloth upholstery (5-doors), P155/80R13 SBR tires on styled steel wheels.

Prices are accurate at time of printing; subject to manufacturer's change.

OPTIONAL EQUIPMENT:

	Retail Price	Dealer Invoice	Low Price
3-speed automatic transmission	450	383	415
5-speed manual transmission	75	64	69
Power steering	225	191	205
Cloth bucket seats	28	24	22
Custom cloth bucket seats	130	111	120
Custom two-tone paint	183	156	168
Air conditioning	675	574	621
Performance axle ratio	21	18	19
Heavy-duty battery	26	22	24
Power brakes	105	89	97
Chromed bumpers	25	21	23
Heavy-duty cooling system			
w/o air conditioning	70	60	64
w/air conditioning	40	34	37
Custom exterior pkg., 3-door	139	118	128
5-door	154	131	142
Rear defogger	145	123	133
California emissions pkg.	99	84	91
Tinted glass	105	89	97
Engine block heater	20	17	18
Left remote & right manual mirrors	53	45	49
Left remote mirror	34	29	31
Bodyside moldings	50	43	46
AM/FM radio	92	78	85
AM/FM stereo	119	101	109
AM delete (credit)	51	43	43
Exterior sport decor	132	112	121
Power steering	225	191	205
Tilt steering column	125	106	115

PONTIAC 1000

	Retail Price	Dealer Invoice	Low Price
3-door sedan	$5959	$5363	$5541
5-door sedan	6099	5489	5670
Destination charge	290	290	290

STANDARD EQUIPMENT (included in above prices):

1.6-liter (98-cid) 4-cylinder engine, 4-speed manual transmission, bumper guards and rub strips, front air dam, mini console, lockable glovebox, rocker panel and bodyside moldings, AM radio, reclining front vinyl bucket seats, one-piece folding rear seatback, P155/80R13 SBR tires on styled steel wheels.

OPTIONAL EQUIPMENT:

Option Group 1	835	710	770
Air conditioning, tinted glass, power brakes.			

Prices are accurate at time of printing; subject to manufacturer's change.

Option Group 2	988	840	910
Group 1 plus tilt steering wheel, left remote and right manual mirrors.			
5-speed manual transmission	75	64	69
3-speed automatic transmission	450	383	415
Air conditioning (tinted glass req.)	675	574	620
HD battery & engine block heater	44	37	40
Rear defogger	145	123	133
California emissions pkg.	99	84	91
Tinted glass (A/C req.)	105	89	97
Power steering	225	191	205
AM/FM radio	92	78	85
AM/FM ST	119	101	109
AM delete (credit)	(56)	(48)	(48)
Genor cloth trim	30	26	28
Glass sunroof	350	298	320
Wheel trim rings	39	33	36

Chevrolet Corsica/Beretta

Chevrolet Corsica

Due out at mid-year, the Corsica 4-door sedan and Beretta 2-door coupe will fill the void created in Chevrolet's lineup when the compact Citation X-car was discontinued at the end of the 1985 model year. Corsica and Beretta are sized between the subcompact Cavalier and mid-size Celebrity and Chevy says they also will be priced between those two (prices weren't announced by press time). Other GM divisions replaced the X-car with the N-body compacts (Buick Skylark/Somerset, Oldsmobile Calais and Pontiac Grand Am), but Chevy didn't get a version of that design, so Corsica and Beretta will be Chevrolet exclusives. The sporty Beretta will eventually replace the much larger, rear drive Monte Carlo coupe. Corsica and Beretta share drivetrains and chassis, but they share no exterior sheet metal and have different dashboards. The reworked 2.0-liter 4-cylinder engine standard in the Cavalier also will be standard in the new compacts, while Chevy's 2.8-liter V-6 will be optional. Both models have standard 4-way adjustable front bucket seats, while Beretta's dashboard gains a standard tachometer and different controls. Underneath, Beretta has an F41 sport suspension and P195/70R14 tires, while Corsica comes with a softer suspension and P185/80R13 tires standard. The sport suspension and larger tires are optional on Corsica. A firmer handling suspension and P205/60R15 tires are available on Beretta as part of a GT option package. Test drives of early production models showed acceleration is only adequate with the standard 4-cylinder engine and optional 3-speed automatic transmission. The V-6 furnishes much livelier performance, whether teamed with the automatic or standard 5-speed manual transmission. Corsica's base suspension is competent, but the F41 suspension standard on Beretta, optional on Corsica, gives these cars more sporting road manners. The Corsica and Beretta are attractively styled compacts that give every indication of being well thought out and well-built. With Chevy's marketing muscle, they're good bets to become top sellers.

Specifications

	2-door coupe	4-door sedan
Wheelbase, in.	103.4	103.4
Overall length, in.	187.2	183.4
Overall width, in.	68.0	68.0
Overall height, in.	52.6	52.7
Front track, in.	55.6	55.6
Rear track, in.	56.5	55.1
Curb weight, lbs.	2550	2491
Cargo vol., cu. ft.	13.5	13.5
Fuel capacity, gal.	13.6	13.6
Seating capacity	5	5
Front headroom, in.	38.0	38.9
Front shoulder room, in.	55.3	55.4
Front legroom, max., in.	43.4	43.4
Rear headroom, in.	36.6	37.4
Rear shoulder room, in.	55.1	55.6
Rear legroom, min., in.	33.7	35.0

Body/Chassis

Drivetrain layout: transverse front engine/front-wheel drive.
Front suspension: MacPherson struts, lower control arms, coil springs, stabilizer bar. **Rear suspension:** semi-independent, beam axle, trailing arms, coil springs stabilizer bar (optional, Corsica). **Steering:** rack and pinion, power assisted, 2.9 turns lock-to-lock. **Turn diameter, ft.:** 35.1. **Front brakes:** 9.7-in. discs. **Rear brakes:** 7.9-in. drums. **Construction:** unit.

Powertrains	ohv I-4	ohv V-6
Displacement, l/cu. in.	2.0/121	2.8/173
Compression ratio	9.0:1	8.9:1
Fuel delivery	TBI	PFI
Net bhp @ rpm	90 @ 5600	125 @ 4500
Net torque @ rpm	108 @ 3200	160 @ 3600
Availability	S	O
Final drive ratios		
5-speed OD manual	3.83:1	3.61:1
3-speed automatic	3.18:1	3.18:1

KEY: bbl = barrel (carburetor); **bhp** = brake horsepower; **torque** = pounds/feet; **Cal.** = California only; **TBI** = throttle body (single-point) fuel injection; **PFI** = port (multi-point) fuel injection; **MFI** = mechanical fuel injection; **ohv** = overhead valve; **ohc** = overhead cam; **dohc** = double overhead cam; **I** = inline engine; **V** = V engine; **flat** = horizontally opposed engine; **D** = diesel; **T** = turbocharged; **OD** = overdrive transmission; **S** = standard; **O** = optional.

PRICES

CHEVROLET CORSICA AND BERETTA
(prices not available at time of publication)

STANDARD EQUIPMENT: Corsica (4-door sedan): 2.0-liter (121-cid) TBI 4-cylinder engine, 5-speed manual transmission, power steering, power brakes, composite halogen headlamps, beltline and bodyside moldings, clearcoat paint, reclining front bucket seats, four-way driver's seat adjustments, soft vinyl door panel trim with cloth inserts and storage pockets, lockable glovebox, driver's side storage compartment, tachometer, coolant temperature and oil pressure gauges, trip odometer, soft-feel steering wheel, headlamps-on warning, rear shoulder belts, full wheel covers, P185/80R13 all-season tires on styled steel wheels. **Beretta** (2-door coupe) adds: F41 sport suspension, dual sport mirrors, console, tinted glass, P195/70R14 all-season tires.

MAJOR OPTIONS will include: 2.8-liter (173-cid) PFI V-6 engine, 3-speed automatic transmission, F41 sport suspension with P195/70R14 tires (Corsica), GT package on Beretta (includes 2.8-liter V-6, blackout exterior trim

Chevrolet Beretta

with charcoal accents, custom cloth interior trim, fold-down rear center armrest), Z51 Performance Handling Package (available on Beretta with 2.8 V-6; includes rally-tuned suspension, P205/60R15 Goodyear Eagle GT "Plus 4" performance tires on 15-inch styled wheels).

Chevrolet Corvette

Chevrolet Corvette Roadster

Few changes have been made to the Corvette coupe and convertible for 1987. The standard 5.7-liter V-8 now has roller hydraulic lifters, resulting in 10 more horsepower (now 240). A new optional electronic system monitors tire pressure to warn the driver of low air pressure in any of the four tires. The system is sensitive to any tire dropping one pound of pressure below a pre-set limit, activating a dashboard warning light. Pressure sensors are mounted at each wheel, along with radio transmitters powered by generators that convert mechanical energy from the moving wheels into electrical energy. The system requires no external wires or connections and it weighs less than two pounds. There is little that is subtle about the Corvette, one of the most overt performance cars you can buy. The 5.7-liter provides blistering acceleration and a top speed of over 150 mph. Corvette's stiff suspension and huge tires give it amazing cornering ability that lets you accelerate around 90-degree turns. When it comes time to stop, the standard anti-lock brakes do the job safely, even on wet or snow-packed surfaces. However, slippery roads are bad news for the high-performance tires, so you'll lose a lot of traction for acceleration and cornering. Bumpy roads are bad news also, since there's little give to the suspension, so the occupants and the body absorb most of the road shock. Chevrolet designed the Corvette to be a race car first, a street car second. Whether this car is appropriate for you depends on your priorities.

Specifications

	2-door coupe	2-door conv.
Wheelbase, in.	96.2	96.2
Overall length, in.	176.5	176.5
Overall width, in.	71.0	71.0
Overall height, in.	46.7	46.4
Front track, in.	59.6	59.6
Rear track, in.	60.4	60.4
Curb weight, lbs.	3216	3279
Cargo vol., cu. ft.	17.9	6.6
Fuel capacity, gal.	20.0	20.0
Seating capacity	2	2
Front headroom, in.	36.5	36.5
Front shoulder room, in.	54.1	54.1
Front legroom, max., in.	42.6	42.6
Rear headroom, in.	—	—
Rear shoulder room, in.	—	—
Rear legroom, min., in.	—	—

Body/Chassis

Drivetrain layout: longitudinal front engine/rear-wheel drive.
Front suspension: unequal length upper and lower control arms,

transverse single-leaf springs, stabilizer bar. **Rear suspension:** five-links, upper and lower control arms, transverse single-leaf springs, stabilizer bar. **Steering:** rack and pinion, power assisted, 2.4 turns lock-to-lock. **Turn diameter, ft.:** 40.1. **Front brakes:** 11.5-in. discs. **Rear brakes:** 11.5-in. discs. **Construction:** unit.

Powertrains

	ohv V-8
Displacement, l/cu. in.	5.7/350
Compression ratio	9.0:1
Fuel delivery	PFI
Net bhp @ rpm	240 @ 4000
Net torque @ rpm	345 @ 3200
Availability	S
Final drive ratios	
4-speed OD manual	3.07:1
4-speed OD automatic	2.59:1[1]

1. 3.07:1 std. on roadster; opt. on others

KEY: bbl = barrel (carburetor); **bhp** = brake horsepower; **torque** = pounds/feet; **Cal.** = California only; **TBI** = throttle body (single-point) fuel injection; **PFI** = port (multi-point) fuel injection; **MFI** = mechanical fuel injection; **ohv** = overhead valve; **ohc** = overhead cam; **dohc** = double overhead cam; **I** = inline engine; **V** = V engine; **flat** = horizontally opposed engine; **D** = diesel; **T** = turbocharged; **OD** = overdrive transmission; **S** = standard; **O** = optional.

PRICES

CHEVROLET CORVETTE	Retail Price	Dealer Invoice	Low Price
3-door coupe	$27999	$23603	$25340
2-door convertible	33172	27961	32170
Destination charge	475	475	475

STANDARD EQUIPMENT (included in above prices):

5.7-liter (350-cid) PFI V-8 engine, 4-speed manual or automatic transmission w/overdrive, power steering, power 4-wheel disc brakes, antilock braking system, theft deterrent system, air conditioning, AM/FM ETR seek & scan radio w/power antenna, tinted glass, dual remote control mirrors, tilt/telescope steering column, power windows, intermittent wipers P245/60VR15 Goodyear Eagle GT tires on cast alloy wheels.

OPTIONAL EQUIPMENT:

Leather seats	400	332	370
Leather sport seats	1025	851	945
Custom two-tone paint	428	355	395
Automatic air conditioning	150	125	138

Prices are accurate at time of printing; subject to manufacturer's change.

Performance axle ratio	22	18	20
Engine oil cooler	110	91	101
Rear defogger & heated outside mirrors	165	137	152
Power door locks	190	156	175
California emissions system	99	82	91
Radiator cooling boost fan	75	62	69
Dual heated power mirrors	35	29	32
Illuminated left visor mirror	58	48	53
Performance Handling Pkg.	795	660	730
Heavy-duty radiator	40	33	37
AM/FM stereo ET cassette	132	110	121
Delco-GM/Bose music system	905	751	835
AM/FM delete (credit)	(256)	(212)	(212)
Removable roof panel	615	510	565
Dual removable roof panels	915	759	840
6-way power driver's seat	240	199	220
Delco-Bilstein shock absorbers	189	157	174
Cruise control	185	154	170
Tire low pressure indicator	325	270	300

Chevrolet Monte Carlo/ Pontiac Grand Prix

Chevrolet Monte Carlo SS

The rear-drive, mid-size Monte Carlo and Grand Prix
coupes, both built from the GM G-body design that debuted
for 1978 and includes the Oldsmobile Cutlass Supreme
and Buick Regal. All of these cars are expected to be gone
by 1988. Monte Carlo is being replaced by the compact
Beretta coupe (see Corsica/Beretta report) and Grand Prix
will be succeeded by a smaller front-drive model next fall.
Monte Carlo is available in two models this year: LS (Lux-

ury Sport) and SS (Super Sport), with the SS available as either a notchback or fastback. Last year's base model has been dropped. A fuel-injected 4.3-liter V-6 is standard in the LS, with new hydraulic valve lifters this year, and a carbureted 5.0-liter V-8 is optional. The SS carries a high-output, carbureted 5.0-liter V-8. Pontiac offers its rear-drive, mid-size coupe four ways: Grand Prix comes in base, LE and Brougham trim, plus there's the fastback 2 + 2 sport model introduced in mid-1986. A 3.8-liter carbureted V-6 is standard in all but the 2 + 2, which comes only with a 5.0-liter V-8. The V-8 and Chevy's 4.3-liter V-6 are optional in all but the 2 + 2. Minor rear styling revisions have been added to both Monte Carlos, while the SS gains the aerodynamic composite headlamps that debuted last year on the LS. The least practical versions of these cars— the SS and 2 + 2 fastbacks—are the ones that makes the most sense to buy these days. These race-car lookalikes have good potential for becoming collectible cars in the years ahead, when big, V-8-powered, rear-drive cars are history. Other than that, there's not much here to recommend over newer, front-drive designs (such as the Celebrity and 6000). For those who prefer rear-wheel drive, we think the Ford Thunderbird is a better choice in an intermediate. This design is nine years old, and that's a long time in the car business.

Specifications	2-door coupe
Wheelbase, in.	108.0
Overall length, in.	200.4
Overall width, in.	71.8
Overall height, in.	54.4
Front track, in.	58.5
Rear track, in.	57.8
Curb weight, lbs.	3283
Cargo vol., cu. ft.	16.2
Fuel capacity, gal.	17.6[1]
Seating capacity	6
Front headroom, in.	37.9
Front shoulder room, in.	56.3
Front legroom, max., in.	42.8
Rear headroom, in.	38.1
Rear shoulder room, in.	55.9
Rear legroom, min., in.	36.5

1. 18.1 w/V-8

Body/Chassis

Drivetrain layout: longitudinal front engine/rear-wheel drive. **Front suspension:** unequal-length upper and lower control arms, coil springs, stabilizer bar. **Rear suspension:** rigid axle, four links, control arms, coil springs (stabilizer bar optional). **Steering:** recirculating ball, power assisted, 3.3 turns lock-to-lock. **Turn diameter, ft.:** 37.1. **Front brakes:** 10.5-in. discs. **Rear brakes:** 9.5-in. drums. **Construction:** unit.

Powertrains	ohv V-6	ohv V-8	ohv V-8
Displacement, l/cu. in.	4.3/262	5.0/305	5.0/305
Compression ratio	9.3:1	9.5:1	9.5:1
Fuel delivery	TBI	4 bbl.	4 bbl.
Net bhp @ rpm	145 @ 4200	150 @ 4000	180 @ 4800
Net torque @ rpm	225 @ 2000	240 @ 2000	225 @ 3200
Availability	S	O	S[1]

1. Monte Carlo SS

Final drive ratios

3-speed automatic	2.29:1		
4-speed OD automatic	2.41:1	2.41:1	3.73:1

KEY: bbl = barrel (carburetor); **bhp** = brake horsepower; **torque** = pounds/feet; **Cal.** = California only; **TBI** = throttle body (single-point) fuel injection; **PFI** = port (multipoint) fuel injection; **MFI** = mechanical fuel injection; **ohv** = overhead valve; **ohc** = overhead cam; **dohc** = double overhead cam; **I** = inline engine; **V** = V engine; **flat** = horizontally opposed engine; **D** = diesel; **T** = turbocharged; **OD** = overdrive transmission; **S** = standard; **O** = optional.

PRICES

CHEVROLET MONTE CARLO	Retail Price	Dealer Invoice	Low Price
LS 2-door coupe	$11306	$9757	$10400
SS 2-door coupe	13463	11619	12385
SS Aero 2-door coupe	14838	12805	13650
Destination charge	414	414	414

STANDARD EQUIPMENT (included in above prices):

4.3-liter (262-cid) TBI V-6 engine, 3-speed automatic transmission, power steering, power brakes, folding front center armrest, cut-pile carpeting, cigar lighter, carpeted lower door panels, vinyl door pull straps, cloth headliner, instrument panel courtesy lights, lockable glovebox, luggage compartment mat, dual outside mirrors, bright lower bodyside moldings, AM radio, cloth front bench seat, full wheel covers, P195/75R14 SBR tires. **SS** adds: 5.0-liter (305-cid) 4 bbl. V-8, 4-speed automatic transmission, gauge package with trip odometer, left remote mirror, blackout exterior moldings, black sport steering wheel, P215/65R15 all-season tires on aluminum wheels.

Prices are accurate at time of printing; subject to manufacturer's change.

OPTIONAL EQUIPMENT:

	Retail Price	Dealer Invoice	Low Price
5.0-liter (305-cid) V-8 engine, LS	440	374	405
4-speed automatic transmission, LS	175	149	161
Cloth 55/45 seat	133	113	122
Cloth bucket seats	147	125	135
Vinyl bench seat	28	24	26
Custom cloth CL 55/45 seat	385	327	355
Custom two-tone paint	214	182	197
Padded vinyl landau roof	260	221	240
Air conditioning	775	659	715
Limited slip differential	100	85	92
Performance axle ratio	21	18	19
Heavy-duty battery	26	22	24
Console	110	94	101
Heavy-duty cooling, w/o A/C	70	60	64
w/A/C	40	34	37
Rear defogger	145	123	133
Power door locks	145	123	133
California emissions system	99	84	91
Gauge package, LS	69	59	63
Tinted glass	120	102	110
Halogen headlamps, SS	25	21	23
Engine block heater	20	17	18
Auxiliary lighting			
w/o T-top roof	33	28	30
w/T-top roof	15	13	14
Left remote & right manual mirrors, LS	53	45	49
Dual remote mirrors, LS	83	71	76
SS	30	26	28
Illuminated passenger visor mirror	50	43	46
Sound systems			
AM/FM ST ET	168	143	155
Above w/cassette & EQ	329	280	305
AM delete (credit)	(56)	(48)	(48)
Power antenna	70	60	64
Premium rear speakers	25	21	23
T-top roof	895	761	825
6-way power driver's seat (55/45 seat req.)	240	204	220
Cruise control	175	149	161
Tilt steering column	125	106	115
Sport suspension, F41 (std. SS)	49	42	45
Tachometer (std. SS)	90	77	83
Power trunklid release	50	43	46
Locking wire wheel covers	199	169	183
Styled rally wheels	56	48	52
Cast aluminum wheels	230	196	210
Power windows	210	179	193
Intermittent wipers	55	47	51

Prices are accurate at time of printing; subject to manufacturer's change.

CONSUMER GUIDE®

Pontiac Grand Prix 2+2

PONTIAC GRAND PRIX

2-door coupe	$11069	$9553	$10405
LE 2-door coupe	11799	10183	11090
Brougham 2-door coupe	12519	10804	11770
2 + 2 2-door coupe	NA	NA	NA
Destination charge	414	414	414

STANDARD EQUIPMENT (included in above prices):

3.8-liter (231-cid) 2 bbl. V-6 engine, 3-speed automatic transmission, power steering, power brakes, lockable glovebox, dual manual mirrors, AM radio, notchback front seat with folding center armrest, P195/75R14 tires. **LE** adds: luxury door panels, added sound insulation, left remote mirror, wide rocker panel and sill moldings. **Brougham** adds: upgraded carpet and door panels, door courtesy lamps, 55/45 front seat, luxury cushion steering wheel, power windows.

OPTIONAL EQUIPMENT:

Option Group 1, base	1313	1116	1210

Air conditioning, AM/FM ST ET, tilt steering column, tinted glass, bodyside moldings, left remote and right manual mirrors, color-keyed seatbelts, luxury cushion steering wheel.

Option Group 2, base	1867	1587	1720

Group 1 plus power windows and door locks, intermittent wipers, lamp group.

Option Group 1, LE	1844	1567	1695

Air conditioning, AM/FM ST ET, power windows and door locks, cruise control, tilt steering wheel, tinted glass, bodyside moldings, intermittent wipers, lamp group, right visor mirror.

Option Group 2, LE	2117	1799	1950

Group 1 plus power seat, remote decklid release, lighted right visor mirror, halogen headlamps.

Prices are accurate at time of printing; subject to manufacturer's change.

	Retail Price	Dealer Invoice	Low Price
Option Group 1, Brougham	1874	1593	1725

Air conditioning, power seat, AM/FM ST ET, cruise control, power door locks, tilt steering column, tinted glass, bodyside moldings, intermittent wipers, lamp group, right visor mirror.

	Retail Price	Dealer Invoice	Low Price
Option Group 2, Brougham	2078	1766	1910

Group 1 plus cornering lamps, remote decklid release, lighted right visor mirror, luggage compartment trim, dual remote mirrors, dome reading lamp, halogen headlamps.

	Retail Price	Dealer Invoice	Low Price
Performance Value Pkg., base	703	598	645
LE	500	425	460

5.0-liter 4 bbl. V-8, bucket seats and console, Rally II wheels, rally gauges.

	Retail Price	Dealer Invoice	Low Price
4.3-liter TBI V-6	200	170	184
5.0-liter 4 bbl. V-8 (4-sp auto trans req.) .	590	502	545
4-sp auto trans (NA w/3.8)	175	149	161
Air conditioning (tinted glass req.)	775	659	715
Limited-slip differential	100	85	92
Cold weather group, w/o HD cooling . . .	44	37	40
w/HD cooling	18	15	16

HD battery and engine block heater.

	Retail Price	Dealer Invoice	Low Price
HD cooling system, w/o A/C	96	82	88
w/A/C	66	56	61
Rear defogger	145	123	133
California emissions pkg.	99	84	91
Rally cluster & trip odometer	71	60	65
Above w/tachometer (stereo req.)	153	130	141
Tinted glass (A/C req.)	120	102	110
Hatch roof	906	770	835
Wide rocker panel moldings, base	86	73	79
Two-tone paint, base & LE	205	174	189
Sport two-tone paint, base	291	247	270
LE	205	174	189
AM/FM ST ET	178	151	164
AM/FM ST ET cassette	300	255	275
AM/FM ST ET cassette w/EQ	450	383	415
AM delete (credit)	(56)	(48)	(48)
Power antenna	70	60	64
Ripple cloth 55/45 seat, base	133	113	122
Reclining bucket seats w/console			
Ripple cloth, base	292	248	270
Pallex cloth, LE	89	76	82
Pallex cloth & leather, LE	389	331	360
Passenger recliner w/bench seat	60	51	55
Power glass sunroof	925	786	850
Y99 rally tuned suspension	50	43	46
Formal padded landau top	337	286	310
Padded landau top	260	221	240
Rally II 14" wheels	125	106	115
Turbo finned aluminum 14" wheels w/locks .	246	209	225
Locking wire wheel covers	214	182	197

Prices are accurate at time of printing; subject to manufacturer's change.

Chevrolet Nova

Chevrolet Nova 4-door

Changes for the 1987 model year are minor and few in number on the Nova: Wider taillights, body-color bumpers and the addition of a rear-window defogger to the standard equipment list. New United Motor Manufacturing Inc., the joint venture in California between General Motors and Toyota, produces the front-drive Nova, nearly identical to the Toyota Corolla. Nova is available as a 4-door sedan or 5-door hatchback, both with a 74-horsepower 1.6-liter 4-cylinder engine. Many wondered if an American car company and the United Auto Workers could successfully produce a Japanese-designed car in the U.S. While the Nova hasn't been a smashing sales success, all indications are that the GM-Toyota venture is producing top-quality cars. Chevrolet claims Nova is ranked first among GM cars in customer satisfaction and has the lowest warranty repair rate. Toyota apparently is convinced also; the company will buy up to 50,000 Corolla FX16 sporty hatchbacks this year that will be built along side Nova at the NUMMI plant (Chevy won't be selling that car). Nova uses Toyota mechanical components, so it figures to have the same kind of reliability and durability as the Japanese-made Corollas. Unfortunately, Chevrolet has raised Nova prices by about $1000 in the past year, so it's not the bargain it once was. It's still a good family subcompact that should provide reliable service.

Specifications

	4-door sedan	5-door sedan
Wheelbase, in.	95.7	95.7
Overall length, in.	166.3	166.3
Overall width, in.	64.4	64.4
Overall height, in.	53.0	52.8
Front track, in.	56.1	56.1
Rear track, in.	55.3	55.3
Curb weight, lbs.	2162	2204
Cargo vol., cu. ft.	12.7	26.0
Fuel capacity, gal.	13.2	13.2
Seating capacity	4	4
Front headroom, in.	38.3	37.9
Front shoulder room, in.	53.9	53.9
Front legroom, max., in.	42.4	42.4
Rear headroom, in.	36.9	35.6
Rear shoulder room, in.	53.7	53.7
Rear legroom, min., in.	31.9	31.9

Body/Chassis

Drivetrain layout: Transverse front engine/front-wheel drive. **Front suspension:** MacPherson struts, lower control arms, coil springs. **Rear suspension:** MacPherson struts, dual links, coil springs, stabilizer bar. **Steering:** rack and pinion, 3.2 turns lock-to-lock. **Turn diameter, ft.:** 30.8. **Front brakes:** 9.6-in. discs. **Rear brakes:** 7.9-in. drums. **Construction:** unit.

Powertrains

	ohc I-4
Displacement, l/cu. in.	1.6/97
Compression ratio	9.0:1
Fuel delivery	2 bbl.
Net bhp @ rpm	74 @ 5200
Net torque @ rpm	86 @ 2800
Availability	S

Final drive ratios
5-speed OD manual	3.72:1
3-speed automatic	3.42:1

KEY: bbl = barrel (carburetor); **bhp** =brake horsepower; **torque** = pounds/feet; **Cal.** = California only; **TBI** = throttle body (single-point) fuel injection; **PFI** = port (multipoint) fuel injection; **MFI** = mechanical fuel injection; **ohv** = overhead valve; **ohc** = overhead cam; **dohc** = double overhead cam; **I** = inline engine; **V** = V engine; **flat** = horizontally opposed engine; **D** = diesel; **T** = turbocharged; **OD** = overdrive transmission; **S** = standard; **O** = optional.

PRICES

CHEVROLET NOVA	Retail Price	Dealer Invoice	Low Price
4-door sedan	$8258	$7457	$7845
5-door sedan	8510	7685	8085
Destination charge	290	290	290

STANDARD EQUIPMENT (included in above prices):

1.6-liter (97-cid) 4-cylinder engine, 5-speed manual transmission, tinted glass, AM radio, rear defogger, black bodyside moldings, child-resistant door locks, locking fuel filler door, reclining front bucket seats, front door pockets, cloth and vinyl seat trim, side window defoggers, trip odometer, coolant temperature gauge, low fuel and door ajar warning lights, cigarette lighter, mist-cycle wipers, optical horn, full-length console, cut-pile carpeting, day/night mirror, P155/80R13 all-season SBR tires on styled steel wheels.

OPTIONAL EQUIPMENT:

Custom two-tone paint	176	150	167
Option Package 2	630	536	600
Automatic transmission, power steering			
Option Package 3	1120	952	1064
Pkg. 2 plus 5-speed, air conditioning, AM/FM ST ET			
Option Package 4	1530	1301	1455
Pkg. 3 plus automatic transmission			
Option Package 5	1480	1258	1380
Pkg. 4 but without rear defogger			
CL Option Package 1, 4-door	2405	2044	1945
5-door	2710	2304	2575
Automatic transmission, AM/FM ST ET, left remote and right manual mirrors, power steering, air conditioning, halogen headlamps, P175/70R13 tires			
CL Option Package 2, 4-door	2625	2231	2500
5-door	2450	2083	2330
CL pkg. 1 content plus 5-speed, cassette stereo, intermittent wipers, cruise control, rear wiper/washer (5-door).			
CL Option Package 3, 4-door	3200	2720	3040
5-door	3630	3085	3450
CL pkg. 2 content plus automatic transmission, power windows and door locks, full wheel covers (4-door), aluminum wheels (5-door).			

All CL Option Packages include windshield tint band, wide black bodyside molding, bodyside stripes, remote decklid and fuel filler releases, luggage compartment trim and lamp, driver's seat height and lumbar support adjustments, velour seat trim, console storage box and armrest, right visor mirror, passenger assist grips, tilt steering column.

Prices are accurate at time of printing; subject to manufacturer's change.

Chevrolet Spectrum

Chevrolet Spectrum 4-door

Five-mph bumpers and a new Turbo model are the biggest changes for 1987 on Spectrum, a front-wheel drive subcompact produced by Isuzu of Japan (which sells its own version as the I-Mark). All Spectrums benefit from flush-fitting composite headlights and 5-mph bumpers that replace last year's 2½-mph bumpers, but the Turbo model's equipment transforms the car from practical transportation to aggressive performer. The Spectrum Turbo, due to arrive around mid-year, comes only as a 4-door sedan in one color—charcoal metallic—with orange accents and body-colored trim. Fog lamps and P185/60R14 tires are part of the Turbo package, as well as special induction and exhaust systems, firmer springs and shock absorbers, front and rear stabilizer bars, and a full instrument cluster. Turbocharging increases horsepower from Spectrum's 1.5-liter 4-cylinder engine to 105 from 70. Other Spectrums have new instrument clusters, steering wheels and interior fabrics, a headlamps-on warning chime and more sound insulation. The Spectrum and nearly identical Isuzu I-Mark are among the also-rans in the subcompact class not because they're bad cars, but because there are better cars available for about the same cost (such as the Honda Civic, Dodge Omni/Plymouth Horizon). To its credit, Spectrum has an economical engine that returns impressive mileage even with automatic transmission, plus a plushy-furnished interior with comfortable seats. However, the engine is noisy and its performance barely adequate with manual transmission, inadequate with automatic. You can do better shopping elsewhere.

Specifications

	3-door sedan	4-door sedan
Wheelbase, in.	94.5	94.5
Overall length, in.	157.4	160.2
Overall width, in.	63.6	63.6
Overall height, in.	52.0	52.0
Front track, in.	54.7	54.7
Rear track, in.	54.3	54.3
Curb weight, lbs.	1947	1989
Cargo vol., cu. ft.	29.7	11.4
Fuel capacity, gal.	11.1	11.1
Seating capacity	4	4
Front headroom, in.	38.0	37.7
Front shoulder room, in.	52.8	52.8
Front legroom, max., in.	41.7	41.7
Rear headroom, in.	37.1	37.6
Rear shoulder room, in.	52.8	52.8
Rear legroom, min., in.	33.0	33.5

Body/Chassis

Drivetrain layout: transverse front engine/front-wheel drive. **Front suspension:** MacPherson struts, lower control arms, coil springs. **Rear suspension:** trailing arms, transverse beam, coil springs. **Steering:** rack and pinion, turns lock-to-lock NA. **Turn diameter, ft.:** 34.8. **Front brakes:** 8.9-in. discs. **Rear brakes:** 7.0-in. drums. **Construction:** unit.

Powertrains

	ohc I-4	ohc I-4T
Displacement, l/cu. in.	1.5/90	1.5/90
Compression ratio	9.6:1	8.0:1
Fuel delivery	2 bbl.	PFI
Net bhp @ rpm	70 @ 5400	105 @ 5400
Net torque @ rpm	87 @ 3400	120 @ 3400
Availability	S	S
Final drive ratios		
5-speed manual	3.58:1	NA
3-speed automatic	3.53:1	

KEY: bbl = barrel (carburetor); **bhp** = brake horsepower; **torque** = pounds/feet; **Cal.** = California only; **TBI** = throttle body (single-point) fuel injection; **PFI** = port (multipoint) fuel injection; **MFI** = mechanical fuel injection; **ohv** = overhead valve; **ohc** =

overhead cam; **dohc** = double overhead cam; **I** = inline engine; **V** = V engine; **flat** = horizontally opposed engine; **D** = diesel; **T** = turbocharged; **OD** = overdrive transmission; **S** = standard; **O** = optional.

PRICES

CHEVROLET SPECTRUM	Retail Price	Dealer Invoice	Low Price
4-door sedan	$7709	$6938	$7400
3-door coupe	7412	6671	7115
Turbo 4-door sedan	NA	NA	NA
Destination charge	290	290	290

STANDARD EQUIPMENT (included in above prices):

1.5-liter (92-cid) 4-cylinder engine, 5-speed manual transmission, power brakes, luggage restraint straps, cargo floor carpet, console, side window and rear defoggers, tinted glass, day/night mirror, wide bodyside moldings, radio prep, reclining cloth and vinyl lowback bucket seats, split folding rear seatback, front door storage pockets, swing-out rear quarter windows, P155/80R13 all-season tires on styled steel wheels. **Turbo** adds: 1.5-liter turbocharged PFI engine, fog lamps, tachometer, turbo boost gauge, voltmeter, oil pressure and coolant temperature gauges, P185/60R14 tires on stamped wheels.

OPTIONAL EQUIPMENT:

Custom Option Package 2, 3-door	825	701	785

Automatic transmission, front seat courtesy lamps, luggage compartment lamp, right visor mirror, full wheel covers, intermittent wipers.

Custom Option Package 3, 3-door	1469	1249	1395

Custom Pkg. 2 plus air conditioning, power steering, tachometer, rear wiper/washer.

Custom Option Package 4, 3-door	1917	1629	1820

Custom Pkg. 3 plus automatic transmission, tilt steering column, remote hatch and fuel filler releases, cargo area cover.

Custom Option Package 2, 4-door	1288	1095	1225

5-speed transmission, front seat courtesy lamps, passenger visor mirror, intermittent wipers, air conditioning, power steering, tachometer, tilt steering column, remote trunk and fuel filler releases.

Custom Option Package 3, 4-door	1166	991	1110

Automatic transmission, front seat courtesy lamps, power steering, air conditioning. Deletes rear defogger.

Custom Option Package 4, 4-door	709	603	675

Automatic transmission, front seat courtesy lamps, passenger visor mirror, intermittent wipers, remote trunk and fuel filler releases.

Custom Option Package 5, 4-door	1638	1392	1555

Option Pkg. 4 plus air conditioning, power steering, tilt steering column.

Air conditioning	660	561	625
Cargo area cover, 3-door	69	59	66
Dual remote sport mirrors	43	37	41
AM ET radio	156	133	148
AM/FM ST ET	301	256	285

Prices are accurate at time of printing; subject to manufacturer's change.

Above w/cassette	423	360	400
Cruise control	175	149	166
Bodyside stripe	53	45	50
Wheel trim rings	52	44	49

Chevrolet Sprint

Chevrolet Sprint 5-door

Taking aim at opposite ends of the subcompact market, the front-drive, Suzuki-built Sprint minicompact goes after both higher gas mileage and higher performance this year. Of course, a different model is being used for each: The Sprint ER, introduced last spring, has a more fuel-efficient axle ratio for 1987 and earned top honors in the EPA fuel economy derby with a city mileage estimate of 54 mpg. The new Sprint Turbo comes with aerodynamic body trim and a choice of two colors, red or white. Horsepower increases to 70 from 48 with the turbocharged 1.0-liter 3-cylinder engine. The Turbo model, available only as a 3-door hatchback with a 5-speed manual transmission, includes a tachometer with turbo indicator light, sport suspension and wider P165/70R12 tires. Other changes in the Sprint lineup include 5-mph bumpers instead of the old 2½-mph bumpers, a new torsion beam rear suspension with coil springs instead of monoleaf springs and a revised instrument panel cluster. The petite, featherweight Sprint is no slouch even with the normally aspirated engine, but most are bought for low-cost, economical transportation, not high performance, and it's hard to beat on that basis, with

Prices are accurate at time of printing; subject to manufacturer's change.

its low base price and small thirst for gasoline, even with automatic transmission. Sprint's tiny size and 1500-pound curb weight are debits in occupant protection, however. Small, lightweight cars are at a disadvantage on the road and their occupants are more likely to be injured in crashes. There aren't many vehicles smaller than the Sprint, so the disadvantages are even greater.

Specifications

	3-door sedan	5-door sedan
Wheelbase, in.	88.4	92.3
Overall length, in.	141.1	145.1
Overall width, in.	60.3	60.3
Overall height, in.	53.1	53.1
Front track, in.	52.4	52.4
Rear track, in.	51.2	51.2
Curb weight, lbs.	1562	1569
Cargo vol., cu. ft.	18.1	NA
Fuel capacity, gal.	8.0	8.0
Seating capacity	4	4
Front headroom, in.	37.0	37.0
Front shoulder room, in.	50.4	50.4
Front legroom, max., in.	42.1	42.1
Rear headroom, in.	36.0	36.0
Rear shoulder room, in.	49.7	49.7
Rear legroom, min., in.	29.1	31.7

Body/Chassis

Drivetrain layout: transverse front engine/front-wheel drive. **Front suspension:** MacPherson struts, lower control arms, coil springs, stabilizer bar. **Rear suspension:** beam axle, monoleaf springs. **Steering:** rack and pinion, 3.5 turns lock-to-lock. **Turn diameter, ft.:** 30.2. **Front brakes:** 8.5-in. discs. **Rear brakes:** 7.1-in. drums. **Construction:** unit.

Powertrains	ohc I-3	ohc I-3	ohc I-3T
Displacement, l/cu. in.	1.0/61	1.0/61	1.0/61
Compression ratio	9.5:1	9.8:1	8.3:1
Fuel delivery	2 bbl.	2 bbl.	PFI
Net bhp @ rpm	48 @ 5100	46 @ 4700	70 @ 5500
Net torque @ rpm	57 @ 3200	78 @ 3200	79 @ 3500
Availability	S	S[1]	S[2]

1. ER   2. Turbo

	ohc I-3	ohc I-3	ohc I-3T
Final drive ratios			
5-speed OD manual	4.10:1	3.79:1	4.10:1
3-speed automatic	3.87:1		

KEY: bbl = barrel (carburetor); **bhp** = brake horsepower; **torque** = pounds/feet; **Cal.** = California only; **TBI** = throttle body (single-point) fuel injection; **PFI** = port (multi-point) fuel injection; **MFI** = mechanical fuel injection; **ohv** = overhead valve; **ohc** = overhead cam; **dohc** = double overhead cam; **I** = inline engine; **V** = V engine; **flat** = horizontally opposed engine; **D** = diesel; **T** = turbocharged; **OD** = overdrive transmission; **S** = standard; **O** = optional.

PRICES

CHEVROLET SPRINT	Retail Price	Dealer Invoice	Low Price
ER 3-door coupe	$6110	$5621	$5925
3-door coupe	5995	5515	5815
Turbo 3-door coupe	7690	7075	7460
5-door sedan	6195	5699	6010
Destination charge	190	190	190

STANDARD EQUIPMENT (included in above prices):

1.0-liter (61-cid) 3-cylinder engine, 5-speed manual transmission, power brakes, front and rear armrests, front and rear ashtrays, illuminated cigar lighter, side window defoggers, left-remote mirror, cloth and vinyl highback reclining front bucket seats, trip odometer, swing-out rear quarter windows (3-doors; roll-down on 5-door), 145/80R12 SBR all-season tires with full-size spare. **ER** has economy gearing. **Turbo** adds: 1.0-liter turbocharged PFI engine, sport suspension, tachometer with turbo light, 165/70R12 tires, white full wheel wheel covers.

OPTIONAL EQUIPMENT:

Custom two-tone paint	255	224	240
Custom Option Package 2 (NA ER)	1369	1205	1300
Air conditioning, rear defogger, tinted glass, tachometer, split folding rear seatback, passenger assist grips, rear wiper/washer, intermittent wipers, wide bodyside moldings, custom seat and door panel trim.			
Option Package 3 (NA ER)	420	370	400
Automatic transmission.			
Custom Option Package 4, base 3-door ..	1719	1513	1635
Automatic transmission, air conditioning, rear defogger, tinted glass, split folding rear seatback, passenger assist grips, rear wiper/washer, intermittent wipers, wide bodyside moldings, custom seat and door panel trim.			
Air conditioning	655	576	620
Console	25	22	24
Left remote and right manual mirrors ...	20	18	19
Bodyside moldings	50	44	48
Front and rear mud guards	30	26	29

Prices are accurate at time of printing; subject to manufacturer's change.

	Retail Price	Dealer Invoice	Low Price
AM ET radio	156	137	148
AM/FM ST ET	301	265	285
Above w/cassette	423	372	400
Cruise control	175	154	166
Sport Package	160	141	152
Sport stripes, mud guards, wheel covers, console.			
Sport stripes	53	47	50
Full wheel covers	52	46	49

Chrysler Fifth Avenue

Chrysler Fifth Avenue

About the only thing that's new with Chrysler's rear-drive luxury sedan is that it will soon be built by AMC in Kenosha, Wis. Chrysler needed another plant to build the Fifth Avenue and similar Dodge Diplomat and Plymouth Gran Fury when it decided to devote space at a St. Louis facility for new extended versions of the Dodge Caravan and Plymouth Voyager. Chrysler's other plants were running at capacity, but AMC's Kenosha plant was running at less than half capacity, so the two automakers struck a deal that has AMC workers assembling Chrysler vehicles, a unique arrangement in U.S. automotive history. Its 5.2-liter V-8 engine and 3-speed automatic transmission are also used in the Diplomat and Gran Fury, which are priced lower than the Fifth Avenue because they have less standard equipment. Fifth Avenue sales continued to be strong in 1986 and Chrysler couldn't be happier since this

Prices are accurate at time of printing; subject to manufacturer's change.

is a high-profit car. The chassis is derived from the mid-70s Dodge Aspen/Plymouth Volare and the proven drivetrain goes further back than that, so the tooling and design costs were recovered ages ago. The Fifth Avenue has substantial standard equipment and Chrysler's 5-year/50,000-mile warranties, plus you get a quiet, smooth drivetrain. It has many faults, however, with the worst being the aged chassis. The rear-drive Fifth Avenue suffers from sloppy handling, a soft suspension that gets pushed around by bumps and poor ride control at highway speeds. It's an old-style American luxury car that with glitzy furnishings and substandard road manners.

Specifications

	4-door sedan
Wheelbase, in.	112.6
Overall length, in.	206.7
Overall width, in.	72.4
Overall height, in.	55.0
Front track, in.	60.5
Rear track, in.	60.0
Curb weight, lbs.	3741
Cargo vol., cu. ft.	15.6
Fuel capacity, gal.	18.0
Seating capacity	6
Front headroom, in.	39.3
Front shoulder room, in.	56.0
Front legroom, max., in.	42.5
Rear headroom, in.	37.7
Rear shoulder room, in.	55.5
Rear legroom, min, in.	37.0

Body/Chassis

Drivetrain layout: longitudinal front engine/rear wheel drive. **Front suspension:** lateral non-parallel control arms, transverse torsion bars, stabilizer bar. **Rear suspension:** rigid axle, semi-elliptic leaf springs. **Steering:** recirculating ball, power assisted, 3.5 turns lock-to-lock. **Turn diameter, ft.:** 40.7. **Front brakes:** 10.8-in. discs. **Rear brakes:** 10.0-in drums. **Construction:** unit.

Powertrains

	ohv V-8
Displacement, l/cu. in.	5.2/318
Compression ratio	9.0:1
Fuel delivery	2 bbl.
Net bhp @ rpm	140 @ 3600

	ohv V-8
	265 @
Net torque @ rpm	2000
Availability	S
Final drive ratios	
3-speed automatic	2.26:1

KEY: bbl = barrel (carburetor); **bhp** =brake horsepower; **torque** = pounds/feet; **Cal.** = California only; **TBI** = throttle body (single-point) fuel injection; **PFI** = port (multipoint) fuel injection; **MFI** = mechanical fuel injection; **ohv** = overhead valve; **ohc** = overhead cam; **dohc** = double overhead cam; **I** = inline engine; **V** = V engine; **flat** = horizontally opposed engine; **D** = diesel; **T** = turbocharged; **OD** = overdrive transmission; **S** = standard; **O** = optional.

PRICES

CHRYSLER FIFTH AVENUE	Retail Price	Dealer Invoice	Low Price
4-door sedan	$15422	$13184	$14265
Destination charge	487	487	487

Retail price does not include $500 Gas Guzzler Tax.

STANDARD EQUIPMENT (included in above prices):

5.2-liter (318-cid) V-8 engine, 3-speed automatic transmission, power steering, power brakes, 60/40 split front bench seat with center armrest, full carpeting including trunk, premium wheel covers, tinted glass, electric rear window defroster, WSW tires, halogen headlamps, padded vinyl roof, air conditioning, AM ETR radio, cloth upholstery, P205/75R15 whitewall tires.

OPTIONAL EQUIPMENT:

Heavy-duty suspension	26	22	24
Power door locks	195	166	179
Power seat, left	240	204	220
Left & right	480	408	440
Cruise control (intermittent wipers req.) ..	179	152	165
Intermittent wipers	58	49	53
Tilt steering column (intermittent wipers req.)	125	106	115
Leather-wrapped steering wheel	60	51	55
Sound systems			
AM & FM stereo ET	155	132	143
AM & FM stereo ET cassette			
w/o Luxury Equipment	399	339	365
w/Luxury Equipment	254	216	235
AM & FM stereo ET cassette w/graphic EQ			
(Ultimate Sound), w/o Luxury Equipment	609	518	560
w/Luxury Equipment	464	394	425
Electric sliding glass sunroof	1076	915	990

Prices are accurate at time of printing; subject to manufacturer's change.

Heavy-duty battery (500 amp)	44	37	40
California emissions package	99	84	91
Illuminated entry system (tilt steering req.) .	75	64	69
Illuminated visor mirror, right	58	49	53
Leather upholstery (60/40 split bench) . . .	395	336	365
Pearl coat paint	40	34	37
Two-tone paint, w/o Luxury Equipment . .	485	412	445
w/Luxury Equipment	148	126	136
Conventional spare tire	93	79	86
Undercoating	43	37	40
Power decklid release	50	43	46
Wire wheel covers	206	175	190
Cast aluminum road wheels			
w/o Luxury Equipment	244	207	225
w/Luxury Equipment	38	32	35
Protection Group	132	112	121
Luxury Equipment Discount Pkg.[1]			
w/o Ultimate Sound	2251	1913	2070
w/Ultimate Sound	2113	1796	1945

Heavy-duty battery, AM/FM stereo ET radio with power amplifier and power antenna, illuminated entry system, illuminated right visor mirror, remote decklid release, power door locks, power front seats, 60/40 leather front bench seat with passenger recliner, cruise control, tilt steering column, leather-wrapped steering wheel, hood stripe, wire wheel covers, electroluminescent opera lights in door applique, intermittent wipers, Protection Group.

DODGE DIPLOMAT

Salon 4-door sedan	$10598	$9426	$10015
SE 4-door sedan	11678	10026	10860
Destination Charge	487	487	487

STANDARD EQUIPMENT (included in above prices):

5.2-liter (318-cid) V-8 engine, 3-speed automatic transmission, power steering, power front disc/rear drum brakes, space-saving spare tire, tinted glass, halogen headlamps, dual horns, AM ET radio, luxury steering wheel, cloth and vinyl bench seat with center armrest, P205/75R15 tires. **SE** adds: front bumper guards, trunk carpeting, trip odometer, ammeter, coolant temperature gauge, cloth headliner, courtesy lights, locking glovebox, bright exterior moldings, vinyl roof, dual remote mirrors, special sound insulation, 60/40 cloth split bench seat.

OPTIONAL EQUIPMENT:

Air conditioning, (auto temp control)	837	711	770
Pearl coat paint	40	34	37
Full vinyl roof	200	170	184
Vinyl bodyside molding	62	53	57
Light Pkg., Salon	128	109	118
SE	90	77	83

Prices are accurate at time of printing; subject to manufacturer's change.

	Retail Price	Dealer Invoice	Low Price
Popular Equipment Discount Pkg., Salon	597	507	550
SE	474	403	436

Rear defogger, dual remote mirrors, Protection Group, AM/FM stereo ET, tilt steering column, intermittent wipers.

	Retail Price	Dealer Invoice	Low Price
Luxury Equipment Discount Pkg., SE	2027	1723	1865

Popular Equipment content plus automatic air conditioning, power windows and door locks, cruise control, illuminated right side visor mirror, wire wheel covers.

	Retail Price	Dealer Invoice	Low Price
Protection group	138	117	127
500-amp battery	44	37	40
Rear defogger	148	126	136
California emissions pkg.	99	84	91
Illuminated entry system (tilt steering req.)	75	64	69
Special body sound insulation	66	56	61
Remote left mirror, Salon	24	20	22
Dual remote mirrors, SE	67	57	62
Illuminated right visor mirror, SE	58	49	53
Upper door frame moldings	46	39	42
Power decklid release	50	43	46
Power door locks	195	166	179
Power driver's seat	240	204	220
Sound systems			
AM & FM stereo ET	155	132	143
AM & FM stereo ET cassette			
w/o Popular or Luxury Equip.	399	339	365
w/Popular or Luxury Equip.	254	216	235
Above w/graphic EQ (Ultimate Sound)			
w/o Popular or Luxury Equip.	609	518	560
w/Popular or Luxury Equip.	464	394	425
Power antenna	70	60	64
Delete standard radio (credit)	(56)	(48)	(48)
Conventional spare tire	93	79	86
Cruise control (int. wipers req.)	179	152	165
Leather-wrapped steering wheel, SE	60	51	55
Tilt steering col. (int. wipers req.)	125	106	115
Power glass sunroof	1076	915	990
Heavy-duty suspension	26	22	24
Premium wheel covers, Salon	96	82	88
Wire wheel covers, SE	224	190	205
Cast aluminum road wheels,			
SE w/o Luxury Equip.	262	223	240
SE w/Luxury Equip.	38	32	35
Intermittent wipers	58	49	53

PLYMOUTH GRAN FURY

	Retail Price	Dealer Invoice	Low Price
4-door sedan	$10598	$9401	$10015
Destination charge	487	487	487

Prices are accurate at time of printing; subject to manufacturer's change.

CONSUMER GUIDE®

STANDARD EQUIPMENT (included in above prices):

5.2-liter (318-cid) V-8 engine, 3-speed automatic transmission, power steering, power front disc/rear drum brakes, space-saving spare tire, tinted glass, halogen headlamps, dual horns, AM ET radio, luxury steering wheel, cloth and vinyl bench seat with center armrest, P205/75R15 tires.

OPTIONAL EQUIPMENT:

Pearl coat paint	40	34	37
Full vinyl roof	200	170	184
Vinyl bodyside molding	62	52	57
60/40 split bench seat w/passenger recliner .	312	265	285
Popular Equipment Discount Pkg.	597	507	550
Dual remote mirrors, rear defogger, protection pkg., trunk dress-up, AM & FM stereo ET, tilt steering column, intermittent wipers.			
Light pkg.	128	109	118
Protection group	138	117	127
Salon Luxury Pkg. (tilt steering req.)	545	463	500
Illuminated entry system, lighted right visor mirror, leather-wrapped steering wheel, bodyside deck stripes, wire wheel covers.			
Auto temp control air conditioning	837	711	770
500-amp battery	44	37	40
Rear defogger	148	126	136
California emissions pkg.	99	84	91
Special body sound insulation	66	56	61
Left remote mirror	24	20	22
Dual remote mirrors	67	57	62
Upper door frame moldings	46	39	42
Power decklid release	50	43	46
Power door locks (opt. mirror(s) req.) . . .	195	166	179
Power windows (opt. mirror(s) req.)	285	242	260
AM & FM stereo ET	155	132	143
AM & FM stereo ET cassette, w/o Popular Equip.	399	339	365
w/Popular Equip.	254	216	235
AM & FM stereo ET cassette w/graphic EQ			
(Ultimate Sound), w/o Popular Equip. . . .	609	518	560
w/Popular Equip.	464	394	425
Delete standard radio (credit)	(56)	(48)	(48)
Conventional spare tire	93	79	86
Cruise control (int. wipers or Popular Equip. req.)	179	152	165
Tilt steering col. (int. wipers req.)	125	106	115
Heavy-duty suspension	26	22	24
Trunk dress-up	56	48	52
Undercoating	43	37	40
Premium wheel covers	96	82	88
Intermittent wipers	58	49	53

Prices are accurate at time of printing; subject to manufacturer's change.

Chrysler LeBaron

Chrysler LeBaron 2-door

Chrysler's compact luxury line has two new faces this year: a 2-door coupe and a convertible. With hidden headlamps, a long hood and short rear deck, and Coke-bottle shape on the sides, the new LeBaron coupe and convertible clearly stand apart from the carryover sedan and station wagon in styling. Underneath the skin, the coupe and convertible are built on a stretched version of the Dodge Daytona front-drive platform, using the base Daytona suspension. The sedan and wagon are built on the K-car platform. The coupe is scheduled to debut in January and the convertible in late spring. Chrysler's 2.5-liter balance-shaft 4-cylinder engine is standard for all LeBarons except the sedan, which comes with a 2.2-liter four. A turbo 2.2 is optional on all. A 5-speed manual is standard on the coupe and convertible, while a 3-speed automatic is standard on the sedan and wagon, optional on the other two. The first generation of front-drive LeBarons were merely gussied-up K-cars, but the new coupe and convertible at least look different than Chrysler's compact family cars. They're not all that much different than the rest of Chrysler's front-drive fleet, since the drivetrains and suspension components are borrowed from other cars. The new coupe has 2.9 inches less rear leg room compared to last year's, despite being 5.8 inches longer overall. The rear seat is even tighter on the convertible. Tastefully styled and plushly furnished, the new LeBaron coupe and convertible need a V-6 engine option to further separate them from the rest of Chrysler's herd of front-drive cars.

Specifications

	2-door coupe	2-door conv.	4-door sedan	5-door wagon
Wheelbase, in.	100.3	100.3	100.3	100.3
Overall length, in.	184.9	184.9	179.2	179.0
Overall width, in.	68.4	68.4	68.0	68.0
Overall height, in.	50.9	52.2	52.9	53.2
Front track, in.	57.5	57.5	57.6	57.6
Rear track, in.	57.6	57.6	57.2	57.2
Curb weight, lbs.	2590	2786	2582	2759
Cargo vol., cu. ft.	33.4	14.0	15.0	67.1
Fuel capacity, gal.	14.0	14.0	14.0	14.0
Seating capacity	5	5	6	6
Front headroom, in.	37.6	38.3	38.6	38.5
Front shoulder room, in.	55.9	55.9	55.4	55.4
Front legroom, max., in.	43.1	43.1	42.2	42.2
Rear headroom, in.	36.3	37.0	37.8	38.5
Rear shoulder room, in.	56.3	45.7	55.9	55.9
Rear legroom, min, in.	33.0	33.0	35.1	34.8

Body/Chassis

Drivetrain layout: transverse front engine/front-wheel drive. **Front suspension:** MacPherson struts, lower control arms, coil springs, stabilizer bar. **Rear suspension:** beam flex axle, trailing arms, coil springs, stabilizer bar. **Steering:** rack and pinion, power assisted, 2.5 turns lock-to-lock coupe & conv.; 3.2 sedan & wagon. **Turn diameter, ft.:** 38.1. **Front brakes:** 10.1-in. discs. **Rear brakes:** 7.9-in drums (8.7-in. wagon). **Construction:** unit.

Powertrains	ohc I-4	ohc I-4T	ohc I-4
Displacement, l/cu. in.	2.2/135	2.2/135	2.5/153
Compression ratio	9.5:1	8.1:1	9.0:1
Fuel delivery	TBI	PFI	TBI
Net bhp @ rpm	97 @ 5200	146 @ 5200	100 @ 4800
Net torque @ rpm	122 @ 3200	170 @ 3600	133 @ 2800
Availability	S	O	S[1]

1. std. coupe, conv. & wgn.

Final drive ratios

	ohc I-4	ohc I-4T	ohc I-4
5-speed OD manual			3.02:1
3-speed automatic	3.02:1	3.02:1	3.02:1

KEY: bbl = barrel (carburetor); **bhp** = brake horsepower; **torque** = pounds/feet; **Cal.** = California only; **TBI** = throttle body (single-point) fuel injection; **PFI** = port (multi-point) fuel injection; **MFI** = mechanical fuel injection; **ohv** = overhead valve; **ohc** = overhead cam; **dohc** = double overhead cam; **I** = inline engine; **V** = V engine; **flat** = horizontally opposed engine; **D** = diesel; **T** = turbocharged; **OD** = overdrive transmission; **S** = standard; **O** = optional.

PRICES

CHRYSLER LE BARON	Retail Price	Dealer Invoice	Low Price
4-door sedan	10707	9362	9980
Town & Country 5-door wagon	12255	10701	11570
Destination charge	426	426	426

STANDARD EQUIPMENT (included in above prices):

2.2-liter (135-cid) TBI 4-cylinder engine, 3-speed automatic transmission, power steering, power brakes, bumper rub strips, full carpeting including trunk/cargo area, headlamps-on chime, cigar lighter, coat hooks, full-length front console, tethered fuel filler cap, tinted glass, halogen headlamps, door courtesy lights, trunk/cargo area and underhood lights, ignition lock light with time delay, lockable glovebox, Message Center (low fuel and washer fluid, door, trunk/liftgate ajar warnings), left remote and right manual mirrors, AM & FM ST ET, padded vinyl landau roof (sedan), cloth and vinyl bench seat, intermittent wipers, premium wheel covers, P185/70R14 SBR whitewall tires. **Town & Country wagon** adds: 2.5-liter (152-cid) TBI 4-cylinder engine, heavy-duty battery, cargo area dress-up, tonneau cover, liftgate wiper/washer.

OPTIONAL EQUIPMENT:

2.5-liter TBI 4-cylinder engine, sedan . . .	279	237	255
2.2-liter PFI turbocharged engine . . . . . ,	678	576	625
Pearl coat paint	40	34	37
High-back bucket seats w/center armrest, console & dual recliners, sedan	366	311	335
Low-back vinyl bucket seats w/center armrest, console & dual recliners, wagon	200	170	184
Popular Equipment Discount Pkg., sedan .	1132	962	1040
Wagon	1408	1197	1295
Rear defogger, tinted glass, AM/FM ST ET radio, trunk dress-up, cruise control, tilt steering column.			
Luxury Equipment Discount Pkg., sedan . .	2154	1831	1980
Wagon	2027	1723	1865
Popular Equipment plus power windows, wire wheel covers, power door locks, power seats, power remote mirrors, power liftgate release on wagon.			
Mark Cross Pkg.	1049	892	965
50/50 reclining leather seats w/dual armrests, seatback pockets, vinyl door panels, leather-wrapped steering wheel.			
Protection Pkg., sedan	204	173	188
Wagon	144	122	132
Rear Defogger Pkg.	192	163	177
Rear defogger, 500-amp battery.			
Deluxe Convenience Pkg.	304	258	280
Cruise control, tilt steering column.			
Air conditioning	782	665	720
California emissions pkg.	99	84	91

Prices are accurate at time of printing; subject to manufacturer's change.

Power Convenience Discount Pkg.	432	367	395
Power windows and door locks.			
Power decklid/liftgate release	50	43	46
Power seat, left or bench	240	204	220
AM & FM ST ET cassette	289	246	265
Leather-wrapped steering wheel	59	50	54
Sport handling suspension	57	48	52
Trunk dress-up	51	43	47
Conventional spare tire	83	71	76
Locking wire wheel covers	176	150	162

CHRYSLER LE BARON COUPE & CONVERTIBLE
(prices not available at time of publication)

STANDARD EQUIPMENT: Highline 2-door coupe: 2.5-liter (153-cid) TBI 4-cylinder engine, 5-speed manual transmission, power steering, power brakes, cloth upholstery, reclining front seats, 60/40 split folding rear seatback, full instrumentation including tachometer, coolant temperature, oil pressure and voltage gauges, trip odometer, mini trip computer, forward center console including cubby box, coin holder and cup holder, full carpeting including trunk, intermittent wipers, optical horn, remote trunklid and fuel filler releases, courtesy/reading lights, carpeted lower door panels, slide-forward passenger seat, P185/70R14 tires. **Premium** adds: vacuum-fluorescent digital instruments, rear head restraints, fold-down rear center armrest, lockable seatback releases. **Convertible** adds to Highline: power top with rear defogger, power windows, vinyl upholstery.

OPTIONS will include: 2.2-liter (135-cid) PFI turbocharged engine, 3-speed automatic transmission, air conditioning, power windows, power door locks, voice alert and electronic navigator, removable sunroof, Light Group (dual lighted visor mirrors, cornering lamps, illuminated entry system, headlamp-off delay), P195/70R14 tires, P205/60R15 tires, alloy wheels.

Chrysler LeBaron GTS/
Dodge Lancer

A stainless steel exhaust system, new lockup torque converter for the optional automatic transmission and a handful of new extra-cost options are planned for the LeBaron GTS and Lancer twins, a pair of front-drive hatchback sedans. The stainless steel exhaust is supposed to resist corrosion longer than the aluminized steel it replaces. The lockup torque converter, designed to improve fuel economy,

Prices are accurate at time of printing; subject to manufacturer's change.

Chrysler LeBaron GTS

comes on the 3-speed automatic transmission only with
the optional 2.5-liter 4-cylinder engine. Among new options are an overhead console with a compass and thermometer and a premium speaker system by Infinity. The
Infinity system, available only with the Ultimate Sound
stereo, will include six speakers, each with its own
amplifier. Introduced for 1985, LeBaron GTS and Lancer
haven't had great impact in the mid-size market. They
provide above-average handling and they can easily hold
five people or mounds of luggage in their roomy interiors.
Where they fall down is in refinement. The interior furnishings are no threat to BMW quality, and neither are
most mechanical parts, though they're well protected by
the 5-year/50,000-mile warranties. The base 2.2-liter 4-cyl-
inder is noisy and lacks the power to move this car swiftly.
The optional 2.5-liter engine has a little more power plus
balancing shafts that help reduce noise and vibration,
making it the best all-around choice. The turbo 2.2 produces the most power, but also the most noise. A quiet,
smooth V-6 engine would improve these cars a lot, but
none is offered. Until one is, the 2.5 is the best engine
available.

Specifications

	5-door sedan
Wheelbase, in.	103.1
Overall length, in.	180.4
Overall width, in.	68.3
Overall height, in.	53.0
Front track, in.	57.6
Rear track, in.	57.2
Curb weight, lbs.	2641
Cargo vol., cu. ft.	42.6

	5-door sedan
Fuel capacity, gal.	14.0
Seating capacity	5
Front headroom, in.	38.3
Front shoulder room, in.	55.8
Front legroom, max., in.	41.1
Rear headroom, in.	37.9
Rear shoulder room, in.	55.9
Rear legroom, min, in.	36.5

Body/Chassis

Drivetrain layout: transverse front engine/front-wheel drive.
Front suspension: MacPherson struts, lower control arms, coil
springs, stabilizer bar. **Rear suspension:** beam flex axle, trailing
arms, coil springs, stabilizer bar. **Steering:** rack and pinion, power
assisted, 2.5 turns lock-to-lock . **Turn diameter, ft.:** 36.2. **Front
brakes:** 10.1-in. discs. **Rear brakes:** 7.9-in. drums. **Construction:** unit.

Powertrains	ohc I-4	ohc I-4T	ohc I-4
Displacement, l/cu. in.	2.2/135	2.2/135	2.5/153
Compression ratio	9.5:1	8.1:1	9.0:1
Fuel delivery	TBI	PFI	TBI
Net bhp @ rpm	97 @ 5600	146 @ 5200	100 @ 4800
Net torque @ rpm	122 @ 3200	170 @ 3600	133 @ 2800
Availability	S	O	O
Final drive ratios			
5-speed OD manual	2.51:1	2.51:1	2.51:1
3-speed automatic	3.02:1	3.02:1	3.02:1

KEY: bbl = barrel (carburetor); **bhp** =brake horsepower; **torque** = pounds/feet; **Cal.**
= California only; **TBI** = throttle body (single-point) fuel injection; **PFI** = port (multi-
point) fuel injection; **MFI** = mechanical fuel injection; **ohv** = overhead valve; **ohc** =
overhead cam; **dohc** = double overhead cam; **I** = inline engine; **V** = V engine; **flat**
= horizontally opposed engine; **D** = diesel; **T** = turbocharged; **OD** = overdrive transmission; **S** = standard; **O** = optional.

PRICES

CHRYSLER LE BARON GTS	Retail Price	Dealer Invoice	Low Price
Highline 5-door sedan	$10152	$9034	$9565
Premium 5-door sedan	11767	10455	11085
Destination charge	426	426	426

STANDARD EQUIPMENT (included in above prices):

2.2-liter (135-cid) TBI 4-cylinder engine, 5-speed manual transmission, power steering, power brakes, AM/FM ST ET, left remote mirror, lockable glovebox w/coin holder, full instrumentation including trip odometer, tachometer, temperature, voltage and oil pressure gauges, tinted glass, cloth and vinyl reclining bucket seats, remote fuel filler and liftgate releases, one-piece fold-down rear seatback, cargo area carpet, P185/70R14 steel-belted all-season radial tires. **Premium** adds: air conditioning, electronic instrumentation (may be deleted), center armrest, inflatable driver's seat . thigh and lumbar support, split folding rear seatback.

OPTIONAL EQUIPMENT:

2.5-liter (153-cid) TBI 4-cylinder engine	279	237	255
2.2-liter PFI turbocharged engine	678	576	625
3-speed automatic transmission	529	450	485
Pearl coat paint	40	34	37
Leather seats & steering wheel trim, Premium	625	531	575
Popular Equipment Discount Pkg.			
Highline w/5-speed	881	749	810
Highline including automatic	1220	1037	1120
Premium w/5-speed	992	843	915
Premium including automatic	1281	1089	1180

Highline: air conditioning, light package, floormats, cruise control, tilt steering column, undercoating. Premium: 2.2-liter turbo engine, cruise control, floormats, tilt steering column, undercoating, luxury wheel covers, P205/60R15 tires.

Console/Lights Convenience Pkg.			
Highline w/o Popular Equipment	228	193	210
Highline w/Popular Equipment	161	137	148
Premium	342	291	315

Light package, lighted visor mirrors, console/armrest, overhead console with compass and outside temperature thermometer.

Deluxe Convenience Pkg.	392	333	360

Tilt steering column, cruise control, floormats, undercoating.

Electronic Features Pkg.			
Premium w/o rear defogger	382	325	350
Premium w/rear defogger	338	287	310

Electronic Voice Alert, 500-amp battery, Electronic Navigator.

Air conditioning, Highline	782	665	720
Rear defogger & 500-amp battery	192	163	177
California emissions pkg.	99	84	91
Power Convenience Discount Pkg.	475	404	435

Power windows and door locks, dual power mirrors.

Power driver's seat	240	204	220
AM & FM ST ET cassette	295	251	270
AM & FM stereo ET cassette w/EQ			
(Ultimate Sound)	505	429	465
Removable glass sunroof			
w/o Console/Lights Convenience Pkg.	372	316	340
w/Console/Lights Convenience Pkg.	197	167	181
Sport handling suspension (optional tire size			
or tire/wheel combination req.)	26	22	24

Prices are accurate at time of printing; subject to manufacturer's change.

Cast aluminum 14″ road wheels	322	274	295
15″ tires and wheel covers	282	240	260
Cast aluminum road wheels w/15″ tires . .	604	513	555
Premium w/Popular Equipment	322	274	295
Rear wiper/washer	126	107	116
P195/70R14 handling tires	101	86	93

DODGE LANCER

5-door sedan	$9852	$8770	$9280
ES 5-door sedan	10806	9609	10180
Destination charge	426	426	426

STANDARD EQUIPMENT (included in above prices):

2.2-liter (135-cid) TBI 4-cylinder engine, 5-speed manual transmission, power steering, power brakes, AM/FM ST ET, tinted glass, passenger assist straps, left remote mirror, lockable glovebox w/coin holder, full instrumentation including trip odometer, tachometer, temperature, voltage and oil pressure gauges, cloth and vinyl reclining bucket seats, remote fuel filler and liftgate releases, one-piece fold-down rear seatback, cargo area carpet, P185/70R14 steel-belted all-season radial tires. **ES adds:** electronic instrumentation (may be deleted), center armrest, inflatable driver's seat thigh and lumbar support, split folding rear seatback, intermittent wipers, sport handling package, 195/70R14 SBR performance tires.

OPTIONAL EQUIPMENT:

2.5-liter (153-cid) TBI 4-cylinder engine . .	279	237	255
2.2-liter turbo engine	678	576	625
3-speed automatic transmission	529	450	485
Air conditioning	782	664	720
Pearl coat paint	40	34	37
Leather seats, ES	625	531	575
Popular Equipment Discount Pkg., base . .	881	749	810
Base incl. auto trans	1220	1037	1120
ES	1442	1226	1325
ES incl. auto trans	1821	1548	1675

Base: air conditioning, light pkg., front and rear floormats, cruise control, tilt steering column, undercoating. ES: base content plus 2.2-liter turbo engine, P205/60 15″ tires on cast aluminum road wheels.

Console/Lights Convenience Pkg.			
Base w/o Popular Equip.	228	194	210
Base w/Popular Equip.	161	137	148
ES	342	291	315

Overhead console with compass, outside temperature thermometer, sunglass holder, garage door opener holder, map lights, lighted visor mirrors, console w/armrest, light pkg.

Deluxe Convenience Pkg.	392	333	360

Cruise control, tilt steering column, front and rear floormats, undercoating.

Electronic Features			
ES w/o rear defogger	681	579	625

Prices are accurate at time of printing; subject to manufacturer's change

	Retail Price	Dealer Invoice	Low Price
ES w/rear defogger	637	541	585
Electronic instrument cluster, electronic navigator, voice alert, 500-amp battery, headlamp extinguish feature.			
Rear defogger (incl. 500-amp battery) . . .	192	163	177
California emissions pkg.	99	84	91
Power Convenience Discount Pkg.	475	404	435
Power windows and door locks.			
Power driver's seat	240	204	220
AM & FM ST ET cassette	295	251	270
Above w/EQ (Ultimate Sound)	505	429	465
Removable glass sunroof			
w/o Power Convenience Pkg.	372	316	340
w/Power Convenience Pkg.	197	167	181
Sport handling suspension	26	22	24
Cast aluminum 14" road wheels, base . . .	310	264	285
15" wheels and tires, base (NC on ES) . . .	282	240	282
w/aluminum wheels, base	592	503	545
w/aluminum wheels, ES	190	162	175
Rear wiper/washer	126	107	116
P195/70R14 SBR handling tires, base . . .	101	86	93

Chrysler New Yorker

Chrysler New Yorker Turbo

The standard automatic transmission gains an electronic lockup torque converter and electronic speed control has been added as a new option for the front-drive New Yorker, Chrysler's flagship luxury sedan. The lockup torque converter is supposed to improve fuel economy by eliminating slip between the engine and drive shafts. It's installed in the 3-speed automatic transmission only with the standard 2.5-liter 4-cylinder engine, not the optional turbocharged 2.2-liter. The new electronic speed control system—or cruise control—replaces an old system that operated on engine vacuum. Also new this year is a speaker option for the Ultimate Sound stereo system. Built by Infinity Systems, the package incudes six speakers, each with its own amplifier. Built on a stretched K-car chassis also used for the Dodge 600 and Plymouth Caravelle, the New Yorker is much plusher than its siblings, rivaling the Fifth Avenue in luxury. The interior is quite roomy, with space for five adults, and the deep trunk can carry plenty of luggage. The standard 2.5-liter 4-cylinder engine gives the New Yorker uninspired acceleration, with only 100 horsepower for a 2800-pound sedan. The optional turbo 2.2 furnishes much livelier acceleration at the expense of refinement. The turbocharged engine develops a nasty growl and a lot of vibration under throttle, both of which are out of place in a luxury sedan. Unfortunately Chrysler doesn't offer a V-6 engine in the New Yorker, which would be an appropriate option for a car of this size and market position.

Specifications

	4-door sedan
Wheelbase, in.	103.3
Overall length, in.	187.2
Overall width, in.	68.0
Overall height, in.	53.1
Front track, in.	57.6
Rear track, in.	57.2
Curb weight, lbs.	2757
Cargo vol., cu. ft.	17.1
Fuel capacity, gal.	14.0
Seating capacity	6
Front headroom, in.	38.6
Front shoulder room, in.	55.4
Front legroom, max., in.	42.2
Rear headroom, in.	37.3
Rear shoulder room, in.	55.9
Rear legroom, min, in.	38.0

Body/Chassis

Drivetrain layout: transverse front engine/front-wheel drive. **Front suspension:** MacPherson struts, lower control arms, coil springs, stabilizer bar. **Rear suspension:** beam flex axle, trailing arms, coil springs, stabilizer bar. **Steering:** rack and pinion, power assisted, 3.2 turns lock-to-lock. **Turn diameter, ft.:** 35.6. **Front brakes:** 10.1-in. discs. **Rear brakes:** 8.9-in. drums. **Construction:** unit.

Powertrains	ohc I-4	ohc I-4T
Displacement, l/cu. in.	2.5/153	2.2/135
Compression ratio	9.0:1	8.1:1
Fuel delivery	TBI	PFI
Net bhp @ rpm	100 @ 4800	146 @ 5200
Net torque @ rpm	136 @ 2800	170 @ 3600
Availability	S	O
Final drive ratios		
3-speed automatic	3.02:1	3.02:1

KEY: bbl = barrel (carburetor); **bhp** = brake horsepower; **torque** = pounds/feet; **Cal.** = California only; **TBI** = throttle body (single-point) fuel injection; **PFI** = port (multipoint) fuel injection; **MFI** = mechanical fuel injection; **ohc** = overhead cam; **dohc** = double overhead cam; **I** = inline engine; **V** = V engine; **flat** = horizontally opposed engine; **D** = diesel; **T** = turbocharged; **OD** = overdrive transmission; **S** = standard; **O** = optional.

PRICES

CHRYSLER NEW YORKER	Retail Price	Dealer Invoice	Low Price
4-door sedan	$14396	$12362	$13100
Destination charge	487	487	487

STANDARD EQUIPMENT (included in above prices):

2.5-liter (153-cid) TBI 4-cylinder engine, 3-speed automatic transmission, power brakes, power steering, power decklid release, power fuel filler door release, Light Group, AM & FM ST ET, luxury steering wheel, premium wheelcovers, front and rear bumper guards, console, tinted glass, power windows, electronic instrumentation, Electronic Voice Alert, cornering lamps, dual power outside mirrors, bodyside stripes, trunk dress-up, landau padded vinyl roof w/coach lamps, intermittent wipers, overhead console, rear head restraints, P185/75R14 whitewall tires.

OPTIONAL EQUIPMENT:

2.2-liter (135-cid) turbocharged engine . .	678	576	625
Delete 2.2 turbo, w/Luxury Equipment (credit)	(678)	(576)	(576)
Pearl coat paint	40	34	37
Luxury Equipment Discount Package	3703	3146	3405

2.2-liter turbo engine, rear defogger, 500-amp battery, power antenna, lighted visor mirrors, bodyside molding, power door locks, dual power seats, cruise control, leather-wrapped steering

Prices are accurate at time of printing; subject to manufacturer's change

wheel, tilt steering column, undercoating, illuminated entry system, 50/50 leather seats, automatic air conditioning, compass and outside temperature readouts, floormats, automatic rear load leveling, wire wheel covers; cloth seat trim is available at no cost.

Deluxe Convenience Pkg.	304	258	280
Cruise control, tilt steering column.			
Protection Pkg.	148	126	136
Rear defroster pkg.	192	163	177
Rear defogger, 500-amp. battery.			
Auto temp. control air conditioning	925	786	850
California emissions pkg.	99	84	91
Power door locks	195	166	179
Power driver's seat	240	204	220
AM & FM ST ET cassette	289	246	265
AM & FM ST ET cassette w/EQ (Ultimate Sound)	499	424	460
Conventional spare tire	83	71	76
Leather-wrapped steering wheel	59	50	54
Sport handling suspension	57	48	52
Wire wheel covers	176	150	162
Cast aluminum 14" wheels			
w/o Luxury Equipment	283	241	260
w/Luxury Equipment	107	91	98

Dodge Aries/ Plymouth Reliant

The front-drive Aries and Reliant K-cars, Chrysler's identical family compacts, lose last year's mid-price SE series but gain front bucket seats as standard equipment. Dropping the SE series leaves base 2- and 4-door sedans and the upscale LE series for all three Aries/Reliant body styles (2-door, 4-door and wagon). That may only be the first step in streamlining the K-car lines; Chrysler reportedly is planning to give the Aries and Reliant the "America" treatment that has been successful on the Dodge Omni and Plymouth Horizon subcompacts. That would probably include eliminating the LE series, making more equipment standard and offering only a few options to reduce production costs and retail prices. Chrysler has moved in that direction the past two years, lumping popular options into discounted packages. With bucket seats now standard, a 3-place bench seat with fold-down center armrest is optional at no cost on LE models. We've always rated the

Prices are accurate at time of printing; subject to manufacturer's change

Dodge Aries 4-door

K-cars highly as sensible family transportation and good
value for the money, and that hasn't changed. A fully-
equipped LE sedan with the 2.5-liter engine, automatic
transmission, air conditioning and the Premium Discount
Package still costs less than $11,000, plus the K-cars are
backed by Chrysler's 5-year/50,000-mile warranties. The
optional 2.5 engine and automatic is the best drivetrain
combination available. The 2.5 is smoother, quieter and
more powerful than the standard 2.2, and it gives the K-
cars lively acceleration without much loss in fuel economy.
Handling is improved on LE models with the addition of
14-inch tires, while the base sedans suffer some loss of
grip with narrower 13-inch rubber. Overall, these aren't
the most modern compacts or the best performing, but
there aren't many others that offer as much value in a
family car.

Specifications

	2-door sedan	4-door sedan	5-door wagon
Wheelbase, in.	100.3	100.3	100.3
Overall length, in.	178.9	178.9	179.0
Overall width, in.	67.9	67.9	67.9
Overall height, in.	52.5	52.9	53.3
Front track, in.	57.6	57.6	57.6
Rear track, in.	57.2	57.2	57.2
Curb weight, lbs.	2317	2323	2448
Cargo vol., cu. ft.	15.0	15.0	67.7

	2-door sedan	4-door sedan	5-door wagon
Fuel capacity, gal.	14.0	14.0	14.0
Seating capacity	6	6	6
Front headroom, in.	38.2	38.6	38.5
Front shoulder room, in.	55.0	55.4	55.4
Front legroom, max., in.	42.2	42.2	42.2
Rear headroom, in.	37.0	37.8	38.5
Rear shoulder room, in.	58.8	55.9	55.9
Rear legroom, min, in.	35.1	35.4	34.8

Body/Chassis

Drivetrain layout: transverse front engine/front-wheel drive. **Front suspension:** MacPherson struts, lower control arms, coil springs, stabilizer bar. **Rear suspension:** beam flex axle, trailing arms, coil springs, stabilizer bar. **Steering:** rack and pinion, 4.0 turns lock-to-lock. **Turn diameter, ft.:** 34.8. **Front brakes:** 9.3-in. discs. **Rear brakes:** 7.9-in. drums. **Construction:** unit.

Powertrains	ohc I-4	ohc I-4
Displacement, l/cu. in.	2.2/135	2.5/153
Compression ratio	9.5:1	9.0:1
Fuel delivery	TBI	TBI
Net bhp @ rpm	97 @ 5200	100 @ 4800
Net torque @ rpm	122 @ 3200	133 @ 2800
Availability	S	O
Final drive ratios		
5-speed OD manual	2.51:1	
3-speed automatic	2.78:1	3.02:1

KEY: bbl = barrel (carburetor); **bhp** =brake horsepower; **torque** = pounds/feet; **Cal.** = California only; **TBI** = throttle body (single-point) fuel injection; **PFI** = port (multi-point) fuel injection; **MFI** = mechanical fuel injection; **ohv** = overhead valve; **ohc** = overhead cam; **dohc** = double overhead cam; **I** = inline engine; **V** = V engine; **flat** = horizontally opposed engine; **D** = diesel; **T** = turbocharged; **OD** = overdrive transmission; **S** = standard; **O** = optional.

PRICES

DODGE ARIES/PLYMOUTH RELIANT	Retail Price	Dealer Invoice	Low Price
2-door sedan	$7879	$7166	$7445
4-door sedan	7879	7166	7445
LE 2-door sedan	8364	7435	7820
LE 4-door sedan	8364	7435	7820
LE 5-door wagon	8808	7826	8235
Destination charge	410	410	410

Prices are accurate at time of printing; subject to manufacturer's change

STANDARD EQUIPMENT (included in above prices):

2.2-liter (135-cid) TBI 4-cylinder engine, 5-speed manual transmission, power brakes, front bench seat with center armrest, vinyl upholstery, upper door frame and belt moldings, halogen headlamps, full carpeting, P175/80R13 blackwall radial tires. **LE** adds: left remote mirror, special sound insulation, bumper rub strips, AM ET radio, cloth bench seat, intermittent wipers, luxury steering wheel, carpeted lower door panels, woodtone dash and door panel appliques, digital clock, luxury wheel covers, dual horns, map, glovebox and trunk lamps, wide black bodyside moldings, black sill moldings.

OPTIONAL EQUIPMENT:

2.5-liter (153-cid) engine, LE (auto trans req.)	279	237	255
3-speed automatic transmission	529	450	485
Air conditioning (tinted glass req.)	782	664	720
Pearl coat paint	40	34	37
Cloth & vinyl bench seat, base	NC	NC	NC
Vinyl bench seat w/center armrest, LE . . .	NC	NC	NC
Above w/cloth & vinyl	NC	NC	NC
Basic Equipment Pkg., base	262	223	240
AM mono ET, left remote mirror, intermittent wipers, deluxe wheel covers.			
Popular Equipment Discount Pkg., LE sedans	720	612	660
Wagon	739	628	680
Automatic transmission, power steering, tinted glass, AM & FM ST ET, dual remote mirrors, uprated sound insulation, trunk dress-up, tonneau cover (wagon), deluxe wheel covers, P185/70R14 blackwall tires.			
Premium Equipment Discount Pkg.,			
LE 2-door	1228	1044	1130
LE 4-door	1278	1086	1175
Wagon	1549	1317	1425
Popular Equipment plus rear defogger, power door locks, cruise control, tilt steering column, rear wiper/washer and luggage rack (wagon).			
Light Pkg.	56	48	52
Tinted glass (A/C req.)	120	102	110
Full console, LE (NA w/bench seat)	152	129	140
Rear defogger	148	126	136
California emissions pkg.	99	84	91
Front & rear floormats	45	38	41
Luggage rack, wagon	126	107	116
Power door locks, LE 2-door	145	123	133
LE 4-door, wagon	195	166	179
Power steering	240	204	220
AM & FM ST ET, base w/o Basic Equip. . . .	268	228	245
Base w/Basic Equip., LE	155	132	143
AM & FM ST ET cassette, LE (Popular			
or Premium Equip. req.)	254	216	235
Conventional spare tire (13″)	73	62	67
Conventional spare tire (14″)	83	71	76

Prices are accurate at time of printing; subject to manufacturer's change

Cruise control	179	152	165
Tilt steering col., LE (cruise control req.) .	125	106	115
HD suspension	59	50	54
Undercoating	43	37	40
Cast aluminum 14" road wheels, LE			
w/Popular or Premium Equip.	322	274	295
w/o Popular or Premium Equip.	370	315	340
Rear wiper/washer, wagon	126	107	116
Woodtone exterior applique, wagon			
w/o Popular or Premium Equip.	274	233	250
w/Popular or Premium Equip.	226	192	210
P185/70R14 tires, LE (req. w/road wheels)			
w/o Popular or Premium Equip.	162	138	149
w/Popular or Premium Equip.	68	58	63

Dodge Caravan/ Plymouth Voyager

Dodge Caravan Extended

Chrysler is stretching its minivans this year and introducing a V-6 engine option, though neither of those will be available until mid-year. The stretched versions of the identical front-drive Caravan and Voyager gain seven inches in wheelbase, 14.6 inches in overall length and 300 pounds in curb weight. Dodge also will have a stretched version of its Mini Ram Van cargo model. Cargo volume grows to 155 cubic feet with the seats removed, 30 more than the standard-size models. Stretched models will have 3.5 to 4.5 inches more leg room between the front and middle seats, depending on seating arrangements. Chrysler's 2.5-liter balance-shaft 4-cylinder engine will be standard on the stretched Caravan and a new 3.0-liter V-6 built by Mitsubishi will be optional. Rated at 140 horsepower, the overhead cam V-6 has multi-point fuel injection (one injector for each cylinder). It will replace the Mitsubishi 2.6-liter four as the optional engine when it goes on sale, probably around March. A carbureted 2.2-liter four remains the base engine in the standard-size Caravan/Voyager; the 2.6 will be optional until the V-6 arrives. Other changes are a redesigned grille flanked by new aerodynamic headlamps, a stainless steel exhaust system that is supposed to last longer than aluminized steel and a separate rear heater as a new option. We haven't driven the stretched models or the new V-6 engine, and Chrysler hasn't released prices for either. The new V-6 engine should answer our biggest complaint: not enough power. The 104-horsepower 2.6-liter four that has been the strongest engine offered had marginal power for merging into expressway traffic or hauling a full load. With 36 more horsepower, the V-6 should be much more capable. The carbureted 2.6 also has a history of driveability problems that Chrysler could never fully solve (hard starting, stalling and rough idling among them). Maximum trailer-towing weight increases to 2750 pounds (from 2000 last year) with the V-6, an indication of the new engine's strength. The standard-size Caravan feels more like a car than a van, both in handling and ride, making it our favorite among the compact vans for passenger use. This year's prices are considerably higher than last year's, so plan on doing some hard bargaining to get a good deal.

Specifications	4-door van	4-door van
Wheelbase, in.	112.0	119.1
Overall length, in.	179.5	190.5
Overall width, in.	69.6	69.6
Overall height, in.	64.2	65.0
Front track, in.	59.9	59.9
Rear track, in.	62.1	62.1
Curb weight, lbs.	3003	3304

	4-door van	4-door van
Cargo vol., cu. ft.	125.0	150.0
Fuel capacity, gal.	15.0[1]	15.0[1]
Seating capacity	5[2]	8
Front headroom, in.	39.0	39.0
Front shoulder room, in.	58.4	58.4
Front legroom, max., in.	38.2	38.2
Rear headroom, in.	37.7	37.6
Rear shoulder room, in.	NA	NA
Rear legroom, min, in.	37.7	NA

1. 20.0 opt.   2. 6, 7 or 8 opt.

Body/Chassis

Drivetrain layout: transverse front engine/front-wheel drive. **Front suspension:** MacPherson struts, lower control arms, coil springs, stabilizer bar. **Rear suspension:** tubular beam axle, leaf springs. **Steering:** rack and pinion, power assisted, 3.2 turns lock-to-lock. **Turn diameter, ft.:** 41.0/43.2. **Front brakes:** 10.1-in. discs. **Rear brakes:** 8.6-in. drums. **Construction:** unit.

Powertrains	ohc I-4	ohc I-4	ohc I-4	ohc V-6
Displacement, l/cu. in.	2.2/135	2.5/153	2.6/156	3.0/187
Compression ratio	9.0:1	9.0:1	8.7:1	8.85:1
Fuel delivery	2 bbl.	TBI	2 bbl.	PFI
Net bhp @ rpm	95 @ 5200	102 @ 4800	104 @ 4800	144 @ 4800
Net torque @ rpm	121 @ 3200	138 @ 2800	142 @ 2800	175 @ 2800
Availability	S	S[1]	O	O[2]

1. extended wagon; late availability   2. late availability

Final drive ratios

5-speed manual	2.76:1	2.76:1		
3-speed automatic	3.22:1	3.22:1	3.02:1	3.22:1

KEY: bbl = barrel (carburetor); **bhp** = brake horsepower; **torque** = pounds/feet; **Cal.** = California only; **TBI** = throttle body (single-point) fuel injection; **PFI** = port (multi-point) fuel injection; **MFI** = mechanical fuel injection; **ohv** = overhead valve; **ohc** = overhead cam; **dohc** = double overhead cam; **I** = inline engine; **V** = V engine; **flat** = horizontally opposed engine; **D** = diesel; **T** = turbocharged; **OD** = overdrive transmission; **S** = standard; **O** = optional.

PRICES

DODGE CARAVAN/ PLYMOUTH VOYAGER	Retail Price	Dealer Invoice	Low Price
4-door van	$10411	$9262	$9805
SE 4-door van	10875	9670	10245

Prices are accurate at time of printing; subject to manufacturer's change

	Retail Price	Dealer Invoice	Low Price
LE 4-door van	11741	10432	11060
Destination charge	480	480	480

STANDARD EQUIPMENT (included in above prices):

2.2-liter (135-cid) 4-cylinder 2 bbl. engine, 5-speed overdrive manual transmission, power steering, power brakes, front and rear bumper rub strips, liftgate wiper/washer, headlamps-on chime, cigarette lighter, intermittent wipers, electronic digital clock, side window demisters, tinted glass, halogen headlamps, inside hood release, tethered fuel cap, day/night mirror, left outside remote control door mirror, AM electronic tune radio, P185/75R14 steel-belted radial tires. **Special Edition** adds: high-back reclining front seats, front folding center armrests, dual-note horn, soft cloth trim panels with carpeted lower insert, road wheels. **Limited Edition** adds: AM & FM stereo ET, deluxe sound insulation, dual black remote control door mirrors, upper and lower bodyside moldings, center woodgrain applique, highback front reclining bucket seats, luxury steering wheel.

OPTIONAL EQUIPMENT:

	Retail Price	Dealer Invoice	Low Price
2.6-liter (156-cid) 4-cylinder engine (auto trans req.)	354	301	325
3-speed automatic transmission	532	452	490
Air conditioning	840	714	775
Pearl coat paint	46	39	42
Two-tone paint, SE (NC on LE)	236	201	215
Low-back cloth bucket seats, base	45	38	41
High-back vinyl bucket seats	NC	NC	NC
Cloth bench seat trim, base	NC	NC	NC
Seating packages			
6-passenger, base & SE	96	82	88
SE w/Popular Equipment (credit)	(20)	(17)	(17)
7-passenger, SE & LE	389	331	360
8-passenger, SE w/Popular & Travel Equip. (credit)	(20)	(17)	(17)
SE w/Travel Equip.	96	82	88
SE w/Popular Equip.	369	314	340
SE	485	412	445
Converta-Bed w/5-pass. seating			
SE & LE w/Travel Equip.	153	130	141
All models	542	461	500
Converta-Bed w/6-pass. seating			
Base & SE	638	542	585
SE w/Popular & Travel Equip.	133	113	122
Base & SE w/Popular Equip.	522	444	480

Prices are accurate at time of printing; subject to manufacturer's change

SE w/Travel Equip.	249	212	230
Popular Equipment Discount Pkg., base . .	501	426	460
SE w/5- or 6-pass.	1130	961	1040
SE w/7- or 8-pass.	1153	980	1060
LE w/5-pass.	931	791	855
LE w/7-pass.	954	811	880

Light package, gauge package, intermittent wipers, AM/FM ST ET w/clock, dual-note horn, cruise control, power liftgate release, dual remote mirrors, deluxe sound insulation, luxury steering wheel, lighted visor mirror, overhead console (LE only).

Luxury Equipment Discount Pkg.

LE w/5-pass.	1422	1209	1310
LE w/7-pass.	1445	1228	1330

Popular Equipment Package plus tilt steering wheel, dual power mirrors, power front door windows, power door locks, power driver's seat.

Travel Equipment Discount Pkg., SE	1538	1307	1415
w/Popular or Luxury Equip.	1481	1259	1365

2.6-liter engine, 7-passenger seating, sunscreen glass, remote control rear vent windows, 20-gallon fuel tank, 500-amp. battery.

Gauge pkg. w/gauge alert	92	78	85
Rear compartment heater, SE & LE	267	227	245
Light group, base & SE	140	119	129
LE	130	111	120
Sport road wheels, SE & LE	505	429	465
500-amp battery	57	48	52
Rear defogger	165	140	152
California emissions pkg.	99	84	91
Sunscreen glass (remote mirrors req.) . . .	406	345	375
Luggage rack	140	119	129
Vinyl bodyside molding	62	53	57
Dual remote mirrors, base & SE	78	66	72
Power door locks	203	173	187
Power liftgate release	49	42	45
Power driver's seat, SE & LE	251	213	230
Power front windows, SE & LE	212	180	195
Sound systems			
AM & FM ST ET, base & SE	155	132	143
AM & FM ST ET cassette, base & SE . .	416	353	385
Base & SE w/Popular Equip., LE . . .	261	222	240
AM & FM ST ET cassette w/EQ			
(Ultimate Sound), SE	613	521	565
SE w/Popular Equip., LE	458	389	420
AM delete, base & SE (credit)	(56)	(48)	(48)
AM & FM ST delete, LE (credit)	(211)	(179)	(179)
Cruise control	207	176	190
Tilt steering column	122	104	112
Heavy-duty suspension	68	58	63
P205/70R14 SBR tires	130	111	120
Conventional spare tire	104	88	96
Wire wheel covers, SE & LE	239	203	220
Styled steel road wheels, base	67	57	62

Prices are accurate at time of printing; subject to manufacturer's change

Dodge/Plymouth Colt

Dodge Colt 3-door

Built by Mitsubishi and sold in identical form through Dodge and Plymouth dealers, the front-drive Colt subcompact has new styling forward of the windshield and new cable shift linkage on manual shift models. The new front styling includes a full-width hood, new fenders and grille, flush aerodynamic headlamps and a revised bumper. Mitsubishi sells its own version of the Colt under the Mirage nameplate. The Mirage gets similar styling changes. Last year's model lineup remains: A 3-door hatchback and 4-door sedan are available in base E and mid-level DL trim, while the 4-door also comes in top-line Premier trim. A turbo engine package is available on the DL hatchback and Premier sedan. The 4-door sedan has been available only through Dodge and Plymouth dealers the past two years, but this year Mitsubishi also will offer a Mirage 4-door. Chrysler's captive imports offer decent value for the money when you stick with the E and DL models and don't go overboard with options. They do especially well as low-cost, economical transportation with manual transmission. With the extra-cost automatic, the base 1.5-liter engine loses some of its zip, uses more gas and generates more noise. Unless you're dead set on automatic, manual shift is the better choice. Noise is a problem on all models since both engines tend to be vocal when worked hard and the interiors aren't well insulated against road noise. Neither are the interiors very roomy, making it tight for four adults, especially in the hatchbacks.

Specifications

	3-door sedan	4-door sedan
Wheelbase, in.	93.7	93.7
Overall length, in.	157.3	169.1
Overall width, in.	63.8	63.8
Overall height, in.	53.5	53.5
Front track, in.	55.5	55.5
Rear track, in.	52.8	52.8
Curb weight, lbs.	1984	2051
Cargo vol., cu. ft.	11.7	10.9
Fuel capacity, gal.	11.9	11.9
Seating capacity	5	5
Front headroom, in.	37.7	37.7
Front shoulder room, in.	52.8	52.8
Front legroom, max., in.	40.5	40.5
Rear headroom, in.	36.7	37.0
Rear shoulder room, in.	54.3	52.6
Rear legroom, min, in.	30.7	30.7

Body/Chassis

Drivetrain layout: transverse front engine/front-wheel drive. **Front suspension:** MacPherson struts, lower control arms, coil springs, stabilizer bar. **Rear suspension:** independent; trailing arms, coil springs, stabilizer bar. **Steering:** rack and pinion, 4.2 turns lock-to-lock. **Turn diameter, ft.:** 30.5. **Front brakes:** 9.4-in. discs. **Rear brakes:** 7.0-in. drums. **Construction:** unit.

Powertrains

	ohc I-4	ohc I-4T
Displacement, l/cu. in.	1.5/90	1.6/98
Compression ratio	9.4:1	7.6:1
Fuel delivery	2 bbl.	TBI
Net bhp @ rpm	68 @ 5500	105 @ 5500
Net torque @ rpm	85 @ 3500	122 @ 3500
Availability	S	S

Final drive ratios

4-speed manual	3.45:1	
5-speed OD manual	4.02:1	4.20:1
3-speed automatic	3.60:1	3.64:1

KEY: bbl = barrel (carburetor); **bhp** = brake horsepower; **torque** = pounds/feet; **Cal.** = California only; **TBI** = throttle body (single-point) fuel injection; **PFI** = port (multi-point) fuel injection; **MFI** = mechanical fuel injection; **ohv** = overhead valve; **ohc** = overhead cam; **dohc** = double overhead cam; **I** = inline engine; **V** = V engine; **flat** = horizontally opposed engine; **D** = diesel; **T** = turbocharged; **OD** = overdrive transmission; **S** = standard; **O** = optional.

PRICES

DODGE/PLYMOUTH COLT	Retail Price	Dealer Invoice	Low Price
E 3-door sedan	$6056	$5405	$5850
DL 3-door sedan	7152	6222	6950
E 4-door sedan	7290	6342	7090
DL 4-door sedan	7677	6679	7480
Premier 4-door sedan	8638	7515	8440
Destination charge	200	200	200

STANDARD EQUIPMENT (included in above prices):

E 1.5-liter (90-cid) 4-cylinder 2 bbl. engine, 4-speed manual transmission (3-door; 5-speed on 4-door), power brakes, passenger assist grips (4-door), carpeting including cargo compartment, side window demisters, locking fuel filler door, upshift indicator light, coolant temperature gauge, trip odometer, dual manual mirrors, front mud guards, vinyl low-back reclining bucket seats, folding rear seatback, flip-open rear quarter windows (3-door; roll-down on sedan), 145/80R13 tires on styled steel wheels. **DL** adds: 5-speed manual transmission, bumper rub strips, cigar lighter, rear defogger, day/night mirror, remote left mirror, wide vinyl bodyside moldings, velour upholstery, trunk light (sedan), 155/80R13 SBR tires with hubcaps and trim rings. **Premier** adds: rear center armrest, digital clock, remote decklid release, remote fuel filler door release, tinted glass, halogen headlamps, dual power mirrors. right visor mirror, velour sport bucket seats, split folding rear seatbacks, variable intermittent wipers, P185/60HR14 SBR tires on aluminum wheels.

OPTIONAL EQUIPMENT:

3-speed automatic transmission (NA E 3-door)	434	360	410
Air conditioning	664	551	631
Carpet protectors	26	22	25
DL Turbo pkg., DL 3-door	1248	1036	1185

1.6-liter (97-cid) turbocharged 4-cylinder TBI engine, front air dam and rear dual spoilers, uprated suspension, side sill extension, driver's foot rest, sport front seats, tachometer, sport steering wheel, maintenance free battery, tinted glass, halogen headlamps, 185/60HR14 tires.

Turbo Pkg., Premier	720	598	685

Turbocharged engine, turbo boost gauge, ventilated front disc brakes, sport steering wheel.

Rear defogger, E	34	28	32
Digital clock, DL	47	39	45
Driver's seat height control, DL & Premier	19	16	18
Tinted glass, E & DL	60	50	57
Dual power mirrors, DL	72	60	68
Vinyl side molding, E	54	45	51
Two-tone paint, Premier	152	126	144
Power steering, DL & Premier	218	181	205

Prices are accurate at time of printing; subject to manufacturer's change

CONSUMER GUIDE®

Radio prep, E	64	53	61
AM/FM ST, E & DL	192	159	182
AM/FM ST ET, Premier	252	209	240
AM/FM ST ET cassette, DL & Premier	384	319	365
Above w/EQ, DL & Premier	625	519	595
Cast aluminum wheels, E	306	254	290
DL	208	173	198
Luggage rack, 4-doors	87	72	83
Cloth & vinyl upholstery, E	43	36	41
Rear wiper/washer, 3-doors	107	89	102
Variable intermittent wipers, DL	51	42	48

Dodge/Plymouth Colt Vista

Dodge Colt Vista

The rear-seat in the 7-passenger Colt Vista has been redesigned to fold flat and extend the cargo floor, plus an adjustable roof rack is available as a new option. The 2-place
rear seat formerly had only a folding rear seatback; now
it also pivots forward for more cargo room at the rear.
Built by Mitsubishi, Chrysler's Japanese partner, and sold
in identical form through Dodge and Plymouth stores, the
Colt Vista is available with front-wheel drive or on-demand 4-wheel-drive that can be used on smooth, dry pavement. Both models are powered by an 88-horsepower 2.0-
liter 4-cylinder engine. One of the most unusual and ver-
satile wagons on the market, the Colt Vista can seat up
to seven people, or the seats can be folded out to be used
as beds, or you can haul a good deal of luggage in the
expanded rear cargo area. With four doors and a rear

liftgate, it's easy to load people and cargo. The 4WD system is engaged with the push of a button to give you the extra traction when you need it. The 2.0-liter engine has to work pretty hard in this car with only 88 horsepower for nearly 2600 pounds of curb weight on the front-drive model and nearly 2900 pounds on the 4WD model. Add in four or five people and the engine is overmatched, especially with automatic transmission. Base prices are reasonably low and a 5-year/50,000-mile rust warranty is standard, making this an attractive vehicle from a value standpoint. We would give a lot of thought to the modest engine output before deciding on this as our carry-all family wagon.

Specifications

	5-door 4WD wagon	5-door wagon
Wheelbase, in.	103.3	103.3
Overall length, in.	174.6	174.6
Overall width, in.	64.6	64.6
Overall height, in.	59.4	57.3
Front track, in.	55.5	55.5
Rear track, in.	54.1	54.1
Curb weight, lbs.	2888	2557
Cargo vol., cu. ft.	63.9	63.9
Fuel capacity, gal.	14.5	13.2
Seating capacity	7	7
Front headroom, in.	38.3	38.3
Front shoulder room, in.	53.1	53.1
Front legroom, max., in.	38.8	38.8
Rear headroom, in.	38.3	38.3
Rear shoulder room, in.	53.2	53.2
Rear legroom, min, in.	36.5	36.5

Body/Chassis

Drivetrain layout: transverse front engine/front-wheel drive or 4WD. **Front suspension:** Mac Pherson struts, lower control arms, coil springs, stabilizer bar. **Rear suspension:** independent; trailing arms, coil springs, stabilizer bar. 4WD: independent; semi-trailing arms, torsion bar. **Steering:** rack and pinion, 4.2 turns lock-to-lock manual, 3.4 power. **Turn diameter, ft.:** 34.8. **Front brakes:** 9.5-in. discs. 4WD 10.3-in. **Rear brakes:** 8.0-in. drums, 4WD: 9-in. **Construction:** unit.

Powertrains	ohc I-4
Displacement, l/cu. in.	2.0/122
Compression ratio	8.5:1

	ohc I-4
Fuel delivery	2 bbl.
Net bhp @ rpm	88 @ 5000
Net torque @ rpm	108 @ 3500
Availability	S
Final drive ratios	
5-speed OD manual	3.19:1
3-speed automatic	3.19:1[1]

1. NA with 4WD

KEY: bbl = barrel (carburetor); **bhp** = brake horsepower; **torque** = pounds/feet; **Cal.** = California only; **TBI** = throttle body (single-point) fuel injection; **PFI** = port (multi-point) fuel injection; **MFI** = mechanical fuel injection; **ohv** = overhead valve; **ohc** = overhead cam; **dohc** = double overhead cam; **I** = inline engine; **V** = V engine; **flat** = horizontally opposed engine; **D** = diesel; **T** = turbocharged; **OD** = overdrive transmission; **S** = standard; **O** = optional.

PRICES

DODGE/PLYMOUTH COLT VISTA	Retail Price	Dealer Invoice	Low Price
5-door wagon	$10158	$8634	$9600
5-door wagon, 4wd	11371	9665	10745
Destination charge	200	200	200

STANDARD EQUIPMENT (included in above prices):

2.0-liter (122-cid) 4-cylinder 2 bbl. engine, 5-speed manual transmission, power brakes, five passenger assist handles, cut-pile carpeting including cargo area, cigar lighter, rear defogger, side window demisters, remote fuel filler door release, coolant temperature gauge, trip odometer, tinted glass, map pockets in front doors and seatbacks, wide bodyside moldings, front mud guards, cloth and vinyl lowback reclining front seats, split-back folding rear bench seats, variable intermittent wipers, P165/80R13 SBR tires. **4WD** adds: power steering, dual outside mirrors, rear mud guards, 185/70R14 SBR tires.

OPTIONAL EQUIPMENT:

3-speed automatic transmission (NA 4wd)	433	359	410
Air conditioning	689	572	655
Carpet protectors	26	22	25
Custom pkg., 2wd	302	251	285
4wd	259	215	245

Dual power mirrors, velour seats, carpeted lower door panels, dual visor mirrors, digital clock, two map lights, front and rear courtesy lights, P185/70R13 tires (2wd only).

Limited slip differential, 4wd	170	141	162

Prices are accurate at time of printing; subject to manufacturer's change

	Retail Price	Dealer Invoice	Low Price
Luggage rack	120	100	114
Two-tone paint	199	165	189
Power door locks	135	112	128
Power steering, 2wd	218	181	205
Power windows	189	157	180
AM/FM ST	192	159	182
AM/FM ST ET cassette	372	309	355
Cruise control	151	125	143
Cast aluminum wheels	242	201	230
Liftgate wiper/washer	107	89	102

Dodge Daytona

Dodge Daytona

Dodge's front-drive sport coupe gets new front and rear styling, a new model lineup and a more powerful turbocharged engine. While Daytona carries on, the similar Chrysler Laser has been dropped. This year's lineup consists of base coupe, luxury Pacifica and high-performance Shelby Z. All Daytonas have concealed, pop-up dual headlamps instead of last year's exposed four lamps and a redesigned rear end with wide taillamps. Chrysler's 2.5-liter balance-shaft 4-cylinder engine is standard in the base Daytona, replacing a 2.2-liter four. The 146-horsepower turbocharged 2.2 is optional in the base Daytona, standard in the Pacifica. That engine is now called Turbo I because a new 174-horsepower version called Turbo II debuts as standard equipment in the Shelby Z. The Turbo II has an intercooler, stronger internal parts and higher boost pressure, plus it's hooked to a stronger 5-speed manual transmission. If you want automatic on the Shelby Z, you can get it only with the Turbo I engine. All Daytonas have new analog instrument clusters with 125-mph electrically driven speedometers standard. Dodge emphasizes performance with the Daytona, and you get plenty of it with either turbocharged engine. The Shelby Z outperforms most V-6-powered cars and some V-8s. The Shelby Z comes with a stiff suspension and wide high-performance tires that give it great handling and tight grip in hard cornering, but at the expense of ride comfort. There's almost no give to the Shelby Z's suspension, so you'll feel every bump. The Pacifica's suspension isn't as stiff and the tires are less aggressive, but it's in the same league. The base model is moderately firm and rides on smaller tires. Our advice is to try before you buy, since these are macho-style performance coupes. One of the best selling points is the 5-year/ 50,000-mile powertrain warranty, good protection for those who flog their cars.

Specifications	3-door coupe
Wheelbase, in.	97.0
Overall length, in.	175.0
Overall width, in.	69.3
Overall height, in.	50.4
Front track, in.	57.6
Rear track, in.	57.6
Curb weight, lbs.	2676
Cargo vol., cu. ft.	33.0
Fuel capacity, gal.	14.0
Seating capacity	4
Front headroom, in.	37.1
Front shoulder room, in.	55.9
Front legroom, max., in.	42.4
Rear headroom, in.	34.3
Rear shoulder room, in.	53.6
Rear legroom, min, in.	30.0

Body/Chassis

Drivetrain layout: transverse front engine/front-wheel drive. **Front suspension:** MacPherson struts, lower control arms, coil springs, stabilizer bar. **Rear suspension:** beam flex axle, trailing arms, coil springs, stabilizer bar. **Steering:** rack and pinion, power assisted, 2.5 turns lock-to-lock. **Turn diameter, ft.:** 34.3. **Front brakes:** 10.1-in. discs. **Rear brakes:** 8.9-in. drums. **Construction:** unit.

Powertrains	ohc I-4	ohc I-4T	ohc I-4T
Displacement, l/cu. in.	2.5/135	2.2/135	2.2/135
Compression ratio	9.0:1	8.1:1	8.1:1
Fuel delivery	TBI	PFI	PFI
Net bhp @ rpm	100 @ 4800	146 @ 5200	174 @ 4800
Net torque @ rpm	136 @ 2800	170 @ 3600	200 @ 3200
Availability	S[1]	S[2]	S[3]

1. base   2. Pacifica   3. Shelby Z

Final drive ratios

5-speed OD manual	2.57:1	2.57:1	2.57:1
3-speed automatic	3.02:1	3.02:1	3.02:1

KEY: bbl = barrel (carburetor); **bhp** =brake horsepower; **torque** = pounds/feet; **Cal.** = California only; **TBI** = throttle body (single-point) fuel injection; **PFI** = port (multipoint) fuel injection; **MFI** = mechanical fuel injection; **ohv** = overhead valve; **ohc** = overhead cam; **dohc** = double overhead cam; **I** = inline engine; **V** = V engine; **flat** = horizontally opposed engine; **D** = diesel; **T** = turbocharged; **OD** = overdrive transmission; **S** = standard; **O** = optional.

PRICES

DODGE DAYTONA (1986 prices)	Retail Price	Dealer Invoice	Low Price
3-door coupe	$9013	$8006	$8470
Turbo Z 3-door coupe	11301	10020	10625
Destination charge	426	426	426

STANDARD EQUIPMENT (included in above prices):

2.2-liter (135-cid) fuel-injected TBI 4-cylinder engine, power brakes, power steering, 5-speed manual transmission, carpeting, console, halogen headlamps w/optical horn, dual remote control door mirrors, power tailgate release, AM & FM stereo ET, rear spoiler, leather-wrapped steering wheel, premium wheel covers, deluxe intermittent wipers, tinted glass, P185/70R14 blackwall tires on aluminum wheels. Turbo adds: turbocharged PFI engine, Light Group, cargo trim/quiet sound package, power outside mirrors, bodyside moldings, P205/60R15 raised black letter tires.

OPTIONAL EQUIPMENT:

2.2-liter turbo engine (incl. 195/70R14 tires), base	990	842	910

Prices are accurate at time of printing; subject to manufacturer's change.

2.5-liter 4-cylinder engine, base	279	237	255
3-speed automatic transmission	504	428	465
Air conditioning	757	643	695
Popular Equipment Discount Pkg. w/A/C			
Base	806	685	740
Base w/T-bar roof	841	715	775
Turbo Z	897	762	825
Popular Equipment w/o A/C			
Base	249	212	230
Base w/T-bar roof	284	241	260
Turbo Z	340	289	315

Air conditioning, power remote mirrors, tilt steering column, rear defogger, cruise control, light group.

Cargo Trim/Quiet Sound Group			
Turbo Z w/o Popular Equipment	252	214	230
Turbo Z w/Popular Equipment	233	198	215

Added cargo area carpeting and sound insulation, tonneau cover.

Sun/Sound/Shade Discount Pkg.			
w/o T-bar roof	626	532	575
w/T-bar roof	294	250	270

T-bar roof, rear window louvers, AM stereo/FM stereo ET cassette.

C/S Handling Package, Turbo Z	183	156	168
Power door locks	130	111	120
Power windows	195	166	179
Power seat, left	225	191	205
Cruise control	179	152	165
Rear window wiper/washer (defogger req.) .	125	106	115
Power remote mirrors	56	48	52
Tilt steering column	115	98	106
AM & FM ST ET cassette	244	207	225
AM/FM ST ET cassette w/EQ			
(Ultimate Sound) w/Sun/Sound/Shade . .	454	386	420
w/o Sun/Sound/Shade	210	179	193
Flip up/removable glass sunroof	332	282	305
Sport seats w/inflatable driver's side supports			
Leather, base	959	815	882
Leather, Turbo Z	674	482	520
Cloth & vinyl, base	392	333	360
Conventional spare tire (w/185/70R14 tires			
only)	83	71	76
P195/70R14 tires, base	92	78	85
Electronic Features (voice alert & trip computer)			
Base	583	496	535
Turbo Z	272	231	250
T-bar roof (incl. power windows & mirrors, reading lamps)			
w/o Popular Equipment	1372	1166	1260
Base w/Popular Equipment	1351	1148	1245
Turbo Z w/Popular Equipment	1295	1101	1015

Prices are accurate at time of printing; subject to manufacturer's change.

Dodge Omni/Charger

Dodge Omni America

The America model of the Omni hatchback sedan, launched in May as an early 1987 model, has been a major success for Chrysler in the small-car arena. The America program streamlines production and lowers costs by offering Omni and the identical Plymouth Horizon in only one price series, with three option packages and three individual options. Chrysler eliminated 702 parts by cutting equipment variations and options. The only engine offered is a carbureted 2.2-liter four, with a choice of 5-speed manual or 3-speed automatic transmissions. The sporty Charger hatchback coupe is offered two ways: base Charger with the same engine as Omni and similar options and the high-performance Shelby Charger with a turbocharged 2.2. Chrysler scored another coup by taking its oldest front-drive car (Omni/Horizon debuted for 1978), making more equipment standard and lowering the price. There is much to recommend the Omni America. Even with a recent price increase it's still an outstanding value at less than $8000 with automatic and air conditioning, and it comes with Chrysler's 5-year/50,000-mile warranties. The 2.2-liter has enough power to handle both automatic transmission and air conditioning without turning anemic, plus it returns decent gas mileage. On the minus side, the interior is cramped compared to newer subcompacts and the driving position is ungainly. Chrysler has had a hit-and-miss workmanship record with these cars. Some are assembled tight as a drum, others come out the door with sloppy assembly quality. Dollar-conscious shoppers should still put this car at the top of their list; there's no better value among sub-compacts.

Specifications

	Omni 5-door sedan	Charger 3-door coupe
Wheelbase, in.	99.1	96.5
Overall length, in.	163.2	174.8
Overall width, in.	66.8	66.1
Overall height, in.	53.0	50.7
Front track, in.	56.1	56.1
Rear track, in.	55.7	56.1
Curb weight, lbs.	2237	2290
Cargo vol., cu. ft.	33.0	32.4
Fuel capacity, gal.	13.0	13.0
Seating capacity	5	5
Front headroom, in.	38.1	37.2
Front shoulder room, in.	51.7	52.2
Front legroom, max., in.	42.1	42.5
Rear headroom, in.	36.9	34.4
Rear shoulder room, in.	51.5	50.9
Rear legroom, min, in.	33.3	28.7

Body/Chassis

Drivetrain layout: transverse front engine/front-wheel drive. **Front suspension:** MacPherson struts, lower control arms, coil springs, stabilizer bar. **Rear suspension:** beam flex axle, trailing arms, coil springs, stabilizer bar on 3-doors. **Steering:** rack and pinion, 3.6 turns lock-to-lock. **Turn diameter, ft.:** 38.1. **Front brakes:** 9.0-in. discs (10.0-in. on Shelby). **Rear brakes:** 7.9-in. drums (8.9-in. on Shelby). **Construction:** unit.

Powertrains

	ohc I-4	ohc I-4T
Displacement, l/cu. in.	2.2/135	2.2/135
Compression ratio	9.0:1	8.1:1
Fuel delivery	2 bbl.	PFI
Net bhp @ rpm	96 @ 5200	146 @ 5200
Net torque @ rpm	119 @ 3200	170 @ 3600
Availability	S	S[1]

1. Shelby

Final drive ratios

5-speed manual	2.20:1	2.57:1
3-speed automatic	2.78:1	

KEY: **bbl** = barrel (carburetor); **bhp** =brake horsepower; **torque** = pounds/feet; **Cal.** = California only; **TBI** = throttle body (single-point) fuel injection; **PFI** = port (multi-point) fuel injection; **MFI** = mechanical fuel injection; **ohv** = overhead valve; **ohc** = overhead cam; **dohc** = double overhead cam; **I** = inline engine; **V** = V engine; **flat** = horizontally opposed engine; **D** = diesel; **T** = turbocharged; **OD** = overdrive transmission; **S** = standard; **O** = optional.

PRICES

DODGE OMNI AND CHARGER	Retail Price	Dealer Invoice	Low Price
Omni America 5-door sedan	$5799	$5277	$5700
Charger 3-door coupe	7199	6554	7000
Shelby Charger 3-door coupe	9840	8931	9400
Destination charge, Omni	320	320	320
Charger	386	386	386

STANDARD EQUIPMENT (included in above prices):

Omni and Charger: 2.2-liter (135-cid) 4-cylinder 2 bbl. engine, 5-speed manual transmission, power brakes, rear defogger, rear wiper/washer, rallye instrument cluster (trip odometer, tachometer, coolant temperature, oil pressure and voltage gauges), tinted glass, luggage compartment light, black bodyside moldings, left remote mirror, right visor mirror, folding shelf panel, intermittent wipers, urethane lower body protection, tethered fuel filler cap, cloth and vinyl upholstery, lockable glovebox, remote liftgate release (Charger), P165/80R13 tires on styled steel wheels. **Shelby Charger** adds: 2.2-liter turbocharged PFI 4-cylinder engine, close-ratio 5-speed manual transmission, power steering, sport suspension, sport front seats, AM & FM ST ET cassette, illuminated right visor mirror, map light, removable glass sunroof, two-tone paint, front and rear spoilers and side sill extensions, P205/50VR15 tires on aluminum wheels.

OPTIONAL EQUIPMENT:

Basic Pkg. (auto trans & power steering)	776	660	715
Manual Transmission Discount Pkg. (NA Shelby)	575	489	530

Power steering, AM & FM ST ET, highback front bucket seats, upgraded cargo area trim, center console with coin holder, cubby box, cupholder, ash receiver light.

Automatic Transmission Discount Pkg. (NA Shelby)	1009	858	930

Manual Transmission Discount Pkg. plus 3-speed automatic transmission.

Air conditioning (discount pkg. req.)	701	596	645
California emissions pkg.	99	84	91
AM & FM ST ET cassette (discount pkg. req.)	246	209	225

Prices are accurate at time of printing; subject to manufacturer's change.

Dodge Shadow/ Plymouth Sundance

Dodge Shadow ES 3-door

Shadow and Sundance, nearly identical front-drive compacts, went on sale during the summer as 5-door hatchbacks. Both lines gained sporty 3-door hatchback models in the fall. Known internally as the P-car, Shadow and Sundance are built on the same platform as the Dodge Daytona, but come with a firmer standard suspension and more standard equipment than most domestic cars. The same suspension is used on all models with either the base fuel-injected 2.2-liter engine or the optional turbocharged 2.2, though turbo models get high-performance tires instead of all-season radials of the same size (P185/70R14) The Shadow ES package (not offered on Sundance) adds P205/50VR15 unidirectional radials on cast-aluminum wheels. Shadow and Sundance are aimed at the baby-boom generation as an alternative to sporty imports and Chrysler will make a strong sales pitch to women, whom the company expects will buy nearly half the P-cars. In base form, Shadow and Sundance exhibit sportier handling than most small cars and a firm, well-controlled ride. The drivetrains are familiar pieces from other front-drive Chrysler cars. The base 2.2 engine is adequate with automatic transmission, a better choice over the standard 5-speed manual since the shift linkage still lacks precision. The optional turbo engine provides a major improvement in performance and a big increase in noise over the base engine, which isn't the quietest 4-cylinder around either. Rear seat leg and head room are marginal for adults and it's a tight squeeze through the rear doors on the 5-door hatchback, but Chrysler expects most buyers will be single or young marrieds who won't use the back seat that much. All models have folding rear seatbacks that give them good cargo-carrying ability. With a generous amount of standard equipment, there aren't that many options available. The prices aren't bad either; a well-equipped Shadow or Sundance 3-door with automatic, air conditioning, the Popular Equipment Package and a stereo with cassette player is under $10,000, and there aren't many comparable cars that can match that.

Specifications

	3-door sedan	5-door sedan
Wheelbase, in.	97.0	97.0
Overall length, in.	171.7	171.7
Overall width, in.	67.3	67.3
Overall height, in.	52.7	52.7
Front track, in.	57.6	57.6
Rear track, in.	57.2	57.2
Curb weight, lbs.	2520	2558
Cargo vol., cu. ft.	33.3	33.0
Fuel capacity, gal.	14.0	14.0
Seating capacity	5	5
Front headroom, in.	38.3	38.3
Front shoulder room, in.	54.4	54.7
Front legroom, max., in.	41.5	41.5
Rear headroom, in.	37.4	37.4
Rear shoulder room, in.	52.5	54.5
Rear legroom, min, in.	20.1	20.1

Body/Chassis

Drivetrain layout: transverse front engine/front-wheel drive. **Front suspension:** MacPherson struts, lower control arms, coil springs, stabilizer bar. **Rear suspension:** beam flex axle, trailing arms, coil springs, stabilizer bar. **Steering:** rack and pinion, power assisted, 2.5 turns lock-to-lock. **Turn diameter, ft.:** 36.2. **Front brakes:** 9.3-in. discs (10.1-in w/turbo). **Rear brakes:** 7.9-in. drums. **Construction:** unit.

Powertrains	ohc I-4	ohc I-4T
Displacement, l/cu. in.	2.2/135	2.2/135
Compression ratio	9.5:1	8.1:1
Fuel delivery	TBI	PFI

	ohv I-4	ohv I-4TD
Net bhp @ rpm	97 @ 5200	146 @ 5200
Net torque @ rpm	122 @ 3200	170 @ 3600
Availability	S	O
Final drive ratios		
5-speed manual	2.51:1	2.51:1
3-speed automatic	3.02:1	3.02:1

KEY: bbl = barrel (carburetor); **bhp** = brake horsepower; **torque** = pounds/feet; **Cal.** = California only; **TBI** = throttle body (single-point) fuel injection; **PFI** = port (multi-point) fuel injection; **MFI** = mechanical fuel injection; **ohv** = overhead valve; **ohc** = overhead cam; **dohc** = double overhead cam; **I** = inline engine; **V** = V engine; **flat** = horizontally opposed engine; **D** = diesel; **T** = turbocharged; **OD** = overdrive transmission; **S** = standard; **O** = optional.

PRICES

DODGE SHADOW	Retail Price	Dealer Invoice	Low Price
3-door	$7499	$6824	$7160
5-door	7699	7004	7350
Destination charge	382	382	382

STANDARD EQUIPMENT (included in above prices):

2.2-liter (135-cid) TBI 4-cylinder engine, 5-speed manual transmission, power steering, power brakes, cloth upholstery, full carpeting including lower door panels and cargo area, tachometer, coolant temperature and voltage gauges, reclining front bucket seats, folding rear seatback, mini-console with storage bin, headlamps-on chime, urethane lower body coating, AM radio, remote manual mirrors, passenger visor mirror, intermittent wipers, rear coat hooks, side window demisters, tethered fuel filler cap, halogen headlamps, remote hatch release, wide bodyside moldings, optical horn, pivoting/removable rear shelf panel, P185/70R14 all-season tires on styled steel wheels.

OPTIONAL EQUIPMENT:

Turbo Engine Pkg.	806	685	740

2.2-liter turbocharged engine, Message Center, vacuum/turbo boost gauge, performance tires.

3-speed automatic transmission	529	450	485
Pearl coat paint	40	34	37
ES Pkg.	1720	1462	1580
w/Popular Equipment	1541	1310	1420
w/Light Pkg.	1696	1442	1560

2.2-liter turbocharged engine, full console w/center armrest, 60/40 folding rear seatback, dual power mirrors, AM & FM ST ET, leather-wrapped steering wheel, premium bucket seats, map light, P205/50VR15 undirectional tires on aluminum wheels.

Prices are accurate at time of printing; subject to manufacturer's change.

	Retail Price	Dealer Invoice	Low Price
Popular Equipment Discount Pkg., 3-door .	341	290	315
5-door	353	300	325
Rear defogger, Light Pkg., AM & FM ST ET.			
Deluxe Convenience Pkg.	304	258	280
Cruise control and tilt steering column.			
Light Pkg., 3-door	88	75	81
5-door	100	85	92
Protection Pkg.	88	75	81
Air conditioning (tinted glass req.)	694	590	640
Full console w/armrest	146	124	134
Rear defogger	148	126	136
California emissions pkg.	99	84	91
Tinted glass	105	89	97
Dual power mirrors (console req.)	48	41	41
Power windows (console req.), 3-door . .	210	179	193
5-door	285	242	260
Power door locks, 3-door	145	123	133
5-door	195	166	179
AM & FM ST ET	155	132	143
AM & FM ST ET cassette	399	339	365
w/ES or Popular Equip.	244	207	225
Removable glass sunroof	365	310	335
Conventional spare tire	83	71	76
w/cast aluminum wheels	160	136	147
Cast aluminum 14″ wheels	306	260	280

PLYMOUTH SUNDANCE

	Retail Price	Dealer Invoice	Low Price
3-door	$7599	$6914	$7260
5-door	7799	7094	7450
Destination charge	382	382	382

STANDARD EQUIPMENT (included in above prices):

2.2-liter (135-cid) TBI 4-cylinder engine, 5-speed manual transmission, power steering, power brakes, cloth upholstery, full carpeting including lower door panels and cargo area, tachometer, coolant temperature and voltage gauges, reclining front bucket seats, 60/40 split folding rear seatback, mini-console with storage bin, headlamps-on chime, urethane lower body coating, AM radio, remote manual mirrors, passenger visor mirror, intermittent wipers, rear coat hooks, side window demisters, tethered fuel filler cap, halogen headlamps, remote hatch release, wide bodyside moldings, optical horn, pivoting/removable rear shelf panel, P185/70R14 all-season tires on styled steel wheels.

OPTIONAL EQUIPMENT:

Turbo engine pkg.	806	685	740
2.2-liter turbocharged engine, Message Center, vacuum/turbo boost gauge, performance tires.			

Prices are accurate at time of printing; subject to manufacturer's change.

CONSUMER GUIDE®

3-speed automatic transmission	529	450	485
Pearl coat paint	40	34	37
Popular Equipment Discount Pkg., 3-door .	341	290	315
5-door	353	300	325
Rear defogger, Light Pkg., AM & FM ST ET.			
Deluxe Convenience Pkg.	304	258	280
Cruise control, tilt steering column.			
Light Pkg., 3-door	88	75	81
5-door	100	85	92
Protection Pkg.	88	75	81
Air conditioning (tinted glass req.)	694	590	640
Full console w/armrest	146	124	134
Rear defogger	148	125	136
California emissions pkg.	99	84	91
Tinted glass	105	89	97
Dual power mirrors (console req.)	48	41	44
Power windows (console req.), 3-door . .	210	179	193
5-door	285	245	260
Power door locks, 3-door	145	123	133
5-door	195	166	179
AM & FM ST ET	155	132	143
AM & FM ST ET cassette			
w/o Popular Equip.	399	339	365
w/Popular Equipment	244	207	225
Removable glass sunroof	365	310	335
Conventional spare tire	83	71	76
w/cast aluminum wheels	163	139	150
Cast aluminum wheels	318	270	295

Ford Aerostar

Passenger versions of the Aerostar, Ford's rear-drive, compact van, have a 3.0-liter V-6 as the standard engine this year, hitched to either a 5-speed manual or 4-speed overdrive automatic transmission. Last year's base engine, a 2.3-liter 4-cylinder, remains standard in the cargo van, with the V-6 optional. The fuel-injected 3.0 V-6, introduced in the Ford Taurus/Mercury Sable, replaced a carbureted 2.8-liter V-6 as the top engine in Aerostar late in the 1986 model year. Other changes are the additions of electric remote control mirrors and special seats that convert to a bed as new options. Swing-out dual rear doors have been added as an option on cargo vans; passenger versions still have a one-piece liftgate. Aerostar follows traditional van design with its rear-drive chassis. That makes for ample

Prices are accurate at time of printing; subject to manufacturer's change.

Ford Aerostar

trailer-towing ability (4900 pounds with the right options) and a maximum payload of 2040 pounds (on cargo vans), plus there's generous interior space, so fitting seven people doesn't call for a lot of squeezing. The 3.0 V-6 now standard in passenger Aerostars produces about 30 more horsepower than last year's 2.8 V-6, and the extra horsepower is needed to overcome the hefty base curb weight of 3300 pounds. The 3.0 V-6 feels adequate in the Aerostar, while the 2.8 struggled from a standing start. Overall, the Aerostar is much closer in concept and execution to the rear-drive Chevrolet Astro than the front-drive Dodge Caravan/ Plymouth Voyager, making it appealing to those who need more brawn than Chrysler's mini vans can provide.

Specifications

	4-door van
Wheelbase, in.	118.9
Overall length, in.	174.9
Overall width, in.	71.7
Overall height, in.	72.6
Front track, in.	61.5
Rear track, in.	60.0
Curb weight, lbs.	3500
Cargo vol., cu. ft.	140.3
Fuel capacity, gal.	17.0
Seating capacity	5[1]
Front headroom, in.	39.6
Front shoulder room, in.	60.0

	4-door van
Front legroom, max., in.	41.4
Rear headroom, in.	37.7
Rear shoulder room, in.	NA
Rear legroom, min., in.	39.8

1. 7 opt.

Body/Chassis

Drivetrain layout: longitudinal front engine/rear-wheel drive.
Front suspension: upper and lower control arms, coil springs.
Rear suspension: upper and lower control arms, coil springs.
Steering: rack and pinion, power assist, turns lock-to-lock NA.
Turn diameter, ft.: 39.8. **Front brakes:** 10.3-in. discs. **Rear brakes:** 10.0-in. drums. **Construction:** unit.

Powertrains

	ohv V-6
Displacement, l/cu. in.	3.0/182
Compression ratio	9.3:1
Fuel delivery	PFI
Net bhp @ rpm	140 @ 4800
Net torque @ rpm	160 @ 3000
Availability	S

Final drive ratios

5-speed manual	3.45:1
3-speed automatic	3.45:1

KEY: bbl = barrel (carburetor); **bhp** =brake horsepower; **torque** = pounds/feet; **Cal.** = California only; **TBI** = throttle body (single-point) fuel injection; **PFI** = port (multipoint) fuel injection; **MFI** = mechanical fuel injection; **ohv** = overhead valve; **ohc** = overhead cam; **dohc** = double overhead cam; **I** = inline engine; **V** = V engine; **flat** = horizontally opposed engine; **D** = diesel; **T** = turbocharged; **OD** = overdrive transmission; **S** = standard; **O** = optional.

PRICES

FORD AEROSTAR	Retail Price	Dealer Invoice	Low Price
4-door van	$10582	$9520	$10040
Destination charge	450	450	450

STANDARD EQUIPMENT (included in above prices):

3.0-liter (182-cid) PFI V-6 engine, 5-speed manual transmission, power steering, power brakes, 5-passenger seating, maintenance-free battery, tinted glass, black fold-away outside mirrors, front air dam, bright flush

Prices are accurate at time of printing; subject to manufacturer's change.

aluminum wheel covers, sliding rear side windows, three coat hooks, courtesy lights, dashboard vanity panel, full-length 16-oz. carpet, scuff plates, inside fuel filler release, cloth headliner, front dome light, step well lamp, front/rear cigar lighter, day/night mirror, AM radio, low-back vinyl front bucket seats, vinyl rear bench seat, spare tire cover, visor mirrors, three bodyside storage bins. **XL** trim adds (for prices see options): bright griller, two-tone rocker area accent paint, dual cloth captain's chairs with recliners and armrests, digital clock, AM/FM stereo radio, intermittent wipers. **XLT** trim adds: dual-note horn, bodyside pinstripes, styled wheel covers, dual premium cloth captain's chairs with power lumbar support and map pockets, carpeted lower door panels with map pockets, electronic instrument cluster, rear grab handle, leather steering wheel, illuminated visor mirrors.

OPTIONAL EQUIPMENT:

4-speed automatic transmission	607	516	560
Limited-slip rear axle	248	210	230
California emissions pkg.	84	72	77
7-pass. seating	354	301	325
w/XLT & quad captain's chairs	585	498	540
Cloth seats w/standard trim			
w/5-pass. seating	106	90	98
w/7-pass. seating	159	135	146
Air conditioning	846	719	780
High-capacity A/C & aux. heater	1422	1209	1310
Heavy-duty battery	49	41	45
Supercool radiator	57	49	52
Rear defogger & wiper/washer			
w/standard trim & 5-pass.	271	230	250
Others	221	188	205
Electronic instrument cluster	180	153	166
Privacy glass	409	347	375
Engine block heater, w/A/C	33	28	30
w/o A/C	63	54	57
Light Group	157	134	144
Black outside swing-away mirrors	52	45	48
Bodyside moldings, w/standard or XL trim .	63	54	58
w/XLT trim	35	30	32
Two-tone paint, w/XL trim	134	114	123
w/XLT trim	91	78	84
Roof rack	141	120	130
Delete underbody spare tire (credit)	(22)	(19)	(19)
Cruise control & tilt steering col.	296	251	272
Trailer towing pkg., w/A/C	283	240	260
w/o A/C	330	281	305
Styled wheel covers	43	36	40
Power windows and door locks	370	314	340
AM/FM ST ET	211	179	194
AM/FM ST ET w/cassette	102	87	94

Prices are accurate at time of printing; subject to manufacturer's change

Super Sound System, w/415A pkg.	305	259	280
w/other packages	409	347	375

Preferred Equipment Packages
Content not available at time of publication.

402A (7 pass., std. trim)	354	301	325
405A (5 pass., XL trim)	906	770	835
407A (7 pass., XL trim)	1149	976	1055
410A (7 pass., XL trim)	1821	1548	1675
411A (7 pass., XL trim)	2671	2270	2455
412A (5 pass., XLT trim)	1258	1070	1155
413A (7 pass., XLT trim)	1581	1344	1455
415A (7 pass., XLT trim)	3235	2750	2975
416A (7 pass., XLT trim)	3709	3152	3410

Ford Escort & EXP/ Mercury Lynx

Ford EXP Luxury Coupe

Single-point fuel injection replaces a 2-barrel carburetor on the base 1.9-liter 4-cylinder engine for the Escort and Lynx, while the sporty Escort GT and Lynx XR3 still come with a high-output 1.9-liter four with multi-point injection (one injector for each cylinder). The Escort LX series has been dropped and the L series renamed GL, so Escort comes in three flavors for 1987: Base Pony (3-door hatchback

Prices are accurate at time of printing; subject to manufacturer's change.

only), mid-level GL (3- and 5-door hatchbacks and 5-door wagon), and top-line GT (3-door only). The nearly identical Mercury Lynx will be offered in a similar lineup. The base L series is relegated to an entry-level 3-door hatchback, while the upscale GS is offered in 3- and 5-door hatchback and 5-door wagon guise. The sporty XR3 continues only as a 3-door hatchback. Starting with January production, Escort and Lynx will be equipped with automatic front seat belts. The motorized belts will pivot around front seat occupants when the doors are closed, and retract when the doors are opened. A split fold-down rear seat and fold-down center armrest are new options. The 2-seat EXP, built on the Escort's front-drive chassis, was resurrected as a 1986½ model with new styling and listed as part of the Escort lineup instead of as a separate model. EXP comes two ways: Luxury Coupe or Sport Coupe. Mercury dealers will get a replacement for Lynx during 1987, a new subcompact called Tracer that is designed by Mazda, Ford's Japanese partner, and built in Mexico. The new subcompact will be based on the Mazda 323 chassis but will have different styling and will be marketed as a sporty, upscale model. Ford is expected to introduce a smaller subcompact built by the Korean company, Kia, next spring in California as a lower-priced model to be sold alongside Escort. Heading into its sixth model year, Escort remains Ford's best-selling line, offering reasonable fuel economy and acceptable performance with the base 1.9-liter engine. Despite its attractive base prices, Escort isn't a price leader in this class when you start adding options such as air conditioning, power steering and automatic transmission. However, Ford groups popular options into money-saving packages that help keep prices reasonable, so check those out when shopping. If you're looking for low-cost transportation, one of these without many options could still prove to be decent value among small cars, but it no longer impresses us as exceptional in any area.

Specifications	Escort 3-door sedan	Escort 5-door sedan	Escort 5-door wagon	EXP 3-door coupe
Wheelbase, in.	94.2	94.2	94.2	94.2
Overall length, in.	166.9	166.9	168.0	168.4
Overall width, in.	65.9	65.9	65.9	65.9

	Escort 3-door sedan	Escort 5-door sedan	Escort 5-door wagon	EXP 3-door coupe
Overall height, in.	53.5	53.5	53.3	50.9
Front track, in.	54.7	54.7	54.7	54.7
Rear track, in.	56.0	56.0	56.0	56.0
Curb weight, lbs.	2180	2222	2274	2291
Cargo vol., cu. ft.	16.4	16.4	28.0	NA
Fuel capacity, gal.	13.0	13.0	13.0	13.0
Seating capacity	4	4	4	2
Front headroom, in.	37.9	37.9	37.9	36.6
Front shoulder room, in.	51.3	51.3	51.3	51.3
Front legroom, max., in.	41.5	41.5	41.5	41.7
Rear headroom, in.	37.3	37.3	38.2	—
Rear shoulder room, in.	51.6	51.4	51.6	—
Rear legroom, min, in.	35.1	35.1	35.1	—

Body/Chassis

Drivetrain layout: tranverse front engine/front-wheel drive.
Front suspension: MacPherson struts, trailing arms, lower control arms, coil springs, stabilizer bar. **Rear suspension:** modified MacPherson struts, trailing arms, lower control arms, coil springs. **Steering:** rack and pinion, 3.5 turns lock-to-lock manual; 3.0 power. **Turn diameter, ft.:** 35.7. **Front brakes:** 9.3-in. discs. **Rear brakes:** 7.1-in. drums (8.0 on 5-doors). **Construction:** unit.

Powertrains

	ohc I-4	ohc I-4	ohc I-4D
Displacement, l/cu. in.	1.9/114	1.9/114	2.0/121
Compression ratio	9.0:1	9.0:1	22.7:1
Fuel delivery	TBI	PFI	MFI
Net bhp @ rpm	90 @ 4600	115 @ 5200	58 @ 3600
Net torque @ rpm	106 @ 3400	120 @ 4400	84 @ 3000
Availability	S	S[1]	O[2]

1. Escort GT, EXP Sport Coupe   2. diesel models

Final drive ratios

4-speed OD manual	2.85:1[1]		
5-speed OD manual	3.52:1	3.73:1	3.52:1
3-speed automatic	3.26:1		

1. 3.52 on GL

KEY: bbl = barrel (carburetor); **bhp** = brake horsepower; **torque** = pounds/feet; **Cal.** = California only; **TBI** = throttle body (single-point) fuel injection; **PFI** = port (multipoint) fuel injection; **MFI** = mechanical fuel injection; **ohv** = overhead valve; **ohc** = overhead cam; **dohc** = double overhead cam; **I** = inline engine; **V** = V engine; **flat** = horizontally opposed engine; **D** = diesel; **T** = turbocharged; **OD** = overdrive transmission; **S** = standard; **O** = optional.

PRICES

FORD ESCORT/EXP	Retail Price	Dealer Invoice	Low Price
Pony 3-door sedan	$6586	$6057	$6300
GL 3-door sedan	6949	6247	6560
GL 5-door sedan	7163	6438	6760
GL 5-door wagon	7444	6688	7025
GT 3-door sedan	8815	7908	8320
EXP 3-door Luxury Coupe	7745	6956	7311
EXP 3-door Sport Coupe	8920	8002	8420
Destination charge	309	309	309

STANDARD EQUIPMENT (included in above prices):

Pony: 1.9-liter (114-cid) TBI 4-cylinder engine, 4-speed manual transmission, power brakes, carpeting, halogen headlamps, package tray, lowback cloth and vinyl reclining front bucket seats, folding rear bench seat, front ashtray, cigar lighter, two coat hooks, consolette, door scuff plates, side window demisters, optical horn, P175/80R13 tires on styled steel wheels. **GL adds:** bodyside paint stripes, matte black rocker panel trim, rear ashtray, cargo area cover (wagon), liftgate carpeting (wagon), carpeted lower door panels with storage bins, AM radio, cloth seat trim, P175/80R13 tires (3-door), P165/80R13 (5-door and wagon). **GT adds:** high-output PFI engine, remote fuel filler and liftgate releases, upgraded sound insulation, power steering, performance suspension, front and rear spoilers, fog lights, dual power mirrors, blackout exterior treatment, bodyside moldings, wheel spats and rocker panel moldings, front center armrest, two rear ashtrays, console with graphic systems display, passenger grab handles, tachometer, trip odometer, coolant temperature gauge, dual visor mirrors, cloth sport front bucket seats, AM/FM stereo radio, split fold-down rear seatback, leather-wrapped steering wheel, P195/60HR15 tires on alloy wheels. **EXP Luxury Coupe** adds to base Escort: 5-speed manual transmission, cargo area carpeting, cargo floor rub strips and retainer bar, cargo area, glovebox and ashtray lights, headlamps-on chime, grey bodyside moldings, fold-down center armrest, overhead console with digital clock and stopwatch, door panel map pockets, front seat grab handles, liftgate courtesy lights, AM/FM stereo radio, P185/70R14 tires. **EXP Sport Coupe** has Luxury Coupe equipment plus Escort GT content.

OPTIONAL EQUIPMENT:

2.0-liter (121-cid) diesel engine	NC	NC	NC
5-speed manual transmission, Escort . . .	76	64	70
3-speed automatic transmission, GL	490	417	450
EXP Luxury Coupe	415	352	380
Premium Equipment Group, GL w/gas engine	496	421	455
GL w/diesel engine	409	347	375

Bumper guards and rub strips, overhead console with digital clock, tachometer, trip odometer and coolant temperature gauge, dual power mirrors, power steering.

Prices are accurate at time of printing; subject to manufacturer's change.

CONSUMER GUIDE®

Bumper rub strips	48	40	44
Overhead console w/clock	82	69	75
Tachometer, trip odometer & coolant temp gauge	87	74	80
Dual power mirrors	88	75	81
Power steering	235	200	215
Climate Control Group			
GL w/gas engine, EXP Luxury Coupe	920	782	845
GL w/diesel, GT or EXP Sport Coupe	893	759	820
Air conditioning, heavy-duty battery, rear defogger, tinted glass, intermittent wipers.			
Air conditioning	688	585	635
Heavy-duty battery	27	23	25
Rear defogger	145	123	133
Tinted glass	105	89	97
Intermittent wipers	55	47	51
Luxury Group, GL	395	336	365
Light/Security Group, front center armrest, cruise control, split folding rear seatback, tilt steering column.			
Light/Security Group, GL	91	78	84
GT	67	57	62
Front center armrest, Escort	55	47	51
Cruise control	176	149	162
Split folding rear seatback, Escort	49	41	45
Tilt steering column	124	106	114
Convenience Group, EXP Luxury Coupe	473	388	435
EXP Sport Coupe	309	253	285
Cargo area cover, dual power mirrors, dual visor mirrors (lighted right), cruise control, power steering, tilt steering column.			
Cargo area cover, EXP	59	50	54
Dual power mirrors, EXP	88	75	81
Visor mirrors (lighted right), EXP	50	43	46
Sun and Sound Group, EXP Luxury Coupe	597	489	550
EXP Sport Coupe	566	481	520
Overhead console w/graphic systems monitor, removable sunroof, AM/FM ST w/cassette, Premium Sound System.			
Console w/graphic systems monitor, EXP	56	48	52
Removable sunroof, EXP	355	302	325
AM/FM ST w/cassette, EXP	148	125	136
Premium Sound System	138	117	127
Luggage rack	110	93	101
Wide vinyl insert moldings	50	43	46
Clearcoat paint, GL & EXP	91	78	84
Two-tone clearcoat paint, GT	152	130	140
Two-tone paint, GL	156	133	144
GT	61	52	56
AM radio	39	33	36
AM/FM ST, Pony	159	135	146
GL	120	102	110
AM/FM ST w/cassette, Pony	306	260	280
GL	267	227	245

Prices are accurate at time of printing; subject to manufacturer's change.

	Retail Price	Dealer Invoice	Low Price
GT, EXP	148	125	136
Vinyl trim	24	21	22
Pivoting front vent windows	63	54	58
Cast aluminum wheels	293	249	270
Styled road wheels	195	166	179
Rear wiper/washer	126	107	116

MERCURY LYNX

	Retail Price	Dealer Invoice	Low Price
L 3-door sedan	$6716	$6174	$6380
GS 3-door sedan	7094	6377	6740
GS 5-door sedan	7308	6567	6945
GS 5-door wagon	7590	6818	7210
XR3 3-door sedan	8897	7981	8450
Destination charge	309	309	309

STANDARD EQUIPMENT (included in above prices):

L: 1.9-liter (114-cid) TBI 4-cylinder engine, 4-speed manual transmission, power brakes, carpeting, cigar lighter, consolette, door scuff plates, side window demisters, reclining front bucket seats with vinyl facings, P165/80R13 tires on styled steel wheels. **GS** adds: bodyside paint stripes, cargo area cover, carpeted lower door panels with storage bins, rear quarter panel storage bins, tailgate ajar alert light (wagon), AM radio, cloth seat trim, folding rear seatback. **XR3** adds: PFI engine, 5-speed manual transmission, remote liftgate and fuel filler releases, dual-note horn, added sound insulation, fog lamps, halogen headlamps, rear spoiler, wheel spats, vinyl fold-down center armrest, upgraded carpeting, console with graphic alert display, cloth door panels, lockable glovebox, tachometer, trip odometer, coolant temperature gauge, dual visor mirrors, AM/FM ST radio, passenger grab handles, sport seats, split fold-down rear seatback, sport suspension, leather-wrapped steering wheel, P195/60HR15 tires on aluminum wheels.

OPTIONAL EQUIPMENT:

2.0-liter diesel engine, L & GS	NC	NC	NC
5-speed manual transmission, L & GS	76	64	70
3-speed automatic transmission, GS	490	417	450
Climate Control Group, GS	865	735	795
XR3	838	712	770
Content not available at time of publication.			
Comfort/Convenience Group, GS	327	278	300
Overhead console w/digital clock, intermittent wipers, trip odometer, tachometer, temperature gauge.			
Air conditioning	688	585	635

Prices are accurate at time of printing; subject to manufacturer's change.

Bumper guards	56	48	52
Bumper rub strips	48	40	44
Rear defogger	145	123	133
Tinted glass	105	89	97
Dual power mirrors	88	75	81
Wide vinyl bodyside molding	50	43	46
Clearcoat metallic paint	91	78	84
Two-tone paint	156	133	144
AM/FM ST, L	159	135	146
GS	120	102	110
AM/FM ST ET cassette, GS	267	227	245
XR3	148	125	136
Premium Sound System	138	117	127
Speed control	176	149	162
Power steering	235	200	215
Tilt steering col., w/o Comfort/Conv.	179	152	165
w/Comfort/Conv.	124	106	114
Split fold-down rear seatback	49	41	45
Front center armrest	55	47	51
Polycast wheels	128	109	118
Vinyl seat trim	24	21	22
Heavy-duty battery	27	23	25
Rear wiper/washer	126	107	116
Engine block heater	18	16	17
Deluxe luggage rack	110	93	101
AM radio delete, GS (credit)	(39)	(33)	(33)
AM/FM ST stelete, XR3 (credit)	(159)	(135)	(135)
Vinyl seat trim, L	24	21	22

Ford LTD Crown Victoria/ Mercury Grand Marquis

Since air conditioning and tinted glass are ordered on nearly all full-size Fords and Mercurys, both have been made standard for 1987. The rear-drive LTD Crown Victoria also gains an electronic digital clock as standard equipment, plus other minor equipment changes. The Grand Marquis gains an electronic search tune AM/FM stereo as standard, replacing a manual-tune radio. The Crown Vic and nearly identical Grand Marquis continue to be offered as 2- and 4-door sedans and a 5-door station wagon, all with a fuel-injected 5.0-liter V 8 and 4-speed overdrive automatic transmission. Sales of both models

Prices are accurate at time of printing; subject to manufacturer's change.

Ford LTD Crown Victoria 4-door

declined during 1986, despite lower gasoline prices, usually a boon for big car sales. However, Ford's current plans are to keep both in production at least to the end of the decade. Part of the dying breed of full-size, rear-drive cars that America used to love, the Crown Victoria and Grand Marquis were introduced for 1979 in this design. The 5.0-liter V-8 gained multi-point fuel injection last year, which helped driveability and performance, but did little or nothing for mileage (under 15 mpg in city driving in our tests). The roomy interior holds six people, the spacious trunk swallows several suitcases easily and these are quiet, refined luxury cruisers. However, they're much happier going in a straight line than around corners, when substantial body lean, lots of tire scrubbing and slow responses to the helm earn them poor marks for handling. Still, the Crown Vic and Grand Marquis are good choices in traditional domestic family cars for those who like full-size motoring with V-8 power.

Specifications

	2-door sedan	4-door sedan	5-door wagon
Wheelbase, in.	114.3	114.3	114.3
Overall length, in.	211.0	211.0	215.0
Overall width, in.	77.5	77.5	79.3
Overall height, in.	55.3	55.3	57.1
Front track, in.	62.2	62.2	62.2
Rear track, in.	62.0	62.0	62.0
Curb weight, lbs.	3724	3741	3920
Cargo vol., cu. ft.	22.4	22.4	88.2
Fuel capacity, gal.	18.0	18.0	18.0

	2-door sedan	4-door sedan	5-door wagon
Seating capacity	6	6	6
Front headroom, in.	37.9	37.9	38.8
Front shoulder room, in.	61.6	61.6	61.6
Front legroom, max., in.	43.5	43.5	43.5
Rear headroom, in.	37.2	37.2	39.1
Rear shoulder room, in.	61.0	61.6	61.6
Rear legroom, min, in.	39.3	39.3	37.9

Body/Chassis

Drivetrain layout: longitudinal front engine/rear-wheel drive. **Front suspension:** unequal length upper and lower control arms, coil springs, gas-pressurized shock absorbers, stabilizer bar. **Rear suspension:** rigid axle, four links, coil springs. **Steering:** recirculating ball, power assisted, 3.4 turns lock-to-lock. **Turn diameter, ft.:** 39.1. **Front brakes:** 11.0-in. discs. **Rear brakes:** 10.0-in. drums (11.0-in. wagons). **Construction:** body on frame.

Powertrains

	ohv V-8
Displacement, l/cu. in.	5.0/302
Compression ratio	8.9:1
Fuel delivery	PFI
Net bhp @ rpm	150 @ 3200
Net torque @ rpm	270 @ 2000
Availability	S
Final drive ratios	
4-speed OD automatic	2.73:1[1]

1. 3.08 w/optional Traction-Lok axle

KEY: bbl = barrel (carburetor); **bhp** = brake horsepower; **torque** = pounds/feet; **Cal.** = California only; **TBI** = throttle body (single-point) fuel injection; **PFI** = port (multipoint) fuel injection; **MFI** = mechanical fuel injection; **ohv** = overhead valve; **ohc** = overhead cam; **dohc** = double overhead cam; **I** = inline engine; **V** = V engine; **flat** = horizontally opposed engine; **D** = diesel; **T** = turbocharged; **OD** = overdrive transmission; **S** = standard; **O** = optional.

PRICES

FORD LTD CROWN VICTORIA	Retail Price	Dealer Invoice	Low Price
2-door coupe	$14709	$12617	$13505
4-door sedan	14349	12311	13170
LX 2-door coupe	15378	13186	14115
LX 4-door sedan	15410	13213	14145
5-door wagon	14315	12282	13140
Country Squire 5-door wagon	14567	12407	13375
LX 5-door wagon	15489	13281	14220

Prices are accurate at time of printing; subject to manufacturer's change.

	Retail Price	Dealer Invoice	Low Price
LX Country Squire 5-door wagon	15741	13495	14450
Destination charge	480	480	480

STANDARD EQUIPMENT (included in above prices):

5.0-liter (302-cid) PFI V-8 engine, 4-speed automatic transmission, power steering, power brakes, front and rear bumper guards, air conditioning, tinted glass, rocker panel moldings, digital clock, 18-ounce color-keyed carpeting, cigar lighter, quartz sweephand illuminated clock, woodtone instrument panel applique, carpeted lower door panels, tethered fuel cap, halogen headlamps, dual-note horn, glovebox, ashtray and trunk lights, left remote mirror, passenger visor mirror, vinyl insert bodyside moldings, carpeted package tray (4-door), automatic parking brake release, AM/FM stereo radio, padded rear half vinyl roof with French seams, cloth and vinyl reclining front bench seats, deluxe wheel covers, P205/75R15 tires. Wagon adds: heavy-duty rear brakes, removable load floor carpeting, 3-way doorgate, cargo area lamp, vinyl upholstery, fold-down second seat, lockable side and underfloor storage compartments, power doorgate window. Country Squire adds: simulated woodgrain bodyside and doorgate trim. LX adds to base equipment: power windows, additional woodtone instrument panel trim, rear seat center armrest (exc. wagon), digital clock, luxury door panels with pull straps and full-length armrests, light group, low fuel and oil level warning lights, seatback map pockets, dual illuminated visor mirrors, dual facing rear seats (wagon), cloth or vinyl split bench seat with dual recliners, carpeted spare tire cover (exc. wagon).

OPTIONAL EQUIPMENT:

Traction-Lok axle	100	85	92
P215/70R15 tires	72	61	66
Conventional spare tire	73	62	67
Automatic A/C & rear defogger	211	179	194
Autolamp system	73	62	67
Heavy-duty battery	27	23	25
Bumper rub strips	59	50	54
Convenience group, exc. LX	135	115	124
w/Power Lock Group	85	73	78
Remote decklid or tailgate release, intermittent wipers, trip odometer, low fuel & oil warning lights.			
Cornering lamps	68	58	63
Rear defogger	145	123	133
Engine block heater	18	16	17
Illuminated entry system	82	69	75
Light group	48	40	44
Power lock group, 2-doors	207	176	190
4-doors & wagons	257	219	235
Power door locks, remote fuel door release.			
Deluxe luggage rack	115	97	106

Prices are accurate at time of printing; subject to manufacturer's change.

Right remote mirror	46	39	42
Vinyl insert bodyside moldings	66	56	61
Two-tone paint/tape treatment	117	100	108
AM/FM ST ET w/cassette	137	116	126
Power antenna	76	64	70
AM/FM radio delete (credit)	(206)	(175)	(175)
Premium Sound System	168	143	155
Power driver's seat	251	214	230
Dual power seats	502	476	460
Dual facing rear seats, wagon	173	147	159
Cruise control	176	149	162
Leather-wrapped steering wheel	59	50	54
Tilt steering column	124	106	114
Automatic load-leveling suspension	200	170	184
Heavy-duty/handling suspension	26	22	24
Heavy-duty trailer towing pkg., sedans	387	329	355
Wagons	399	339	365

Heavy-duty battery, trailer towing suspension, transmission and power steering oil coolers, wiring harness, heavy-duty flasher system, conventional spare tire, 3.27 axle, heavy-duty rear brakes (sedans), heavy-duty U-joint, extra heavy-duty radiator, dual exhausts.

Tripminder computer	215	182	198
Pivoting front vent windows	79	67	73
Locking wire wheel covers	212	180	195
Cast aluminum wheels	390	332	360
Power windows & mirrors	393	334	360
Intermittent wipers	55	47	51
Brougham half vinyl roof	665	565	610
Split bench seat	139	118	128
All-vinyl seat trim	34	29	31
Duraweave vinyl seat trim	96	82	88
Leather seat trim	418	356	385

MERCURY GRAND MARQUIS

GS 4-door sedan	$15163	$13016	$13950
LS 2-door sedan	15478	13283	14240
LS 4-door sedan	15621	13405	14370
Colony Park GS 5-door wagon	15500	13302	14260
Colony Park LS 5-door wagon	16029	13752	14745
Destination charge	480	480	480

STANDARD EQUIPMENT (included in above prices):

GS: 5.0-liter (302-cid) PFI V-8 engine, 4-speed overdrive automatic transmission, power steering, power brakes, air conditioning, P215/75R15 WSW steel-belted radial tires, deluxe sound package, rocker panel and wheellip moldings, tinted glass, dual remote mirrors, wheel covers, dual-note horn, flight bench seat, full carpeting, gas-filled shock absorbers, halogen headlamps, AM/FM stereo radio, color-keyed seatbelts, wide lower bodyside

Prices are accurate at time of printing; subject to manufacturer's change.

moldings, power windows, vinyl roof, deluxe wheel covers, analog clock, left remote-control door mirror, hood/decklid paint stripes, seatbelt warning chimes, automatic parking brake release. LS adds: visor vanity mirror, luxury interior and trunk trim, dual-beam dome lamp. Colony Park has Marquis equipment plus 3-way tailgate, power tailgate window, carpeted load floor, heavy-duty frame, woodgrain exterior applique, fold-down rear seat, conventional spare tire.

OPTIONAL EQUIPMENT:

P215/70R15 tires	72	61	66
Conventional spare tire	73	62	67
Automatic climate control	211	179	194
Power antenna	76	64	70
Autolamp Delay System	73	62	67
Bumper rub strips	59	50	54
Digital clock	61	52	56
Convenience Group, w/o Power Lock Group	135	115	124
w/Power Lock Group	85	73	78

Intermittent wipers, power decklid/tailgate release, trip odometer, low fuel, oil & washer fluid warning lights.

Cornering lamps	68	58	63
Rear defogger	145	123	133
Illuminated entry system	82	69	75
Light Group	48	40	44
Power Lock Group, 2-door	207	176	190
4-doors, wagons	257	219	235

Includes remote fuel filler & trunk releases.

Deluxe luggage rack	115	97	106
Dual illuminated visor mirrors	109	92	100
Bodyside protection moldings	66	56	61
Two-tone paint w/tape stripes	129	110	119
AM/FM ST ET cassette	137	116	126
AM/FM ST ET delete (credit)	(206)	(175)	(175)
Premium Sound System	168	143	155
Formal coach vinyl roof	665	565	610
Power driver's seat	251	214	230
Dual power seats	502	427	460
Dual facing rear seats, wagon	173	147	159
Speed control	176	149	162
Leather-wrapped steering wheel	59	50	54
Tilt steering column	124	106	114
Automatic load leveling	200	170	184
Heavy-duty suspension	26	22	24
Trailer tow III pkg., sedans	387	329	355
Wagons	399	339	365

Heavy-duty suspension, wiring harness, transmission and steering oil coolers, conventional spare tire, heavy-duty flasher, heavy-duty rear brakes (sedans), 3.55 Traction-Lok axle, heavy-duty radiator, dual exhaust system.

Cloth seat trim, wagons	54	46	50

Prices are accurate at time of printing; subject to manufacturer's change.

CONSUMER GUIDE®

Vinyl seat trim (sedans)	34	29	31
Leather seat trim	418	355	385
Tripminder computer	261	222	240
Pivoting front vent windows	79	67	73
Locking wire wheel covers	183	155	168
Cast aluminum wheels	361	307	330
Traction-Lok axle	100	85	92
California emissions pkg.	99	84	91
Engine block heater	18	16	17

Ford Mustang

Ford Mustang LX 3-door

Major styling changes and a new instrument panel give
Ford's "pony car" a fresh look for 1987, while buyers will
have fewer models and powertrains to choose from. The
slow-selling turbocharged SVO model has been dropped,
leaving a base LX model and high-performance GT. The
similar Mercury Capri also has been dropped. This is the
first major restyling since the current design was introduced for 1979, marked mainly by new front and rear
fascia, aerodynamic headlamps and prominent lower bodyside moldings. A lower air dam with integrated fog lamps
and air scoops sets the GT apart from the LX at the front,
plus the GT hatchback coupe carries a large decklid spoiler
and the taillamps are covered by slotted applique for a
louvered effect. The 5.0-liter V-8 standard in the GT, optional in the LX, gains 25 horsepower (to 225) through
new cylinder heads and induction revisions. The 3.8-liter

V-6 has been dropped as an option, leaving a 2.3-liter 4-cylinder engine as the only alternative to the V-8. Standard in the LX, the 2.3 gains multi-point fuel injection in place of a 1-barrel carburetor, and this year comes with either a 5-speed manual or 4-speed overdrive automatic. There's a huge gap in horsepower and performance between those two engines, and Ford clearly plans on selling mostly V-8-powered Mustangs this year. This year's horsepower increase keeps the Mustang GT even with the Chevrolet Camaro IROC-Z, which can be ordered with a 225-horsepower 5.7-liter Corvette V-8 for 1987. Mustang holds a few advantages: a 5-speed manual is available for those who prefer to shift for themselves, while 5.7-liter Camaros come only with automatic transmission. The Mustang GT claims a slight advantage in straight-line acceleration, while the Camaro IROC-Z would win a one-on-one race around most twisting road courses. Ford's biggest advantage is in price, with the Mustang GT a couple of thousand dollars cheaper than a comparably equipped IROC-Z.

Specifications

	2-door coupe	3-door coupe	2-door conv.
Wheelbase, in.	100.5	100.5	100.5
Overall length, in.	179.6	179.6	179.6
Overall width, in.	69.1	69.1	69.1
Overall height, in.	52.1	52.1	51.9
Front track, in.	56.6	56.6	56.6
Rear track, in.	57.0	57.0	57.0
Curb weight, lbs.	2724	2782	3214
Cargo vol., cu. ft.	9.9	12.3	6.4
Fuel capacity, gal.	15.4	15.4	15.4
Seating capacity	4	4	4
Front headroom, in.	37.0	37.0	37.6
Front shoulder room, in.	55.4	55.4	55.4
Front legroom, max., in.	41.7	41.7	41.7
Rear headroom, in.	35.9	35.6	37.0
Rear shoulder room, in.	54.3	54.3	48.9
Rear legroom, min, in.	30.7	30.7	30.7

Body/Chassis

Drivetrain layout: longitudinal front engine/front-wheel drive.
Front suspension: modified MacPherson struts, lower control arms, coil springs, stabilizer bar (gas-pressurized shock absorbers on GT). **Rear suspension:** rigid axle, four links, coil springs, stabilizer bar optional (standard on GT). **Steering:** rack and pin-

ion, power assisted, 3.0 turns lock-to-lock (2.5 on GT). **Turn diameter, ft.: 37.4. Front brakes:** 10.0-in. discs. **Rear brakes:** 9.0-in. drums. **Construction:** unit.

Powertrains	ohc I-4	ohv V-8
Displacement, l/cu. in.	2.3/140	5.0/302
Compression ratio	9.5:1	9.2:1
Fuel delivery	PFI	PFI
Net bhp @ rpm	90 @ 3800	225 @ 4000
Net torque @ rpm	130 @ 2800	300 @ 3200
Availability	S[1]	S[2]

1. LX   2. GT; opt. LX

Final drive ratios

5-speed OD manual	3.45:1	2.73:1[1]
4-speed OD automatic	3.73:1	2.73:1[1]

1. 3.08 opt.

KEY: bbl = barrel (carburetor); **bhp** = brake horsepower; **torque** = pounds/feet; **Cal.** = California only; **TBI** = throttle body (single-point) fuel injection; **PFI** = port (multipoint) fuel injection; **MFI** = mechanical fuel injection; **ohv** = overhead valve; **ohc** = overhead cam; **dohc** = double overhead cam; **I** = inline engine; **V** = V engine; **flat** = horizontally opposed engine; **D** = diesel; **T** = turbocharged; **OD** = overdrive transmission; **S** = standard; **O** = optional.

PRICES

FORD MUSTANG	Retail Price	Dealer Invoice	Low Price
LX 2-door coupe	$8271	$7448	$7815
LX 3-door coupe	8690	7821	8210
LX 2-door convertible	13052	11704	12300
GT 3-door coupe	12106	10861	11410
GT 2-door convertible	15852	14196	14940
Destination charge	374	374	374

STANDARD EQUIPMENT (included in above prices):

LX: 2.3-liter (140-cid) PFI 4-cylinder engine, 5-speed manual transmission, power steering, power brakes, intermittent wipers, bumper rub strips, halogen headlamps, dual remote mirrors, black bodyside moldings, rear spoiler, full carpeting, cigar lighter, console with armrest, cargo area cover on 3-door, carpeted lower door panels, lockable glovebox, side window demisters, tachometer, trip odometer, oil pressure, voltage and coolant temperature gauges, dual visor mirrors, AM/FM ST ET, lowback reclining front bucket seats, cloth upholstery, split fold-down rear seatback (3-door), optical horn, turbine wheel covers, P195/75N14 tires. **Convertible** adds: power top, tinted glass, luggage rack, footwell courtesy lights. **GT** adds to LX equipment:

Prices are accurate at time of printing; subject to manufacturer's change.

5.0-liter (302-cid) PFI V-8 engine, 5-speed manual transmission, Traction-Lok axle, low oil level, coolant and washer fluid warnings, heavy-duty battery, dual outlet exhaust system, remote fuel door release, tinted glass, tilt steering column, rocker panel moldings and rear wheel spats, driver's footrest, map lights, articulated sport seats, P225/60VR16 Goodyear Eagle GT Gatorback tires on aluminum wheels.

OPTIONAL EQUIPMENT:

5.0-liter engine pkg., LX	1885	1603	1735
Includes GT chassis, tires and wheels.			
4-speed automatic transmission	515	437	475
Climate Control Group, LX coupes w/2.3 .	1005	853	925
LX coupes w/5.0	978	830	900
LX conv. w/2.3	740	628	680
LX coupe w/5.0	713	605	655
GT coupe	858	729	790
GT conv.	713	605	655
Air conditioning, heavy-duty battery, rear defogger, tinted glass.			
Air conditioning	788	670	725
Rear defogger	145	123	133
Tinted glass	120	102	110
Climate Control Group w/Premium Sound instead of rear defogger			
LX coupes w/2.3	1028	873	945
LX coupes w/5.0	1001	850	920
LX conv. w/2.3	908	771	835
LX conv. w/5.0, GT	881	748	810
Climate Control Group w/Custom Equipment Group and Premium Sound instead of rear defogger			
LX coupes w/2.3	860	730	790
LX coupes w/5.0	833	707	765
LX conv. w/2.3	740	628	680
LX conv. w/5.0, GT	713	605	655
Custom Equipment Group, LX coupes . . .	624	531	575
LX conv.	538	458	495
GT coupe	500	425	460
GT conv.	414	352	380
Graphic EQ, dual power mirrors, lighted visor mirrors, tilt steering column, power windows.			
Graphic EQ	218	186	200
Dual power mirrors	60	51	55
Lighted visor mirrors	100	85	92
Tilt steering column, LX	124	106	114
Power windows, coupes	222	189	205
Convertibles	296	252	270
Special Value Group, LX w/5.0	735	624	675
GT	519	441	475
Power Lock Group (includes remote fuel filler & decklid/hatch releases. AM/FM ST ET w/cassette, speed control, styled road wheels.			

Prices are accurate at time of printing; subject to manufacturer's change

Power Lock Group, LX	244	207	225
GT	206	175	190
AM/FM ST ET w/cassette	137	116	126
Speed control	176	149	162
Styled road wheels, LX	178	151	164
Bodyside molding insert stripe	49	41	45
AM/FM ST ET delete (credit)	(206)	(175)	(175)
Flip-up/open-air sunroof	355	302	325
T roof, LX	1737	1417	1600
LX w/Climate Control Group	1667	1417	1535
LX w/Special Value Group	1543	1311	1420
LX w/Custom Equipment Group	1505	1279	1385
GT	1608	1366	1480
GT W/Special Value Group	1401	1191	1290
GT w/Custom Equipment Group	1341	1140	1235
Premium Sound System	168	143	155
Wire wheel covers, LX	98	83	90
California emissions pkg.	99	84	91
Leather articulated sport seats, LX conv.	780	663	720
GT conv.	415	352	380
Vinyl seat trim	29	25	27

Ford Taurus/Mercury Sable

Ford Taurus LX 4-door

Introduced mid-way through the 1986 model year, the slickly styled, hot-selling Taurus and Sable are carryovers except for minor equipment changes. Late in the '87 model year, a 4-speed overdrive automatic transmission will become available at extra cost with Taurus' base 2.5-liter 4-cylinder engine. Until then, the 2.5 will be offered with a 5-speed manual transmission (on the MT-5 model only) or 3-speed automatic (L and GL models only). A 3.0-liter V-6 and the overdrive automatic are standard on the Taurus LX, optional on the L and GL. Sable is being offered only with the V-6 engine and the overdrive automatic this year and air conditioning is now standard on the top-line LS series. The front-drive, mid-size Taurus and Sable are available in 4-door sedan and 5-door wagon styling. The sedans share none of their sheetmetal, but the wagons use the same body panels from the windshield on back. Taurus and Sable are the most impressive new domestic cars to come along in many years, combining contemporary styling with ample interior and cargo room, while providing uncommonly good road manners. A sport suspension is not offered as an option, unusual for a domestic sedan, but none is needed. The base suspension gives them flat, neutral cornering, and the moderately firm power steering responds directly to drive input and snaps back to center promptly at the end of a turn. The ride is firmer than on most domestic cars, though Sable is a little softer than Taurus, making these cars feel more like European sedans. The V-6 engine is a much better choice than the noisy 4-cylinder engine, providing more power and better behavior with automatic transmission. Even with the V-6, acceleration is only adequate from a standstill; the engine is much livelier from a flying start, giving Taurus and Sable good passing ability. Overall, we've been highly impressed by these cars and so far we have not uncovered any major faults that would keep us from recommending them—including the prices.

Specifications	4-door sedan	5-door wagon
Wheelbase, in.	106.0	106.0
Overall length, in.	188.4	188.4
Overall width, in.	70.6	70.6
Overall height, in.	54.3	55.1
Front track, in.	61.5	61.5
Rear track, in.	60.5	59.9
Curb weight, lbs.	2982	3186
Cargo vol., cu. ft.	17.0	45.7
Fuel capacity, gal.	16.0	16.0

	4-door sedan	5-door wagon
Seating capacity	4	5
Front headroom, in.	38.3	28.6
Front shoulder room, in.	57.5	57.5
Front legroom, max., in.	41.7	41.7
Rear headroom, in.	37.6	38.3
Rear shoulder room, in.	57.5	57.5
Rear legroom, min, in.	37.5	36.6

Body/Chassis

Drivetrain layout: transverse front engine/front-wheel drive. **Front suspension:** MacPherson struts, coil springs, control arms, stabilizer bar. **Rear suspension:** sedan: MacPherson struts, coil springs, parallel suspension arms. Wagon: upper and lower control arms, coil springs, stabilizer bar. **Steering:** rack and pinion, power assisted, 2.5 turns lock-to-lock. **Turn diameter, ft.:** 39.8. **Front brakes:** 10.1-in. discs. **Rear brakes:** 8.9-in. drums. **Construction:** unit.

Powertrains	ohv I-4	ohv V-6
Displacement, l/cu. in.	2.5/153	3.0/182
Compression ratio	9.0:1	9.3:1
Fuel delivery	TBI	PFI
Net bhp @ rpm	90 @ 4400	140 @ 4800
Net torque @ rpm	140 @ 4800	160 @ 3000
Availability	S	O[1]

1. std. LX

Final drive ratios

5-speed OD manual	3.73:1	
3-speed automatic	3.26:1	
4-speed OD automatic		3.37:1

KEY: bbl = barrel (carburetor); **bhp** = brake horsepower; **torque** = pounds/feet; **Cal.** = California only; **TBI** = throttle body (single-point) fuel injection; **PFI** = port (multipoint) fuel injection; **MFI** = mechanical fuel injection; **ohv** = overhead valve; **ohc** = overhead cam; **dohc** = double overhead cam; **I** = inline engine; **V** = V engine; **flat** = horizontally opposed engine; **D** = diesel; **T** = turbocharged; **OD** = overdrive transmission; **S** = standard; **O** = optional.

PRICES

FORD TAURUS	Retail Price	Dealer Invoice	Low Price
L 4-door sedan	$10650	$9156	$10010
L 5-door wagon	11870	10192	11160
GL 4-door sedan	11622	9982	10925

Prices are accurate at time of printing; subject to manufacturer's change.

	Retail Price	Dealer Invoice	Low Price
GL 5-door wagon	12802	10985	12035
MT-5 4-door sedan	12074	10366	11350
MT-5 5-door wagon	12654	10859	11895
LX 4-door sedan	14633	12541	13755
LX 5-door wagon	15243	13059	14330
Destination charge	426	426	426

STANDARD EQUIPMENT (included in above prices):

L: 2.5-liter (153-cid) 4-cylinder TBI engine, 3-speed automatic transmission (3.0-liter, 182-cid PFI V-6 and 4-speed OD automatic on wagon), power steering, power brakes, childproof rear door locks, day/night mirror, locking glovebox, side window defoggers, bodyside moldings, AM radio, carpeted trunk or cargo area, front door curb lights and map pockets, urethane lower door and rocker panel coating, luggage rack (wagon), left remote and right manual mirrors, full wheel covers, flight bench seat w/driver's recliner and fold-down center armrest, driver's foot rest, cigar lighter, 60/40 split bench rear seat (wagon), P195/70R14 tires. **MT-5** adds: 5-speed manual transmission (sedan), air conditioning, tilt steering column, digital clock, luxury sound package, upshift light, intermittent wipers, body color grille, fold-down rear center armrest (sedans), rear compartment heat ducts, tachometer, front seatback map pockets, cargo tiedown net (wagon), reclining front bucket seats with console. **GL** adds to L equipment: 3.0-liter V-6 engine (wagon), 4-speed OD automatic transmission (wagon), tinted glass, light group, trip odometer, dual electric mirrors, AM/FM search-tune radio, split bench seat with console, P205/70R14 tires. **LX** adds: air conditioning, power door locks, automatic brake release, power windows, luxury wheel covers, cargo tiedown hooks (sedan), dual illuminated visor mirrors, tilt steering wheel, cornering lamps, finned wheel covers, power driver's seat.

OPTIONAL EQUIPMENT:

3.0-liter V-6 engine, L & GL	672	571	620
Exterior accent group, MT-5 sedan	91	78	84
MT-5 wagon	49	41	45
Automatic air conditioning, LX	183	155	168
GL	945	803	870
Manual air conditioning	788	670	725
Autolamp system	73	62	67
Heavy-duty battery	27	23	25
Cargo area cover, wagons	66	56	61
Digital clock	78	66	72
Cornering lamps	68	58	63
Rear defogger	145	123	133
Engine block heater	18	16	17

Prices are accurate at time of printing; subject to manufacturer's change.

CONSUMER GUIDE®

Remote fuel door & decklid release	91	78	84
w/remote liftgate release, wagons	41	35	38
Extended range fuel tank	46	39	42
Tinted glass	120	102	110
Illuminated entry system	82	69	75
Electronic instrument cluster	351	299	325
Keyless entry system	202	172	186
Light group, L, GL & MT-5 sedans	48	40	44
L, GL & MT-5 wagons	52	45	48
Diagnostic alert lights	89	76	82
Load floor extension, wagons	66	56	61
Power door locks	195	166	179
Dual power mirrors, L sedan	96	82	88
L wagon	59	50	54
Dual illuminated visor mirrors, L	116	98	107
GL & MT-5	104	88	96
Rocker panel moldings	55	47	51
Power moonroof	741	630	680
Clearcoat paint	183	155	168
Automatic parking brake release	12	10	11
AM/FM ST ET	141	120	130
AM/FM ST w/cassette, L	268	228	245
GL, MT-5 & LX	137	116	126
Premium sound system	168	143	155
Power antenna	76	54	70
AM delete (credit), L	(65)	(55)	(55)
AM/FM stereo delete (credit), GL, MT-5 &			
LX	(206)	(175)	(175)
Rear-facing third seat, wagons	155	132	143
Reclining passenger seat	45	38	41
Power driver's seat	251	214	230
Dual power seats, LX	502	427	460
Others	251	214	230
Speed control	176	149	162
Tilt steering column	124	106	114
Leather-wrapped steering wheel	59	50	54
Paint stripe	57	49	52
Heavy-duty suspension	26	22	24
Sliding vent windows	79	67	73
Rear wiper/washer, wagons	126	107	116
Finned wheel covers, L, GL & MT-5	65	55	60
Locking spoked wheel covers			
L, GL & MT-5	205	174	189
LX	140	119	129
Aluminum wheels, L, GL & MT-5	390	332	360
LX	326	277	300
Styled road wheels, L, GL & MT-5	178	151	164
LX	113	96	104

Prices are accurate at time of printing; subject to manufacturer's change.

	Retail Price	Dealer Invoice	Low Price
Power windows	296	252	272
Insta-Clear windshield	250	213	230
Intermittent wipers	55	47	51
California emissions pkg.	99	84	91
Split bench seats	276	234	255
Leather seat trim	415	352	380
Vinyl seat trim	39	33	36

MERCURY SABLE

	Retail Price	Dealer Invoice	Low Price
GS 4-door sedan	$12340	$10602	$11475
LS 4-door sedan	14544	12475	13525
GS 5-door sedan	12904	11081	12000
LS 5-door wagon	15089	12939	14035
Destination charge	426	426	426

STANDARD EQUIPMENT (included in above prices):

GS: 3.0-liter, (182-cid) PFI V-6, 4-speed automatic transmission, power steering, power brakes, flip-up tailgate window (wagon), bumber rub strips, halogen headlamps, cornering lamps, luggage rack (wagon), left remote and right manual door mirrors, front fold-down center armrest, rear folding armrest on sedan, side window defoggers, fully trimmed luggage compartment with light, day/night mirror, dual visor mirrors, driver's foot rest, locking glovebox, passenger assist handles, load floor tiedown hooks (wagon), tachometer, temperature gauge and trip odometer, cloth flight bench seat with driver's recliner, P205/70R14 tires. **LS** adds: air conditioning, power windows, digital clock, remote decklid release (sedan), remote fuel filler release, light group, automatic parking brake release, intermittent wipers, dual power door mirrors, urethane lower door and rocker panel coating, diagnostic warning lights, front seatback map pockets, cargo tiedown net (wagon), AM/FM stereo radio, twin-comfort lounge seats with dual recliners and power lumbar support adjusters, 60/40 split rear seatback on wagon.

OPTIONAL EQUIPMENT:

Conventional spare tire	73	62	67
Automatic air conditioning	945	803	870
Manual air conditioning	788	670	725
Autolamp System	73	62	67
Automatic parking brake release	12	10	11
Digital clock	78	66	72
Dual illuminated visor mirrors	99	84	91
Electronic instrument cluster	351	299	325
Insta-Clear heated windshield	250	213	230
Intermittent wipers	55	47	51
Keyless entry system	202	172	186

Prices are accurate at time of printing; subject to manufacturer's change.

CONSUMER GUIDE®

Power moonroof	741	630	680
Rear defogger	145	123	133
Sliding vent windows	79	67	73
Cruise control	176	149	162
Tilt steering column	124	106	115
Tinted glass	120	102	110
Light Group, GS sedan	48	40	44
GS wagon	52	45	48
Heavy-duty battery	27	23	25
Heavy-duty suspension	26	22	24
Extended range fuel tank	46	39	42
California emissions system	99	84	91
Power antenna	76	64	70
Power door locks, GS sedans	285	243	260
GS wagons	237	201	220
LS	195	166	179
6-way power driver's seat	251	214	230
Dual power seats	502	427	460
Power windows	296	252	270
AM/FM ST ET cassette	137	116	126
Premium Sound System	168	143	155
AM/FM ST ET delete (credit)	(206)	(175)	(175)
Clearcoat paint	183	155	168
Cast aluminum wheels	335	285	310
Locking wire wheel covers	150	128	138
Polycast wheels	123	105	113
Leather-wrapped steering wheel	59	50	54
Leather trim	415	352	380
Vinyl trim	39	33	36
Twin comfort seats, GS	195	166	179
Bucket seats, GS (NC LS)	195	166	179
Picnic tray, wagons	66	56	61
Rear facing third seat, wagons	155	132	143
Rear window wiper/washer, wagons	126	107	116
Luggage rack delete, wagons (credit)	(115)	(97)	(97)
Engine block heater	18	16	17

Ford Tempo/Mercury Topaz

Four-wheel-drive appears this year on a new Tempo model and as a new option package for the similar Topaz, offering "shift-on-the-fly" capability (meaning 4WD can be engaged on the move) via an electric switch mounted on the dashboard. Ford calls the new system "All Wheel Drive" and that's the name that will appear on cars so equipped. It is a part-time 4WD system meant for slippery conditions,

Prices are accurate at time of printing; subject to manufacturer's change.

Mercury Topaz All Wheel Drive 2-door

not smooth, dry pavement, that can be shifted in or out of
4WD at any speed. The 4WD option includes a high-output
2.3-liter 4-cylinder engine and new 3-speed automatic
transmission. The new transmission replaces last year's
3-speed automatic on front-drive models as well and will
be available with the high-output engine (previously available only with a 5-speed manual). Power steering is now
standard on Tempo and nitrogen gas-filled shock absorbers
are standard on Topaz. The driver-side air bag, previously
a limited-production option, has been made a regular production option. The addition of 4-wheel-drive has renewed
our interest in Ford's front-drive compacts, which have
aged quickly since they were introduced as early 1984
models. The 4WD option is great to have in nasty weather,
where the added traction can keep you out of trouble. We
also like the air bag option for the extra protection it provides in case you do get into serious trouble. The biggest
shortcomings are under the hood, where the 2.3-liter 4-cyl-
inder engine produces marginal power in both base and
high-output tune, especially with automatic transmission.

Specifications

	2-door sedan	4-door sedan
Wheelbase, in.	99.9	99.9
Overall length, in.	176.5	176.5
Overall width, in.	68.3	68.3
Overall height, in.	52.7	52.7
Front track, in.	54.9	54.9
Rear track, in.	57.6	57.6
Curb weight, lbs.	2462[1]	2515[2]
Cargo vol., cu. ft.	13.2	13.2

	2-door sedan	4-door sedan
Fuel capacity, gal.	15.4[3]	15.4[3]
Seating capacity	5	5
Front headroom, in.	37.5	37.5
Front shoulder room, in.	53.4	53.4
Front legroom, max., in.	41.5	41.5
Rear headroom, in.	36.9	36.9
Rear shoulder room, in.	54.0	53.4
Rear legroom, min, in.	36.0	36.0

1. 2667 w/4-wheel drive   2. 2720 w/4-wheel drive   3. 13.7 w/4-wheel drive

Body/Chassis

Drivetrain layout: transverse front engine/front-wheel drive (4WD optional). **Front suspension:** MacPherson struts, coil springs, lower control arms, stabilizer bar. **Rear suspension:** MacPherson struts, coil springs, four trailing links. **Steering:** rack and pinion, power assisted, turns lock-to-lock NA. **Turn diameter, ft.:** 38.7. **Front brakes:** 9.3-in. discs. **Rear brakes:** 8.0-in. drums. **Construction:** unit.

Powertrains	ohv I-4	ohv I-4
Displacement, l/cu. in.	2.3/141	2.3/141
Compression ratio	9.0:1	9.0:1
Fuel delivery	TBI	TBI
	86 @	94 @
Net bhp @ rpm	3800	4000
	120 @	126 @
Net torque @ rpm	3200	3200
Availability	S	S[1]

1. All-Wheel Drive & Sport GL/GS Sport

Final drive ratios

5-speed OD manual[1]	3.33:1	3.73:1
3-speed automatic	3.07:1	3.07:1[2]

1. NA All-Wheel Drive   2. 3.09 w/4WD

KEY: bbl = barrel (carburetor); **bhp** = brake horsepower; **torque** = pounds/feet; **Cal.** = California only; **TBI** = throttle body (single-point) fuel injection; **PFI** = port (multi-point) fuel injection; **MFI** = mechanical fuel injection; **ohv** = overhead valve; **ohc** = overhead cam; **dohc** = double overhead cam; **I** = inline engine; **V** = V engine; **flat** = horizontally opposed engine; **D** = diesel; **T** = turbocharged; **OD** = overdrive transmission; **S** = standard; **O** = optional.

PRICES

FORD TEMPO	Retail Price	Dealer Invoice	Low Price
GL 2-door sedan	$8160	$7338	$7700
GL 4-door sedan	8310	7471	7840

Prices are accurate at time of printing; subject to manufacturer's change.

	Retail Price	Dealer Invoice	Low Price
Sport GL 2-door sedan	8909	8004	8405
Sport GL 4-door sedan	9059	8138	8545
LX 2-door sedan	9321	8371	8795
LX 4-door sedan	9520	8548	8980
All Wheel Drive 2-door sedan	10044	9014	9475
All Wheel Drive 4-door sedan	10194	9148	9620
Destination charge	398	398	398

STANDARD EQUIPMENT (included in above prices):

GL: 2.3-liter (140-cid) TBI 4-cylinder engine, 5-speed manual transmission, power steering, power brakes, tethered fuel cap, upshift indicator, intermittent wipers, halogen headlamps, wide bodyside moldings, urethane lower body protection, one front and two rear ashtrays, cigar lighter, full carpeting, two coat hooks, consolette, carpeted lower door panels, lockable glovebox, AM ET radio, rocker sill scuff plates, cloth reclining bucket seats, optical horn, dual visor mirrors, deluxe wheel covers, P185/70R14 all-season SBR tires. **All Wheel Drive** adds: high-specific-output engine, 4-wheel drive, tachometer, coolant temperature gauge, trip odometer, cloth center armrest, luxury carpeting, cloth door panels, three passenger assist handles, illuminated front footwells, AM/FM ST ET, upgraded upholstery, seatback map pockets, tinted galss, styled road wheels. **LX** deletes 4-wheel drive and adds: illuminated entry system, power door locks, remote decklid and fuel door releases, tilt steering column, touring suspension, trip odometer, woodtone instrument panel applique. **Sport GL** adds to GL: performance suspension, tinted glass, AM/FM ST ET, dual power mirrors, tachometer and coolant temperature guage, blackout exterior treatment, sport seats, leather-wrapped steering wheel, center armrest, light group, alloy wheels.

OPTIONAL EQUIPMENT:

3-speed automatic transmisson	482	409	445
Select GL Pkg., w/AM/FM ST ET	191	162	176
w/o radio	124	105	114
Tinted glass, dual power mirrors.			
Tinted glass	120	102	110
Dual power mirrors	111	94	102
AM/FM ST ET	93	79	86
Power Equipment Group			
Power Lock Group (includes remote fuel filler and trunk releases), power driver's seat, power windows.			
2-door GL, Sport or All Wheel Drive	560	475	515
4-door GL, Sport or All Wheel Drive	635	540	585
LX 2-door	323	275	295
LX 4-door	347	295	320

Prices are accurate at time of printing; subject to manufacturer's change.

Power Lock Group, 2-doors	237	201	220
4-doors	288	245	265
Power driver's seat	251	214	230
Power windows, 2-doors	222	189	205
4-doors	296	252	270
Convenience Group			
GL	643	546	590
Select GL	565	480	520
Sport GL	418	355	385
LX	371	315	340
All Wheel Drive	510	433	470

Front center armrest, Premium Sound System, AM/FM ST ET cassette, speed control, tilt steering column.

Front center armrest	55	47	51
Premium Sound System	138	117	127
AM/FM ST ET cassette, GL	250	213	230
LX or Select GL	157	134	144
Speed control	176	149	162
Tilt steering column	124	106	114
Lower accent paint treatment	78	66	72
Air bag, GL	815	692	750
LX	751	639	690
Air conditioning	773	657	710
Console	116	98	107
Rear defogger	145	123	133
Sport instrument cluster	87	74	80
Decklid luggage rack	115	97	106
AM/FM ST	93	79	86
AM/FM ST ET cassette, GL	250	213	230
LX, Select GL or All Wheel Drive	157	134	144
AM delete (credit), GL	(65)	(55)	(55)
AM/FM ST delete (credit), LX or All-Wheel Drive	(157)	(134)	(134)
Sport GL or w/Convenience Group	(315)	(267)	(267)
Styled road wheels	178	151	164
California emissions pkg.	99	84	91
Clearcoat metallic paint	91	78	84

MERCURY TOPAZ

GS 2-door sedan	$8664	$7790	$8185
GS 4-door sedan	8814	7923	8330
GS Sport 2-door sedan	9319	8373	8805
GS Sport 4-door sedan	9469	8506	8950
LS 4-door sedan	10266	9216	9700
Destination charge	398	398	398

STANDARD EQUIPMENT (included in above prices):

GS: 2.3-liter (140-cid) TBI 4-cylinder engine, 5-speed manual transmission,

Prices are accurate at time of printing; subject to manufacturer's change.

power steering, power brakes, tethered fuel cap, trip odometer, tachometer, coolant temperature gauge, upshift indicator light, halogen headlamps, dual power mirrors, urethane lower body protection, 10-ounce cut-pile carpeting, consolette, carpeted lower door panels, lockable glovebox, AM/FM ST ET, door scuff plates, cloth seats with vinyl facings, visor mirrors, P185/70R14 tires. **GS Sport** adds: high-output engine, 3.73 axle ratio, leather-wrapped steering wheel, performance suspension, console with graphic alert monitor, sport seats, two rear grab handles, P185/65R365 tires on TR-type aluminum wheels. **LS** adds to GS equipment: digital clock, power decklid and fuel filler releases, rear defogger, illuminated entry system, Light Group, power windows and door locks, touring suspension, intermittent wipers, illuminated door lock bezels, fold-down center armrest, 18-ounce carpeting, full console with graphic alert monitor, upgraded door panels, two rear passenger assist handles, woodtone instrument panel applique, footwell lamps, illuminated visor mirrors, AM/FM ST ET cassette, seatback map pockets, cloth upholstery, tilt steering column, performance tires.

OPTIONAL EQUIPMENT:

3-speed automatic transmission	482	409	445
Comfort/Convenience Pkg., GS	409	347	375
GS Sport	368	313	340
Fold-down center armrest, intermittent wipers, digital clock, Light Group, remote fuel filler & decklid releases.			
All Wheel Drive Pkg.	915	777	840
Four-wheel drive, high-output engine, automatic transmission.			
Air conditioning	773	657	710
Rear defogger	145	123	133
Clearcoat metallic paint	91	78	84
Power Lock Group (std. LS), 2-doors	237	201	220
4-door	288	245	265
2-doors w/Comfort/Conv.	156	133	144
4-doors w/Comfort/Conv.	207	176	190
Lower bodyside accent paint, GS	78	66	72
GS Sport & LS	118	101	109
Premium Sound System	138	117	127
Speed control	176	149	162
Tilt steering column	124	106	114
Polycast road wheels	178	151	164
Decklid luggage rack	115	97	106
Power windows, 2-doors	222	189	205
4-doors	296	252	270
Air bag, GS	815	692	750
GS w/Comfort/Conv., LS	751	639	690
AM/FM ST delete (credit), GS & GS Sport	(157)	(134)	(134)
AM/FM cassette delete (credit), LS	(315)	(267)	(267)
AM/FM ST ET cassette, GS	157	134	144
Heavy-duty battery	27	23	25
Engine block heater	18	16	17

Prices are accurate at time of printing; subject to manufacturer's change.

Power driver's seat	251	214	230
California emissions pkg.	99	84	91

Ford Thunderbird/ Mercury Cougar

Ford Thunderbird Turbo Coupe

The Ford and Mercury personal-luxury coupes get new styling and powertrain lineups for 1987. Thunderbird retains a similar silhouette, but gets all new sheetmetal, aero headlamps, full-width taillamps and flush-mounted side glass. The similar Cougar also gains aero headlamps, flush-fitting glass and full-width taillamps, plus a new greenhouse design. Several functional changes have been made: The Thunderbird Turbo Coupe gets the intercooled 2.3-liter 4-cylinder engine from the defunct SVO Mustang, plus 4-wheel disc brakes with anti-lock feature, electronic Automatic Ride Control, P225/60VRl6 unidirectional tires and unique front styling with functional hood scoops. A 4-speed overdrive automatic is optional on the Turbo Coupe and standard with the base 3.8-liter V-6 on other models; last year's 3-speed automatic has been shelved. Last year's top-line Elan model has been renamed LX, and a new Sport model with a 5.0-liter V-8 standard has been added. On the Cougar, the V-8 is now standard in the sporty XR-7 instead of the turbocharged 2.3-liter 4-cylinder engine offered previously. A 4-speed overdrive automatic transmission is now standard on all Cougars and last year's GS series has been dropped, making the LS the base Cougar for 1987. Until the price of gas rises appreciably, the V-8 is our favorite engine for the Thunderbird and Cougar, giving these rear-drive coupes plenty of get-up-and-go and smooth, unobtrusive driveability with the 4-speed automatic transmission. The penalty, of course, is in the V-8's thirst for fuel. The Turbo Coupe has impressive performance, especially with manual transmission, but the turbocharged 2.3 loses 40 horsepower with automatic, and nearly all Thunderbirds are sold with automatic transmission. Too bad the anti-lock brakes new for this year are available only on the Turbo Coupe, which hasn't been that big a seller in previous years. Thunderbird and Cougar are class acts in nearly every respect; quiet, plushly furnished, comfortable seats and above average ride and handling. With either, you'll be getting a well-designed, well-built intermediate that shows you don't need front-wheel drive to be contemporary.

Specifications

	2-door coupe
Wheelbase, in.	104.2
Overall length, in.	202.1
Overall width, in.	71.1
Overall height, in.	53.4
Front track, in.	58.1
Rear track, in.	58.5
Curb weight, lbs.	3133
Cargo vol., cu. ft.	14.6
Fuel capacity, gal.	22.1
Seating capacity	5
Front headroom, in.	37.7
Front shoulder room, in.	56.3
Front legroom, max., in.	42.0
Rear headroom, in.	36.9
Rear shoulder room, in.	55.2
Rear legroom, min, in.	34.3

Body/Chassis

Drivetrain layout: longitudinal front engine/rear-wheel drive. **Front suspension:** modified MacPherson struts, lower control arms, coil springs, gas-pressurized shock absorbers, stabilizer bar. **Rear suspension:** rigid axle, four links, coil springs, gas-pressurized shock absorbers, stabilizer bar optional. **Steering:** rack and pinion, power assisted, 3.0 turns lock-to-lock. **Turn diameter, ft.:** 39.4. **Front brakes:** 10.0-in. discs. **Rear brakes:** 9.0-in. drums. **Construction:** unit.

Powertrains	ohv V-6	ohv V-8	ohc I-4T
Displacement, l/cu. in.	3.8/232	5.0/302	2.3/140
Compression ratio	8.7:1	8.9:1	8.0:1
Fuel delivery	TBI	PFI	PFI
Net bhp @ rpm	120 @ 3600	150 @ 3200	190 @ 4600[1]
Net torque @ rpm	205 @ 1600	270 @ 2000	240 @ 3400
Availability	S	O	S[2]

1. 150 bhp @ 4400 and 200 lb-ft @ 3000 w/automatic transmission   2. Turbo Coupe

Final drive ratios

5-speed OD manual			3.55:1
4-speed OD automatic	3.27:1	2.73:1	3.73:1

KEY: bbl = barrel (carburetor); **bhp** = brake horsepower; **torque** = pounds/feet; **Cal.** = California only; **TBI** = throttle body (single-point) fuel injection; **PFI** = port (multipoint) fuel injection; **MFI** = mechanical fuel injection; **ohv** = overhead valve; **ohc** = overhead cam; **dohc** = double overhead cam; **I** = inline engine; **V** = V engine; **flat** = horizontally opposed engine; **D** = diesel; **T** = turbocharged; **OD** = overdrive transmission; **S** = standard; **O** = optional.

PRICES

FORD THUNDERBIRD	Retail Price	Dealer Invoice	Low Price
2-door coupe	$13028	$11187	$11945
Sport 2-door coupe	15065	12918	13815
LX 2-door coupe	15357	13167	14080
Turbo Coupe	16600	14223	15220
Destination charge	432	432	432

STANDARD EQUIPMENT (included in above prices):

3.8-liter (242-cid) TBI V-6 engine, 4-speed automatic transmission, power steering, power brakes, air conditioning, tethered fuel cap, tinted glass, left remote mirror, black wide bodyside moldings, luxury wheel covers, 16-ounce carpeting, quartz sweephand clock, consolette, vinyl door panels with storage bins, lockable glovebox, electronic instrument panel with trip odometer and service interval reminder, analog fuel and coolant temperature gauges, side window demisters, ashtray, glovebox and trunk lights, polyester trunk mat, dual visor mirrors, AM/FM ST ET, split bench seat, cloth upholstery, optical horn, P215/70R14 tires. **LX** adds: illuminated entry system, power door lock, remote fuel filler and trunk releases, automatic parking brake release, speed control, tilt steering column, intermittent wipers, dual power mirrors, bright rocker panel moldings, fold-down front center armrest, 20-ounce carpeting, digital clock, cloth door panels with courtesy lights, quarter panel courtesy lights, Light Group, carpeted trunk, AM/FM ST ET cassette, split bench seat with four-way headrests, leather-wrapped steering wheel, styled steel wheels. **Sport** adds to base equipment: 5.0-liter (302-cid) PFI V-8

Prices are accurate at time of printing; subject to manufacturer's change.

engine, heavy-duty battery, handling suspension, dual power mirrors, exterior blackout treatment, accent stripes, digital clock, center console, Light Group, carpeted trunk, bucket seats, P215/70HR14 tires on styled steel wheels. **Turbo Coupe** adds: 2.3-liter (140-cid) PFI turbocharged 4-cylinder engine, 5-speed manual transmission, Traction-Lok axle, 4-wheel disc brakes with anti-lock feature, remote fuel door release, automatic ride control, intermittent wipers, fog lamps, lower charcoal accent paint, fold-down center armrest, 20-ounce carpeting, analog instrument cluster with tachometer, turbo boost gauge, coolant temperature, ampere and oil pressure gauges, articulated sport seats with power lumbar support and power backrest and cushion bolsters, leather-wrapped steering wheel, P225/60VR16 Goodyear Eagle GT Gatorback tires on alloy wheels.

OPTIONAL EQUIPMENT:

5.0-liter V-8, base & LX	639	543	590
4-speed automatic transmission, Turbo	515	437	475
Heavy-duty battery	27	23	25
Electronic Equipment Group, base	634	539	585
Sport, Turbo Coupe	365	310	335
LX	577	490	530
Keyless entry system, automatic climate control.			
Luxury Light/Convenience Group, base	461	392	425
Base w/Electronic Equipment	379	322	350
Sport & Turbo	426	362	390
Sport & Turbo w/Electronic Equipment	344	292	315
LX	244	207	225
Autolamp system, cornering lamps, lighted visor mirrors, illuminated entry system, Light Group.			
Dual power seats, base, LX & Sport	302	257	280
LX w/articulated seats, Turbo	251	214	230
Power antenna	76	64	70
Digital clock, base	61	52	56
Rear defogger	145	123	133
Engine block heater	18	16	17
Power Lock Group	249	211	230
Power door locks, remote fuel filler & trunk releases.			
Dual power mirrors	96	82	88
Power moonroof, base, Sport or Turbo	841	715	775
LX or w/Luxury/Light Group	741	630	680
AM/FM ST ET delete (credit)	(206)	(175)	(175)
AM/FM ST ET cassette	137	116	126
Graphic EQ	218	186	200
Premium Sound System	168	143	155
Power driver's seat	251	214	230
Speed control	176	149	162
Leather-wrapped steering wheel	59	50	54
Tilt steering column	124	106	114
Locking wire wheel covers, LX	90	77	83

Prices are accurate at time of printing; subject to manufacturer's change.

Cast aluminum wheels, LX	221	188	203
Base	343	291	315
Styled road wheels	122	104	112
Power windows	222	189	205
Intermittent wipers	55	47	51
California emissions pkg.	99	84	91
Two-tone paint, base	218	186	200
LX	163	139	150
Clearcoat paint	183	155	168
Articulated sport seats (std. Turbo)	183	155	168
Vinyl trim	37	31	34
Leather trim	415	352	380

MERCURY COUGAR

LS 2-door coupe	$13630	$11700	$12540
XR-7 2-door coupe	15660	13425	14405
Destination charge	432	432	432

STANDARD EQUIPMENT (included in above prices):

LS: 3.8-liter (232-cid) TBI V-6 engine, 4-speed automatic transmission, power steering, power brakes, air conditioning, dual-note horn, halogen headlamps, electronic instruments, left remote-control door mirror, bodyside and decklid accent stripes, vinyl-insert bodyside moldings, deluxe wheel covers, full carpeting, seatbelt reminder chimes, cloth-and-vinyl door panel trim, brushed instrument panel applique, AM/FM stereo, individual reclining front seats, quartz analog clock, center console, four-spoke luxury steering wheel, cloth-and-vinyl upholstery, trip odometer, tinted glass, right remote-control convex door mirror, rocker panel moldings, hood accent striping, luxury wheel covers, luxury floor carpeting, carpeted seat cushion side facings, luxury door panel trim, woodtone instrument panel applique, quar-ter-trim courtesy lights, illuminated passenger visor mirror, velour cloth upholstery, electronic digital clock, P215/70R14 tires. **XR-7** adds: 5.0-liter (302-cid) PFI V-8 engine, 5-speed manual transmission, handling suspension, P205/70HR14 BSW tires, polycast wheels, tinted glass, higher-effort power steering, analog gauge cluster including tachometer, leather wrapped steering wheel, Traction-Lok axle.

OPTIONAL EQUIPMENT:

5.0-liter PFI V-8 engine, LS	639	543	590
Conventional spare tire	73	62	67
Locking wire wheel covers	212	180	195
Polycast wheels, LS	178	151	164
Power Lock Group	249	211	230
includes remote fuel filler & trunk releases.			
Power windows	222	189	205
Power moonroof	841	715	775

Prices are accurate at time of printing; subject to manufacturer's change.

	Retail Price	Dealer Invoice	Low Price
Power driver's seat	251	214	230
Dual power seats, LS	554	471	510
XR-7	502	427	460
AM/FM ST ET cassette	137	116	126
AM/FM ST ET delete (credit)	(206)	(175)	(175)
Premium Sound System	168	143	155
Power antenna	71	60	65
Graphic EQ	218	186	200
Clearcoat metallic paint	183	155	168
Two-tone paint	163	139	150
Rear half luxury vinyl roof	260	221	240
Leather seat trim	415	352	380
Automatic air conditioning	162	138	149
Heavy-duty battery	27	23	25
Engine block heater	18	16	17
Rear defogger	145	123	133
Intermittent wipers	55	47	51
Automatic parking brake release	12	10	11
Headlamp Convenience Group Automatic dimmer, Autolamp Delay System.	176	149	162
Keyless entry system	202	172	186
Cornering lamps	68	58	63
Light Group	35	30	33
Dual illuminated visor mirrors	100	85	92
Speed control	176	149	162
Leather-wrapped steering wheel, LS	59	50	54
Electronic digital clock	61	52	56
Illuminated entry system	82	69	75
Electronic instrument cluster	330	281	305
Tilt steering column	124	106	114
California emissions pkg.	99	84	91

Honda Accord

All-new last year, the latest edition of the Accord continued
to be a hot item among buyers despite escalating prices
and remained one of the 10 best selling cars in the U.S.
Changes for this year are limited to new colors and the
addition of automatic front seat belts to Accord hatchbacks
after the start of 1987 production. The current Accord generation is offered in 3-door hatchback and 4-door sedan
body styles. Both are assembled at Honda's Ohio plant and
shipped to dealers in most parts of the country, as the

Prices are accurate at time of printing; subject to manufacturer's change.

Honda Accord LXi 4-door

percentage of imported Accords continues to decline. Two engines are offered: A carbureted 2.0-liter 4-cylinder in the DX and LX models and a fuel-injected 2.0 in the LXi. Both are available with a 5-speed manual or 4-speed automatic transmission. The latest Accord is roomier and somewhat plusher than before and still offers competent road manners, good gas mileage and a comfortable ride. There's not that much difference on paper between the carbureted and fuel-injected engines, but the injected version feels much livelier on the road, both from a standing start and in highway passing. Either engine works quite well with automatic transmission and returns impressive mileage. These aren't sport sedans, yet they're quite agile and have above average handling ability. In short, they're among the most refined and capable family cars available. The standard equipment is generous for all models, but Accord's base prices are much higher than a year ago because of the decline in the value of the U.S. dollar. In the past year, prices have increased $1300 on the LX sedan and around $1800 on the LXi sedan, which is now just under $15,000. That's a lot of money for a 4-cylinder, compact sedan. For that reason, our favorite remains the LX sedan, which has nearly everything the LXi offers for about $1600 less. Despite the higher prices, the Accord is still a fine buy today that will have good resale value down the road.

Specifications

	3-door coupe	4-door sedan
Wheelbase, in.	102.4	102.4
Overall length, in.	174.8	178.5

	3-door coupe	4-door sedan
Overall width, in.	66.7	66.7
Overall height, in.	52.6	53.3
Front track, in.	58.3	58.3
Rear track, in.	58.1	58.1
Curb weight, lbs.	2454	2568
Cargo vol., cu. ft.	19.0	14.0
Fuel capacity, gal.	15.8	15.8
Seating capacity	5	5
Front headroom, in.	38.0	38.7
Front shoulder room, in.	55.1	54.9
Front legroom, max., in.	42.8	42.8
Rear headroom, in.	36.5	37.1
Rear shoulder room, in.	54.5	54.5
Rear legroom, min, in.	30.2	32.4

Body/Chassis

Drivetrain layout: transverse front engine/front-wheel drive. **Front suspension:** upper and lower wishbones, coil springs concentric with shock absorbers, radius rods, stabilizer bar. **Rear suspension:** upper and lower wishbones, trailing arms, coil sprints concentric with shock absorbers, stabilizer bar on LXi models. **Steering:** rack and pinion, power assisted, 2.5 turns lock-to-lock. **Turn diameter, ft.:** 34.1. **Front brakes:** 9.5-in. discs. **Rear brakes:** 7.9-in. drums. **Construction:** unit.

Powertrains	ohc I-4	ohc I-4
Displacement, l/cu. in.	2.0/119	2.0/119
Compression ratio	9.2:1	9.4:1
Fuel delivery	2 bbl.	PFI
Net bhp @ rpm	98 @ 5500	110 @ 5500
Net torque @ rpm	109 @ 3500	114 @ 4500
Availability	S[1]	S[2]

1. DX, LX   2. LXi only

Final drive ratios

Final drive ratios		
5-speed OD manual	4.07:1	4.07:1
4-speed OD automatic	4.07:1	4.07:1

KEY: bbl = barrel (carburetor); **bhp** = brake horsepower; **torque** = pounds/feet; **Cal.** = California only; **TBI** = throttle body (single-point) fuel injection; **PFI** = port (multipoint) fuel injection; **MFI** = mechanical fuel injection; **ohv** = overhead valve; **ohc** = overhead cam; **dohc** = double overhead cam; **I** = inline engine; **V** = V engine; **flat** = horizontally opposed engine; **D** = diesel; **T** = turbocharged; **OD** = overdrive transmission; **S** = standard; **O** = optional.

PRICES

HONDA ACCORD

	Retail Price	Dealer Invoice	Low Price
DX 3-door coupe, 5-speed	$9795	$8228	$9595
DX 3-door coupe, automatic	10325	8673	10125
DX 4-door sedan, 5-speed	10625	8925	10425
DX 4-door sedan, automatic	11155	9370	11055
LX 4-door sedan, 5-speed	12799	10751	12600
LX 4-door sedan, automatic	13329	11196	13130
LXi 3-door coupe, 5-speed	12785	10739	12585
LXi 3-door coupe, automatic	13315	11185	13115
LXi 4-door sedan, 5-speed	14429	12120	14230
LXi 4-door sedan, automatic	14959	12566	14760
Destination charge	209	209	209

These models sell at or above retail in many locations.

STANDARD EQUIPMENT (included in above prices):

DX: 2.0-liter (119-cid) 4-cylinder engine, 5-speed manual or 4-speed automatic transmission as above, power steering, power brakes, cruise control (sedan only), tinted glass, locking fuel filler door with remote release, remote hatch/trunklid release, intermittent wipers, tachometer, trip odometer, quartz digital clock, remote-control left door mirror, rear defogger, adjustable steering wheel, left door map pocket, swing-out rear side windows (coupe), roll-down rear door windows (sedan), cargo area/trunk light, rear window wiper/washer (coupe), full carpeting, front bucket seats with reclining backrests, electronic warning system, full wheel covers, halogen headlamps, low-fuel warning lamp, rear seat center armrest (sedan), split fold-down rear seatback (coupe), childproof rear door locks (sedan), full wheel covers, rear seat heater ducts (sedan), bodyside protection moldings, front mud guards, 185/70R13 tires. **LX** adds: power antenna, AM/FM stereo cassette radio, air conditioning, dual electric remote-control door mirrors, power windows, power door locks, right front door map pocket, fold-down rear seatback, upgraded interior trim. **LXi** deletes power antenna and door locks on coupe and adds: PFI engine, custom alloy wheels (sedan), power moonroof with sunshade (sedan), cruise control (coupe), "full logic" sound system (sedan), luxury interior trim.

OPTIONS are available as dealer-installed accessories; prices may vary.

Honda Civic

A 4-wheel-drive system that engages automatically in slippery conditions debuts this fall on the Civic 4WD wagon.

Prices are accurate at time of printing; subject to manufacturer's change.

Honda Civic Si 3-door

Honda calls the system Real Time 4WD; it is similar to the system introduced last year on the Volkswagen Vanagon Syncro. Under normal conditions power is sent only to the front wheels, but when road conditions demand additional traction, a viscous coupling engages automatically to send power to the rear wheels as well, eliminating the need to engage 4WD through a transfer case. Real Time 4WD automatically disengages when the wagon is back on a dry surface. The Civic wagon formerly was available with a part-time 4WD system engaged by a dashboard switch. The 4WD model comes only with a 6-speed manual transmission that includes a lower gear for extra traction. Other Civics are carryovers from last year except for new exterior colors. U.S.-built Civic sedans started showing up in Honda showrooms earlier this fall. The Civic scores highly for providing good gas mileage and good performance, a combination that eludes many car companies, at attractive prices. They're much higher now than a year ago, but a DX hatchback or Civic sedan should still be under $10,000 with air conditioning and a stereo. Civics are tiny on the outside, but impressively roomy inside. The Civics are even more impressive on the road. The 1.5-liter engines (fuel-injected in the Si and carbureted in the others) give the Civics lively acceleration and satisfying mileage, plus they perform with commendable smoothness and refinement. They're space efficient, fuel efficient and lots of fun to drive.

Specifications

	3-door sedan	4-door sedan	5-door wagon
Wheelbase, in.	93.7	96.5	96.5
Overall length, in.	150.0	163.4	157.1
Overall width, in.	64.0	64.0	63.9
Overall height, in.	52.6	54.5	58.3
Front track, in.	55.1	55.1	55.1
Rear track, in.	55.7	55.7	55.7
Curb weight, lbs.	1863	1940	2015
Cargo vol., cu. ft.	14.5	12.1	56.6
Fuel capacity, gal.	11.9	12.1	12.1
Seating capacity	4	4	4
Front headroom, in.	37.6	38.1	39.2
Front shoulder room, in.	53.9	53.5	53.0
Front legroom, max., in.	43.3	40.3	38.9
Rear headroom, in.	35.2	36.7	38.0
Rear shoulder room, in.	53.0	52.0	52.4
Rear legroom, min, in.	18.9	32.8	35.9

Body/Chassis

Drivetrain layout: transverse front engine/front-wheel drive. **Front suspension:** MacPherson struts, lower control arms, lateral torsion bars, stabilizer bar. **Rear suspension:** beam axle, trailing links, coil springs, stabilizer bar (except base, Civic 3-door and Civic DX). **Steering:** rack and pinion, turns lock-to-lock NA. **Turn diameter, ft.:** 29.5 3-door, 30.2 4-door, wagon. **Front brakes:** 9.0-in. discs. **Rear brakes:** 7.1-in. drums. **Construction:** unit.

Powertrains

	ohc I-4	ohc I-4	ohc I-4
Displacement, l/cu. in.	1.3/81	1.5/91	1.5/91
Compression ratio	10.0:1	9.2:1	8.7:1
Fuel delivery	3 bbl.	3 bbl.	PFI
Net bhp @ rpm	60 @ 5500	76 @ 6000	91 @ 5500
Net torque @ rpm	73 @ 3500	84 @ 3500	93 @ 4500
Availability	S[1]	S[2]	S[3]

1. base 3d only   2. others except Si   3. Si 3d only

Final drive ratios

4-speed OD manual	3.72:1		
5-speed OD manual		4.07:1	4.27:1
4-speed OD automatic		3.59:1	

KEY: bbl = barrel (carburetor); **bhp** = brake horsepower; **torque** = pounds/feet; **Cal.** = California only; **TBI** = throttle body (single-point) fuel injection; **PFI** = port (multipoint) fuel injection; **MFI** = mechanical fuel injection; **ohv** = overhead valve; **ohc** =

overhead cam; **dohc** = double overhead cam; **I** = inline engine; **V** = V engine; **flat** = horizontally opposed engine; **D** = diesel; **T** = turbocharged; **OD** = overdrive transmission; **S** = standard; **O** = optional.

PRICES

HONDA CIVIC	Retail Price	Dealer Invoice	Low Price
3-door sedan, 4-speed	$5799	$5219	$5600
DX 3-door sedan, 5-speed	7489	6366	7290
DX 3-door sedan, automatic	7989	6791	7790
Si 3-door sedan, 5-speed	8899	7564	8700
5-door wagon, 5-speed	8330	7081	8130
5-door wagon, automatic	8830	7506	8630
4-door sedan, 5-speed	8455	7187	8255
4-door sedan, automatic	9180	7803	8980
4WD 5-door wagon, 6-speed	9695	8421	9495
Destination charge	209	209	209

These models sell at or above retail in many locations.

STANDARD EQUIPMENT (included in above prices):

1.3-liter (81-cid) 4-cylinder engine, 4-speed manual transmission, locking fuel filler door, front bucket seats with reclining backrests, cargo area/trunk light, hatch/trunklid-open warning light, manual remote-control left door mirror, trip odometer, fold-down rear seatback (exc. sedan), all-vinyl interior trim, full interior carpeting, front mud guards, 175/70R13 tires. **DX** adds: 1.5-liter (91-cid) 4-cylinder engine, 5-speed manual or 4-speed automatic overdrive transmission as above, wheel trim rings, tilt-adjustable steering column, rear window wiper/washer, bodyside protection moldings, tinted glass, intermittent wipers, rear defogger, remote hatch/trunklid release, 3-spoke steering wheel, split rear seatback with recliners, rear seat headrests, swing-open rear side windows. **Si** adds to DX equipment: PFI engine, body-color bumpers and front chin spoiler, full wheel covers, upgraded tires, halogen headlamps, dual remote-control door mirrors, tilt/removable glass sunroof, cloth interior trim, door map pockets, center console with cassette tape storage, quartz digital clock, tachometer. **Sedan** deletes split rear seatback from DX equipment and adds: childproof rear door locks, roll-down rear door windows, rear passenger assist handles, visor vanity mirror, cloth interior trim, rear seat heater ducts, front door map pockets, 3-spoke steering wheel, quartz digital clock, tachometer, halogen headlamps. **Wagon** adds to DX equipment: childproof rear door locks, roll-down rear door windows, rear passenger assist handles, underdash stowage shelf, front door map pockets, stowage drawer under right front seat, rear seat heater ducts, 3-spoke steering wheel, halogen headlamps, tachometer. **4WD wagon** deletes 3-spoke steering wheel from wagon equipment and adds: 4-wheel drive, 6-speed manual transmission, all-season tires, rear mud guards.

OPTIONS are available as dealer-installed accessories; prices may vary.

Prices are accurate at time of printing; subject to manufacturer's change.

CONSUMER GUIDE®

Honda Civic CRX

Honda Civic CRX

The Civic-based 2-seat CRX hatchbacks continue unchanged from last year except for new exterior colors. Three versions are again offered: Fuel-saver CRX HF (carbureted 1.5-liter engine), CRX 1.5 (carbureted engine with three valves per cylinder) and boy-racer CRX Si (fuel-injected engine). The Si also has a power sunroof and two of last year's major additions, 60-series performance radials mounted on 14-inch alloy wheels. For those who need only a 2-seater, the CRX offers more bang for the buck and practicality than anything else on the market. The fuel-miser HF has less performance than the other two CRX models, but is among the stingiest cars in gas consumption. The CRX 1.5 is much livelier, but still returns impressive mileage that will keep operating costs down. The Si's spirited fuel-injected 1.5 is the most potent CRX engine and the Si has the best handling. The other two CRX models also acquit themselves well on the road, so don't think you have to buy the Si to get good roadability. For such a small car, the CRX easily accommodates people over six feet tall. The driver's seat goes well back from the steering wheel and pedals, while the passenger enjoys plenty of room for stretching out and head room is at least adequate. Behind the seats, there's ample cargo room for a twosome, though there's nothing to keep your cargo from sliding into the front cabin in a hard stop. There's plenty of value in the CRX line, but check with your insurance agent first about rates on a CRX; the insurance industry is negative about sporty cars in general and 2-seaters in particular.

Specifications

	3-door coupe
Wheelbase, in.	86.6
Overall length, in.	144.6
Overall width, in.	63.9
Overall height, in.	50.8
Front track, in.	55.1
Rear track, in.	55.7
Curb weight, lbs.	1713
Cargo vol., cu. ft.	20.2
Fuel capacity, gal.	10.8
Seating capacity	2
Front headroom, in.	37.6
Front shoulder room, in.	52.6
Front legroom, max., in.	42.7
Rear headroom, in.	—
Rear shoulder room, in.	—
Rear legroom, min, in.	—

Body/Chassis

Drivetrain layout: transverse front engine/front-wheel drive.
Front suspension: MacPherson struts, lower control arms, lateral torsion bars, stabilizer bar. **Rear suspension:** beam axle, trailing links, coil springs, stabilizer bar (except CRX HF). **Steering:** rack and pinion, 4.0 turns lock-to-lock. **Turn diameter, ft.:** 28.2. **Front brakes:** 9.0-in. discs. **Rear brakes:** 7.1-in. drums. **Construction:** unit.

Powertrains

	ohc I-4	ohc I-4	ohc I-4
Displacement, l/cu. in.	1.5/91	1.5/91	1.5/91
Compression ratio	10.0:1	9.2:1	8.7:1
Fuel delivery	3 bbl.	3 bbl.	PFI
Net bhp @ rpm	58 @ 4800	76 @ 6000	91 @ 5500
Net torque @ rpm	79 @ 2500	84 @ 3500	93 @ 4500
Availability	S[1]	S[2]	S[3]

1. HF only   2. CRX 1.5 only   3. Si only

Final drive ratios

5-speed OD manual	2.95:1	4.27:1	4.27:1
4-speed OD automatic		3.95:1	

KEY: bbl = barrel (carburetor); **bhp** =brake horsepower; **torque** = pounds/feet; **Cal.** = California only; **TBI** = throttle body (single-point) fuel injection; **PFI** = port (multi-point) fuel injection; **MFI** = mechanical fuel injection; **ohv** = overhead valve; **ohc** = overhead cam; **dohc** = double overhead cam; **I** = inline engine; **V** = V engine; **flat** = horizontally opposed engine; **D** = diesel; **T** = turbocharged; **OD** = overdrive transmission; **S** = standard; **O** = optional.

PRICES

HONDA CIVIC CRX

	Retail Price	Dealer Invoice	Low Price
HF 3-door coupe, 5-speed	$7639	$6493	$7440
1.5 3-door coupe, 5-speed	7975	6779	7775
1.5 3-door coupe, automatic	8475	7204	8275
Si 3-door coupe, 5-speed	9395	7986	9195
Destination charge	209	209	209

These models sell at or above retail in many locations.

STANDARD EQUIPMENT (included in above prices):

HF: 1.5-liter (91-cid) 4-cylinder engine, 5-speed overdrive manual transmission, power brakes, sport suspension, rear spoiler, remote-control left door mirror, tinted glass, halogen headlamps, remote hatch release, remote fuel filler door release, intermittent wipers, electric rear-window defroster, bucket seats with reclining backrests, cloth interior trim, locking storage compartment in rear floor, tachometer, trip odometer, custom alloy wheels, hatch-open warning lamp, bodyside rub moldings. **CRX 1.5** deletes alloy wheels from HF equipment and adds: upgraded tires, full wheel covers, dual remote-control door mirrors, door map pocket, quartz digital clock. **Si** adds: PFI engine, 60-series tires, 14-inch custom alloy wheels, body-color rear spoiler and front bumper/chin spoiler, body-color rocker panel extensions, power sunroof, rear wiper/washer, center console with cassette tape storage.

OPTIONS are available as dealer-installed accessories; prices may vary.

Honda Prelude

Prelude, Honda's oldest model in its U.S. lineup, is carried over unchanged for 1987, expected to be the last year for the current generation. The front-drive Prelude debuted during the 1983 model year in its current design. A restyled Prelude, probably with some mechanical changes, could arrive as early as next spring. Until then, Prelude will still be offered in base form with a 1.8-liter 4-cylinder engine fed by dual sidedraft carburetors and the racier Si model with a fuel-injected 2.0-liter 4-cylinder engine. Just as some people don't show their age, neither do some cars. Not that the Prelude is old by absolute standards, but there are newer Japanese rivals such as the Nissan Pulsar and 200SX, Toyota Celica and Subaru XT. Still, Prelude

Prices are accurate at time of printing; subject to manufacturer's change.

Honda Prelude

looks fresh and performs with the best of the sporty coupes.
Prelude offers all-around capability on the road, a high
level of refinement and comfort and an impressive array
of convenience features. It's the kind of car that is enjoyable
tearing around a race track or just cruising down the in-
terstate. The ride is firm and can become jiggly on badly
broken pavement, though it's not the rock-hard ride of
some high-performance coupes. The interior doesn't offer
much room in any direction; the rear seat is useless for
anyone but small children and six-footers will be short of
head room in front. Otherwise, though, we continue to be
impressed with this classy front-drive coupe. The Prelude
Si offers better performance, but not enough to justify a
$3000 price difference over the base model, which remains
our favorite.

Specifications

	2-door coupe
Wheelbase, in.	96.5
Overall length, in.	169.1
Overall width, in.	66.5
Overall height, in.	51.0
Front track, in.	57.9
Rear track, in.	57.9
Curb weight, lbs.	2293
Cargo vol., cu. ft.	9.1
Fuel capacity, gal.	15.8
Seating capacity	4
Front headroom, in.	37.3
Front shoulder room, in.	54.5

	2-door coupe
Front legroom, max., in.	43.2
Rear headroom, in.	33.9
Rear shoulder room, in.	51.9
Rear legroom, min., in.	26.1

Body/Chassis

Drivetrain layout: transverse front engine/front-wheel drive. **Front suspension:** double wishbone, upper and lower control arms, coil springs, stabilizer bar. **Rear suspension:** independent; MacPherson struts, lower control arms, coil springs, stabilizer bar. **Steering:** rack and pinion, power assisted, 3.1 turns lock-to-lock. **Turn diameter, ft.:** 34.1. **Front brakes:** 9.1-in. discs. **Rear brakes:** 9.1-in. discs. **Construction:** unit.

Powertrains	ohc I-4	ohc I-4
Displacement, l/cu. in.	1.8/113	2.0/119
Compression ratio	9.1:1	9.4:1
Fuel delivery	2×1 bbl.	PFI
Net bhp @ rpm	100 @ 5500	110 @ 5500
Net torque @ rpm	107 @ 4000	114 @ 4500
Availability	S[1]	S[2]

1. base model   2. Si only

Final drive ratios
5-speed OD manual	4.07:1	4.07:1
4-speed OD automatic	3.88:1	3.88:1

KEY: bbl = barrel (carburetor); **bhp** =brake horsepower; **torque** = pounds/feet; **Cal.** = California only; **TBI** = throttle body (single-point) fuel injection; **PFI** = port (multi-point) fuel injection; **MFI** = mechanical fuel injection; **ohv** = overhead valve; **ohc** = overhead cam; **dohc** = double overhead cam; **I** = inline engine; **V** = V engine; **flat** = horizontally opposed engine; **D** = diesel; **T** = turbocharged; **OD** = overdrive transmission; **S** = standard; **O** = optional.

PRICES

HONDA PRELUDE	Retail Price	Dealer Invoice	Low Price
2-door coupe, 5-speed	$11995	$10076	$11795
2-door coupe, automatic	12525	10521	12325
2.0 Si 2-door coupe, 5-speed	14945	12554	14745
2.0 Si 2-door coupe, automatic	15475	12999	15275
Destination charge	209	209	209

These models sell at or above retail in many locations.

Prices are accurate at time of printing; subject to manufacturer's change.

STANDARD EQUIPMENT (included in above prices):

1.8-liter (113-cid) 4-cylinder engine, 5-speed manual or 4-speed automatic transmission as above, power 4-wheel disc brakes, speed-variable power steering, full wheel covers, halogen headlamps, tilt steering wheel, dual remote-control door mirrors, tinted glass, front mud guards, electronic warning system, power moonroof, trunk light, fade-out interior light, door map pockets, low-fuel warning lamp, right front passenger assist handle, quartz digital clock/calendar, trip odometer, tachometer, AM/FM ET stereo cassette, electric rear-window defroster, intermittent wipers, remote trunklid release, fold-down rear seatback with lock, remote fuel filler door release, front bucket seats with reclining backrests, cloth interior trim, full interior carpeting, 185/70R13 tires. **2.0 Si** adds: 2.0-liter (122-cid) 4-cylinder PFI engine, upgraded tires, power door mirrors, leather-wrapped steering wheel, cruise control, power windows, upgraded sound system with 7-band graphic equalizer, driver's seat lumbar support adjuster, body-color rear bumper and lip spoiler, body-color front bumper/spoiler, upgraded interior trim, Michelin V-rated tires on custom alloy wheels.

OPTIONS are available as dealer-installed accessories; prices may vary.

Hyundai Excel

Hyundai Excel 3-door

Aerodynamic headlamps and a new grille will give the Korean-made Excel a different look at the front, while under the skin the suspension will be firmer and the front stabilizer bar larger for better handling. The other major change coming for 1987 is that the optional 3-speed automatic transmission gains a lockup torque converter that is supposed to improve fuel economy by eliminating slippage between the engine and drive shafts. The Excel, a front-drive subcompact, was introduced in the U.S. last February in 4-door sedan and 5-door hatchback styling; a 3-door hatchback was added in June. Hyundai has dealers in 31 states that form an arc around the center of the U.S. The company will be expanding into more states this year and expects to have dealers in the 48 contiguous states by the end of calendar 1987, with the Midwest scheduled to come last. The front-drive Excel is built on the same platform as the Japanese-made Mitsubishi Mirage and Dodge/Plymouth Colt and uses the same 1.5-liter 4-cylinder engine, transmissions and many suspension components as the Mirage and Colt. Hyundai builds some of those components under license from Mitsubishi and buys others from the Japanese company. The Excel's body and interior are designed and built by Hyundai, the first Korean company to sell cars in the U.S. Hyundai easily shattered first-year sales records for imported cars by offering cars with low base prices and more standard equipment than most competitors, showing that price and value are important factors in many buying decisions. The entry-level Excel is still $4995, but even the highest-priced GLS models don't go much over $8000 even with the few available options added in. Since the Excel is based on the Mitsubishi Mirage and Dodge/Plymouth Colt design, the performance should be about the same. However, an Excel GLS 3-door we tested with a 5-speed manual transmission was surprisingly sluggish from a standing start. The Excel acquitted itself well on the road, showing competent handling (with the help of the optional alloy wheels and P195/70R13 tires) and a comfortable ride for a subcompact. Overall, we're pretty impressed with the Excel's value for the money, considering what you get for $8000 or less. We still rank the Dodge Omni/Plymouth Horizon slightly higher because of its more powerful 2.2-liter engine and longer powertrain and rust warranties. Also, the Excel's performance isn't as brisk as the Honda Civic's or Toyota Tercel's.

Specifications	3-door sedan	4-door sedan	5-door sedan
Wheelbase, in.	93.7	93.7	93.7
Overall length, in.	160.9	168.0	160.9

	3-door sedan	4-door sedan	5-door sedan
Overall width, in.	63.1	63.1	63.1
Overall height, in.	54.1	54.1	54.1
Front track, in.	54.1	54.1	54.1
Rear track, in.	52.8	52.8	52.8
Curb weight, lbs.	2127	2150	2127
Cargo vol., cu. ft.	26.6	11.2	26.0
Fuel capacity, gal.	10.6[1]	10.6[1]	10.6[1]
Seating capacity	4	4	4
Front headroom, in.	37.5	37.5	37.5
Front shoulder room, in.	52.1	52.1	52.1
Front legroom, max., in.	40.9	40.9	40.9
Rear headroom, in.	36.9	36.9	36.9
Rear shoulder room, in.	51.6	51.6	51.6
Rear legroom, min., in.	32.4	32.4	32.4

1. 13.2 gals. on GLS w/automatic

Body/Chassis

Drivetrain layout: transverse front engine/front-wheel drive.
Front suspension: MacPherson struts, lower control arms, coil
springs, stabilizer bar. **Rear suspension:** independent; trailing
arms, coil springs, stabilizer bar. **Steering:** rack and pinion, 3.9
turns lock-to-lock. **Turn diameter, ft.:** 33.8. **Front brakes:** 9.0-in.
discs. **Rear brakes:** 7.1-in. drums. **Construction:** unit.

Powertrains

	ohc I-4
Displacement, l/cu. in.	1.5/90
Compression ratio	9.5:1
Fuel delivery	2 bbl.
Net bhp @ rpm	68 @ 5500
Net torque @ rpm	82 @ 3500
Availability	S

Final drive ratios

4-speed manual	3.47:1
5-speed OD manual	3.47:1
3-speed automatic	3.60:1

KEY: bbl = barrel (carburetor); **bhp** = brake horsepower; **torque** = pounds/feet; **Cal.**
= California only; **TBI** = throttle body (single-point) fuel injection; **PFI** = port (multi-
point) fuel injection; **MFI** = mechanical fuel injection; **ohv** = overhead valve; **ohc** =
overhead cam; **dohc** = double overhead cam; **I** = inline engine; **V** = V engine; **flat**
= horizontally opposed engine; **D** = diesel; **T** = turbocharged; **OD** = overdrive transmission; **S** = standard; **O** = optional.

PRICES

HYUNDAI EXCEL

	Retail Price	Dealer Invoice	Low Price
Base 3-door sedan, 4-speed	$4995	$4496	$4895
GL 3-door sedan, 5-speed	5995	5276	5795
GL 3-door sedan, automatic	6415	5641	6215
GLS 3-door sedan, 5-speed	6645	5648	6445
GLS 3-door sedan, automatic	7065	6013	6865
Base 5-door sedan, 4-speed	5295	4766	5195
GL 5-door sedan, 5-speed	6295	5540	6095
GL 5-door sedan, automatic	6715	5905	6515
GLS 5-door sedan, 5-speed	6945	5903	6745
GLS 5-door sedan, automatic	7365	6268	7165
GL 4-door sedan, 5-speed	6445	5672	6245
GL 4-door sedan, automatic	6865	6037	6665
GLS 4-door sedan, 5-speed	7095	6031	6895
GLS 4-door sedan, automatic	7515	6396	7315
Destination charge	225	225	225

STANDARD EQUIPMENT (included in above prices):

1.5-liter (90-cid) 4-cylinder engine, 4-speed manual, 5-speed manual or 3-speed automatic transmission as above, power brakes, maintenance-free battery, front and rear mud flaps, rear stone guards, rear defogger, side window defoggers, variable intermittent wipers, locking fuel filler door, coolant temperature gauge, trip odometer, graphic display, low fuel warning light, day/night mirror, illuminated lockable glovebox, under-dash parcel tray, cargo area light, illuminated cigar lighter and ashtray, three assist grips, dual coat hooks, driver's footrest, reclining front bucket seats, three-position rear seatbacks, rear seat headrests, vinyl upholstery, full carpeting including cargo area, front and rear armrests, detachable cargo area cover, rear seat heater ducts, P155/80R13 Goodyear Corsa GT all-season tires on styled steel wheels with full-size spare. GL adds: hub covers and wheel trim rings, dual remote mirrors, tinted glass, bodyside moldings, rear wiper/washer (5-door), remote hatch or trunk release, remote fuel filler release, front door map pockets, dual rear ashtrays, cloth and vinyl upholstery, cloth door panel trim, full center console, analog quartz clock. GLS adds: AM/FM ST ET cassette, tachometer, visor and glovebox mirrors, front passenger underseat storage tray, driver's seat height and lumbar support adjuster, full cloth upholstery, upgraded carpeting, digital quartz clock, luxury steering wheel, cloth headliner.

OPTIONAL EQUIPMENT:

Excel Option Pkg., Base	175	131	166
Right remote mirror, tinted glass, bodyside molding.			
Alloy wheels & 5 P175/70R13 tires	320	240	305

Prices are accurate at time of printing; subject to manufacturer's change.

	Retail Price	Dealer Invoice	Low Price
Air conditioning	675	506	640
Passive restraint system	75	56	71
AM/FM ST ET cassette, exc. GLS	295	177	280
w/Dolby & 4 speakers, GL	415	249	395
GLS	120	72	114
Power sunroof	375	281	355
Power steering	230	195	220

Isuzu I-Mark

Isuzu I-Mark 3-door

New front-end styling and a new turbocharged sport model will be the major changes to the I-Mark, Isuzu's front-drive subcompact. Flush-mounted, composite headlamps (halogen high and low beams mounted in a single unit), built-in fog lamps, a grille-less nose and new contoured front fenders are the major changes at the front. Last year's 2.5-mph bumpers have been replaced by new bumpers rated for 5-mph crashes. Inside, controls for lights and wipers have been relocated so the driver can reach them without taking his hands off the steering wheel. The new turbocharged RS model will arrive next March, boasting 110-horsepower from its 1.5-liter 4-cylinder engine, a larger front air dam, rear spoiler, thicker rear stabilizer bar and P185/60R14 tires on alloy wheels. The turbocharged 1.5 also gets multipoint fuel injection instead of a 2-barrel carburetor. I-Mark is sold in nearly identical form as the Chevrolet Spectrum.

Chevy will field a turbocharged Spectrum only in 4-door styling, while the RS also will be available as a 3-door hatchback. I-Mark has two other trim levels: S, added last year as a price leader, and base trim. I-Mark becomes a little more distinctive from Spectrum this year in styling and trim, but the two cars are still nearly identical mechanically. Their main virtues are low price and high gas mileage, plus more comfortable seats than you usually find in Japanese subcompacts. Overall, I-Mark doesn't match cars such as the Civic and Tercel in performance and roadability, and it has no real price advantage over the Dodge Omni/Plymouth Horizon America.

Specifications

	3-door sedan	4-door sedan
Wheelbase, in.	94.5	94.5
Overall length, in.	157.4	160.2
Overall width, in.	63.5	63.5
Overall height, in.	54.1	54.1
Front track, in.	54.7	54.7
Rear track, in.	54.3	54.3
Curb weight, lbs.	1923	1937
Cargo vol., cu. ft.	29.7	11.3
Fuel capacity, gal.	11.1	11.1
Seating capacity	5	5
Front headroom, in.	38.0	37.7
Front shoulder room, in.	52.8	52.8
Front legroom, max., in.	41.7	41.7
Rear headroom, in.	37.1	37.6
Rear shoulder room, in.	52.8	52.8
Rear legroom, min, in.	33.3	33.5

Body/Chassis

Drivetrain layout: transverse front engine/front-wheel drive.
Front suspension: MacPherson struts, lower control arms, coil springs. **Rear suspension:** trailing arm, transverse beam, coil springs. **Steering:** rack and pinion, turns lock-to-lock NA. **Turn diameter, ft.:** 34.8. **Front brakes:** 8.9-in. discs. **Rear brakes:** 7.0-in. drums. **Construction:** unit.

Powertrains	ohc I-4	ohc I-4T
Displacement, l/cu. in.	1.5/90	1.5/90
Compression ratio	9.6:1	8.0:1
Fuel delivery	2 bbl.	PFI

	ohc I-4	ohc I-4T
Net bhp @ rpm	70 @ 5400	110 @ 5400
Net torque @ rpm	87 @ 3400	120 @ 3500
Availability	S	S[1]

1. RS

Final drive ratios

5-speed OD manual	3.58:1	3.83:1
3-speed automatic	3.53:1	3.53:1

KEY: bbl = barrel (carburetor); **bhp** = brake horsepower; **torque** = pounds/feet; **Cal.** = California only; **TBI** = throttle body (single-point) fuel injection; **PFI** = port (multi-point) fuel injection; **MFI** = mechanical fuel injection; **ohv** = overhead valve; **ohc** = overhead cam; **dohc** = double overhead cam; **I** = inline engine; **V** = V engine; **flat** = horizontally opposed engine; **D** = diesel; **T** = turbocharged; **OD** = overdrive transmission; **S** = standard; **O** = optional.

PRICES

ISUZU I-MARK (1986 prices)	Retail Price	Dealer Invoice	Low Price
S 4-door sedan, 5-speed	$7189	$6470	$6890
S 4-door sedan, automatic	7619	6836	7320
S 3-door sedan, 5-speed	6999	6299	6700
S 3-door sedan, automatic	7429	6665	7130
Base 4-door sedan, 5-speed	7979	6860	7680
Base 4-door sedan, automatic	8409	7226	8110
Base 3-door sedan, 5-speed	7869	6766	8570
Base 3-door sedan, automatic	8299	7132	8000
Destination charge	249	249	249

STANDARD EQUIPMENT (included in above prices):

S: 1.5-liter (90-cid) 2 bbl. 4-cylinder engine, power brakes, passenger assist grips, cargo area cover (3-doors), cut-pile carpeting, remote fuel filler and trunk/hatch releases, halogen headlamps, luggage compartment light, lockable glovebox, dual power mirrors, door map pockets, wide bodyside moldings, reclining front bucket seats, split fold-down rear seatback, trip odometer, rear wiper/washer (3-doors), intermittent wipers, P175/70R13 all-season SBR tires on alloy wheels. **Base** adds: digital clock, rear defogger, tinted glass, tilt steering column, tachometer.

OPTIONAL EQUIPMENT:

Air conditioning	680	578	645
Front console (NA S)	30	24	29
Cruise control (NA S)	195	160	185
Carpet mats (NA S)	50	30	48

Prices are accurate at time of printing; subject to manufacturer's change.

AM/FM ST radio	. . . .	250	150	240
AM/FM ST ET cassette	. . . .	410	287	390
AM/FM ST ET cassette w/EQ (NA S)	. . . .	520	364	495
Sunroof (NA S)	. . . .	300	240	285
Power steering (NA S)	. . . .	220	187	210

Isuzu Impulse

Isuzu Impulse

A limited-production turbocharged RS model with a special suspension and white exterior treatment will debut early in 1987 as the major change for Isuzu's eye-catching sport coupe. The RS will come with a handling package, 205/60R14 tires and limited-slip rear differential. The only color available will be white, with body-color mirrors, wheels and door handles and gray accents on the bumpers, spoiler and rocker panels. The base Impulse and Impulse Turbo are largely carryovers for 1987. The price-leader Impulse S introduced last spring has been dropped, so all models again come with air conditioning and power windows standard. Isuzu's rear-drive coupe arrived in the U.S. in spring 1983 and the high-fashion styling overshadowed Impulse's ordinary performance until late in the 1985 model year, when the turbocharged/intercooled model was introduced. Acceleration is quite brisk and the Turbo's taut suspension gives it impressive handling on smooth surfaces. Rough pavement can result in bump-steer and momentary traction loss, and the ride gets thumpy and jolting. As with most sport coupes, interior room is sparse. Tall drivers will have to hunker down because of the low roof and the small back seat offers only token room for adults. Even base models are fully equipped, so you don't have to spend a fortune on options, so Impulse offers fairly good value for the money against most competitors. However, styling remains its biggest lure since similar performance is available at similar cost in cars like the Honda Prelude and Toyota Celica GT-S.

Specifications

	3-door coupe
Wheelbase, in.	96.1
Overall length, in.	172.6
Overall width, in.	65.2
Overall height, in.	51.4
Front track, in.	53.3
Rear track, in.	53.9
Curb weight, lbs.	2727
Cargo vol., cu. ft.	29.4
Fuel capacity, gal.	15.1
Seating capacity	4
Front headroom, in.	36.9
Front shoulder room, in.	54.5
Front legroom, max., in.	41.9
Rear headroom, in.	35.8
Rear shoulder room, in.	54.0
Rear legroom, min, in.	28.1

Body/Chassis

Drivetrain layout: longitudinal front engine/rear-wheel drive. **Front suspension:** double wishbone arms, coil springs, gas-filled shock absorbers, stabilizer bar. **Rear suspension:** rigid axle, three links, coil springs, gas-filled shock absorbers, stabilizer bar. **Steering:** rack and pinion, power assisted, turns lock-to-lock NA. **Turn diameter, ft.:** 31.5. **Front brakes:** 9.8-in. discs. **Rear brakes:** 10.5-in. discs. **Construction:** unit.

Powertrains	ohc I-4	ohc I-4T
Displacement, l/cu. in.	1.9/119	2.0/122
Compression ratio	9.2:1	7.9:1
Fuel delivery	PFI	PFI
Net bhp @ rpm	90 @ 5000	140 @ 5400
Net torque @ rpm	146 @ 3000	166 @ 3000
Availability	S	S

Final drive ratios	ohc I-4	ohc I-4T
5-speed OD manual	3.91:1	3.91:1
4-speed OD automatic	3.91:1	3.91:1

KEY: bbl = barrel (carburetor); **bhp** = brake horsepower; **torque** = pounds/feet; **Cal.** = California only; **TBI** = throttle body (single-point) fuel injection; **PFI** = port (multipoint) fuel injection; **MFI** = mechanical fuel injection; **ohv** = overhead valve; **ohc** = overhead cam; **dohc** = double overhead cam; **I** = inline engine; **V** = V engine; **flat** = horizontally opposed engine; **D** = diesel; **T** = turbocharged; **OD** = overdrive transmission; **S** = standard; **O** = optional.

PRICES

ISUZU IMPULSE (1986 prices)	Retail Price	Dealer Invoice	Low Price
Base 3-door coupe, automatic	$12619	$10845	$12120
Base 3-door coupe, 5-speed	12059	10369	11560
Turbo 3-door coupe, automatic	14999	12894	14500
Turbo 3-door coupe, 5-speed	14439	12418	13940
S 3-door coupe, 5-speed	10699	9629	10200
Destination charge	249	249	249

STANDARD EQUIPMENT (included in above prices):

1.9-liter (119-cid) 4-cylinder PFI engine, 5-speed manual or 4-speed automatic transmission as above, power steering, power 4-wheel disc brakes, air conditioning, power windows, power door locks, digital clock with time delay, tinted glass, dual power remote mirrors, passenger visor mirror, adjustable lumbar support, tilt steering column with memory, rear spoiler, trip computer, adjustable folding rear seatbacks, P195/60R14 tires on turbine-style alloy wheels. **Turbo** adds: front air dam, sport seats with 7-way driver's side adjustment, AM/FM stereo ET, anti-theft device. **S** deletes air conditioning, cruise control, and rear wiper/washer from base equipment.

OPTIONAL EQUIPMENT:

Leather interior & digital instruments			
Turbo	780	624	740
Parcel shelf, power mirrors & door locks,			
Base	100	85	95
Air conditioning, S	695	591	660
Premium audio w/EQ, Base	595	446	565
Digital Drive Monitor, Base	120	102	114
AM/FM ST ET, Base & S	280	238	265

Lincoln Continental/Mark VII

Minor equipment changes are in store for the similar Continental sedan and Mark VII coupe until mid-year, when

Prices are accurate at time of printing; subject to manufacturer's change.

Lincoln Continental

the Mark VII is due to receive some styling changes. Sales of the mid-size Mark VII and Continental have been sluggish, while the full-size Lincoln Town Car has exceeded Ford's expectations, so the company hopes the new styling will spur more interest in the downsized Lincoln coupe, which will probably remain in rear-drive form with a V-8 engine for the next few years. The Continental sedan, however, will be redesigned for 1988 on a stretched front-drive Taurus/Sable platform and come only with V-6 engines, including a 3.8-liter unit that will eventually be offered with a supercharger. All Continentals and Mark VIIs gained anti-lock brakes as standard equipment last year, a welcome addition, but the most roadworthy model remained the Mark VII LSC with its high-output V-8, handling suspension and high-performance tires. The LSC's V-8 furnishes strong acceleration, brisk passing response and loafs along quietly and comfortably at cruising speeds. Mileage, however, remains a weak point. We averaged less than 16 mpg even with a lot of expressway driving. Interior furnishings are plush, the LSC's standard equipment impressively complete. The price for all this is high against most cars, but actually quite reasonable compared to the high-priced European coupes such as the BMW 635CSi, Jaguar XJ-S and Mercedes-Benz 560SEC. Other rivals include GM's front-drive luxury coupes (Eldorado, Riviera and Toronado), and the LSC outscores those cars in our book.

Specifications	Mark VII 2-door coupe	Continental 4-door sedan
Wheelbase, in.	108.5	108.5
Overall length, in.	202.8	200.7

	Mark VII 2-door coupe	Continental 4-door sedan
Overall width, in.	70.9	73.6
Overall height, in.	54.2	55.6
Front track, in.	58.4	58.4
Rear track, in.	59.0	59.0
Curb weight, lbs.	3722	3799
Cargo vol., cu. ft.	14.2	14.7
Fuel capacity, gal.	22.1	20.3
Seating capacity	5	5
Front headroom, in.	37.8	38.5
Front shoulder room, in.	56.0	57.6
Front legroom, max., in.	42.0	42.0
Rear headroom, in.	37.1	37.7
Rear shoulder room, in.	57.8	57.8
Rear legroom, min., in.	36.9	38.3

Body/Chassis

Drivetrain layout: longitudinal front engine/rear-wheel drive. **Front suspension:** modified MacPherson struts, lower control arms, electronically controlled air springs, automatic level control, gas-pressurized shocks, stabilizer bar. **Rear suspension:** rigid axle, four links, electronically controlled air springs, automatic level control, gas-pressurized shocks, stabilizer bar. **Steering:** rack and pinion, power assisted, 3.0 turns lock-to-lock. **Turn diameter, ft.:** 40.0. **Front brakes:** 10.9-in. discs. **Rear brakes:** 11.3-in. discs. **Construction:** unit.

Powertrains	ohv V-8	ohv V-8
Displacement, l/cu. in.	5.0/302	5.0/302
Compression ratio	8.9:1	8.9:1
Fuel delivery	PFI	PFI
Net bhp @ rpm	150 @ 3200	200 @ 4000
Net torque @ rpm	270 @ 2000	285 @ 3000
Availability	S	S[1]

1. Mark VII LSC

Final drive ratios

4-speed OD automatic	2.73:1[1]	3.27:1

1. 3.08 w/optional Traction-Lok axle

KEY: bbl = barrel (carburetor); **bhp** = brake horsepower; **torque** = pounds/feet; **Cal.** = California only; **TBI** = throttle body (single-point) fuel injection; **PFI** = port (multi-point) fuel injection; **MFI** = mechanical fuel injection; **ohv** = overhead valve; **ohc** = overhead cam; **dohc** = double overhead cam; **I** = inline engine; **V** = V engine; **flat** = horizontally opposed engine; **D** = diesel; **T** = turbocharged; **OD** = overdrive transmission; **S** = standard; **O** = optional.

PRICES

LINCOLN CONTINENTAL	Retail Price	Dealer Invoice	Low Price
4-door sedan	$25484	$21602	$23065
Givenchy 4-door sedan	27899	23630	25250
Destination charge	524	524	524

STANDARD EQUIPMENT (included in above prices):

5.0-liter (302-cid) PFI V-8 engine, 4-speed automatic transmission, power steering, power 4-wheel disc brakes, anti-lock braking system, compass and thermometer with Ice Alert, power decklid pulldown, remote fuel filler and decklid releases, rear defogger, heated outside mirrors, power windows and door locks, power mini-vent windows, tethered fuel cap, tinted glass, automatic headlight dimmer, Autolamp delay system, illuminated entry system, keyless entry system, low engine oil alert light, engine compartment light, automatic parking brake release, cruise control, variable intermittent wipers, bumper rub strips, coach lamps, halogen headlamps, cornering lamps, dual power mirrors, four lighted ashtrays with cigar lighters, 30-ounce floor carpet, 10-ounce luggage compartment carpet, carpeted lower door panels, spare tire cover, coat hooks, reading lamps, consolette with storage compartment, fold-down front center armrest, lighted front door armrest storage bins, roof rail assist handles, rear seat headrests, rear compartment heat ducts, woodtone instrument panel applique, electronic instrument panel, message center and systems monitor, cloth interior trim, front and rear courtesy and footwell lights, luggage compartment and glovebox lights, floormats, dual lighted visor mirrors, AM/FM ST ET cassette, power front seats with recliners, optical horn, P215/70R15 tires on aluminum wheels.
Givenchy adds: dual-shade paint, leather interior trim, front seat cushion map pockets, wire-spoke aluminum wheels.

OPTIONAL EQUIPMENT:

Traction-Lok axle	101	85	93
Puncture sealant tires	200	168	184
Wire-spoke aluminum wheels, base	693	582	640
Anti-theft alarm system	200	168	184
Power glass moonroof	1319	1068	1215
Brushed aluminum upper bodyside molding .	74	62	68
Automatic day/night mirror	89	75	82
Bodyside protection molding	70	59	64
Dual-shade paint	320	269	294
Ford JBL Audio System	506	425	465
Glamour paint	268	225	245
Leather seat trim, base	560	471	454
California emissions pkg.	99	84	91
Engine block heater	26	22	24

Prices are accurate at time of printing; subject to manufacturer's change

CONSUMER GUIDE®

LINCOLN MARK VII

2-door coupe	$23246	$19709	$21155
Bill Blass Designer Series 2-door coupe	24837	21046	22600
LSC 2-door coupe	24837	21046	22600
Destination charge	524	524	524

STANDARD EQUIPMENT (included in above prices):

5.0-liter (302-cid) PFI V-8, 4-speed automatic transmission, power steering, power 4-wheel disc brakes, anti-lock braking system, electronic air suspension with automatic level control, automatic temperature control air conditioning, overhead console with warning lights and reading lamps, power decklid release, defroster group, power windows and door locks, remote fuel door release, tinted glass, headlamp convenience group, illuminated entry system, electronic instrument panel with message center, dual heated power mirrors, AM/FM ST ET cassette, six-way power bucket seats, cruise control, tilt steering column, intermittent wipers, full-length console with lockable compartment, side window defoggers, P215/70R15 tires on aluminum wheels. **LSC** adds: high-output engine, 3.27 axle ratio, analog instrumentation including tachometer and coolant temperature gauge, leather interior trim including steering wheel, shift knob, and console, handling suspension, P215/65R15 tires on wider aluminum wheels. **Bill Blass** adds to base: prairie mist metallic clearcoat paint, bodyside and decklid paint stripes, Sandalwood seat trim in choice of leather, UltraSuede or cloth/leather, wire-spoke aluminum wheels.

OPTIONAL EQUIPMENT:

Traction-Lok axle	101	85	93
Puncture sealant tires	200	168	184
Wire spoke aluminum wheels, base	693	582	640
Anti-theft alarm system	200	168	184
Power glass moonroof	1319	1108	1215
Automatic day/night mirror	89	75	82
Glamour paint	268	225	245
Leather seat trim	560	471	515
Engine block heater	26	22	24
California emissions pkg.	99	83	91

Lincoln Town Car

A compact disc player is scheduled to be added as a new option to the full-size Town Car, which outsells the Continental and Mark VII combined by nearly three to one. Corrosion protection is improved through wider use of gal-

Lincoln Town Car

vanized sheetmetal, the standard battery is upgraded to 84 amps from 71, a conventional spare tire and premium sound system are standard, and the top-line Cartier Designer Series gets new color schemes and seat fabrics. Besides the Cartier model, Town Car also is sold in base and Signature Series trim. More items are lumped with the Comfort/convenience option package, leaving fewer individual options this year. Long on room, long on comfort, long on refinement, and just plain long, the Town Car continues to set the sales pace for Lincoln, while the smaller Continental and Mark VII get a bigger share of the development and advertising budget. Lincoln buyers traditionally have judged value in pounds and inches, and the Town Car provides plenty of both, especially compared to the downsized Continental and Mark VII. No wonder then that Town Car sales were up in 1986 while Continental sales fell. There's really only one direct competitor left for the Town Car, the Cadillac Brougham, also full-size, rear-drive and powered by a V-8 engine. Choosing one over the other is a coin toss for us, since both provide disappointing performance by today's standards and equal amounts of room and comfort. For those who still covet the traditional American luxury car, this is at least as good as a bet as the Cadillac. The choice is yours.

Specifications	4-door sedan
Wheelbase, in.	117.3
Overall length, in.	219.0

	4-door sedan
Overall width, in.	78.1
Overall height, in.	55.9
Front track, in.	62.2
Rear track, in.	62.0
Curb weight, lbs.	4051
Cargo vol., cu. ft.	22.4
Fuel capacity, gal.	18.0
Seating capacity	6
Front headroom, in.	39.0
Front shoulder room, in.	60.7
Front legroom, max., in.	43.5
Rear headroom, in.	38.2
Rear shoulder room, in.	60.7
Rear legroom, min., in.	42.1

Body/Chassis

Drivetrain layout: longitudinal front engine/rear-wheel drive.
Front suspension: unequal-length upper and lower control arms,
coil springs, gas-pressurized shock absorbers, stabilizer bar. **Rear
suspension:** rigid axle, four links, coil springs, gas-pressurized
shock absorbers. **Steering:** recirculating ball, power assisted, 3.4
turns lock-to-lock. **Turn diameter, ft.:** 40.0. **Front brakes:** 11.1-
in. discs. **Rear brakes:** 10.0-in drums. **Construction:** body on
frame.

Powertrains	ohv V-8
Displacement, l/cu. in.	5.0/302
Compression ratio	8.9:1
Fuel delivery	PFI
Net bhp @ rpm	150 @ 3200
Net torque @ rpm	270 @ 2000
Availability	S

Final drive ratios
4-speed OD automatic	3.08:1[1]

1. 3.27 w/optional Traction-Lok axle

KEY: bbl = barrel (carburetor); **bhp** = brake horsepower; **torque** = pounds/feet; **Cal.**
= California only; **TBI** = throttle body (single-point) fuel injection; **PFI** = port (multi-
point) fuel injection; **MFI** = mechanical fuel injection; **ohv** = overhead valve; **ohc** =
overhead cam; **dohc** = double overhead cam; **I** = inline engine; **V** = V engine; **flat**
= horizontally opposed engine; **D** = diesel; **T** = turbocharged; **OD** = overdrive transmission; **S** = standard; **O** = optional.

PRICES

LINCOLN TOWN CAR	Retail Price	Dealer Invoice	Low Price
4-door sedan	$22837	$19369	$21010
Signature Series 4-door sedan	25743	21810	23685
Cartier Edition 4-door sedan	27026	22888	24865
Destination charge	542	542	542

STANDARD EQUIPMENT (included in above prices):

Town Car: 5.0-liter (302-cid) PFI V-8 engine, 4-speed automatic transmission, power steering, power brakes, power vent and door windows, automatic temperature control air conditioning, tilt steering wheel, automatic parking brake release, tinted glass, front bumper guards, front and rear bumper rub strips, hood accent stripes, cornering lamps, coach lamps, bodyside accent stripes, full wheel covers, dual power mirrors, variable intermittent wipers, cruise control, full vinyl roof w/padded rear roof pillars, Twin-Comfort lounge front seats w/six-way power driver's seat and dual fold-down center armrests, rear seat folding center armrest, AM/FM ST ET cassette, premium sound system, analog clock, passenger assist handles, full carpeting including lower door panels, electronic warning chimes, full interior courtesy lighting, luggage compartment and spare tire trim defroster group, tethered fuel cap, P215/70R15 tires w/full-size spare. **Town Car Signature** adds: 3.27 axle ratio, coach roof, manual front passenger seatback recliner, pleat-pillow-style upholstery, seatback assist straps and map pockets, door and quarter trim woodtone accents. **Town Car Cartier** adds: two-tone paint, full textured-vinyl roof, platinum bodyside moldings, turbine-spoke aluminum wheels, leather-wrapped steering wheel.

OPTIONAL EQUIPMENT:

Traction-Lok axle	101	85	93
Puncture sealant tires	200	168	184
Locking wire wheel covers			
Cartier (credit)	(137)	(115)	(115)
Base	341	286	315
Lacy spoke aluminum wheels, Signature . .	137	115	126
Others	478	401	440
Turbine spoke aluminum wheels, Signature .	137	115	126
Base	478	401	440
Wire spoke aluminum wheels, Cartier . . .	395	332	365
Signature	532	447	490
Base	873	733	805
Electronic instrument panel	822	691	755
Keyless illuminated entry system	209	175	192

Prices are accurate at time of printing; subject to manufacturer's change.

CONSUMER GUIDE®

Anti-theft alarm system	200	168	184
Power glass moonroof	1319	1108	1215
Preferred Equipment Pkg.	694	583	640

Power decklid pulldown, illuminated visor mirrors, automatic headlight dimmer, autolamp delay system, dual power seats, rear floormats.

Leather-wrapped steering wheel	115	96	106
Automatic day/night mirror	89	75	82
Automatic load leveling	202	170	186
Bodyside protection molding	70	59	64
Carriage roof, Signature	726	610	670
Others	1069	898	985
Valino luxury coach roof	343	288	315
Ford JBL Audio System	506	425	465
Compact Disc player (Ford JBL req.)	864	726	795
Dual shade paint	320	269	295
Glamour paint	268	225	245
Leather seat trim, Signature	469	394	430
Base	531	446	490
Engine block heater	26	22	24
California emissions pkg.	99	83	91
Dual exhaust system	83	69	76
100-amp. alternator	67	56	62
Class III Trailer Tow Pkg.			
High altitude	463	389	425
Others	546	458	500

For 5000-lb. maximum gross trailer weight/750-lb. tongue load. Includes HD suspension and cooling, transmission and power steering fluid oil coolers, 3.55 Traction-Lok axle, HD U-joints, trailer wiring harness, HD turn signals and flashers, HD rear brakes, automatic load leveling suspension, dual exhaust system.

Mazda RX-7

An anti-lock brake system (ABS) will be available as a new option on the RX-7 Turbo and GXL models as the major change for 1987 on Mazda's rotary-powered sports car. The RX-7 was redesigned for last year and the second generation debuted with a 2+2 model in addition to a 2-seater. A turbocharged 2-seater arrived in mid-1986. For this year, models with the 5-speed manual transmission will have a starter interlock that requires the clutch pedal be pushed all the way in before the car can be started. A 146-horsepower 1.3-liter twin-rotor engine is standard in the base and GXL, while the turbocharged engine is rated at 182 horsepower. The redesigned RX-7 had a tough act

Prices are accurate at time of printing; subject to manufacturer's change

Mazda RX-7 Turbo

to follow, since the original rotary-powered sports car showed impressive staying power over its 7-year run. The 1.3-liter engine gives the RX-7 plenty of zip in normally aspirated form, and tire-scorching power in turbocharged form. Those who buy automatic transmission will miss out on some of the performance and a lot of the rotary engine's free-revving nature. Handling is quite good and the RX-7 has great agility, plus highly capable brakes even without the newly available ABS. Interior room is still tight for tall people, and the rear seat on the 2+2 model is a joke; it's a squeeze for one person to sit sideways. Despite the ever escalating prices, the RX-7 remains a fine value among sports cars because of its competent design, complete equipment and, most of all, the rotary engine's reputation for longevity.

Specifications

	3-door coupe
Wheelbase, in.	95.7
Overall length, in.	168.9
Overall width, in.	66.5
Overall height, in.	49.8
Front track, in.	57.1
Rear track, in.	56.7
Curb weight, lbs.	2625[1]
Cargo vol., cu. ft.	19.5
Fuel capacity, gal.	16.6
Seating capacity	2[2]
Front headroom, in.	37.2
Front shoulder room, in.	52.8

	3-door coupe
Front legroom, max., in.	46.9
Rear headroom, in.	33.0[3]
Rear shoulder room, in.	NA
Rear legroom, min., in.	NA

1. 2850 lbs., Turbo   2. 4, 2 + 2   3. 2 + 2

Body/Chassis

Drivetrain layout: longitudinal front engine/rear-wheel drive.
Front suspension: MacPherson struts, lower control arms, coil springs, stabilizer bar. **Rear suspension:** independent, trailing arms, camber control links, coil springs, stabilizer bar. **Steering:** rack and pinion, 3.5 turns lock-to-lock. **Turn diameter, ft.:** 32.2.
Front brakes: 9.8-in. discs (10.9-in. GXL, Turbo). **Rear brakes:** 10.3-in. discs (10.7-in. GXL, Turbo). **Construction:** unit.

Powertrains	2-rotor Wankel	2-rotor Wankel turbo
Displacement, l/cu. in.	1.3/80	1.3/80
Compression ratio	9.4:1	8.5:1
Fuel delivery	PFI	PFI
Net bhp @ rpm	146 @ 6500	182 @ 6500
Net torque @ rpm	138 @ 3500	183 @ 3500
Availability	S[1]	S[2]

1. Base, GXL   2. Turbo

Final drive ratios

5-speed OD manual	4.10:1	4.10:1
4-speed OD automatic	3.91:1	

KEY: bbl = barrel (carburetor); **bhp** = brake horsepower; **torque** = pounds/feet; **Cal.** = California only; **TBI** = throttle body (single-point) fuel injection; **PFI** = port (multi-point) fuel injection; **MFI** = mechanical fuel injection; **ohv** = overhead valve; **ohc** = overhead cam; **dohc** = double overhead cam; **I** = inline engine; **V** = V engine; **flat** = horizontally opposed engine; **D** = diesel; **T** = turbocharged; **OD** = overdrive transmission; **S** = standard; **O** = optional.

PRICES

MAZDA RX-7	Retail Price	Dealer Invoice	Low Price
3-door coupe	$14199	$12358	$14000
Luxury 3-door coupe	15799	13602	15600
Sport 3-door coupe	15749	13559	15550
2 + 2 3-door coupe	14699	12793	14500
Luxury 2 + 2 3-door coupe	16299	14038	16100

Prices are accurate at time of printing; subject to manufacturer's change.

	Retail Price	Dealer Invoice	Low Price
GXL 3-door coupe	18449	15779	18250
GXL 2 + 2 3-door coupe	18949	16206	18750
Turbo 3-door coupe	20399	17446	20200

Destination charge varies by region. These models sell at or above retail in many locations.

STANDARD EQUIPMENT (included in above prices):

1.3-liter (80-cid) PFI rotary engine, power 4-wheel disc brakes, 5-speed manual transmission, quartz halogen headlamps, multi-adjustable fabric sport seats, full instrumentation, remote hatch and fuel filler releases, day/night mirror, passenger visor mirror, cargo area lamp, luggage hold-down straps, center console with armrest, digital clock, carpeting, AM/FM stereo ET, dual remote mirrors, bodyside moldings, rear defogger, front air dam, P185/70HR14 tires on steel wheels. **Luxury** adds: power mirrors, power sunroof, tinted windshield sunshade, cassette player with 100-watt amplifier, alloy wheels. **Sport** adds to base equipment: front air dam, side sill extensions, rear spoiler, power steering, power mirrors, sport suspension, 205/60VR15 tires on alloy wheels. **GXL** adds: power steering, limited slip differential, Auto Adjusting Suspension, rear wiper/washer, power sunroof, leather steering wheel with tilt feature, velour seats, courtesy lamps, cruise control, power windows, lockable storage box, air conditioning, cassette player, graphic EQ, P205/60VR15 tires on aluminum wheels. **Turbo** deletes power steering and adds turbocharged, intercooled engine, uprated suspension and brakes, 205/55VR16 Goodyear Eagle GT tires on 7-inch-wide alloy wheels.

OPTIONAL EQUIPMENT:

4-speed automatic transmission (NA Sport & Turbo)	595	506	565
Anti-lock braking system, GXL & Turbo . .	1300	1105	1235
Air conditioning (std. GXL & Turbo)	795	636	755
Aluminum wheels, base	395	316	375
Leather pkg., GXL	730	584	695
Burglar alarm, GXL & Turbo	180	140	171
Compact Disc player, GXL & Turbo	715	576	680
Power sunroof, Sport	570	456	540
Power steering, Turbo	395	340	375
Graphic EQ, Luxury	140	105	133
Cassette deck, base & Sport	169	120	160
Cruise control, base, Luxury & Sport . . .	200	150	190
Armrest	50	38	48
Floormats	49	34	47

Prices are accurate at time of printing; subject to manufacturer's change.

Mazda 323

Mazda 323 4-door

All-new last year, the front-drive 323 subcompact replaced the GLC and was available in 3-door hatchback and 4-door sedan form. This year a 5-door station wagon built on the same platform joins the 323 lineup, the first time Mazda has offered a station wagon since the GLC wagon was retired in 1983. The wagon comes with 60/40 split rear seatbacks that lay flat to create nearly 57 cubic feet of cargo space. The wagon is available in base or Deluxe trim, while the hatchback comes in base or Deluxe and the sedan in Deluxe and top-line Luxury trim. The 323 came out longer and heavier than the GLC, with a roomier interior and more cargo space. To handle the extra size and weight, engine displacement was increased to 1.6 liters from 1.5 and horsepower jumped by 14 to 82. Mazda moved upmarket with its new subcompact, in size and performance. Still, the short wheelbase limits interior length, though this is no "crampact." Cargo space on the sedan is quite impressive as the deep trunk easily swallows small suitcases. With the 5-speed manual transmission, performance is at least adequate, highway mileage gets well above 30 mpg and the 1.6-liter engine behaves in fairly refined fashion. Expect less performance and mileage, more noise with the 3-speed automatic transmission. On balance, this is a competent car that offers above-average performance, room and value against other subcompacts, and is well worth looking at. The base and Deluxe versions offer the best value-per-dollar.

Specifications

	3-door sedan	4-door sedan	5-door wagon
Wheelbase, in.	94.5	94.5	94.5
Overall length, in.	161.8	169.7	169.7
Overall width, in.	64.8	64.8	64.8
Overall height, in.	54.7	54.7	55.5
Front track, in.	54.7	54.7	54.7
Rear track, in.	55.7	55.7	55.7
Curb weight, lbs.	2060	2115	2170
Cargo vol., cu. ft.	10.5	14.7	56.8
Fuel capacity, gal.	11.9	11.9	11.9
Seating capacity	5	5	5
Front headroom, in.	38.4	38.4	38.4
Front shoulder room, in.	52.8	52.8	51.9
Front legroom, max., in.	41.5	41.5	41.5
Rear headroom, in.	37.0	37.4	37.4
Rear shoulder room, in.	52.8	52.8	51.9
Rear legroom, min., in.	34.7	34.7	34.7

Body/Chassis

Drivetrain layout: transverse front engine/front-wheel drive. **Front suspension:** MacPherson struts, lower control arms, coil springs, stabilizer bar. **Rear suspension:** independent struts, trailing arms, trapezoidal links, coil links, stabilizer bar. **Steering:** rack and pinion, 3.6 turns lock-to-lock. **Turn diameter, ft.:** 30.8. **Front brakes:** 9.4-in. discs. **Rear brakes:** 7.9-in. drums. **Construction:** unit.

Powertrains

	ohc I-4
Displacement, l/cu. in.	1.6/97
Compression ratio	9.3:1
Fuel delivery	PFI
Net bhp @ rpm	82 @ 5000
Net torque @ rpm	92 @ 2500
Availability	S

Final drive ratios

4-speed OD manual	4.10:1
5-speed OD manual	4.10:1
3-speed automatic	3.63:1

KEY: bbl = barrel (carburetor); **bhp** =brake horsepower; **torque** = pounds/feet; **Cal.** = California only; **TBI** = throttle body (single-point) fuel injection; **PFI** = port (multipoint) fuel injection; **MFI** = mechanical fuel injection; **ohv** = overhead valve; **ohc** = overhead cam; **dohc** = double overhead cam; **I** = inline engine; **V** = V engine; **flat** = horizontally opposed engine; **D** = diesel; **T** = turbocharged; **OD** = overdrive transmission; **S** = standard; **O** = optional.

PRICES

MAZDA 323	Retail Price	Dealer Invoice	Low Price
3-door sedan	$6099	$5616	$6000
5-door wagon	8299	7267	8100
Deluxe 3-door sedan	7699	6737	7500
Deluxe 4-door sedan	8299	7267	8100
Deluxe 5-door wagon	8899	7792	8700
Luxury 4-door sedan	8899	7792	8700

Destination charge varies by region.

STANDARD EQUIPMENT (included in above prices):

1.6-liter (97-cid) PFI 4-cylinder engine, 4-speed manual transmission (sedan; 5-speed on wagon), bodyside moldings, front mud flaps, tinted glass, trip odometer, rear package tray, luggage compartment trim. **Deluxe** adds: 5-speed manual transmission, stone guards, intermittent wipers, remote fuel filler and hatch releases, carpeting, passenger assist grips with coat hangers, day/night rearview mirror, passenger visor mirror, cloth seats, split folding rear seatbacks, AM/FM stereo ET. **Deluxe wagon** adds to base: luxury door trim, wide bodyside moldings, driver's seat height and lumbar support adjustments, storage compartment under passenger seat, headlamps-on reminder, rear wiper/washer, 175/70SR13 SBR tires. **Luxury** adds to Deluxe sedan: tilt steering column, 5-way adjustable seats, dual power remote mirrors, cargo area or trunk light, spotlight, door courtesy lights, console, tachometer, digital clock, warning light package, headlight reminder chime, illuminated entry system, cloth visors and headliner, underseat tray, center armrest.

OPTIONAL EQUIPMENT:

3-speed automatic transmission (NA base)	430	387	410
Sunroof, 4-doors	320	272	305
Power moonroof, Deluxe wagon	550	468	525
175/70R13 tires & alloy wheels, Deluxe exc. wagon	395	316	375
Aluminum wheels, Deluxe wagon & Luxury 4-door	320	256	305
Power steering (NA base)	230	196	220
Power Pkg., Deluxe wagon & Luxury 4-door	550	468	525
Cruise control, power steering, windows & door locks.			
Air conditioning	715	576	680
Floormats	49	35	47
AM/FM ST ET, base wagon	295	236	280
AM/FM ST ET cassette (NA base)	395	300	375

Prices are accurate at time of printing; subject to manufacturer's change.

Mazda 626

Mazda 626 4-door

A 4-speed electronically controlled overdrive automatic replaces a 3-speed automatic as the optional transmission in the front-drive 626 compact line, now Mazda's oldest U.S. model as it heads into its fifth season. A 5-speed manual transmission remains standard. The new transmission includes a lockup torque converter and "economy" and "power" shift modes, with the power mode providing more responsive acceleration. Deluxe models now ride on 185/70SR14 tires, two sizes wider than last year, and wider wheels. Last year, new front and rear styling, fuel injection for the standard 2.0-liter engine and the addition of the GT model with a turbocharged 2.0 gave the 626 a fresh appearance and more performance, but the 626 is now one of the oldest Japanese models available in the U.S. Mazda's Japanese rivals have redesigned their compacts since the 626 was introduced, and all have gained interior room, not one of the 626's strong points. Head and leg room are limited in all models, especially the coupe. With the addition of fuel injection and 11 horsepower last year, the 2.0-liter engine produces more satisfactory performance, though it's still not as potent or refined as Honda's 2.0. We're still impressed by the 626's road manners. The suspension is slightly firmer than most rivals', giving the 626 a stable, comfortable ride and competent cornering ability that puts this car near the head of its class. Even though this is an "old" design by Japanese standards, there's still much to recommend it, including a competitive price.

Specifications

	2-door coupe	4-door sedan	5-door sedan
Wheelbase, in.	98.8	98.8	98.8
Overall length, in.	177.8	177.8	177.8
Overall width, in.	66.5	66.5	66.5
Overall height, in.	53.7	55.5	53.7
Front track, in.	56.3	56.3	56.3
Rear track, in.	56.1	56.1	56.1
Curb weight, lbs.	2450	2450	2555
Cargo vol., cu. ft.	13.3	13.7	21.0
Fuel capacity, gal.	15.8	15.8	15.8
Seating capacity	5	5	5
Front headroom, in.	37.6	38.4	37.6
Front shoulder room, in.	54.9	54.9	54.9
Front legroom, max., in.	41.9	41.4	41.9
Rear headroom, in.	36.8	37.8	36.7
Rear shoulder room, in.	52.5	54.7	54.7
Rear legroom, min., in.	33.3	36.4	33.3

Body/Chassis

Drivetrain layout: transverse front engine/front-wheel drive.
Front suspension: MacPherson struts, lower control arms, coil
springs, electronically adjustable shock absorbers (GT), stabilizer
bar. **Rear suspension:** MacPherson struts, trailing arms,
trapezoidal links, electronically adjustable shock absorbers (GT),
stabilizer bar. **Steering:** rack and pinion, 3.8 turns lock-to-lock
manual, 3.0 power. **Turn diameter, ft.:** 33.5. **Front brakes:** 9.8-
in. discs. **Rear brakes:** 9.1-in. drums. **Construction:** unit.

Powertrains	ohc I-4	ohc I-4T
Displacement, l/cu. in.	2.0/122	2.0/122
Compression ratio	8.6:1	7.8:1
Fuel delivery	PFI	PFI
Net bhp @ rpm	93 @ 5000	120 @ 5000
Net torque @ rpm	115 @ 2500	150 @ 3000
Availability	S[1]	S[2]

1. DX, LX   2. GT

Final drive ratios
5-speed OD manual	4.10:1	4.10:1
4-speed OD automatic	3.70:1	

KEY: bbl = barrel (carburetor); **bhp** =brake horsepower; **torque** = pounds/feet; **Cal.**
= California only; **TBI** = throttle body (single-point) fuel injection; **PFI** = port (multi-
point) fuel injection; **MFI** = mechanical fuel injection; **ohv** = overhead valve; **ohc** =
overhead cam; **dohc** = double overhead cam; **I** = inline engine; **V** = V engine; **flat**
= horizontally opposed engine; **D** = diesel; **T** = turbocharged; **OD** = overdrive transmission; **S** = standard; **O** = optional.

PRICES

MAZDA 626

	Retail Price	Dealer Invoice	Low Price
Deluxe 4-door sedan	$9899	$8587	$9700
Luxury 4-door sedan	11699	10019	11500
GT 4-door sedan	13149	11261	12950
Deluxe 2-door coupe	9949	8681	9750
Luxury 2-door coupe	11899	10191	11700
GT 2-door coupe	13449	11517	13250
Luxury 5-door Touring Sedan	12399	10619	12200
GT 5-door Touring Sedan	14049	12031	13850

Destination charge varies by region. These models sell at or above retail in many locations.

STANDARD EQUIPMENT (included in above prices):

Deluxe: 2.0-liter (122-cid) PFI 4-cylinder engine, power brakes, intermittent wipers, dual remote mirrors, digital clock, rear seat heat ducts, remote fuel filler and trunk releases, locking glovebox, full carpeting, rear defogger, storage pockets in front door panels and seat backs, velour upholstery, open-style headrests, 6-way adjustable seats, split folding rear seatback, AM/FM stereo ET, P185/70SR14 tires on steel wheels. **Luxury** adds: power steering, variable intermittent wipers, dual power mirrors, 9-way adjustable seats, rear wiper/washer (5-door), power antenna, full console with armrest, cruise control, power windows, power door locks, rear seat center armrest (4-door), door courtesy lamps, cassette deck. **GT** adds: turbocharged engine, 4-wheel disc brakes, Auto Adjusting Suspension, bronze tinted glass, head-lamp washers, dual exhaust pipes, sport steering wheel, graphic EQ, P195/60R15 tires on alloy wheels.

OPTIONAL EQUIPMENT:

4-speed automatic transmission (NA GT) .	675	594	640
Automatic Suspension System, Luxury . . .	310	264	295
Power steering, Deluxe	290	247	275
Power sunroof, Luxury	530	424	505
Power moonroof, GT	640	512	610
Aluminum wheels, Deluxe & Luxury	360	288	340
195/60R15 tires & aluminum wheels, Luxury 2- & 5-doors	695	556	660
Digital instrument panel, GTs	550	432	525
w/Automatic Suspension, Luxury models .	700	576	665
AM/FM ST ET cassette	395	300	375
Cruise control, Deluxe	200	150	190
Graphic EQ, Deluxe & Luxury	140	105	133
Air conditioning	765	612	725

Prices are accurate at time of printing; subject to manufacturer's change.

CONSUMER GUIDE®

Floormats	49	35	47
Luxury armrest, Luxury & Turbo	49	38	47
Full console w/armrest, Deluxe	79	61	75

Mercedes-Benz S-Class

Mercedes-Benz 560 SEL

The 560SEC coupe, 560SL coupe/roadster and the long-wheelbase sedans in the S-Class are carryovers from 1986, with one exception. The 300SDL Turbo sedan gains a trap oxidizer for reduced exhaust emissions, a move being made on all of Mercedes' 6-cylinder diesel models. The 300SDL was a late arrival for 1986, going on sale at the end of March. Other S-Class sedans are the 420SEL and 560SEL, both powered by gas V-8 engines. There's much to like about these cars since they are built with the finest materials and Old World craftsmanship, plus they provide top-notch road manners with the added protection of standard anti-lock brakes and, just in case, a driver-side air bag and front seat belt tensioning retractors activated in frontal collisions. The new 6-cylinder diesel engine introduced last spring was a pleasant surprise, being smoother, quieter and more powerful than its 5-cylinder predecessor. It's still no match for the refined performance of Mercedes' V-8 engines, however, which furnish great amounts of power with unmatched smoothness. In case you haven't been paying attention, Mercedes has been stressing performance the past few years; the 5.6-liter V-8 is within two horsepower of the Corvette's 5.7-liter V-8. This kind of luxury, performance and safety equipment costs a small fortune to acquire, insure and maintain, but you get a pretty big chunk of it back when you're ready to trade for a new one. You're also protected by a generous warranties: 4 years/ 50,000 miles, and they'll come to you if the car breaks down.

Specifications

	560SL 2-door coupe/ roadster	560SEC 2-door coupe	300SDL, 560SEL 4-door sedan	420SEL 4-door sedan
Wheelbase, in.	96.7	112.0	120.9	121.1
Overall length, in.	180.3	199.2	208.1	208.1
Overall width, in.	70.5	72.0	71.7	71.7
Overall height, in.	50.8	55.6	56.7	56.7
Front track, in.	57.6	61.2	61.2	61.2
Rear track, in.	57.7	60.1	60.1	60.1
Curb weight, lbs.	3705	3890	4035	3835
Cargo vol., cu. ft.	6.6	14.9	15.2	15.2
Fuel capacity, gal.	25.5	27.1	27.1	27.1
Seating capacity	2	4	5	5
Front headroom, in.	36.5	37.8	38.6	38.6
Front shoulder room, in.	51.6	57.2	56.2	56.2
Front legroom, max., in.	42.2	41.9	41.9	41.9
Rear headroom, in.	—	36.7	37.2	37.2
Rear shoulder room, in.	—	54.2	55.7	55.7
Rear legroom, min, in.	—	30.6	39.6	39.6

Body/Chassis

Drivetrain layout: longitudinal front engine/rear-wheel drive. **Front suspension:** upper and lower control arms, coil springs, gas-pressurized shock absorbers, stabilizer bar. **Rear suspension:** independent; semi-trailing arms, coil springs, gas-pressurized shock absorbers, stabilizer bar. **Steering:** recirculating ball, variable-ratio power assisted, 2.9 turns lock-to-lock. **Turn diameter, ft.:** 34.4 SL; 38.1 SEC; 40.6 SEL. **Front brakes:** 11.0-in. discs. **Rear brakes:** 11.0-in. discs. **Construction:** unit.

Powertrains

	ohc I-6TD	ohc V-8	ohc V-8
Displacement, l/cu. in.	3.0/183	4.2/256	5.6/338
Compression ratio	22.0:1	9.0:1	9.0:1
Fuel delivery	MFI	PFI	PFI
Net bhp @ rpm	143 @ 4600	201 @ 5200	238 @ 4800[1]
Net torque @ rpm	195 @ 2400	228 @ 3600	287 @ 2500
Availability	S	S	S

1. 227 bhp in 560SL

Final drive ratios	ohc I-6TD	ohc V-8	ohc V-8
4-speed automatic	2.88:1	2.47:1	2.47:1

KEY: **bbl** = barrel (carburetor); **bhp** = brake horsepower; **torque** = pounds/feet; **Cal.** = California only; **TBI** = throttle body (single-point) fuel injection; **PFI** = port (multi-point) fuel injection; **MFI** = mechanical fuel injection; **ohv** = overhead valve; **ohc** = overhead cam; **dohc** = double overhead cam; **I** = inline engine; **V** = V engine; **flat** = horizontally opposed engine; **D** = diesel; **T** = turbocharged; **OD** = overdrive transmission; **S** = standard; **O** = optional.

PRICES

MERCEDES-BENZ S-CLASS	Retail Price	Dealer Invoice	Low Price
300SDL 4-door sedan	$47000	$37600	$46800
420SEL 4-door sedan	52000	41600	51800
560SEL 4-door sedan	615000	49200	61300
560SEC 2-door coupe	68000	54400	67800
560SL 2-door coupe/roadster	55300	44240	55100
Destination charge	NA	NA	NA

West Coast prices are slightly higher. These models sell at or above retail in many locations. Add Gas Guzzler Tax of $1050 on 420SEL, $1300 on 560SL, and $1500 on 560SEL and 560SEC.

STANDARD EQUIPMENT (included in above prices):

300SDL: 3.0-liter (183-cid) 6-cylinder turbocharged diesel 6-cylinder engine, 4-speed automatic transmission, power four-wheel disc brakes, anti-lock braking system, power steering, central locking, automatic climate control, power windows, Supplemental Restraint System, rear defogger, halogen headlamps with wipe/wash system, front bucket seats with eight-way power adjustment and two-position driver's side memory, leather upholstery, folding front center armrest, retractable rear head restraints, lighted visor mirrors, cruise control, tinted glass, front seatback parcel nets, rear reading lamps, full carpeting including trunk, front door map pockets, intermittent wipers, dual heated remote mirrors (power right), tachometer, coolant temperature and oil pressure gauges, anti-theft alarm system, 205/65R15 tires on alloy wheels. **420SEL** adds: 4.2-liter (256-cid) PFI V-8 engine. **560SEL** adds: 5.6-liter (338-cid) PFI V-8 engine, power rear seat adjuster, heated front and rear seats. **560SEC** deletes rear reading lamps and power rear seat adjuster. **560SL** deletes power right mirror, parcel nets, power seats; adds folding convertible top and removable steel top.

OPTIONAL EQUIPMENT:

California emissions pkg., 300SDL	350	350	350
Power orthopedic front backrests, each . .	275	220	260
560SL	90	72	86

Prices are accurate at time of printing; subject to manufacturer's change

	Retail Price	Dealer Invoice	Low Price
Heated front seats (std. 560SEL & SEC) . .	435	348	415
Heated rear seats, 300SDL, 420SEL	435	348	415
Power rear seat, 300SDL, 420SEL	580	464	550
Four-place seating, 300SDL, 420SEL	2480	1984	2355
560SEL	1900	1520	1805
Protective metal undershielding, 420 &			
560 models	140	112	133

Mercedes-Benz 190

Mercedes-Benz 190E 2.6

Two new models are being added to the compact 190 Series, both due to arrive in January. The 2.6-liter 6-cylinder engine that also powers the mid-size 260E sedan is being installed in this body to create the 190E 2.6. Horsepower is rated at 158 and the 190E 2.6 will be available with manual and automatic transmissions. The 5-cylinder diesel engine that debuted last year in the 190D 2.5 gets turbocharged this year for a gain of 30 horsepower (to 123) in the new 190D 2.5 Turbo. The normally aspirated diesel model is carried over unchanged. The gas-powered 190E 2.3 gets a boost in compression (to 9:1 from 8:1) and nine more horsepower (to 130), while the limited-production 190E 2.3-16, with a high-performance 16-valve engine, is carried over unchanged. All 190s get new aerodynamic halogen headlamps and a revised automatic air conditioning system. Headlamp washers are now standard on the 190E 2.3-16, optional on others. The 190-Series has the same materials, craftsmanship and engineering as the larger Mercedes, but it's built to smaller scale here. Mer-

Prices are accurate at time of printing; subject to manufacturer's change.

cedes' Supplemental Restraint System (driver-side air bag and emergency retractors for the front seat belts) is standard on all models, and anti-lock brakes are standard on the high-performance 190E 2.3-16, optional on the others. The 190E, the most popular model in this group, provides satisfying performance with either manual or automatic transmission; acceleration is brisk, passing response prompt and engine behavior exemplary. Nimble, responsive handling is complemented by good wet-road adhesion. In short, the 190E offers exceptional road manners, as it should at this price. There's little head or leg room in the rear seat, which is divided by the driveline hump that also takes up some foot room in the rear-drive 190. If you can afford the price and can make do with limited rear seat room, this is a top-quality sedan with fine performance and reassuring safety features.

Specifications

	4-door sedan
Wheelbase, in.	104.9
Overall length, in.	175.0
Overall width, in.	66.1
Overall height, in.	54.4
Front track, in.	56.6
Rear track, in.	55.8
Curb weight, lbs.	2780
Cargo vol., cu. ft.	11.7
Fuel capacity, gal.	16.5
Seating capacity	5
Front headroom, in.	38.0
Front shoulder room, in.	53.5
Front legroom, max., in.	41.9
Rear headroom, in.	36.7
Rear shoulder room, in.	53.2
Rear legroom, min, in.	30.9

Body/Chassis

Drivetrain layout: longitudinal front engine/rear-wheel drive. **Front suspension:** modified MacPherson struts, lower control arms, coil springs, gas-pressurized shock absorbers, stabilizer bar. **Rear suspension:** independent; five links, coil springs, gas-pressurized shock absorbers, stabilizer bar. **Steering:** recirculating ball, power assisted, 3.3 turns lock-to-lock. **Turn diameter, ft.:** 34.8. **Front brakes:** 10.3-in. discs. **Rear brakes:** 10.2-in. discs. **Construction:** unit.

Powertrains	ohc I-4	dohc I-4	ohc I-6	ohc I-5D	ohc I-5TD
Displacement, l/cu. in. .	2.3/140	2.3/140	2.6/159	2.5/152	2.5/152
Compression ratio	9.0:1	9.7:1	9.2:1	22.0:1	22.0:1
Fuel delivery	PFI	PFI	PFI	MFI	MFI
	130 @	167 @	158 @	93 @	123 @
Net bhp @ rpm	5100	5800	5800	4600	4600
	146 @	162 @	162 @	122 @	168 @
Net torque @ rpm . . .	3500	4750	4600	2800	2400
Availability	S	S	S	S	S
Final drive ratios					
5-speed OD manual . .	3.27:1	3.27:1	3.27:1	3.42:1	
4-speed automatic	3.27:1	3.27:1	3.27:1	3.07:1	2.65:1

KEY: **bbl** = barrel (carburetor); **bhp** =brake horsepower; **torque** = pounds/feet; **Cal.** = California only; **TBI** = throttle body (single-point) fuel injection; **PFI** = port (multipoint) fuel injection; **MFI** = mechanical fuel injection; **ohv** = overhead valve; **ohc** = overhead cam; **dohc** = double overhead cam; **I** = inline engine; **V** = V engine; **flat** = horizontally opposed engine; **D** = diesel; **T** = turbocharged; **OD** = overdrive transmission; **S** = standard; **O** = optional.

PRICES

MERCEDES-BENZ 190	Retail Price	Dealer Invoice	Low Price
190D 2.5 4-door sedan, 5-speed	$26400	$21120	$26200
190D 2.5 4-door sedan, automatic	27100	21680	26900
190D 2.5 Turbo 4-door sedan, automatic .	29800	23840	29600
190E 2.3 4-door sedan, 5-speed	26400	21120	26200
190E 2.3 4-door sedan, automatic	27100	21680	26900
190E 2.3-16 4-door sedan, 5-speed	39600	31680	39400
190E 2.3-16 4-door sedan, automatic . . .	40300	32240	40100
190E 2.6 4-door sedan, 5-speed	30300	24240	30100
190E 2.6 4-door sedan, automatic	31000	24800	30800
Destination charge	NA	NA	NA

West Coast prices are slightly higher on all models. These models sell at or above retail in many locations.

STANDARD EQUIPMENT (included in above prices):

2.5-liter (152-cid) 5-cylinder diesel engine (190D 2.5), 2.3-liter (140-cid) PFI 4-cylinder engine (190E 2.3), 5-speed manual or 4-speed automatic transmission as above, power steering, power four-wheel disc brakes, automatic climate control system, Supplemental Restraint System, central locking, power windows, cruise control, intermittent wipers, rear defogger, reclining front bucket seats, M-B Tex vinyl upholstery, aerodynamic halogen headlamps, fog lamps, dual heated mirrors (power right), AM/FM ST ET cassette, tachometer, coolant temperature and oil pressure gauges, quartz

Prices are accurate at time of printing; subject to manufacturer's change.

clock, lighted visor mirrors, 185/65R15 SBR tires on forged alloy wheels. **190D 2.5 Turbo and 190E 2.6** add: 2.5-liter turbocharged diesel engine (190D Turbo) or 2.6-liter (159-cid) gasoline engine (190E 2.6), anti-lock braking system, special front air dam. **190E 2.3-16** adds: 2.3-liter DOHC 16-valve engine, limited-slip differential, digital stopwatch, power front seats with driver's side memory, rear sport bucket seats, black leather upholstery, automatic level control, leather-wrapped steering wheel and shift knob, metallic paint, anti-theft alarm system, voltmeter, oil temperature gauge, 205/55VR15 tires.

OPTIONAL EQUIPMENT:

Anti-lock braking system, 190D, 190E 2.3 .	1515	1212	1440
dAnti-theft alarm system (std. 2.3-16) . . .	450	360	430
California emissions pkg.	350	350	350
Rear seat head restraints	255	204	240
Metallic paint (std. 2.3-16)	340	272	325
Power front seats (std. 2.3-16)	830	664	790
Power orthopedic front backrests (each)			
(NA 2.3-16)	275	220	260
Reinforced front seat frames, each			
(NA 2.3-16)	25	20	24
Heated front seats	435	348	415
Leather upholstery (std. 2.3-16)	1285	1028	1220
Velour upholstery (NA 2.3-16)	1265	1028	1200
Protective metal undershielding, 190D . . .	90	72	86
190E 2.3, 2.6	40	32	38
Headlamp wipe/wash system (std. 2.3-16) .	240	192	220

Mercedes-Benz 260/300

Introduced in the U.S. last year, Mercedes' mid-size series has been expanded with the 300D Turbo sedan and 300TD Turbo station wagon, which went on sale in July as early '87s, and the 260E, which arrived in October. The 260E is the same sedan as the 300E, but uses a new 2.6-liter 6-cylinder engine derived from the 300E's 3.0-liter six through a smaller piston bore. The 2.6 engine also is available in the new 190E 2.6. The 260E has 19 less horsepower than the 300E, less standard equipment and a lower base price. The 300E, the best-selling Mercedes in North America, is unchanged for 1987. The 300D Turbo sedan and 300TD Turbo wagon are powered by a turbocharged 3.0-liter 6-cylinder diesel rated at 143 horsepower. Anti-lock brakes and

Mercedes-Benz 300 TD Turbo

the Supplemental Restraint System (air bag and emergency front seat belt retractors) are standard on the 260E and all 300 models. The 260/300 sedan fits between the compact 190 and larger S-Class in size and price, and is Mercedes' best all-around model in our estimation. We've tried the 300E and 300D Turbo and were highly impressed by both. The 300E's gas 6-cylinder engine provides fine acceleration and excellent passing response with commendable smoothness and refinement. The 300D Turbo's diesel engine is impressively quiet and smooth for a diesel, and it only feels sluggish when first starting out. The new 300 sedans are much more athletic than the old ones, showing flat cornering ability, fine roadholding and good stability at high speeds. The roomy interior can hold five adults and the trunk has ample luggage space, with the load liftover at bumper level.

Specifications	4-door sedan	5-door wagon
Wheelbase, in.	110.2	110.2
Overall length, in.	187.2	188.2
Overall width, in.	68.5	68.5
Overall height, in.	56.9	59.8
Front track, in.	58.9	58.9
Rear track, in.	58.6	58.6
Curb weight, lbs.	3220[1]	3670
Cargo vol., cu. ft.	14.6	76.8
Fuel capacity, gal.	18.5	18.5
Seating capacity	5	5
Front headroom, in.	36.9	36.9
Front shoulder room, in.	55.9	55.9
Front legroom, max., in.	41.7	41.7
Rear headroom, in.	36.9	36.9

	4-door sedan	5-door wagon
Rear shoulder room, in.	55.7	55.7
Rear legroom, min, in.	33.5	33.5

1. 3370 lbs., 300D Turbo

Body/Chassis

Drivetrain layout: longitudinal front engine/rear-wheel drive. **Front suspension:** gas-pressurized struts, coil springs, control arms, stabilizer bar. **Rear suspension:** independent; gas-pressurized shock absorbers, five links, coil springs, stabilizer bar (self-leveling feature on wagon). **Steering:** recirculating ball, power-assisted turns lock-to-lock NA. **Turn diameter, ft.:** 36.7. **Front brakes:** 11.0-in. discs. **Rear brakes:** 11.0-in. discs. **Construction:** unit.

Powertrains	ohc I-6	ohc I-6	ohc I-6TD
Displacement, l/cu. in.	2.6/159	3.0/181	3.0/183
Compression ratio	9.2:1	9.2:1	22.0:1
Fuel delivery	PFI	PFI	MFI
Net bhp @ rpm	158 @	177 @	143 @
	5800	5700	4600
Net torque @ rpm	162 @	188 @	195 @
	4600	4400	2400
Availability	S	S	S
Final drive ratios			
5-speed OD manual	3.27:1	3.07:1	
4-speed automatic	3.27:1	3.07:1	2.65:1

KEY: bbl = barrel (carburetor); **bhp** = brake horsepower; **torque** = pounds/feet; **Cal.** = California only; **TBI** = throttle body (single-point) fuel injection; **PFI** = port (multipoint) fuel injection; **MFI** = mechanical fuel injection; **ohv** = overhead valve; **ohc** = overhead cam; **dohc** = double overhead cam; **I** = inline engine; **V** = V engine; **flat** = horizontally opposed engine; **D** = diesel; **T** = turbocharged; **OD** = overdrive transmission; **S** = standard; **O** = optional.

PRICES

MERCEDES-BENZ 260/300	Retail Price	Dealer Invoice	Low Price
260E 4-door sedan, 5-speed	$33700	$26960	$33500
260E 4-door sedan, automatic	34500	27600	34300
300D Turbo 4-door sedan, automatic . . .	39500	31600	39300
300TD Turbo 5-door wagon, automatic . .	42500	34000	42300
300E 4-door sedan, 5-speed	38600	30880	38400
300E 4-door sedan, automatic	39500	31600	39300
Destination charge	NA	NA	NA

West coast prices are slightly higher. These models sell at or above retail in many locations.

STANDARD EQUIPMENT (included in above prices):

260E: 2.6-liter (159-cid) PFI 4-cylinder engine, 5-speed manual or 4-speed automatic transmission, anti-lock braking system, aerodynamic halogen headlamps, Supplemental Restraint System, rear headrests, exterior bulb failure and low fluid level warning indicators, heated mirrors (power right), automatic climate control system, central locking, power windows, 195/65R15 tires (V-rated on 260E). **300D Turbo and 300E** add: 3.0-liter (181-cid) PFI gasoline 6-cylinder or 3.0-liter (183-cid) 6-cylinder turbocharged diesel engine, headlamp wipe/wash system, anti-theft alarm system, power telescopic steering column adjustment, fuel line and engine block heaters (300D). **300D Turbo wagon** adds: turbodiesel engine, automatic level control, roof rack, rear wiper/washer.

OPTIONAL EQUIPMENT:

Anti-theft alarm system, 260E	510	408	485
California emissions pkg.	350	350	350
Rear reading lamps	70	56	67
Metallic paint, 260E	375	300	355
Partition net & luggage cover, 300TD . . .	375	300	355
Power orthopedic front backrests, each . .	275	220	260
Reinforced front seat frames, each	25	20	24
Heated front seats	435	348	415
Rear facing third seat, 300TD	940	752	895
Leather upholstery	1285	1028	1220
Velour upholstery	1265	1012	1200
Electrically adjustable steering col., 260E .	275	220	260
Protective metal undershielding, 260E & 300E	90	72	86

Merkur Scorpio & XR4Ti

Scorpio, a V-6 powered sedan, was supposed to debut late in calendar year 1986 as the second German-made car under the fledgling Merkur label, but Ford Motor Co. now says the earliest Scorpio will arrive in the U.S. is next spring and there's a chance a V-8 powered Scorpio will be offered next year. The XR4Ti is a carryover except that larger wheels and tires are standard for 1987. Standard wheel/tire diameter is now 15 inches; wheel width remains 5½ inches and tire size 195/60HR. The rear-drive, turbocharged sport coupe, sold through Lincoln-Mercury dealers who hold Merkur franchises, got off to a disappointing start in the U.S. market when it was introduced for 1985, though sales picked up somewhat for 1986. The rear-drive

Prices are accurate at time of printing; subject to manufacturer's change.

Merkur XR4Ti

Scorpio, Europe's 1986 "Car of the Year," is a 5-door hatch-back sedan that initially will have a 2.9-liter V-6 and anti-lock braking system in U.S. trim. We haven't driven the Scorpio and specifications and prices weren't available, so our comments here concern the XR4Ti. The XR4Ti is a sports coupe that offers good performance and plenty of room for adults. Its turbocharged 2.3-liter engine has plenty of spunk and performs quietly and smoothly with the manual transmission. You'll lose 40 horsepower and a whole lot of acceleration with automatic transmission. The suspension is soft enough for good bump absorption, yet firm enough to give the XR4Ti balanced handling and quick steering response. This is a good car that is finally catching on in the U.S. Now the bad news: The base price is up by $1500 over last year.

Specifications

	3-door coupe
Wheelbase, in.	102.7
Overall length, in.	178.4
Overall width, in.	68.0
Overall height, in.	53.8
Front track, in.	57.2
Rear track, in.	57.8
Curb weight, lbs.	2920
Cargo vol., cu. ft.	17.1
Fuel capacity, gal.	15.0
Seating capacity	5
Front headroom, in.	38.5
Front shoulder room, in.	53.9
Front legroom, max., in.	41.0
Rear headroom, in.	37.7

	3-door coupe
Rear shoulder room, in.	54.1
Rear legroom, min, in.	34.4

Body/Chassis

Drivetrain layout: longitudinal front engine/rear-wheel drive.
Front suspension: modified MacPherson struts, lower control arms, gas-filled shock absorbers, stabilizer bar. **Rear suspension:** independent; semi-trailing arms, coil springs, gas-filled shock absorbers. **Steering:** rack and pinion, power assisted, 3.6 turns lock-to-lock. **Turn diameter, ft.:** 35.4. **Front brakes:** 10.2-in. discs. **Rear brakes:** 10.0-in. drums. **Construction:** unit.

Powertrains

	ohc I-4T
Displacement, l/cu. in.	2.3/140
Compression ratio	8.0:1
Fuel delivery	PFI
Net bhp @ rpm	175 @ 5000[1]
Net torque @ rpm	200 @ 3000[1]
Availability	S

1. 145 bhp @ 4400 and 180 lb-ft @ 3600 with automatic transmission.

Final drive ratios
5-speed OD manual	3.64:1
3-speed automatic	3.36:1

KEY: bbl = barrel (carburetor); **bhp** = brake horsepower; **torque** = pounds/feet; **Cal.** = California only; **TBI** = throttle body (single-point) fuel injection; **PFI** = port (multi-point) fuel injection; **MFI** = mechanical fuel injection; **ohv** = overhead valve; **ohc** = overhead cam; **dohc** = double overhead cam; **I** = inline engine; **V** = V engine; **flat** = horizontally opposed engine; **D** = diesel; **T** = turbocharged; **OD** = overdrive transmission; **S** = standard; **O** = optional.

PRICES

MERKUR XR4Ti	Retail Price	Dealer Invoice	Low Price
3-door coupe	$17832	$15834	$16440
Destination charge	142	142	142

STANDARD EQUIPMENT (included in above prices):

2.3-liter (140-cid) PFI turbocharged 4-cylinder engine, 5-speed manual transmission, power steering, power brakes, rear defogger, bronze tinted glass, dual-note horn, cruise control, intermittent wipers, rear wiper/washer, halogen foglamps and headlamps, dual heated power mirrors, bodyside molding, metallic paint, flip-out rear quarter windows, air conditioning, folding rear center armrest, full cut-pile carpeting, electronic multi-function clock, console with cassette storage and armrest, cloth door panel trim, door map pockets, lighted lockable glovebox, Graphic Information Module (door ajar, low air temperature and bulb outage monitor), three passenger assist handles, side window demisters, tachometer, coolant temperature and turbo boost gauges, warning lights (oil pressure, oil level, low fuel, low coolant, low washer fluid, front brake pad wear), footwell courtesy lights with time delay, cargo area tiedowns and net, front seatback map pockets, lighted right visor mirror, rear package tray with storage box, AM/FM ST ET cassette, cloth seat trim, dual sport seats with stepless recliners, driver's seat height adjuster, asymmetrically split folding rear seatback, 195/60HR15 Pirelli P6 tires on aluminum wheels.

OPTIONAL EQUIPMENT:

3-speed automatic transmission	427	363	395
Heated front seats	183	155	168
Gray leather interior	890	752	820
Tilt/slide screened moonroof	549	466	505

Mitsubishi Cordia/Tredia

Mitsubishi Tredia LS

The front-drive Cordia coupe and Tredia sedan share drivetrains and chassis equipment and both are largely carryover models this year. An electronically-tuned stereo radio with cassette player is now standard, interior fabrics are new and the base Tredia sedan has been dropped, making the Tredia L the lowest-priced model. Power windows are a new option on Cordia. Engine choices remain a carbureted 2.0-liter four or turbocharged 1.8-liter four. A new feature on all 1987 Mitsubishi cars and trucks is a 3-year/ 36,000-mile warranty covering specific electronic components. Among the components are cruise control, alternator, and electronically controlled transmissions. With a

96.3-inch wheelbase and overall length of about 173 inches, the Cordia and Tredia are either large subcompacts or small compacts. Both models offer the usual Japanese virtues of good assembly quality and a lot of standard equipment for the money, though when you add in options they aren't bargains. The non-turbo 2.0-liter engine is more than adequate for these cars with manual shift and only adequate with automatic transmission. Mileage should be good with either transmission. The turbo 1.8 offers a lot more go power (nearly 30 more horsepower), but comes only with a 5-speed manual transmission.

Specifications

	Cordia 3-door coupe	Tredia 4-door sedan
Wheelbase, in.	96.3	96.3
Overall length, in.	173.0	172.4
Overall width, in.	65.4	65.4
Overall height, in.	49.4	51.6
Front track, in.	55.5	55.5
Rear track, in.	54.1	54.1
Curb weight, lbs.	2337	2370
Cargo vol., cu. ft.	NA	13.6
Fuel capacity, gal.	12.8	12.8
Seating capacity	4	4
Front headroom, in.	36.8	37.6
Front shoulder room, in.	52.8	52.8
Front legroom, max., in.	41.3	40.9
Rear headroom, in.	35.6	36.4
Rear shoulder room, in.	50.0	52.8
Rear legroom, min, in.	30.3	34.3

Body/Chassis

Drivetrain layout: transverse front engine/front-wheel drive. **Front suspension:** MacPherson struts, lower control arms, coil springs, stabilizer bar. **Rear suspension:** independent; trailing arms, coil springs, stabilizer bar. **Steering:** rack and pinion, 4.2 turns lock-to-lock manual; 2.9 power. **Turn diameter, ft.:** 32.2. **Front brakes:** 9.5-in. discs. **Rear brakes:** 8.0-in. drums. **Construction:** unit.

Powertrains

	ohc I-4	ohc I-4T
Displacement, l/cu. in.	2.0/122	1.8/110
Compression ratio	8.5:1	7.5:1
Fuel delivery	2 bbl.	TBI
Net bhp @ rpm	88 @ 5000	116 @ 5500

	ohc I-4	ohc I-4T
	108 @	129 @
Net torque @ rpm	3500	3000
Availability	S	S
Final drive ratios		
5-speed OD manual	3.19:1	3.47:1
3-speed automatic	3.19:1	

KEY: bbl = barrel (carburetor); **bhp** =brake horsepower; **torque** = pounds/feet; **Cal.** = California only; **TBI** = throttle body (single-point) fuel injection; **PFI** = port (multipoint) fuel injection; **MFI** = mechanical fuel injection; **ohv** = overhead valve; **ohc** = overhead cam; **dohc** = double overhead cam; **I** = inline engine; **V** = V engine; **flat** = horizontally opposed engine; **D** = diesel; **T** = turbocharged; **OD** = overdrive transmission; **S** = standard; **O** = optional.

PRICES

MITSUBISHI CORDIA	Retail Price	Dealer Invoice	Low Price
L 3-door coupe, 5-speed	$9759	$8319	$9260
L 3-door coupe, automatic	10189	8679	9790
Turbo 3-door coupe, 5-speed	11329	9597	10830
Destination charge	219	219	219

STANDARD EQUIPMENT (included in above prices):

L: 2.0-liter (122-cid) 4-cylinder 2 bbl. engine, 5-speed manual or 3-speed automatic transmission as above, power steering, power brakes, carpet, cigar lighter, coin holder, console, rear defogger, remote fuel filler and hatch releases, full instrumentation, warning light cluster, trip odometer, tinted glass with dark upper windshield band, halogen headlamps, door map pockets, dual remote manual mirrors, right visor mirror, bodyside moldings, mud guards, AM/FM stereo ET cassette, sport front seats with see-through headrests and driver's lumbar support adjuster, passenger seat walk-in feature, split fold-down rear seatback, front seat storage bin, variable intermittent wipers, P185/70R13 all season tires. **Turbo** adds: 1.8-liter (109-cid) turbocharged 4-cylinder engine, 5-speed, front air dam and rear spoiler, cruise control, H-rated tires.

OPTIONAL EQUIPMENT:

Air conditioning	698	572	665
Sunroof	278	222	265
Power front windows	142	113	135
Rear wiper/washer	112	89	106

MITSUBISHI TREDIA

L 4-door sedan, 5-speed	$9369	$8032	$8870
L 4-door sedan, automatic	9789	8389	9290
LS 4-door sedan, automatic	10379	8898	9880
Turbo 4-door sedan, 5-speed	10429	8887	9930
Destination charge	219	219	219

Prices are accurate at time of printing; subject to manufacturer's change.

STANDARD EQUIPMENT (included in above prices):

L: 2.0-liter (122-cid) 2 bbl. 4-cylinder engine, 5-speed manual or 3-speed automatic transmission as above, power steering, power brakes, full carpeting, quartz digital clock, rear defogger, side window demisters, remote fuel filler and decklid releases, reclining front cloth bucket seats, dual remote mirrors, bodyside moldings, driver's seat lumbar support adjuster, tilt steering column, tachometer, coolant temperature gauge, trip odometer, intermittent wipers, rear center armrest, passenger assist grips, front mud guards, tinted glass, carpeted lower door panels, passenger visor mirror, console with storage bin, P185/70R13 tires on styled steel wheels. **LS** adds: cruise control, power windows and door locks, power mirrors. **Turbo** adds to L: 1.8-liter (109-cid) TBI turbocharged engine, front air dam extension, performance suspension, turbo boost and oil pressure gauges, sport steering wheel, 195/60HR14 tires on alloy wheels.

OPTIONAL EQUIPMENT:

Air conditioning   698   572   665

Mitsubishi Galant

Mitsubishi Galant

Mitsubishi's front-drive luxury sedan is available with a 5-speed manual transmission for the first time. Previously, only a 4-speed overdrive automatic was offered on Galant, introduced for the 1985 model year. Other changes include making an electronic theft deterrent system and electrically heated outside mirrors standard and leather upholstery a new option. Mitsubishi says driveability and engine performance are improved this year through internal modifications. Specific electronic components are covered for 3 years/36,000 miles under a new provision added to Mitsubishi's warranty. Among the components are cruise control, alternator, automatic air conditioner, and

Prices are accurate at time of printing; subject to manufacturer's change.

electronically controlled automatic transmissions, power steering and suspension. We haven't driven the 1987 Galant, so we can't say whether this year's engine changes really have improved performance and driveability. We found last year's to be smooth and quiet, but not particularly potent with automatic transmission; performance should be at least a little better with this year's manual transmission. Our most recent Galant test car also was equipped with the optional ECS package, an expensive option group that adds 4-wheel disc brakes and larger tires (which we appreciate) and electronic suspension controls that change ride height and firmness. We found there was little absorbency in all the settings, and it was uncomfortably jiggly in the firmest, and it provided minimal apparent improvement in handling. Our conclusion: It was something we could easily live without. Among Galant's strong points are its impressive list of standard features and modest base price compared to rivals in the low end of the premium sedan class. It lacks the performance of the 6-cylinder Nissan Maxima or Toyota Cressida, but is priced well below those two and comes comparably equipped.

Specifications

	4-door sedan
Wheelbase, in.	102.4
Overall length, in.	183.1
Overall width, in.	66.7
Overall height, in.	51.6
Front track, in.	56.9
Rear track, in.	55.3
Curb weight, lbs.	2811
Cargo vol., cu. ft.	NA
Fuel capacity, gal.	15.9
Seating capacity	5
Front headroom, in.	38.3
Front shoulder room, in.	55.5
Front legroom, max., in.	40.3
Rear headroom, in.	37.1
Rear shoulder room, in.	55.0
Rear legroom, min, in.	36.5

Body/Chassis

Drivetrain layout: transverse front engine/front-wheel drive.
Front suspension: MacPherson struts, lower control arms, coil springs, stabilizer bar (electronic level control optional). **Rear suspension:** beam axle, trailing arms, coil springs, stabilizer bar

(electronic level control optional). **Steering:** rack and pinion, electronically power assisted, 2.3 turns lock-to-lock. **Turn diameter, ft.:** 34.8. **Front brakes:** 10.4-in. discs. **Rear brakes:** 8.0-in. drums. **Construction:** unit.

Powertrains	ohc I-4
Displacement, l/cu. in.	2.4/143
Compression ratio	8.5:1
Fuel delivery	PFI
Net bhp @ rpm	110 @ 4500
Net torque @ rpm	138 @ 3500
Availability	S
Final drive ratios	
5-speed OD manual	3.41:1
4-speed OD automatic	3.19:1

KEY: bbl = barrel (carburetor); **bhp** = brake horsepower; **torque** = pounds/feet; **Cal.** = California only; **TBI** = throttle body (single-point) fuel injection; **PFI** = port (multipoint) fuel injection; **MFI** = mechanical fuel injection; **ohv** = overhead valve; **ohc** = overhead cam; **dohc** = double overhead cam; **I** = inline engine; **V** = V engine; **flat** = horizontally opposed engine; **D** = diesel; **T** = turbocharged; **OD** = overdrive transmission; **S** = standard; **O** = optional.

PRICES

MITSUBISHI GALANT	Retail Price	Dealer Invoice	Low Price
4-door sedan, 5-speed	$13999	$11865	$13500
4-door sedan, automatic	14669	12343	14170
Destination charge	219	219	219

STANDARD EQUIPMENT (included in above prices):

2.4-liter (143-cid) PFI 4-cylinder engine, 5-speed manual or 4-speed automatic transmission as above, automatic temperature control air conditioning, power steering, power brakes, power windows, power door locks, cruise control, 6-way adjustable driver's seat, rear window defogger, multi-adjustable rear seat, AM/FM ST/ET cassette, power antenna, intermittent wipers, maintenance-free battery, tinted glass, bodyside moldings, velour upholstery, 185/70HR14 tires.

OPTIONAL EQUIPMENT:

ECS Pkg.	663	544	630
Electronically controlled suspension, 4-wheel disc brakes, 195/60HR15 tires.			
AM & FM ST ET w/cassette & EQ	336	235	320
Power sunroof	530	424	505
Leather seats	609	487	580

Prices are accurate at time of printing; subject to manufacturer's change.

Mitsubishi Mirage

Mitsubishi Mirage Turbo

A 4-door sedan that has been available for two years as
the Dodge/Plymouth Colt finally bows under Mitsubishi's
own nameplate in the U.S. Only a 3-door hatchback Mirage
was available before, with either a carbureted 1.5-liter
4-cylinder engine or turbocharged, fuel-injected 1.6 (which
gains three horsepower this year, to 105). The sedan will
be offered only with the 1.5-liter engine. Mirage (and the
Dodge/Plymouth Colt) also has new sheetmetal from the
windshield forward and aerodynamic halogen headlamps.
Mirage's 1.5-liter engine and front-drive chassis are also
used in the Korean-built Hyundai Excel. Hyundai buys
components from Mitsubishi or builds them under license
for the Excel. Mitsubishi will start buying Korean-built
cars from Hyundai early next year for sale under its own
name in the U.S. The Korean subcompact will be based
on the Excel, but will not be called Mirage and will be
priced as an entry-level model. Since Mirage is nearly
identical to the Dodge/Plymouth Colt, look for a Chrysler
version if there isn't a Mitsubishi dealer near you. Mirage
has the same virtues and vices as Colt, with high mileage,
low base bases and a 5-year/50,000-mile rust warranty
among the strong points. Mitsubishi's new 3-year/36,000-
mile coverage of electronic components includes the electronically controlled 3-speed automatic transmission available on Mirage. The base Mirage engine lacks the
smooth refinement and brisk performance of the Honda

Civic's 1.5, but has proven to be a fairly reliable 4-cylinder engine. If you're looking for reliable low-cost transportation, you should look at Mirage or the similar Colt.

Specifications

	3-door sedan	4-door sedan
Wheelbase, in.	93.7	93.7
Overall length, in.	157.3	169.1
Overall width, in.	63.8	64.4
Overall height, in.	53.5	53.5
Front track, in.	55.5	55.5
Rear track, in.	52.8	52.8
Curb weight, lbs.	2018	2095
Cargo vol., cu. ft.	NA	NA
Fuel capacity, gal.	11.9	11.9
Seating capacity	4	4
Front headroom, in.	37.7	36.7
Front shoulder room, in.	52.8	54.3
Front legroom, max., in.	40.6	40.6
Rear headroom, in.	36.7	37.0
Rear shoulder room, in.	52.8	54.3
Rear legroom, min, in.	30.7	30.7

Body/Chassis

Drivetrain layout: transverse front engine/front-wheel drive. **Front suspension:** MacPherson struts, lower control arms, coil springs, stabilizer bar. **Rear suspension:** independent; trailing arms, coil springs, stabilizer bar (except base model). **Steering:** rack and pinion, 4.2 turns lock-to-lock (3.7 Turbo). **Turn diameter, ft.:** 30.5. **Front brakes:** 9.5-in. discs. **Rear brakes:** 7.0-in. drums. **Construction:** unit.

Powertrains

	ohc I-4	ohc I-4T
Displacement, l/cu. in.	1.5/90	1.6/97
Compression ratio	9.4:1	7.6:1
Fuel delivery	2 bbl.	TBI
Net bhp @ rpm	68 @ 5500	105 @ 5500
Net torque @ rpm	85 @ 3500	122 @ 3500
Availability	S	S[1]

1. Turbo

Final drive ratios

4-speed manual	3.15:1	
5-speed OD manual	3.67:1	3.67:1
3-speed automatic	3.17:1	3.17:1

KEY: bbl = barrel (carburetor); **bhp** = brake horsepower; **torque** = pounds/feet; **Cal.** = California only; **TBI** = throttle body (single-point) fuel injection; **PFI** = port (multipoint) fuel injection; **MFI** = mechanical fuel injection; **ohv** = overhead valve; **ohc** = overhead cam; **dohc** = double overhead cam; **I** = inline engine; **V** = V engine; **flat** = horizontally opposed engine; **D** = diesel; **T** = turbocharged; **OD** = overdrive transmission; **S** = standard; **O** = optional.

PRICES

MITSUBISHI MIRAGE	Retail Price	Dealer Invoice	Low Price
3-door sedan, 4-speed	$6059	$5530	$5730
L 3-door sedan, 5-speed	7319	6354	6820
L 3-door sedan, automatic	7729	6714	7430
4-door sedan, 5-speed	7859	6821	7560
4-door sedan, automatic	8269	7181	7870
Turbo 3-door sedan, 5-speed	8479	7320	7980
Turbo 3-door sedan, automatic	9109	7861	8610
Destination charge	219	219	219

STANDARD EQUIPMENT (included in above prices):

1.5-liter (90-cid) 2bbl. 4-cylinder engine, 4-speed manual transmission, power brakes, halogen headlamps, front mud guards, locking fuel filler door, reclining lowback vinyl front bucket seats, walk-in passenger seat feature, fold-down rear seatback, assist grips, trip odometer, coolant temperature gauge, upshift indicator, console, flip-out rear quarter windows, needled carpeting, P145/80R13 tires on styled steel wheels. **L** adds: tinted glass, wide bodyside moldings, dual remote mirrors, cloth sport seats with map pockets, cargo area cover, cut-pile carpeting, carpeted lower door panels with map pockets, quartz analog clock, day/night mirror, rear defogger, full wheel covers, P155/80R13 tires. **4-door** adds: remote fuel filler and decklid releases, split fold-down rear seatback. **Turbo** adds: 1.6-liter (97-cid) TBI 4-cylinder engine, engine oil cooler (with automatic transmission), performance suspension, front air dam, side sill extensions, roof spoiler, tachometer, turbo boost gauge, intermittent wipers, turbo-style steering wheel, black hubcaps and trim rings, 185/60HR14 tires.

OPTIONAL EQUIPMENT:

Radio accommodation pkg., base	76	53	72
Air conditioning	677	555	645
Rear defogger, base	35	28	33
AM/FM ST cassette (NA base)	385	269	365
AM/FM ST (NA Turbo)	234	164	220
Power sunroof, Turbo	461	369	440
Cast alloy wheels, Turbo	265	212	250
Rear wiper/washer, L & Turbo	112	89	106

Prices are accurate at time of printing; subject to manufacturer's change.

Mitsubishi Starion

Mitsubishi Starion ESI-R

The rear-drive, turbocharged Starion comes with automatic front shoulder belts for 1987 to satisfy the federal requirement that 10 percent of each manufacturer's cars be equipped with passive restraint systems. The belts pivot around front-seat occupants when the doors are closed; lap belts still have to be buckled manually. Also new this year is a standard theft deterrent system that sounds an alarm, flashes the headlights and disables the starting system if the car is broken into, plus the outside mirrors are now electrically heated, and specific electronic components are covered by a 3-year/36,000-mile warranty. Among the components are cruise control, alternator, automatic air conditioner, and rear anti-lock brake system. Two versions of Starion are available: the 145-horsepower LE and the 176-horsepower ESI-R with an intercooler for the turbocharger, wider tires and special exterior trim. Starion has been sold as the Dodge/Plymouth Conquest in recent years, but for '87 it will be marketed as the Chrysler Conquest (same car, new name). We tested a 1986 ESI-R with the intercooled engine and anti-lock rear brakes and found it provided outstanding acceleration and passing response, fine braking, responsive handling and reassuring roadholding. There's not much head room in front and minimal space in any direction in the rear. Mitsubishi packs more standard equipment into the Starion than Chrysler does with the similar Conquest, so the base price is higher and the options list shorter. With either the base turbo 2.6 or the intercooled 2.6, you get fine performance; the ESI-R just has more of it.

Specifications

	3-door coupe
Wheelbase, in.	95.9
Overall length, in.	173.2
Overall width, in.	66.8
Overall height, in.	50.2
Front track, in.	55.5
Rear track, in.	55.1
Curb weight, lbs.	2988
Cargo vol., cu. ft.	19.0
Fuel capacity, gal.	19.8
Seating capacity	4
Front headroom, in.	36.6
Front shoulder room, in.	52.4
Front legroom, max., in.	40.8
Rear headroom, in.	35.4
Rear shoulder room, in.	51.2
Rear legroom, min, in.	29.1

Body/Chassis

Drivetrain layout: longitudinal front engine/rear-wheel drive. **Front suspension:** MacPherson struts, lower control arms, coil springs, stabilizer bar. **Rear suspension:** independent, MacPherson struts, lower control arms, coil springs, stabilizer bar. **Steering:** recirculating ball, power assisted, 3.0 turns lock-to-lock. **Turn diameter, ft.:** 31.5. **Front brakes:** 9.9-in. discs (10.8-in. on ESI-R). **Rear brakes:** 9.6-in. discs (10.4-in. on ESI-R). **Construction:** unit.

Powertrains	ohc I-4T	ohc I-4T
Displacement, l/cu. in.	2.6/156	2.6/156
Compression ratio	7.0:1	7.0:1
Fuel delivery	TBI[1]	TBI[1]
Net bhp @ rpm	145 @ 5000	176 @ 5000
Net torque @ rpm	185 @ 2500	223 @ 2500
Availability	S[2]	S[3]

1. Two injectors   2. LE   3. ESI-R

Final drive ratios

5-speed OD manual	3.55:1	3.55:1
4-speed OD automatic	3.55:1	

KEY: bbl = barrel (carburetor); **bhp** =brake horsepower; **torque** = pounds/feet; **Cal.** = California only; **TBI** = throttle body (single-point) fuel injection; **PFI** = port (multipoint) fuel injection; **MFI** = mechanical fuel injection; **ohv** = overhead valve; **ohc** = overhead cam; **dohc** = double overhead cam; **I** = inline engine; **V** = V engine; **flat** = horizontally opposed engine; **D** = diesel; **T** = turbocharged; **OD** = overdrive transmission; **S** = standard; **O** = optional.

PRICES

MITSUBISHI STARION	Retail Price	Dealer Invoice	Low Price
LE 3-door coupe, 5-speed	$15469	$12837	$14970
LE 3-door coupe, automatic	16039	13314	15540
ESI-R 3-door coupe, 5-speed	17989	14933	17490
Destination charge	219	219	219

STANDARD EQUIPMENT (included in above prices):

2.6-liter (156-cid) turbocharged 4-cylinder engine, 5-speed manual or 4-speed automatic transmission as above, power steering, 4-wheel disc brakes, leather-wrapped steering wheel, power windows, power antenna, detachable cargo cover, carpeting, quartz digital clock, cruise control, tilt steering column, rear defogger, remote fuel filler and hatch releases, full instrumentation, tinted glass, halogen headlamps and fog lamps, map pockets, intermittent wipers, rear wiper/washer, dual power mirrors, right visor mirror, split folding rear seatback, air conditioning, power door locks, AM/FM ST ET cassette with six speakers and graphic equalizer, P215/60HR15 SBR tires on alloy wheels. **ESI-R** adds: intercooled engine, limited-slip differential, rear brake lockup control system, side sill extensions and large fender flares, P205/55VR16 front and P225/50VR16 rear SBR performance tires; deletes right visor mirror and bodyside moldings.

OPTIONAL EQUIPMENT:

Sunroof	278	222	265
Leather seats	389	309	370

CHRYSLER CONQUEST

3-door coupe	$14417	$12110	$13260
Destination charge, 1986	200	200	200

STANDARD EQUIPMENT (included in above prices):

2.6-liter (156-cid) turbocharged 4-cylinder engine, 5-speed overdrive manual transmission, power brakes, power steering, power windows, cast aluminum wheels, steel-belted radial tires, front air dam, cargo area security panel, console, power mirrors, electric rear defroster, illuminated entry system, fog lamps, tachometer, turbo boost gauge, tinted glass, halogen headlamps, power liftgate release, AM/FM stereo radio w/cassette and power antenna,

Prices are accurate at time of printing; subject to manufacturer's change.

lowback reclining front bucket seats, 50/50 split folding rear seatbacks, adjustable steering column, intermittent windshield wipers, P195/70R14 tires.

OPTIONAL EQUIPMENT:

Intercooler Pkg.	2757	2288	2620
Intercooled engine, uprated transmission and clutch, Sure Grip rear axle, AM/FM stereo ET cassette with graphic EQ, leather steering wheel, illuminated vanity mirror, 16" wheels and tires.			
Technica pkg.	351	291	335
Electronic instrument cluster, voice alert system.			
4-speed automatic transmission	576	478	545
Air conditioning	843	700	800
Carpet protectors	26	22	25
AM/FM stereo ET cassette w/graphic EQ	360	299	340
Leather seats	414	343	395
Leather steering wheel	60	50	57
Removable glass sunroof	267	222	255

Nissan Maxima

Nissan Maxima GXE 4-door

A minor facelift gave the front-drive Maxima a new look front and rear for its release last spring an early 1987 model and the model lineup and standard equipment were revised at the same time. A new GXE series replaced the GL series and a 4-speed overdrive automatic transmission was made available on the sporty SE series, which previously had been available only with manual transmission. This fall, the only substantive change will be that motorized automatic front seat belts will become standard to satisfy the federal requirement that 10 percent of each

Prices are accurate at time of printing; subject to manufacturer's change.

manufacturer's cars be equipped with passive restraints. Rear seat shoulder belts became standard when the '87 models were released last spring. Nissan has expanded its warranty coverage on all models to include major powertrain components and electronic systems for 3 years/36,000 miles. Previously, the powertrain warranty was for 2 years/24,000 miles and electronic components were covered for 1 year/12,000 miles. Maxima, Nissan's luxury line, was redesigned to front-wheel drive for the 1985 model year, when it acquired a modified version of the 300ZX sports car's 3.0-liter V-6, a smooth, refined engine that gives it ample acceleration and brisk passing response. The interior is adequate for four adults rather than roomy, but otherwise, Maxima has earned high praise from our staff for its generous amount of standard equipment, good performance and polished road manners. Despite recent price increases, Maxima still is modestly priced against European rivals and the Toyota Cressida, and it stands as a fine value among luxury sedans.

Specifications

	4-door sedan	5-door wagon
Wheelbase, in.	100.4	100.4
Overall length, in.	181.5	184.8
Overall width, in.	66.5	66.5
Overall height, in.	55.1	55.1
Front track, in.	57.5	57.3
Rear track, in.	57.1	56.9
Curb weight, lbs.	3040	3280
Cargo vol., cu. ft.	14.5	NA
Fuel capacity, gal.	15.9	15.9
Seating capacity	5	5
Front headroom, in.	37.0	37.0
Front shoulder room, in.	53.5	53.5
Front legroom, max., in.	42.0	42.0
Rear headroom, in.	36.3	36.3
Rear shoulder room, in.	53.5	53.5
Rear legroom, min, in.	33.0	33.0

Body/Chassis

Drivetrain layout: transverse front engine/front-wheel drive. **Front suspension:** MacPherson struts, lower control arms, coil springs, stabilizer bar. **Rear suspension:** independent; MacPherson struts, parallel links, stabilizer bar. **Steering:** rack and pinion, power assisted, turns lock-to-lock NA. **Turn diameter, ft.:** 35.4. **Front brakes:** discs. **Rear brakes:** discs. **Construction:** unit.

Powertrains	ohc V-6
Displacement, l/cu. in.	3.0/181
Compression ratio	9.0:1
Fuel delivery	PFI
Net bhp @ rpm	152 @ 5200
Net torque @ rpm	167 @ 3600
Availability	S
Final drive ratios	
5-speed OD manual	3.43:1
4-speed OD automatic	3.43:1

KEY: bbl = barrel (carburetor); **bhp** = brake horsepower; **torque** = pounds/feet; **Cal.** = California only; **TBI** = throttle body (single-point) fuel injection; **PFI** = port (multi-point) fuel injection; **MFI** = mechanical fuel injection; **ohv** = overhead valve; **ohc** = overhead cam; **dohc** = double overhead cam; **I** = inline engine; **V** = V engine; **flat** = horizontally opposed engine; **D** = diesel; **T** = turbocharged; **OD** = overdrive transmission; **S** = standard; **O** = optional.

PRICES

NISSAN MAXIMA	Retail Price	Dealer Invoice	Low Price
GXE 4-door sedan, automatic	$16499	$14189	$16300
GXE 5-door wagon, automatic	17399	14963	17200
SE 4-door sedan, 5-speed	16499	14189	16300
SE 4-door sedan, automatic	17249	14819	17050
Destination charge	210	210	210

These models sell at or above retail in many locations.

STANDARD EQUIPMENT (included in above prices):

GXE: 3.0-liter (181-cid) PFI V-6 engine, 4-speed automatic transmission, air conditioning, cruise control, power windows, power door locks, power steering, power brakes, tilt steering column, keyless entry system, halogen headlamps, cornering lamps, bronze tinted glass, AM/FM cassette stereo w/7-band graphic equalizer and automatic volume control, split fold-down rear seat (sedans), sunroof (wagon), anti-theft alarm system, alloy wheels, P195/60HR15 tires. SE adds: 5-speed manual transmission, 3-way adjustable shock absorbers, power sliding glass sunroof, special blackout moldings and trim, rear deck spoiler, sport bucket seats, 4-spoke sport steering wheel, unique woven cloth trim.

OPTIONAL EQUIPMENT:

Power glass sunroof, GXE sedan	700	574	665
Leather trim, GXE sedan	700	574	665

Prices are accurate at time of printing; subject to manufacturer's change.

	Retail Price	Dealer Invoice	Low Price
Electronics Pkg., GXE sedan	700	574	665
Digital instruments, automatic temperature control, trip computer.			
Front air dam & fog lights, SE	255	175	240
Two-tone paint, GXE	250	205	240

Nissan Pulsar NX

Nissan Pulsar NX

Nissan's front-drive coupe has been redesigned for 1987 and it incorporates some unusual features that make it the automotive equivalent of "Transformer" toys. Pulsar is the first car to be conceived and developed at Nissan's California design studio. It's a 2-seater for practical purposes, but has a small vinyl rear bench seat for occasional use. A T-bar roof with removable steel panels is standard, allowing open air motoring. The only body style is a 3-door hatchback coupe, but the hatchback lid also is removable for carrying bulky cargo or just letting in more fresh air. If you don't like the hatchback styling, Nissan dealers will be able to sell you a fiberglass roof that transforms the Pulsar into a squareback coupe. Pulsar uses the same front-drive chassis as the Sentra, but has firmer suspension components and larger tires. Base engine is a 70-horsepower 1.6-liter four, now with single-point fuel injection instead of a 2-barrel carburetor. New this year is a 16-valve 1.6-liter engine with dual overhead cams and multi-point injection, rated at 113 horsepower. The 16-valve engine is standard in the Pulsar SE and comes only with a 5-speed manual transmission. The SE also has P195/60R14 tires and alloy wheels. Nissan's warranties now covers major powertrain components and specific electronic components for 3 years/36,000 miles. The new Pulsar has one of the most flexible body designs ever mounted on wheels. This is really a 2-seater since only small children will fit in the tiny rear seat, but otherwise it's a very practical car that has ample cargo room and a multiple personality. The 16-valve engine is a real character-builder for the Pulsar, changing it from a wheezer to a sprinter (Nissan claims 0-60 mph in under 10 seconds). With 43 more horsepower than the base engine, the 16-valve engine provides a major boost in performance. The old Pulsar was a pretty good seller for Nissan, appealing mainly to young women (65 percent of Pulsar buyers in 1986 were women, an unusually high percentage). Nissan expects more than half of this year's buyers to be men, with the 16-valve engine being one of the main attractions. With base prices of $10,599 for the XE and $11,799 for the 16-valve SE, the new Pulsar is well worth looking at.

Specifications

	3-door coupe
Wheelbase, in.	95.7
Overall length, in.	166.5
Overall width, in.	65.7
Overall height, in.	50.8
Front track, in.	56.7
Rear track, in.	56.7
Curb weight, lbs.	2315[1]
Cargo vol., cu. ft.	NA
Fuel capacity, gal.	13.2
Seating capacity	4
Front headroom, in.	38.0
Front shoulder room, in.	NA
Front legroom, max., in.	44.2
Rear headroom, in.	33.9
Rear shoulder room, in.	NA
Rear legroom, min., in.	31.1

1. 2425 lbs., SE.

Body/Chassis

Drivetrain layout: transverse front engine/front-wheel drive. **Front suspension:** MacPherson struts, lower control arms, coil springs, stabilizer bar. **Rear suspension:** independent; semi-trailing arms, coil springs, stabilizer bar. **Steering:** rack and pinion, 3.2 turns lock-to-lock. **Turn diameter, ft.:** 33.5. **Front brakes:** discs. **Rear brakes:** drums. **Construction:** unit.

Powertrains	ohc I-4	dohc I-4
Displacement, l/cu. in.	1.6/97	1.6/97
Compression ratio	9.4:1	Na
Fuel delivery	TBI	PFI
	70 @	113 @
Net bhp @ rpm	5000	6400
	94 @	99 @
Net torque @ rpm	2800	4800
Availability	S	S
Final drive ratios		
5-speed OD manual	4.47:1	4.47:1
3-speed automatic	3.60:1	

KEY: bbl = barrel (carburetor); **bhp** =brake horsepower; **torque** = pounds/feet; **Cal.** = California only; **TBI** = throttle body (single-point) fuel injection; **PFI** = port (multi-point) fuel injection; **MFI** = mechanical fuel injection; **ohv** = overhead valve; **ohc** = overhead cam; **dohc** = double overhead cam; **I** = inline engine; **V** = V engine; **flat** = horizontally opposed engine; **D** = diesel; **T** = turbocharged; **OD** = overdrive transmission; **S** = standard; **O** = optional.

PRICES

NISSAN PULSAR NX	Retail Price	Dealer Invoice	Low Price
XE 3-door coupe, 5-speed	$10599	—	—
XE 3-door coupe, automatic	11059	—	—
SE 3-door coupe, 5-speed	11799	—	—
Destination charge	210	210	210

Dealer invoice and low price not available at time of publication.

STANDARD EQUIPMENT (included in above prices):

XE: 1.6-liter (97-cid) TBI 4-cylinder engine, 5-speed manual or 3-speed automatic transmission as above, power steering, power brakes, T-bar roof, removable hatchback lid, dual power mirrors, tilt steering column, center console, reclining bucket seats, cloth upholstery, 185/70SR13 tires on steel wheels. **SE** adds: DOHC PFI 16-valve engine, ventilated front disc brakes, body-color front air dam and rocker panels, upgraded upholstery, 195/60R14 tires on alloy wheels.

Prices are accurate at time of printing; subject to manufacturer's change.

OPTIONAL EQUIPMENT:

Air conditioning	715	—	—
Vehicle Security System, SE	175	—	—
Fog lights, SE	145	—	—
Sport graphics	105	—	—

Nissan Sentra

Nissan Sentra GXE 4-door

Nissan's most popular model in the U.S. was redesigned last spring, coming out slightly longer and wider than the previous generation and 200-300 pounds heavier, depending on body style. The Sentra engine from the previous generation was carried over, except that a new version of the 1.6-liter 4-cylinder was introduced in the new sport coupe, using single-point fuel injection in place of the 2-barrel carburetor found on all other models. This fall, the only change is that a 4-wheel-drive station wagon is being added to the lineup. The 4WD system is a part-time system (intended for use only in slippery conditions) with shift-on-the-fly capability, meaning it can be engaged or disengaged on the move through an electronic switch. The 4WD wagon will use the fuel-injected engine and be available only with a 5-speed manual transmission. Nissan's warranties now cover major powertrain components and electronic systems for 3 years/36,000 miles. Previously, the powertrain was covered for 2 years/24,000 miles and electronic components for 1 year/12,000 miles. The new Sentras are quite a bit heavier than the previous models, but there hasn't been any real increase in engine power, so performance may have suffered a little. The new Sentras feel much more solid than the old versions, plus they're quieter because of more sound insulation. Performance is modest, but so are the prices. Sentra is worth looking at for low-cost transportation.

Specifications	2-door sedan	2-door coupe	3-door sedan	4-door sedan	5-door wagon
Wheelbase, in.	95.7	95.7	95.7	95.7	95.7
Overall length, in. . . .	168.7	166.5	162.4	168.7	172.2
Overall width, in.	64.6	65.6	64.6	64.6	64.6
Overall height, in. . . .	54.3	52.2	55.3	54.3	54.3
Front track, in.	56.3	56.5	56.3	56.3	56.3
Rear track, in.	56.3	56.5	56.3	56.3	56.3
Curb weight, lbs.	2200	2258	2238	2231	2304
Cargo vol., cu. ft.	NA	NA	NA	NA	NA
Fuel capacity, gal. . . .	13.2	13.2	13.2	13.2	13.2
Seating capacity	5	4	5	5	5
Front headroom, in. . .	NA	NA	NA	NA	NA
Front shoulder room, in.	NA	NA	NA	NA	NA
Front legroom, max., in.	NA	NA	NA	NA	NA
Rear headroom, in. . . .	NA	NA	NA	NA	NA
Rear shoulder room, in.	NA	NA	NA	NA	NA
Rear legroom, min, in. .	NA	NA	NA	NA	NA

Body/Chassis

Drivetrain layout: transverse front engine/front-wheel drive. **Front suspension:** MacPherson struts, lower control arms, coil springs, stabilizer bar (exc. Standard). **Rear suspension:** trailing links, coil springs, stabilizer bar (exc. Standard). **Steering:** rack and pinion, turns lock-to-lock NA. **Turn diameter, ft.:** 30.2. **Front brakes:** 9.5-in. discs. **Rear brakes:** 7.1-in. drums. **Construction:** unit.

Powertrains	ohc I-4	ohc I-4
Displacement, l/cu. in.	1.6/97	1.6/97
Compression ratio	9.4:1	9.4:1
Fuel delivery	2 bbl.	TBI
Net bhp @ rpm	70 @ 5000	70 @ 5000
Net torque @ rpm	92 @ 2800	94 @ 2800
Availability	S	S[1]

1. Sport Coupe

Final drive ratios	ohc I-4	ohc I-4
5-speed OD manual	3.90:1	4.17:1
3-speed automatic	3.60:1	3.60:1

KEY: bbl = barrel (carburetor); **bhp** =brake horsepower; **torque** = pounds/feet; **Cal.** = California only; **TBI** = throttle body (single-point) fuel injection; **PFI** = port (multi-point) fuel injection; **MFI** = mechanical fuel injection; **ohv** = overhead valve; **ohc** = overhead cam; **dohc** = double overhead cam; **I** = inline engine; **V** = V engine; **flat** = horizontally opposed engine; **D** = diesel; **T** = turbocharged; **OD** = overdrive transmission; **S** = standard; **O** = optional.

PRICES

NISSAN SENTRA	Retail Price	Dealer Invoice	Low Price
Standard 2-door sedan, 5-speed	$6199	$5579	$6000
E 2-door sedan, 5-speed	7499	6524	7300
E 2-door sedan, automatic	8529	7162	8330
XE 2-door sedan, 5-speed	8399	7265	8200
XE 2-door sedan, automatic	9209	7952	9010
E 3-door sedan, 5-speed	7349	6394	7150
E 3-door sedan, automatic	8109	7032	7910
XE 3-door sedan, 5-speed	8449	7308	8250
XE 3-door sedan, automatic	9259	7995	9060
E 4-door sedan, 5-speed	7899	6872	7700
E 4-door sedan, automatic	8659	7510	8460
XE 4-door sedan, 5-speed	8749	7568	8550
XE 4-door sedan, automatic	9559	8255	9360
GXE 4-door sedan, 5-speed	9699	8341	9500
GXE 4-door sedan, automatic	10159	8727	9960
XE 5-door wagon, 5-speed	9099	7871	8900
XE 5-door wagon, automatic	9909	8558	9710
GXE 5-door wagon, 5-speed	10049	8642	9850
GXE 5-door wagon, automatic	10509	9028	10310
XE 4WD 5-door wagon, 5-speed ...	9999	NA	NA
XE 3-door coupe, 5-speed	9399	8130	9200
XE 3-door coupe, automatic	10209	8817	10010
SE 3-door coupe, 5-speed	10399	8943	10200
SE 3-door coupe, automatic	10859	9329	10660
Destination charge	210	210	210

STANDARD EQUIPMENT (included in above prices):

Standard: 1.6-liter (97-cid) 2bbl. 4-cylinder engine, 5-speed manual transmission, power brakes, flip-out rear quarter windows, halogen headlamps, coolant temperature gauge, low brake fluid warning light, rear defogger, taillamp/brake light failure warning, headlamps-on reminder, side window demisters, lowback reclining front bucket seats, passenger seat walk-in

Prices are accurate at time of printing; subject to manufacturer's change.

feature, optical horn, center console, front and rear ashtrays, cigar lighter, full carpeting, 155R13 all-season SBR tires on styled steel wheels. **E** adds: power steering and tilt steering column (automatic models only), tinted glass, dual outside mirrors, black bodyside moldings, half-cover wheel caps, split fold-down rear seatback (3-door), trip odometer, soft door armrests, cargo cover (3-door), upgraded cargo area/trunk trim with carpeting, intermittent wipers. **XE** adds: TBI engine (coupe and 4WD wagon), dual remote mirrors, full wheel covers, cloth seats, tilt steering column, tachometer (coupe), remote decklid/hatch release, day/night mirror, large sunvisors, cargo cover (coupe), upgraded door armrests (coupe), cargo area/trunk light, lockable glovebox, AM/FM ST (automatic models only), passenger assist grips, upgraded door panels, cigar lighter illumination, upgraded cargo area/trunk trim, power steering, rear wiper/washer (3- and 5-doors), 4.167 final drive ratio (coupe), 175/70R13 all-season tires. **GXE** adds: body color bumpers, black wide bodyside moldings, upgraded cloth upholstery, AM/FM ST ET with diversity antenna, variable intermittent wipers, cut-pile carpeting, cloth-covered parcel shelf (sedan), driver's seat lumbar support, high-back rear bench seat (sedan), tachometer, soft-rim steering wheel, dual visor mirrors, large door armrests, large floor console with lid, digital clock, rear door lamp switches, low fuel and washer fluid warning lamps. **SE** adds to XE coupe: body color bumpers, pop-up sunroof, multiple driver's seat adjustments, cut-pile carpeting, dual visor mirrors, low fuel and washer fluid warning lights, digital clock, large console with lid, AM/FM ST ET with diversity antenna, variable intermittent wipers, 185/60R14 tires on alloy wheels.

OPTIONAL EQUIPMENT:

Air conditioning	715	586	680
Alloy wheels, XE 3- and 4-door sedans . .	370	303	350
Pop-up sunroof & alloy wheels, XE coupe .	770	643	730
Two-tone paint, XE coupe	250	205	240
Black bodyside moldings, Standard	45	30	43
Luggage rack, wagons	155	110	147

Nissan Stanza

Stanza, Nissan's family compact sedan, was redesigned and introduced last spring as an early 1987 model. The styling follows that of the Maxima luxury sedan and the front-drive platform and major suspension components are borrowed from the Maxima. Stanza uses the same 97-horsepower 2.0-liter 4-cylinder engine as it did before and it is again available in 4-door sedan and 5-door hatchback body styles. Wheelbase on the new Stanza is three inches

Nissan Stanza GXE 4-door

longer than before and overall length is 4.5 inches greater.
Curb weight is where the biggest difference shows; the
4-door sedan weighs 2770 pounds, 450 more than the previous generation. The Stanza line also includes a 5-door
station wagon with different styling and a different chassis. The wagon is available with front-wheel drive or part-
time 4-wheel drive with shift-on-the-fly engagement. The
wagon uses the same 2.0-liter engine as the sedans, but
rides a shorter wheelbase. All 1987 Nissans are covered
by expanded warranties that cover major powertrain components and electronic systems for 3 years/36,000 miles.
Previously, the powertrain warranty was for 2 years/
24,000 miles and electronic components were covered for
1 year/12,000 miles. The sedans and the wagon are much
different vehicles, but they share a common problem: too
little horsepower for their weight. The 2.0-liter 4-cylinder
engine standard in all models is pulling nearly 2800
pounds on the base 4-door sedan and nearly 3100 pounds
on the 4WD wagon, so it's working much harder than
before. The lack of power shows up when you need a quick
burst of speed for merging into expressway traffic or have
to climb a steep hill. However, all Stanzas offer good value
for the money because of their reasonable prices and
numerous standard features. What they need most is more
horsepower.

Specifications

	4-door sedan	5-door sedan	5-door wagon
Wheelbase, in.	100.4	100.4	99.0
Overall length, in.	177.8	176.2	170.3
Overall width, in.	66.5	66.5	65.6
Overall height, in.	54.9	54.9	64.2
Front track, in.	55.7	55.7	56.3
Rear track, in.	55.7	55.7	54.7
Curb weight, lbs.	2770	2845	2820[1]
Cargo vol., cu. ft.	12.0	22.0	80.0
Fuel capacity, gal.	16.1	16.1	15.9[2]
Seating capacity	5	5	5
Front headroom, in.	38.9	38.9	38.8
Front shoulder room, in.	NA	NA	55.5
Front legroom, max., in.	42.0	42.0	39.4
Rear headroom, in.	37.4	37.4	38.3
Rear shoulder room, in.	NA	NA	NA
Rear legroom, min., in.	33.0	33.0	34.0

1. 3080 lbs., 4WD wagon.   2. 13.2 gals., 4WD wagon

Body/Chassis

Drivetrain layout: transverse front engine/front-wheel drive.
Front suspension: MacPherson struts, lower control arms, coil
springs, stabilizer bar. **Rear suspension:** independent; MacPherson struts, coil springs, stabilizer bar. **Steering:** rack and pinion,
power assisted, turns lock-to-lock NA. **Turn diameter, ft.:** 32.8
(35.4 wagon). **Front brakes:** discs. **Rear brakes:** drums. **Construction:** unit.

Powertrains

	ohc I-4
Displacement, l/cu. in.	2.0/120
Compression ratio	8.5:1
Fuel delivery	PFI
Net bhp @ rpm	97 @ 5200
Net torque @ rpm	114 @ 2800
Availability	S

Final drive ratios

5-speed OD manual	4.17:1
4-speed OD automatic	4.13:1

KEY: bbl = barrel (carburetor); **bhp** =brake horsepower; **torque** = pounds/feet; **Cal.**
= California only; **TBI** = throttle body (single-point) fuel injection; **PFI** = port (multi-
point) fuel injection; **MFI** = mechanical fuel injection; **ohv** = overhead valve; **ohc** =

overhead cam; **dohc** = double overhead cam; **I** = inline engine; **V** = V engine; **flat** = horizontally opposed engine; **D** = diesel; **T** = turbocharged; **OD** = overdrive transmission; **S** = standard; **O** = optional.

PRICES

NISSAN STANZA	Retail Price	Dealer Invoice	Low Price
E 4-door sedan, 5-speed	$10499	$9082	$10300
E 4-door sedan, automatic	11149	9628	10949
GXE 4-door sedan, 5-speed	11899	10293	11700
GXE 4-door sedan, automatic	12549	10839	12350
XE 5-door sedan, 5-speed	11499	9947	11300
XE 5-door sedan, automatic	12149	10493	11950
2WD 5-door wagon	NA	—	—
4WD 5-door wagon	NA	—	—
Destination charge	210	210	210

STANDARD EQUIPMENT (included in above prices):

E: 2.0-liter (120-cid) PFI 4-cylinder engine, 5-speed manual or 4-speed automatic transmission as above, power steering, power brakes, tilt steering column, dual remote mirrors, intermittent wipers, tinted glass, halogen headlamps, dual trip odometers, coolant temperature gauge, analog clock, function warning system (taillamps/brake lights, headlights, door ajar, low fuel and washer fluid), rear defogger, side window demisters, reclining front bucket seats, remote fuel filler and trunk/hatch releases, center console, lockable glovebox, front storage bins, optical horn, right visor mirror, front and rear ashtrays, cigar lighter, needlepunch carpeting, 185/70R14 tires. **XE** adds: power mirrors, dark windshield band, sport front seats, special cloth seat trim, driver's seat height and lumbar support adjustments, tachometer, digital clock, map lights, rear door lamp switch, dual visor mirrors, cloth insert door panels, cut-pile carpet, cargo area cover (hatchback), split fold-down and reclining rear seat, AM/FM ST ET with diversity antenna, variable intermittent wipers, rear wiper/washer. **GXE** adds: upgraded upholstery, seatback pockets, illuminated entry system with fadeout, power windows with driver's door automatic down feature, oil pressure gauge, voltmeter, rear center armrest, trunk pass-through, carpeted rear shelf panel, needlepunch full trunk carpet, cassette deck, cruise control, power door locks, power antenna.

OPTIONAL EQUIPMENT (sedans):

Air conditioning	770	631	730
Power sunroof & alloy wheels, GXE	1100	902	1045
Vehicle security system & wheel locks	175	110	166

Prices are accurate at time of printing; subject to manufacturer's change.

Nissan Van

Nissan Van GXE

Nissan is the latest company to enter the compact van field and they have chosen a name that has a familiar ring to it. It's the Nissan Van, which isn't very original when you consider there's also a Toyota Van. The similarities don't stop there. Like Toyota's Van, Nissan's has rear-wheel drive, a 4-cylinder engine mounted behind the front axle and it holds seven people. Even Nissan's styling is similar to arch-rival Toyota's. Unlike Toyota, Nissan is not offering a 4-wheel-drive Van this year. Nissan is using its 2.4-liter 4-cylinder truck engine, rated at 106 horsepower, in the Van with a choice of 5-speed manual or 4-speed automatic transmissions. Nissan is aiming primarily at the passenger van market. The base XE model comes with front bucket seats, a 2-place middle bench seat and 3-place rear bench. The middle and rear benches can be removed, the 2-place seat can be turned around to face the rear and the 3-place seat can be installed in the middle position for 5-passenger seating. The GXE option package includes twin captain's chairs in the middle that can be rotated to face rearward. With the rear and middle seats removed, cargo capacity is 150 cubic feet and the cargo area is eight feet long, four and a half feet wide. Maximum payload is 1470 pounds. A sliding passenger-side door and split rear liftgate are standard. The split liftgate allows opening either the entire door or only the glass hatch for access to the cargo area. Standard equipment includes power steering, stereo radio and rear defroster. Options include dual sunroofs and air conditioning. We haven't driven the Nissan Van, so we cannot comment on its performance.

Specifications

	4-door van
Wheelbase, in.	92.5
Overall length, in.	178.0
Overall width, in.	66.5
Overall height, in.	72.4
Front track, in.	56.3
Rear track, in.	55.1
Curb weight, lbs.	3265
Cargo vol., cu. ft.	150.0
Fuel capacity, gal.	17.7
Seating capacity	7
Front headroom, in.	39.4
Front shoulder room, in.	57.1
Front legroom, max., in.	39.8
Rear headroom, in.	38.2
Rear shoulder room, in.	57.6
Rear legroom, min., in.	36.4

Body/Chassis

Drivetrain layout: longitudinal mid-engine/rear-wheel drive. **Front suspension:** upper and lower control arms, coil springs, stabilizer bar. **Rear suspension:** solid rear axle, five links, coil springs, stabilizer bar. **Steering:** recirculating ball, turns lock-to-lock NA. **Turn diameter, ft.:** 30.2. **Front brakes:** 10.2-in. discs. **Rear brakes:** 10.2-in. drums. **Construction:** unit.

Powertrains

	ohc I-4
Displacement, l/cu. in.	2.4/146
Compression ratio	8.3:1
Fuel delivery	TBI
Net bhp @ rpm	106 @ 4800
Net torque @ rpm	137 @ 2400
Availability	S
Final drive ratios	
5-speed OD manual	4.39:1
4-speed OD automatic	4.62:1

KEY: bbl = barrel (carburetor); **bhp** = brake horsepower; **torque** = pounds/feet; **Cal.** = California only; **TBI** = throttle body (single-point) fuel injection; **PFI** = port (multi-point) fuel injection; **MFI** = mechanical fuel injection; **ohv** = overhead valve; **ohc** = overhead cam; **dohc** = double overhead cam; **I** = inline engine; **V** = V engine; **flat** = horizontally opposed engine; **D** = diesel; **T** = turbocharged; **OD** = overdrive transmission; **S** = standard; **O** = optional.

PRICES

NISSAN VAN	Retail Price	Dealer Invoice	Low Price
XE 4-door van, 5-speed	$11999	—	—
XE 4-door van, automatic	12799	—	—
GXE 4-door van, automatic	13999	—	—
Destination charge	210	210	210

Dealer invoice and low price not available at time of publication.

STANDARD EQUIPMENT (included in above prices):

XE: 2.4-liter (142-cid) TBI 4-cylinder engine, 5-speed manual or 4-speed automatic transmission as above, power steering, power brakes, 7-passenger seating, front and rear heater ducts, tinted glass, AM/FM ST, halogen headlamps, loop-pile carpeting, tilt steering column, tachometer, rear defogger, intermittent wipers, power right-side mirror, P195/75R14 tires on steel wheels. **GXE** adds: rear wiper/washer, cruise control, power windows and door locks, dual power mirrors, second-row captain's chairs, cassette player, privacy glass.

OPTIONAL EQUIPMENT:

Dual air conditioning w/cooler-heater box	1450	—	—
Dual sunroof pkg., GXE	1250	—	—
Includes front pop-up glass and rear sliding steel sunroofs, cloth headliner, front map lights, P205/70R14 tires on alloy wheels.			
Two-tone paint	250	—	—
Bodyside graphics	120	—	—
Roof luggage rack	155	—	—

Nissan 200SX

Nissan's rear-drive sport coupe gets the 3.0-liter V-6 used in the 300ZX sports car for a big boost in engine displacement and horsepower. The 160-horsepower V-6, standard in the 200SX SE hatchback, replaces a 120-horsepower 1.8-liter turbocharged 4-cylinder as the performance engine in the lineup. A 102-horsepower 2.0-liter 4-cylinder engine remains standard in the XE 2-door notchback and 3-door hatchback. Both engines come with either a 5-speed manual transmission or 4-speed automatic. All models

Prices are accurate at time of printing; subject to manufacturer's change.

Nissan 200SX SE 3-door

have a new hood, bumpers, taillamps and body-colored spoilers front and rear. Interior trim also is new and instrument panel graphics have been revised. The SE's suspension has been modified with larger stabilizer bars and firmer springs and the V-6-powered hatchback rides on 205/60R15 tires mounted on 5-bolt alloy wheels. Warranties on 1987 Nissans have been expanded to cover major powertrain components for 3 years/36,000 miles. The V-6 develops ample torque across a broad range of engine speeds and works well with either the 5-speed manual or 4-speed automatic transmission, so the 200SX is now a threat to V-8-powered sport coupes. The 4-cylinder XE models offer much milder performance, but still have pretty good handling thanks to a moderately firm suspension and good-sized tires. Standard equipment is pretty extensive and the prices aren't at all out of line in this class. The rear-drive 200SX may not be the best choice for areas that get lots of snow, but it impresses us as an attractive rival to sporty coupes such as the Honda Prelude, Toyota Celica, Dodge Daytona, Mazda 626 GT and others.

Specifications	2-door coupe	3-door coupe
Wheelbase, in.	95.5	95.5
Overall length, in.	174.4	174.4
Overall width, in.	65.0	65.0
Overall height, in.	50.4	50.4
Front track, in.	54.7	54.7
Rear track, in.	56.1	56.1
Curb weight, lbs.	2645	2734[1]

	2-door coupe	3-door coupe
Cargo vol., cu. ft.	9.0	17.0
Fuel capacity, gal.	14.0	14.0
Seating capacity	4	4
Front headroom, in.	38.1	38.1
Front shoulder room, in.	NA	NA
Front legroom, max., in.	44.4	44.4
Rear headroom, in.	35.9	34.2
Rear shoulder room, in.	NA	NA
Rear legroom, min., in.	24.1	24.1

1. 2976 lbs., SE

Body/Chassis

Drivetrain layout: longitudinal front engine/rear-wheel drive. **Front suspension:** MacPherson struts, lower control arms, coil springs, stabilizer bar. **Rear suspension:** independent; semi-trailing arms, coil springs, stabilizer bar. **Steering:** rack and pinion, power assisted, 3.0 turns lock-to-lock. **Turn diameter, ft.:** 32.2. **Front brakes:** 9.8-in. discs (10.8-in., SE). **Rear brakes:** 10.2-in. discs (11.4-in., SE). **Construction:** unit.

Powertrains	ohc I-4	ohc V-6
Displacement, l/cu. in.	2.0/120	3.0/181
Compression ratio	8.5:1	9.0:1
Fuel delivery	PFI	PFI
Net bhp @ rpm	102 @ 5200	160 @ 5200
Net torque @ rpm	116 @ 3200	174 @ 4000
Availability	S	S
Final drive ratios		
5-speed OD manual	4.11:1	3.70:1
4-speed OD automatic	4.11:1	3.70:1

KEY: bbl = barrel (carburetor); **bhp** = brake horsepower; **torque** = pounds/feet; **Cal.** = California only; **TBI** = throttle body (single-point) fuel injection; **PFI** = port (multipoint) fuel injection; **MFI** = mechanical fuel injection; **ohv** = overhead valve; **ohc** = overhead cam; **dohc** = double overhead cam; **I** = inline engine; **V** = V engine; **flat** = horizontally opposed engine; **D** = diesel; **T** = turbocharged; **OD** = overdrive transmission; **S** = standard; **O** = optional.

PRICES

NISSAN 200SX	Retail Price	Dealer Invoice	Low Price
XE 2-door coupe, 5-speed	$10849	$9330	$10650
XE 2-door coupe, automatic	11499	9876	11300
XE 3-door coupe, 5-speed	11199	9631	11000

Prices are accurate at time of printing; subject to manufacturer's change.

CONSUMER GUIDE®

XE 3-door coupe, automatic	11849	10177	11650
SE 3-door coupe, 5-speed	14499	12469	14300
SE 3-door coupe, automatic	15149	13015	14950
Destination charge	210	210	210

STANDARD EQUIPMENT (included in above prices):

XE: 2.0-liter (120-cid) PFI 4-cylinder engine, 5-speed manual or 4-speed automatic transmission as above, power steering, power four-wheel disc brakes, dual outside mirrors, variable intermittent wipers, tinted glass, rear defogger, halogen headlamps, bodyside moldings, color-keyed rear spoiler (hatchback), cargo area/trunk light, glovebox light, lighted ignition switch, illuminated ashtray and cigar lighter, 125-mph speedometer, tachometer, coolant temperature, oil pressure and voltage gauges, low brake fluid warning light, low fuel, brake fluid and washer fluid warning lights, headlamp and brake light failure warning, side window demisters, adjustable driver's seat lumbar support, cloth reclining lowback front bucket seats, AM/FM ST ET, power antenna, memory tilt steering column, remote fuel filler and trunk/hatch releases, right visor mirror, needled velour carpeting, 195/60R15 all-season SBR tires on styled steel wheels. **SE** adds: 3.0-liter (181-cid) PFI V-6 engine, Vehicle Security System, cassette deck, body-color front spoiler and rocker panel extensions, power remote mirrors, dark-tint upper windshield band, upgraded upholstery, power windows and door locks, long door armrests, sport steering wheel, cut-pile carpet, front footwell lights, map/courtesy light fadeout, detachable cargo cover, 205/60R15 tires on 5-bolt alloy wheels.

OPTIONAL EQUIPMENT:

Air conditioning	770	631	730
Power Equipment Pkg., XE 2-door	2000	1720	1900
XE 3-door	1800	1548	1710
Power steel sunroof (2-door), pop-up glass sunroof (3-door), dark tint upper windshield band, dual power mirrors, multi-spoke alloy wheels, power windows & door locks, large door armrests, carpeted lower door panels, cassette deck, front footwell lights, map/courtesy light fadeout, detachable cargo cover (3-door), cruise control.			
Sport/Convenience Pkg., SE	516	600	490
Cruise control, pop-up glass sunroof.			
Two-tone paint, SE	250	205	240
Vehicle Security System & wheel locks,			
XE	175	110	166
Fog lights, SE	145	95	138

Nissan 300ZX

Nissan's sports car gets front and rear styling refinements, a firmer suspension and a new turbocharger this year.

Prices are accurate at time of printing; subject to manufacturer's change.

Nissan 300ZX Turbo

Frontal area has been reduced by integrating the hood, bumper and air dam and the auxiliary driving lights have been relocated under the bumper. At the rear, the taillight lenses now stretch across the width of the car. The 2-seat and 2+2 coupes have new wheels with a brushed alloy finish and the turbocharged 2-seater has new wheels with a charcoal finish. The front springs and suspension bushings are firmer on all 300ZX models, the front and rear stabilizer bars are larger and the power steering pump has been recalibrated for improved steering response. The rear disc brakes are now ventilated, same as in the front. Nissan says the new turbocharger has less friction for quicker response and smoother power delivery. Nissan's warranties now cover major powertrain and electronic components for 3 years/36,000 miles. Among the electronic components covered are adjustable shock absorbers (standard on Turbos), trip computer and theft deterrent system. The 300ZX has been criticized for being more of a "boulevard" sports car than rivals such as the Porsche 944, Corvette and Mazda RX-7 Turbo, all which stress performance over comfort and convenience. The Z-car is no wimp, however, since it boasts ample performance even with the normally aspirated engine. The 300ZX also is easier to live with and more comfortable than many competitors. This is a highly refined sports car that can be very enjoyable on a long trip for one or two people.

Specifications

	3-door coupe	3-door 2+2 coupe
Wheelbase, in.	91.3	99.2
Overall length, in.	170.7	178.5
Overall width, in.	67.9	67.9
Overall height, in.	49.7	49.7
Front track, in.	55.7	55.7
Rear track, in.	56.5	56.5
Curb weight, lbs.	3139	3265
Cargo vol., cu. ft.	14.7	20.3
Fuel capacity, gal.	19.0	19.0
Seating capacity	2	4
Front headroom, in.	36.6	37.2
Front shoulder room, in.	54.0	54.2
Front legroom, max., in.	43.6	43.6
Rear headroom, in.	—	34.3
Rear shoulder room, in.	—	NA
Rear legroom, min., in.	—	25.3

Body/Chassis

Drivetrain layout: longitudinal front engine/rear-wheel drive. **Front suspension:** MacPherson struts, lower control arms, coil springs (Turbo: adjustable shock absorbers). **Rear suspension:** independent; semi-trailing arms, coil springs (Turbo: adjustable shock absorbers). **Steering:** rack and pinion, power assisted, 2.8 turns lock-to-lock. **Turn diameter, ft.:** 32.2. **Front brakes:** 10.8-in. discs (11.2-in., Turbo). **Rear brakes:** 11.1-in. discs. **Construction:** unit.

Powertrains

	ohc V-6	ohc V-6T
Displacement, l/cu. in.	3.0/181	3.0/181
Compression ratio	9.0:1	7.8:1
Fuel delivery	PFI	PFI
Net bhp @ rpm	160 @ 5200	200 @ 5200
Net torque @ rpm	174 @ 4000	227 @ 3600
Availability	S	S[1]

1. Turbo only

Final drive ratios

5-speed OD manual	3.70:1	3.70:1
4-speed OD automatic	3.70:1	3.70:1

KEY: bbl = barrel (carburetor); **bhp** =brake horsepower; **torque** = pounds/feet; **Cal.** = California only; **TBI** = throttle body (single-point) fuel injection; **PFI** = port (multipoint) fuel injection; **MFI** = mechanical fuel injection; **ohv** = overhead valve; **ohc** =

overhead cam; **dohc** = double overhead cam; **I** = inline engine; **V** = V engine; **flat** = horizontally opposed engine; **D** = diesel; **T** = turbocharged; **OD** = overdrive transmission; **S** = standard; **O** = optional.

PRICES

NISSAN 300ZX	Retail Price	Dealer Invoice	Low Price
GS 3-door coupe	$18499	—	—
GS 2+2 3-door coupe	20649	—	—
GS 3-door coupe w/T-bar roof	19499	—	—
Turbo 3-door coupe	21399	—	—
Destination charge	210	210	210

Dealer invoice and low price not available at time of publication. These models sell at or above retail in many locations.

STANDARD EQUIPMENT (included in above prices):

GS: 3.0-liter (181-cid) PFI V-6 engine, 5-speed manual transmission, 4-wheel power disc brakes, power steering, air conditioning, AM/FM ST ET cassette, 8-way adjustable front seats, T-bar roof (except base), tilt steering column, anti-theft device, power windows, power door locks, cloth upholstery, tachometer, trip odometer, tinted glass, halogen headlamps, alloy wheels, P215/60R15 steel-belted radial tires. **Turbo** adds: turbocharged engine, adjustable shock absorbers, uprated brakes, black mirrors and trim moldings, Goodyear Eagle GT tires, headlight washers, front spoiler extensions, rear spoiler, turbo boost gauge.

OPTIONAL EQUIPMENT:

4-speed automatic transmission	650	—	—
Electronic Equipment Pkg.	1300	—	—

  Heated mirrors, premium stereo system with graphic EQ and steering-wheel-mounted controls, automatic temperature control, cruise control, eight-way power driver's seat, illuminated entry system.

Leather Trim Pkg., GS w/T-roof, Turbo	1000	—	—
GS 2+2	1150	—	—

  Leather seating surfaces, simulated leather door panel trim, cargo area cover, left visor mirror, bronze-tinted glass, seatbelt tension release.

Digital instrument pkg.	650	—	—

  Includes digital instrument display, trip computer, dual trip odometers and fuel gauges, Auto Check System. Not available on 2-seat GS without T-roof.

Oldsmobile Cutlass Supreme/Buick Regal

These rear-drive intermediates are due to disappear next year in favor of smaller, front-drive models. As a result,

Prices are accurate at time of printing; subject to manufacturer's change.

Oldsmobile Cutlass Supreme 4-door

the final Cutlass Supreme is a virtual '86 rerun. The only discernible change is adoption of aerodynamic composite headlamps, introduced on last year's top-line Salon coupe, for the base and Brougham coupe and sedan. Engine choices are untouched: standard 3.8-liter V-6 and optional 5.0-liter V-8, both still teamed with a 3-speed automatic transmission. The sporty 4-4-2 continues as an option package for the base coupe only. The similar Regal, offered only as a coupe, gets thicker, vertical grille bars as the only exterior change. Recalibrated electronics for the 3.8-liter turbocharged V-6 standard in the limited-production Grand National results in 10 more horsepower (now 245). The Regal T Type disappears as a separate model in favor of option groups that add up to the same thing. The rear-drive Cutlass Supreme and Regal have about as much interior and cargo room as the front-drive Cutlass Ciera and Century, and comparably equipped will probably cost a little less. The base 3.8-liter V-6 is adequate for these cars, but won't provide sterling performance or penny-pinching fuel economy. The V-8s and Regal's turbocharged V-6 improve performance at further expense in fuel economy. The rear-drive Supreme and Regal also have more trouble coping with snow and rain, where the added traction of front-wheel drive pays off in the Ciera and Century.

Specifications

	2-door coupe	4-door sedan
Wheelbase, in.	108.1	108.1
Overall length, in.	200.0	200.4

	2-door coupe	4-door sedan
Overall width, in.	71.6	71.9
Overall height, in.	54.9	55.9
Front track, in.	58.5	58.5
Rear track, in.	57.7	57.7
Curb weight, lbs.	3110	3167
Cargo vol., cu. ft.	15.2	15.2
Fuel capacity, gal.	18.1	18.1
Seating capacity	6	6
Front headroom, in.	38.1	38.7
Front shoulder room, in.	56.2	56.7
Front legroom, max., in.	42.8	42.8
Rear headroom, in.	38.3	37.8
Rear shoulder room, in.	56.1	57.1
Rear legroom, min., in.	36.3	37.0

Body/Chassis

Drivetrain layout: longitudinal front engine/rear-wheel drive. **Front suspension:** unequal-length upper and lower control arms, coil springs, stabilizer bar. **Rear suspension:** rigid axle, four links, control arms, coil springs (stabilizer bar optional). **Steering:** recirculating ball, power assisted, 3.6 turns lock-to-lock V-8s, 4.1 V-6s. **Turn diameter, ft.:** 38.2 coupes, 37.3 sedans. **Front brakes:** 10.5-in. discs. **Rear brakes:** 9.4-in. drums. **Construction:** body on frame.

Powertrains	ohv V-6	ohv V-8	ohv V-8
Displacement, l/cu. in.	3.8/231	5.0/307	5.0/307
Compression ratio	8.0:1	8.0:1	8.0:1
Fuel delivery	2 bbl.	4 bbl.	4 bbl.
Net bhp @ rpm	110 @ 3800	140 @ 3200	170 @ 4000
Net torque @ rpm	190 @ 1600	255 @ 2000	250 @ 2600
Availability	S	O	S[1]

1. 4-4-2

Final drive ratios

3-speed automatic	2.41:1	2.14:1
4-speed OD automatic		2.56:1

KEY: bbl = barrel (carburetor); **bhp** =brake horsepower; **torque** = pounds/feet; **Cal.** = California only; **TBI** = throttle body (single-point) fuel injection; **PFI** = port (multipoint) fuel injection; **MFI** = mechanical fuel injection; **ohv** = overhead valve; **ohc** = overhead cam; **dohc** = double overhead cam; **I** = inline engine; **V** = V engine; **flat** = horizontally opposed engine; **D** = diesel; **T** = turbocharged; **OD** = overdrive transmission; **S** = standard; **O** = optional.

PRICES

OLDSMOBILE CUTLASS SUPREME	Retail Price	Dealer Invoice	Low Price
2-door coupe	$11539	$9958	$10560
4-door sedan	11539	9958	10560
Brougham 2-door coupe	12378	10682	11325
Brougham 4-door sedan	12378	10682	11378
Salon 2-door coupe	12697	10958	11620
Destination charge	414	414	414

STANDARD EQUIPMENT (included in above prices):

3.8-liter (231-cid) 2 bbl. V-6 engine, 3-speed automatic transmission, AM radio, P195/75R14 steel-belted radial tires, full carpeting, day/night mirror, bench seat, power brakes, power steering. **Brougham** adds: custom sport bench seat, upgraded interior and exterior trim, custom sport steering wheel with padded rim, special wheels, ride and handling suspension, reclining front bucket seats, full instrumentation, console. **Salon** adds: special ratio power steering, uprated suspension, halogen high-beam headlamps, rallye instrument cluster, color-coordinated sport mirrors, contour reclining bucket seats, leather wrapped steering wheel, bodyside accent stripes, floor shift, 14 × 6-inch super stock wheels.

OPTIONAL EQUIPMENT:

5.0-liter (307-cid) V-8 4bbl.	590	501	545
4-speed automatic transmission	175	149	161
Air conditioning	775	659	715
Tinted glass	120	102	110
Power windows, 2-doors	210	179	193
4-doors	285	242	260
Contour front bucket seats, base 2-door	57	48	52
Power decklid release	50	43	46
Bodyside moldings	60	51	55
Padded vinyl roof, base 4-door & Salon	260	221	240
T-top roof, 2 doors	895	761	825
Intermittent wipers	55	47	51
Astroroof, base 2-door, Brougham	925	786	850
Landau roof, base 2-door, Brougham	260	221	240
Full vinyl roof, base 4-door, Salon	175	149	161
Rear defogger	145	123	133
Exterior opera lamps, base 4-door, Salon	77	65	71
Left remote & right manual mirrors	61	52	56
Console w/floorshift, base	110	94	101
Illuminated right visor mirror	58	49	53
Firm ride & handling pkg.			
Brougham 2-door	30	26	28
Others	49	42	45

Prices are accurate at time of printing; subject to manufacturer's change

	Retail Price	Dealer Invoice	Low Price
Limited slip differential	100	85	92
Engine block heater	18	15	16
Cruise control	175	149	161
Leather-wrapped steering wheel, base ...	90	77	83
Brougham 4-door	54	46	50
Tilt steering wheel	125	106	115
Aluminum wheels	199	169	183
Locking wire wheel covers	199	169	183
Convenience group, base	57	48	52
Brougham 2-door	42	36	39
Halogen headlamps	15	13	14
High-capacity battery	26	22	24
AM radio delete (credit)	(56)	(48)	(48)
AM/FM ST ET	207	176	190
AM/FM ST ET cassette	354	301	325
AM/FM ST ET w/cassette & EQ	504	428	465
Rally instruments	142	121	131
Exterior lamp monitors	77	65	71
California emissions system	99	84	91
High-capacity radiator	30	26	28
4-4-2 pkg., base 2-door	2577	2190	2370

High output 5.0-liter V-8, dual exhausts, air conditioning, sport exterior treatment, high-capacity cooling system, 3.73 axle ratio, 4-speed automatic, performance suspension, P215/65R15 tires on chrome-style wheels.

BUICK REGAL

2-door coupe	$11562	$9978	$10755
Limited 2-door coupe	12303	10617	11440
Destination charge	414	414	414

STANDARD EQUIPMENT (included in above prices):

3.8-liter (231-cid) 2bbl. V-6 engine, 3-speed automatic transmission, power steering, power brakes, bumper guards and rub strips, cut-pile carpeting, light group (ashtray, engine compartment, trunk, glovebox), lockable glovebox, dual outside mirrors, bodyside, wheel opening and rocker panel moldings, AM radio, notchback bench seat, cloth upholstery, deluxe wheel covers, P195/75R14 SBR tires. **Limited** adds: belt reveal and wide rocker panel moldings, 55/45 front seat, upgraded steering wheel.

OPTIONAL EQUIPMENT:

3.8-liter turbo engine (T pkg. req.)	1422	1209	1310
5.0-liter (307-cid) 4 bbl. V-8	590	502	545
4-speed automatic transmission (turbo or 5.0 req.)	175	149	161
Air conditioning	775	659	715

Prices are accurate at time of printing; subject to manufacturer's change.

Limited slip differential	100	85	92
Heavy-duty battery	26	22	24
Heavy-duty cooling, w/A/C	40	34	37
w/o A/C	70	60	64
Cruise control	175	149	161
Rear defogger	145	123	133
Power door locks	145	123	133
California emissions pkg.	99	84	91
Tinted glass	120	102	110
Tinted windshield	105	89	97
Engine block heater	18	15	17
Headlamps-on indicator	16	14	15
Trip odometer	16	14	15
Electronic instrumentation,	299	254	275
w/Grand National	173	147	159
Door courtesy & warning lights, Ltd	44	37	40
Coach lamps, Ltd	102	87	94
Front seat reading lamps	24	20	22
Tungsten halogen headlamps	25	21	23
Twilight Sentinel	57	48	52
Cornering lamps	57	48	52
Left remote & right manual mirrors	53	45	49
Dual remote mirrors	83	71	76
w/Grand National	30	26	28
Passenger visor mirror	7	6	6
Lighted	58	49	53
Bodyside moldings	60	51	55
Exterior molding pkg., base	110	94	101
Designer's accent paint	205	174	189
Solid special color paint	200	170	184
AM/FM stereo ET	168	143	155
w/cassette	232	197	215
w/cassette & graphic EQ	504	428	465
AM delete (credit)	(56)	(48)	(48)
Extended range speakers	25	21	23
Concert Sound speakers	95	81	87
Power antenna	70	60	64
Astroroof	925	786	850
Hatchroof	895	761	825
Power driver's seat	240	204	220
Passenger seatback recliner	75	64	69
Sport steering wheel	50	43	46
Tilt steering column	125	106	115
Heavy-duty suspension (F40)	27	23	25
Gran Touring suspension (F41)	49	42	45
Theft deterrent system	159	135	146
Landau vinyl top	200	170	184
Heavily padded	260	221	240

Prices are accurate at time of printing; subject to manufacturer's change.

	Retail Price	Dealer Invoice	Low Price
55/45 front seat, base	133	114	122
Bucket seats, base	195	166	179
45/45 leather and vinyl seat, Limited	377	320	345
Trunk trim	47	40	43
Power trunk release	50	43	46
Aluminum wheels	285	242	260
Locking wire wheel covers	199	169	183
Body colored wheels	85	72	78
Power windows	210	179	193
Intermittent wipers	55	47	51
T pkg.	508	432	465

Leather-wrapped steering wheel, uprated suspension, fast-ratio power steering, P215/65R15 tires on aluminum wheels.

	Retail Price	Dealer Invoice	Low Price
Grand National pkg., base	3574	3038	3290

T pkg. plus 3.8-liter turbo engine, 3.42 axle, full-length operating console, air conditioning, spoilers.

	Retail Price	Dealer Invoice	Low Price
Exterior sport pkg., base	100	85	92
Limited	30	25	28

Plymouth Caravelle/ Dodge 600

Plymouth Caravelle

Plymouth's mid-size, front-drive family sedan gains a stainless-steel exhaust system, electronic lockup torque converter for the 3-speed automatic transmission and new extra-cost electronic speed control system. The same changes have been applied to the similar Dodge 600, available only as a 4-door sedan for 1987 since last year's coupe and convertible have been dropped. Chrysler touts the stainless steel exhaust system as being more corrosion resistant than the aluminized steel it replaces. The lockup torque converter, which is supposed to improve fuel economy by eliminating slippage between the engine and transmission, comes only with the optional 2.5-liter 4-cylinder engine. A 2.2-liter four is standard and a turbocharged 2.2 also is available on both Caravelle and 600. These family sedans are built on the same front-drive platform as the Chrysler New Yorker luxury sedan, so you get as much interior room as the more expensive New Yorker. That means there's space for up to six people with the standard front bench seat. The standard 2.2 engine is adequate for the 2600-pound curb weight, but doesn't provide spirited passing power. The optional 2.5 engine has better performance and it's smoother and quieter than the 2.2 because of its balance shafts. If you want maximum performance, the turbocharged 2.2 delivers a much stronger punch, though it's also the noisiest of the three engines. A fully equipped Caravelle or 600 is priced well below Ford or GM's front-drive intermediates, and they come with Chrysler's 5-year/50,000-mile warranties, so there's pretty good value here.

Specifications

	4-door sedan
Wheelbase, in.	103.3
Overall length, in.	185.2
Overall width, in.	68.0
Overall height, in.	53.1
Front track, in.	57.6
Rear track, in.	57.2
Curb weight, lbs.	2589
Cargo vol., cu. ft.	17.1
Fuel capacity, gal.	14.0
Seating capacity	6
Front headroom, in.	38.6
Front shoulder room, in.	55.7
Front legroom, max., in.	42.2
Rear headroom, in.	37.4
Rear shoulder room, in.	56.1
Rear legroom, min., in.	36.7

Body/Chassis

Drivetrain layout: transverse front engine/front-wheel drive.
Front suspension: MacPherson struts, lower control arms, coil springs, stabilizer bar. **Rear suspension:** beam flex axle, trailing arms, coil springs, stabilizer bar. **Steering:** rack and pinion, power assisted, 3.2 turns lock-to-lock. **Turn diameter, ft.:** 35.6. **Front brakes:** 10.0-in. discs. **Rear brakes:** 8.9-in. drums. **Construction:** unit.

Powertrains	ohc I-4	ohc I-4	ohc I-4T
Displacement, l/cu. in.	2.2/135	2.5/153	2.2/135
Compression ratio	9.5:1	9.0:1	8.1:1
Fuel delivery	TBI	TBI	PFI
Net bhp @ rpm	97 @ 5200	100 @ 4800	146 @ 5200
Net torque @ rpm	122 @ 3200	133 @ 3800	170 @ 3600
Availability	S	O	O
Final drive ratios			
3-speed automatic	3.02:1	3.02:1	3.02:1

KEY: bbl = barrel (carburetor); **bhp** = brake horsepower; **torque** = pounds/feet; **Cal.** = California only; **TBI** = throttle body (single-point) fuel injection; **PFI** = port (multipoint) fuel injection; **MFI** = mechanical fuel injection; **ohv** = overhead valve; **ohc** = overhead cam; **dohc** = double overhead cam; **I** = inline engine; **V** = V engine; **flat** = horizontally opposed engine; **D** = diesel; **T** = turbocharged; **OD** = overdrive transmission; **S** = standard; **O** = optional.

PRICES

PLYMOUTH CARAVELLE	Retail Price	Dealer Invoice	Low Price
4-door sedan	$9813	$8588	$9155
SE 4-door sedan	10527	9206	9820
Destination charge	426	426	426

STANDARD EQUIPMENT (included in above prices):

2.2-liter (135-cid) TBI 4-cylinder engine, 3-speed automatic transmission, power steering, power brakes, passenger assist handles, bumper rub strips, full carpeting including trunk, cigar lighter, coat hooks, carpeted door panels, tethered fuel filler cap, remote fuel-filler release, tinted glass, halogen headlamps, door courtesy lights, ash receiver and glovebox lights, lockable glovebox, dual outside mirrors, AM ET radio with digital clock, cloth and vinyl bench seat with fold-down center armrest, trip odometer, coolant temperature and voltage gauges, headlamps-on chime, deluxe bright wheel covers, P185/70R14 SBR tires. **SE** adds: remote decklid release, left remote and right manual mirrors, AM & FM ST ET, reclining front seats with dual fold-down center armrests, luxury wheel covers, intermittent wipers.

Prices are accurate at time of printing; subject to manufacturer's change.

OPTIONAL EQUIPMENT:

2.5-liter (153-cid) TBI 4-cylinder engine	279	237	255
2.2-liter turbo engine	678	576	625
Pearl coat paint	40	34	37
Bodyside protective molding	60	51	55
Popular Equipment Discount Pkg., base	911	774	838
SE	978	831	900
Rear defogger, 500-amp battery, air conditioning, cruise control, tilt steering column, AM & FM ST ET, intermittent wipers, left remote and right manual mirrors.			
Rear defroster pkg.	192	163	177
Rear defogger, 500-amp battery.			
Protection pkg.	204	173	188
Deluxe Convenience Pkg.	304	258	280
Cruise control, tilt steering column.			
Light pkg.	134	113	123
Air conditioning	782	665	720
California emissions pkg.	99	84	91
Dual power mirrors, base w/o Popular Equip.	110	94	101
Base w/Popular Equip., SE	86	73	79
Lighted visor mirrors	116	99	107
Power Convenience Pkg.	432	367	395
Power windows and door locks.			
Power driver's seat	240	204	220
AM & FM ST ET cassette			
Base w/o Popular Equip.	434	369	400
Base w/Popular Equip., SE	289	246	265
Conventional spare tire	83	71	76
European handling suspension	57	48	52
Trunk dress-up	51	43	47
Locking wire wheel covers, base	272	231	250
SE	224	190	205

DODGE 600

4-door sedan	$10010	$8758	$9450
SE 4-door sedan	10672	9331	10075
Destination charge	426	426	426

STANDARD EQUIPMENT (included in above prices):

2.2-liter (135-cid) 4-cylinder TBI engine, 3-speed automatic transmission, power steering, power brakes, intermittent wipers, bumper rub strips, color-keyed carpeting (including door panels and trunk), headlamps-on chime, coat hooks, cloth bucket seats, remote fuel filler door release, console, halogen headlamps, message center, courtesy lights (including hood and trunk), left remote and right manual mirrors, bright exterior moldings, P185/70R14 tires. **SE sedan** adds: front folding armrests, assist handles, remote decklid release, 50/50 cloth and vinyl reclining front seats, cornering lamps.

Prices are accurate at time of printing; subject to manufacturer's change.

OPTIONAL EQUIPMENT:

2.5-liter (153-cid) TBI 4-cylinder engine . .	279	237	255
2.2-liter turbo engine	678	576	625
Pearl coat paint	40	34	37
Vinyl bodyside molding	60	51	55
Popular Equipment Discount Pkg., base . .	911	774	840
SE	978	831	900

Rear defogger, 500-amp battery, AM & FM ST ET, intermittent wipers, left remote and right manual mirrors; includes cruise control and tilt steering column on SE.

Rear defroster pkg. (incl. 500-amp battery) .	192	163	177
Protection pkg.	204	173	188
Deluxe Convenience Pkg.	304	258	280

Cruise control, tilt steering column. Base requires Popular Equipment Discount Pkg.

Light pkg.	134	114	123
Air conditioning	782	665	720
California emissions pkg.	99	84	91
Dual power mirrors, base w/o Popular Equip.	110	94	101
Base w/Popular Equip., SE	86	73	79
Lighted visor mirrors	116	99	107
Power Convenience Discount Pkg.	432	367	395
Power windows and door locks.			
Power seat (left or bench)	240	204	220
AM & FM ST ET cassette			
Base w/o Popular Equip.	434	369	400
Base w/Popular Equip., SE	289	246	265
Conventional spare tire	83	71	76
Sport handling suspension	57	48	52
Trunk dress-up	51	43	47
Locking wire wheel covers	272	231	250
Cast aluminum road wheels	370	315	340

Plymouth Horizon/Turismo

Like their Dodge Omni/Charger stablemates, the Horizon hatchback sedan and Turismo hatchback coupe arrived as early 1987 models in May when Chrysler launched its America program. That limits both models to a single series available with three option packages and only three individual options. A carbureted 2.2-liter 4-cylinder engine is standard in Horizon and Turismo; a 5-speed manual transmission is standard and a 3-speed automatic available as part of a package. Dodge offers the same lineup, plus the turbocharged Shelby Charger. Even with a price increase this fall, a Horizon with air conditioning, automa-

Prices are accurate at time of printing; subject to manufacturer's change.

Plymouth Horizon America

tic transmission, power steering and stereo radio still costs less than $8000 at suggested retail. The standard 2.2-liter engine gives it plenty of gusto and great gas mileage with manual transmission, and more than adequate power and decent mileage with automatic transmission. To top it off, the powertrain and rust warranties cover the car for 5 years/50,000 miles. Horizon debuted for 1978 as Chrysler's first front-drive car and Turismo followed a year later, so these aren't state-of-the-art subcompacts, particularly in interior room and ergonomics. The rear seat is cramped, the folding rear seatback isn't split and doesn't lay flat, the steering wheel is mounted low, and the pedals are too high and close for most drivers. Quality control on these cars hasn't been the best, despite all the experience Chrysler has had building them, particularly with the Turismo. With so many fewer parts now, perhaps workmanship will improve. Despite the flaws, these are the best small-car values on the market today.

Specifications	5-door sedan	3-door coupe
Wheelbase, in.	99.1	96.5
Overall length, in.	163.2	174.8
Overall width, in.	66.8	66.1
Overall height, in.	53.0	50.7
Front track, in.	56.1	56.1
Rear track, in.	55.7	55.7
Curb weight, lbs.	2237	2290
Cargo vol., cu. ft.	36.6	34.3

	5-door sedan	3-door coupe
Fuel capacity, gal.	13.0	13.0
Seating capacity	5	5
Front headroom, in.	38.1	37.2
Front shoulder room, in.	51.7	52.2
Front legroom, max., in.	42.1	42.5
Rear headroom, in.	36.9	34.4
Rear shoulder room, in.	51.5	50.9
Rear legroom, min., in.	33.3	28.7

Body/Chassis

Drivetrain layout: transverse front engine/front-wheel drive. **Front suspension:** MacPherson struts, lower control arms, coil springs, stabilizer bar. **Rear suspension:** semi-independent, beam axle, trailing arms, coil springs (stabilizer bar optional). **Steering:** rack and pinion, 3.6 turns lock-to-lock. **Turn diameter, ft.:** 38.1 Turismo; 39.0 Horizon. **Front brakes:** 9.0-in. discs. **Rear brakes:** 7.9-in drums. **Construction:** unit.

Powertrains

	ohc I-4
Displacement, l/cu. in.	2.2/135
Compression ratio	9.0:1
Fuel delivery	2 bbl.
Net bhp @ rpm	96 @ 5200
Net torque @ rpm	119 @ 3200
Availability	S

Final drive ratios

5-speed OD manual	2.20:1
3-speed automatic	2.78:1

KEY: bbl = barrel (carburetor); **bhp** = brake horsepower; **torque** = pounds/feet; **Cal.** = California only; **TBI** = throttle body (single-point) fuel injection; **PFI** = port (multi-point) fuel injection; **MFI** = mechanical fuel injection; **ohv** = overhead valve; **ohc** = overhead cam; **dohc** = double overhead cam; **I** = inline engine; **V** = V engine; **flat** = horizontally opposed engine; **D** = diesel; **T** = turbocharged; **OD** = overdrive transmission; **S** = standard; **O** = optional.

PRICES

PLYMOUTH HORIZON AND TURISMO		Retail Price	Dealer Invoice	Low Price
Horizon America 5-door sedan		$5799	$5277	$5700
Turismo 3-door coupe		7199	6554	7000
Destination charge, Horizon		320	320	320
Turismo	386	386	386	

Prices are accurate at time of printing; subject to manufacturer's change.

STANDARD EQUIPMENT (included in above prices):

2.2-liter (135-cid) 4-cylinder 2 bbl. engine, 5-speed manual transmission, power brakes, rear defogger, rear wiper/washer, rallye instrument cluster (trip odometer, tachometer, coolant temperature, oil pressure and voltage gauges), tinted glass, luggage compartment light, black bodyside moldings, left remote mirror, right visor mirror, folding shelf panel, intermittent wipers, urethane lower body protection, tethered fuel filler cap, cloth and vinyl upholstery, lockable glovebox, remote liftgate release (Turismo), P165/80R13 tires on styled steel wheels.

OPTIONAL EQUIPMENT:

Basic Pkg. (auto trans & power steering) .	776	660	715
Manual Transmission Discount Pkg.	575	489	530
Power steering, AM & FM ST ET, highback front bucket seats, upgraded cargo area trim, center console with coin holder, cubby box, cupholder, ash receiver light.			
Automatic Transmission Discount Pkg. . . .	1009	858	930
Manual Transmission Discount Pkg. plus 3-speed automatic transmission.			
Air conditioning (Discount Pkg. req.)	701	596	645
California emissions pkg.	99	84	91
AM & FM stereo ET cassette (discount pkg. req.)	246	209	225

Pontiac Bonneville

Pontiac Bonneville

The Bonneville name returns for 1987, but this time on a new front-wheel drive, full-size sedan. Sharing its H-body platform with the Buick LeSabre and Oldsmobile Delta 88, introduced for 1986, Bonneville is aimed at the upscale sporty market and comes only as a 4-door (Buick and Olds offer 2-door coupes). Last year's rear-drive, mid-size Bonneville has been dropped, but the same G-body platform carries on as the Grand Prix. A 4-speed overdrive automatic transmission is teamed with the 3.8-liter V-6 as the only drivetrain available. New front and rear sheetmetal gives Bonneville more of a wedge look than LeSabre or Delta 88. Pontiac offers a base model and a luxury LE, plus a sporty SE option package for the LE. To comply with federal requirements that 10 percent of 1987 cars have passive restraints, GM's automatic front seat belt system will become standard in Bonneville sometime after production starts. For what is still basically a family car, the '87 Bonneville is quite competent, especially the SE. With its firmer suspension, the SE leans less and steers more positively than the base car or LE, but the ride is harsher. The Buick 3.8-liter V-6 furnishes brisk acceleration and relaxed cruising. Overall, the smaller, lighter Bonneville shows just how far American family cars have come in a relatively short time. Though it's not that much different than its H-body siblings, Bonneville has a more focused marketing direction and it is a roomy, competent alternative to premium-priced imports for those who don't relate to traditional Detroit family cars.

Specifications

	4-door sedan
Wheelbase, in.	110.8
Overall length, in.	198.7
Overall width, in.	72.1
Overall height, in.	55.5
Front track, in.	NA
Rear track, in.	NA
Curb weight, lbs.	3316
Cargo vol., cu. ft.	15.5
Fuel capacity, gal.	18.0
Seating capacity	6
Front headroom, in.	38.9
Front shoulder room, in.	NA
Front legroom, max., in.	42.4
Rear headroom, in.	38.2
Rear shoulder room, in.	NA
Rear legroom, min., in.	38.4

Body/Chassis

Drivetrain layout: transverse front engine/front-wheel drive. **Front suspension:** MacPherson struts, lower control arms, coil springs. **Rear suspension:** MacPherson struts, lower control arms, coil springs. **Steering:** rack and pinion, power assisted, turns lock-to-lock NA. **Turn diameter, ft.:** NA. **Front brakes:** 10.0-in. discs. **Rear brakes:** 8.9-in. drums. **Construction:** unit.

Powertrains	ohv V-6
Displacement, l/cu. in.	3.8/231
Compression ratio	8.5:1
Fuel delivery	PFI
Net bhp @ rpm	150 @ 4400
Net torque @ rpm	200 @ 2000
Availability	S

Final drive ratios

4-speed OD automatic	2.73:1[1]

1. 2.97:1 on SE

KEY: bbl = barrel (carburetor); **bhp** = brake horsepower; **torque** = pounds/feet; **Cal.** = California only; **TBI** = throttle body (single-point) fuel injection; **PFI** = port (multi-point) fuel injection; **MFI** = mechanical fuel injection; **ohv** = overhead valve; **ohc** = overhead cam; **dohc** = double overhead cam; **I** = inline engine; **V** = V engine; **flat** = horizontally opposed engine; **D** = diesel; **T** = turbocharged; **OD** = overdrive transmission; **S** = standard; **O** = optional.

PRICES

PONTIAC BONNEVILLE	Retail Price	Dealer Invoice	Low Price
4-door sedan	$13399	$11563	$12325
LE 4-door sedan	14866	12829	13674
Destination charge	475	475	475

STANDARD EQUIPMENT (included in above prices):

3.8-liter (231-cid) PFI V-6 engine, 4-speed automatic transmission, power steering, power brakes, bodyside moldings, cloth door panels with carpeted lower section and map pockets, cloth bench seats, P205/75R14 SBR tires. **LE** adds: power windows, 45/45 split front seat with recliners and upgraded upholstery, front and rear fold-down center armrests, wide bodyside molding.

OPTIONAL EQUIPMENT:

Option Group 1, base	475	388	435
AM/FM ST ET, tilt steering column, intermittent wipers, wide bodyside moldings, left remote and right manual mirrors.			
Option Group 2, base	686	711	630
Group 1 plus power door locks, cruise control, lamp group.			
Option Group 3, base	1389	1181	1280
Group 2 plus power windows, courtesy lamps, power seat, right visor mirror.			
Option Group 1, LE	790	672	725
Power door locks, AM/FM ST ET, cruise control, tilt steering column, lamp group, intermittent wipers, right visor mirror.			

Prices are accurate at time of printing; subject to manufacturer's change.

	Retail Price	Dealer Invoice	Low Price
Option Group 2, LE	1066	906	980
Group 1 plus power driver's seat, cornering lamps, lighted right visor mirror, remote decklid release.			
Option Group 3, LE	1593	1354	1465
Power passenger seat, dual remote mirrors, illuminated entry system, Twilight Sentinel, leather-wrapped steering wheel, remote fuel door release, rear courtesy lamps.			
Option Group 1, SE	580	493	535
Power door locks, AM/FM ST ET, cruise control, lamp group, right visor mirror.			
Option Group 2, SE	856	728	790
Group 1 plus power driver's seat, cornering lamps, lighted right visor mirror, remote decklid release.			
Option Group 3, SE	1333	1133	1226
Group 2 plus power passenger seat, power remote mirrors, illuminated entry system, Twilight Sentinel, remote fuel filler release, rear courtesy lamps.			
Performance Value Pkg. 1, base & LE . . .	215	183	198
Aluminum wheels w/locks, rally gauges.			
Performance Value Pkg., base & LE	356	303	330
Pkg. 1 plus P215/65R15 tires.			
SE Pkg., LE	940	799	865
P215/65R15 tires on aluminum wheels, 2.97 axle ratio, tilt steering column, intermittent wipers, leather-wrapped steering wheel, courtesy and dual reading lamps, Driver Information Center, 45/45 front seat, console, Y99 sport suspension, sport exterior trim.			
Heavy-duty battery & cooling system . . .	66	54	61
Rear defogger	145	123	133
Driver Information Center, LE	125	106	115
Electronic Ride Control	170	145	156
California emissions pkg.	99	84	91
Rally instrument cluster	100	85	92
Decklid luggage carrier	115	98	106
Automatic tilt rearview mirror	80	68	74
Two-tone paint	105	89	97
AM/FM ST ET	178	151	165
AM/FM ST ET cassette	300	255	275
AM/FM ST ET w/cassette & EQ	450	383	415
Above w/Touch Control, base & LE . . .	735	625	675
SE	685	582	630
Bose music system, base & LE	1298	1103	1195
SE	1248	1061	1150
Delete AM radio (credit)	(95)	(81)	(81)
Power antenna	70	60	64
Reclining pass. seat, base (45/45 req.) . .	70	60	64
Dual reclining seats, base (45/45 req.) . . .	140	119	129
45/45 notchback seat, base	133	109	122
w/Leather/Majestic cloth trim, LE	379	322	350
45/45 seat, LE (console req.)	110	94	101
w/Leather/Majestic cloth trim, LE	489	416	450
SE	379	322	350
Power glass sunroof, LE w/o Lamp Group .	1284	1091	1180
LE w/Lamp Group, SE	1254	1066	1155
Y99 sport suspension, base & LE	50	43	46

Prices are accurate at time of printing; subject to manufacturer's change.

Pontiac Fiero

Pontiac Fiero GT

The mid-engine, 2-seat Fiero gets a handful of significant changes for 1987, including revised front and rear fascias for the base Fiero and Sport Coupe, larger fuel tanks across the board and a new 5-speed manual transmission for the V-6 engine. In the base Fiero and Sport Coupe, the standard 2.5-liter 4-cylinder engine has been revamped for six more horsepower and gains GM's multi-coil ignition system. Fuel tank capacity has grown to 12 gallons from 10.2 on all models. The sportier SE model also comes with the 4-cylinder engine and 5-speed manual standard, but offers a multi-point injected 2.8-liter V-6 as an option. With the V-6 comes the new Getrag-designed, GM-produced 5-speed manual transmission shared by GM's other divisions. The performance Fiero, the GT, was revised for a 1986½ introduction with its distinct swept-back pillars and the V-6 engine. The V-6 is the only way to go as far as we're concerned since the base 4-cylinder engine offers only passable performance with the 5-speed and lackluster performance with automatic. The Getrag-designed 5-speed gives the V-6 the extra gear it's sorely needed. The firmer suspension and larger tires on the SE and GT give the Fiero flat cornering and better handling, but the ride is so stiff that a run down a bumpy road crossed by railroad tracks can be punishing. Interior space is tight and cargo space is a joke. Many of Fiero's problems stem from an original decree that this would be a low-cost commuter car; now the emphasis is on performance. A Honda Civic CRX is cheaper and more fun, and the Toyota MR2 is a slicker performance-oriented 2-seater.

Specifications

	2-door coupe
Wheelbase, in.	93.4
Overall length, in.	162.7[1]
Overall width, in.	69.0
Overall height, in.	46.9
Front track, in.	57.8
Rear track, in.	58.7
Curb weight, lbs.	2546
Cargo vol., cu. ft.	5.9
Fuel capacity, gal.	11.9
Seating capacity	2
Front headroom, in.	37.0
Front shoulder room, in.	54.9
Front legroom, max., in.	43.5
Rear headroom, in.	—
Rear shoulder room, in.	—
Rear legroom, min., in.	—

1. 165.1 on GT

Body/Chassis

Drivetrain layout: transverse mid-engine/rear-wheel drive. **Front suspension:** unequal-length upper and lower control arms, coil springs, stabilizer bar. **Rear suspension:** MacPherson struts, lower control arms, coil springs. **Steering:** rack and pinion, 2.9 turns lock-to-lock. **Turn diameter, ft.:** 39.0. **Front brakes:** 11.0-in. discs. **Rear brakes:** 12.6-in. discs. **Construction:** unit.

Powertrains

	ohv I-4	ohv V-6
Displacement, l/cu. in.	2.5/151	2.8/173
Compression ratio	9.0:1	8.5:1
Fuel delivery	TBI	PFI
Net bhp @ rpm	98 @ 4800	135 @ 4400
Net torque @ rpm	135 @ 3200	165 @ 3600
Availability	S	S[1]

1. GT; opt. SE

Final drive ratios

5-speed OD manual	3.35:1	3.61:1
3-speed automatic	2.84:1	3.33:1

KEY: bbl = barrel (carburetor); **bhp** = brake horsepower; **torque** = pounds/feet; **Cal.** = California only; **TBI** = throttle body (single-point) fuel injection; **PFI** = port (multi-point) fuel injection; **MFI** = mechanical fuel injection; **ohv** = overhead valve; **ohc** = overhead cam; **dohc** = double overhead cam; **I** = inline engine; **V** = V engine; **flat** = horizontally opposed engine; **D** = diesel; **T** = turbocharged; **OD** = overdrive transmission; **S** = standard; **O** = optional.

PRICES

PONTIAC FIERO	Retail Price	Dealer Invoice	Low Price
2-door coupe	$8299	$7826	$8000
2-door Sport Coupe	9989	8920	9340
SE 2-door coupe	11239	10036	10565
GT 2-door coupe	13489	12046	12680
Destination charge	320	320	320

STANDARD EQUIPMENT (included in above prices):

2.5-liter (151-cid) TBI 4-cylinder engine, 4-speed manual transmission, power 4-wheel disc brakes, carpeting, center console, tachometer, coolant temperature gauge and voltmeter, locking fuel filler door with remote release, halogen headlamps, left remote and right manual mirrors, black bodyside moldings, day/night mirror, reclining bucket seats, side window defoggers, 13-inch rally wheels, P185/75R14 tires. **Sport Coupe** adds: close-ratio 4-speed manual transmission, performance axle ratio, custom quarter window treatment, deluxe luggage compartment trim, AM radio. **SE** adds: custom reclining seats, 14-inch aluminum wheels, P195/70R14 steel-belted radial tires, Y99 sport suspension, AM radio with integral clock, tinted glass, formula steering wheel, rear deck luggage rack, remote control decklid release. **GT:** adds: 2.8-liter (173-cid) PFI V-6 engine, 5-speed manual transmission, WS6 performance suspension, sport seats, P205/60R15 front and P215/60R15 rear Goodyear Eagle GT tires on aluminum wheels.

OPTIONAL EQUIPMENT:

Option Group 1, base	1317	1119	1210
Sport Coupe	1217	1034	1120
SE	1127	958	1035
Air conditioning, AM/FM ST ET, tilt steering column, tinted glass, intermittent wipers, lamp group on SE.			
Option Group 2, Sport Coupe	1581	1344	1455
SE	1613	1371	1485
Group 1 plus power windows, cruise control and lamp group; SE adds power door locks and right visor mirror.			
Option Group 1, GT	1181	1004	1085
Air conditioning, cruise control, power door locks, dual power mirrors, right visor mirror.			
Performance Value Pkg., Sport Coupe	259	220	240
P195/70R14 tires on aluminum wheels w/locks, Y99 suspension.			
2.8-liter V-6, SE	695	591	640
3-speed automatic transmission	490	417	450
Air conditioning	775	659	715
Heavy-duty battery (V-6 req.)	26	22	24
V-6 heavy-duty cooling, w/o A/C	70	60	64
w/A/C	40	34	37
Rear defogger	145	123	133

Prices are accurate at time of printing; subject to manufacturer's change.

	Retail Price	Dealer Invoice	Low Price
California emissions pkg.	99	84	91
Tinted glass (A/C req.), base & Sport Coupe .	120	102	110
Decklid luggage carrier (NA base)	115	98	106
AM radio, base	122	104	112
AM/FM ST ET, base	317	269	290
Sport Coupe & SE	217	184	200
AM/FM ST ET cassette, base	439	373	405
Sport Coupe & SE	339	288	310
Above w/EQ, Sport Coupe & SE	489	416	450
GT	160	136	145
Above w/Touch Control, Sport Coupe & SE .	529	450	485
GT	200	170	184
Subwoofer (A/C & stereo req.; NA base) .	150	128	138
AM delete (credit) Sport Coupe & SE	(56)	(48)	(48)
AM/FM ST ET cassette delete, GT (credit) .	(373)	(317)	(317)
Suede, leather & Pallex trim, SE & GT . . .	375	319	345
Decklid spoiler, SE & GT	269	229	245
Glass sunroof	375	319	345
Turbo aluminum wheels, Sport Coupe . . .	241	205	220

Pontiac Firebird

Pontiac Firebird GTA

A 5.7-liter V-8 engine is available in a revised Firebird lineup for 1987. Last year's SE series is gone, while both remaining models have new option packages: The base Firebird has the Formula package and the Trans Am the new top-of-the-line GTA package. The Formula package comes with the 5.0-liter 4-barrel V-8 standard and the 5.0-liter tuned-port injected (TPI) V-8 an option with either a 5-speed manual or 4-speed automatic transmission. The

Prices are accurate at time of printing; subject to manufacturer's change.

5.7-liter Corvette V-8, available only with automatic, also is optional on the Formula. The Trans Am's standard engine is the 165-horsepower 4-barrel V-8 with the 5-speed manual. Options include the 5.0-liter TPI V-8, and the 5.7-liter TPI V-8, rated at 210 horsepower by Pontiac, which comes only with automatic. A new optional fully articulating driver's seat becomes available later in the model year, a Pontiac exclusive at GM. That same seat will become standard equipment on the GTA at that time. The 5.7-liter V-8 is standard on the racy GTA, but those who don't want that much engine can order the less potent 5.0-liter TPI V-8 instead. The old saw that there's no substitute for cubic inches is still true today, as evidenced by the arrival of the 5.7-liter V-8 in the Firebird and similar Chevrolet Camaro. This is traditional Detroit performance with a deep exhaust rumble, a stiff, thumpy ride and flashy styling. As always, it's not very practical because of the cramped interior, high insurance costs and low gas mileage. However, it's more practical than the 2-seat Corvette, and now you can get the Corvette's engine.

Specifications

	3-door coupe
Wheelbase, in.	101.0
Overall length, in.	188.0[1]
Overall width, in.	72.0
Overall height, in.	49.7
Front track, in.	60.7
Rear track, in.	61.6
Curb weight, lbs.	3105
Cargo vol., cu. ft.	31.0
Fuel capacity, gal.	15.5[2]
Seating capacity	4
Front headroom, in.	37.0
Front shoulder room, in.	57.7
Front legroom, max., in.	43.0
Rear headroom, in.	35.6
Rear shoulder room, in.	56.3
Rear legroom, min., in.	28.8

1. 191.6 on Trans Am   2. 16.2 w/5.0-liter 4 bbl. V-8

Body/Chassis

Drivetrain layout: longitudinal front engine/rear-wheel drive. **Front suspension:** modified MacPherson struts, lower control arms, coil springs, stabilizer bar. **Rear suspension:** rigid axle, torque tube, longitudinal control arms, coil springs, Panhard rod, stabilizer bar. **Steering:** recirculating ball, power assisted, 2.8 turns lock-to-lock. **Turn diameter, ft.:** 36.7. **Front brakes:** 10.5-in. discs. **Rear brakes:** 9.5-in. drums (discs optional). **Construction:** unit.

Powertrains	ohv V-6	ohv V-8	ohv V-8	ohv V-8	ohv V-8
Displacement, l/cu. in. . .	2.8/173	5.0/305	5.0/305	5.0/305	5.7/350
Compression ratio	8.9:1	9.3:1	9.3:1	9.3:1	9.3:1
Fuel delivery	PFI	4 bbl.	4 bbl.	PFI	PFI
Net bhp @ rpm	135 @ 5100	155 @ 4200	165 @ 4400	205 @ 4400	210 @ 4000
Net torque @ rpm . . .	160 @ 3900	245 @ 2000	250 @ 2400	285 @ 3200	315 @ 3200
Availability	S	O	S[1]	O[2]	S[3]

1. Trans Am   2. Trans Am   3. GTA; opt. on Formula & Trans Am

Final drive ratios

5-speed OD manual . .	3.42:1	3.23:1	3.23:1	3.08:1	
4-speed OD automatic .	3.42:1	2.73:1	2.73:1	2.73:1	2.77:1

KEY: bbl = barrel (carburetor); **bhp** = brake horsepower; **torque** = pounds/feet; **Cal.** = California only; **TBI** = throttle body (single-point) fuel injection; **PFI** = port (multipoint) fuel injection; **MFI** = mechanical fuel injection; **ohv** = overhead valve; **ohc** = overhead cam; **dohc** = double overhead cam; **I** = inline engine; **V** = V engine; **flat** = horizontally opposed engine; **D** = diesel; **T** = turbocharged; **OD** = overdrive transmission; **S** = standard; **O** = optional.

PRICES

PONTIAC FIREBIRD	Retail Price	Dealer Invoice	Low Price
3-door coupe	$10359	$9251	$9735
Trans Am 3-door coupe	13259	11840	12465
Destination charge	414	414	414

STANDARD EQUIPMENT (included in above prices):

2.8-liter (173-cid) PFI V-6 engine, 5-speed manual transmission, power steering, power brakes, center console, full carpeting, reclining front bucket seats, fold-down rear seatback, halogen headlamps, dual outside mirrors, Formula steering wheel, power liftgate pulldown, rear spoiler, dual sport mirrors, P215/65R15 tires on Rally II wheels. **Trans Am** adds: 5.0-liter (305-cid) 4bbl. V-8 engine, black-finish exterior accents, front fender air extractors, wheel opening flares, sport mirrors with left remote, rear spoiler, turbo-cast aluminum wheels, full instrumentation, special suspension, 5-speed manual transmission, 4-way manual seat.

Prices are accurate at time of printing; subject to manufacturer's change.

OPTIONAL EQUIPMENT:

Option Group 1, base & Formula 1273 1082 1170
  Air conditioning, AM/FM ST ET, tilt steering column, tinted glass, bodyside moldings, color-keyed seat belts.
Option Group 2, base 1792 1523 1650
  Formula 1842 1566 1695
  Group 1 plus power windows, cruise control, power door locks, intermittent wipers, lamp group, remote hatch release (Formula).
Option Group 1, Trans Am 1697 1442 1560
  GTA 1701 1446 1565
  Air conditioning, AM/FM ST ET, power windows, cruise control, tilt steering column, tinted glass, bodyside moldings, intermittent wipers, lamp group, color-keyed seatbelts.
Option Group 2, Trans Am 1949 1657 1795
  GTA 1958 1664 1801
  Power door locks, Leather Appointment Group, remote hatch release, interior roof console, right visor mirror, automatic day/night mirror (GTA).
Performance Value Pkg. 1, base 265 225 245
  Deep-dish turbo aluminum wheels, rally gauges w/tachometer
Performance Value Pkg. 2, base 709 603 650
  Pkg. 1 plus 5.0-liter 4bbl. V-8, custom interior.
Performance Value Pkg. 1, Trans Am . . . 839 713 770
  Removable hatch roof with sunshades, custom interior.
Formula Option, base 1070 910 985
  5.0-liter 4bbl. V-8, P245/50VR16 tires on turbo wheels, WS6 Performance Pkg., gauge cluster, rear spoiler, Formula exterior.
GTA Option, Trans Am 2700 2295 2485
  5.7-liter (350-cid) PFI engine, P245/50VR16 tires on gold diamond spoke wheels, WS6 Performance Pkg., engine oil cooler, 4-wheel disc brakes, limited-slip axle, articulating seats w/custom trim, power mirrors, Leather Appointment Group, GTA exterior.
5.0-liter 4bbl. V-8, base 400 340 370
5.0-liter PFI V-8, Formula & Trans Am . . . 745 633 685
  w/GTA (credit) . . . . (300) (255) (255)
5.7-liter PFI V-8, Formula & Trans Am . . . 1045 888 960
  Requires 4-speed automatic, engine oil cooler, WS6 Peformance Pkg 4-wheel disc brakes, limited-slip axle.
5-speed manual transmission GTA (credit) (490) (417) (417)
  Available only when 5.0-liter is substituted for 5.7.
4-speed automatic transmission 490 417 450
Air conditioning (tinted glass req.) 775 659 715
Electronic air conditioning 825 701 760
  Requires tinted glass & electronic instruments.
Limited-slip axle 100 85 92
Heavy-duty battery 26 22 24
Hood decal, Trans Am 95 81 87
Rear defogger 145 123 133
Engine oil cooler 110 94 101
California emissions pkg. 99 84 91
Rally cluster w/tachometer, base 150 128 138
Electronic instruments 275 234 253
  Includes Driver Information Center; requires electronic air conditioning. NA base & Formula.
Tinted glass (A/C req.) 120 102 110
Locking hatch roof 920 782 845

Prices are accurate at time of printing; subject to manufacturer's change.

	Retail Price	Dealer Invoice	Low Price
Power remote mirrors	91	77	84
4-wheel disc brakes (NA base)	179	152	165
AM/FM ST ET	217	184	200
AM/FM ST ET cassette	339	288	310
AM/FM ST ET w/cassette & EQ	489	416	450
Above w/Touch Control	529	449	485
Subwoofer (stereo req.)	150	128	138
AM delete (credit)	(56)	(48)	(48)
Power antenna	70	60	64
Cargo security screen	69	59	63
4-way driver's seat, base & Formula	35	30	32
Custom Interior Trim Packages			
Upgraded seats and door panels, color-keyed seatbelts, split folding rear seats.			
Pallex cloth, w/o power windows	319	271	295
w/power windows	349	297	320
w/leather, T/A w/o power windows	619	526	570
T/A w/power windows	649	552	595
Custom Interior w/articulating seats			
T/A w/o power windows	619	526	570
T/A w/power windows	649	552	595
Y99 suspension, base	50	43	46
WS6 Performance Pkg., T/A	385	327	355
P245/50VR16 tires on turbo wheels, sport suspension.			
Aluminum wheels, base (diamond or turbo)	215	183	198

Pontiac Grand Am

A more powerful base 4-cylinder engine and, later in the model year, a turbocharged 2.0-liter four will boost performance for Grand Am, Pontiac's rendition of the GM N-body compact (Buick Skylark/Somerset and Oldsmobile Calais are the others). The base 2.5-liter four gets six more horsepower (to 98) through new internal parts and GM's multi-coil ignition system that does away with the distributor. When teamed with the new Getrag-designed 5-speed manual transmission, the 2.5 also gains counter-rotating balance shafts to reduce the vibration and noise common to large 4-cylinder engines. The new 5-speed will be available with the 165-horsepower 2.0-liter turbo 4-cylinder engine (also used in the Sunbird) when it arrives at mid-year. A 3.0-liter V-6 available only with a 3-speed automatic remains standard in the SE, optional in the others. SE models

Pontiac Grand Am SE 2-door

have a new analog instrument cluster with a tachometer (optional on base and LE models). Later in the model year GM's automatic front seat belts will become standard on all Grand Ams. The sportiest of GM's three N-body compacts has also been the best seller, easily outpacing the Buick and Oldsmobile versions. Despite another round of improvements this year the 2.5 still comes out as only an average performer at best. It has a little more power, and runs a little quieter and smoother (especially with the 5-speed manual), but lacks the snappy acceleration and brisk passing response of the V-6, which we recommend even though it's an expensive option that comes only with the extra-cost automatic transmission.

Specifications

	2-door coupe	4-door sedan
Wheelbase, in.	103.4	103.4
Overall length, in.	177.5	177.5
Overall width, in.	66.9	67.5
Overall height, in.	52.5	52.5
Front track, in.	55.6	55.6
Rear track, in.	55.2	55.2
Curb weight, lbs.	2492	2565
Cargo vol., cu. ft.	13.0	13.0
Fuel capacity, gal.	13.6	13.6
Seating capacity	5	5
Front headroom, in.	37.7	37.7
Front shoulder room, in.	54.5	54.5
Front legroom, max., in.	42.9	42.9

	2-door coupe	4-door sedan
Rear headroom, in.	37.1	37.1
Rear shoulder room, in.	55.2	55.2
Rear legroom, min., in.	34.3	34.3

Body/Chassis

Drivetrain layout: transverse front engine/front-wheel drive.
Front suspension: MacPherson struts, lower control arms, coil springs, stabilizer bar. **Rear suspension:** beam axle, trailing arms, coil springs, stabilizer bar optional. **Steering:** rack and pinion, power assisted, 2.9 turns lock-to-lock. **Turn diameter, ft.:** 35.4. **Front brakes:** 9.8-in. discs. **Rear brakes:** 7.9-in. drums. **Construction:** unit.

Powertrains	ohc I-4T	ohv I-4	ohv V-6
Displacement, l/cu. in.	2.0/121	2.5/151	3.0/181
Compression ratio	8.0:1	9.0:1	9.0:1
Fuel delivery	PFI	TBI	PFI
Net bhp @ rpm	165 @ 5600	98 @ 4800	125 @ 4900
Net torque @ rpm	175 @ 4000	135 @ 3200	150 @ 2400
Availability	O[1]	S	S[2]

1. SE; late availability   2. SE; opt. on others

Final drive ratios

5-speed OD manual	3.61:1	3.35:1	
3-speed automatic	3.18:1	2.84:1	2.84:1

KEY: bbl = barrel (carburetor); **bhp** = brake horsepower; **torque** = pounds/feet; **Cal.** = California only; **TBI** = throttle body (single-point) fuel injection; **PFI** = port (multipoint) fuel injection; **MFI** = mechanical fuel injection; **ohv** = overhead valve; **ohc** = overhead cam; **dohc** = double overhead cam; **I** = inline engine; **V** = V engine; **flat** = horizontally opposed engine; **D** = diesel; **T** = turbocharged; **OD** = overdrive transmission; **S** = standard; **O** = optional.

PRICES

PONTIAC GRAND AM	Retail Price	Dealer Invoice	Low Price
2-door coupe	$9299	$8304	$8740
4-door sedan	9499	8483	8930
LE 2-door coupe	9999	8929	9340
LE 4-door sedan	10199	9108	9585
SE 2-door coupe	12659	11304	11900
SE 4-door sedan	12899	11519	12125
Destination charge	370	370	370

Prices are accurate at time of printing; subject to manufacturer's change

STANDARD EQUIPMENT (included in above prices):

2.5-liter (151-cid) 4-cylinder TBI engine, 5-speed manual transmission, full console, power steering, power brakes, tinted glass, side window defogger, halogen headlamps, headlamps-on warning, dual horns, acoustic insulation package, upshift indicator light, black left outside mirror, narrow bodyside molding, AM radio, cloth reclining front bucket seats, P185/80R13 all-season SBR tires. **LE** adds: deluxe carpeting, locking glovebox w/lamp, wide bodyside moldings, leather steering wheel, two-tone paint, custom wheel covers. **SE** adds: 3.0-liter PFI V-6, 3-speed automatic transmission, analog gauge cluster with tachometer, leather-wrapped steering wheel, shift knob and parking brake lever, monotone exterior treatment, P215/60R14 tires.

OPTIONAL EQUIPMENT:

Option Group 1, base	1128	959	1040
Air conditioning, AM/FM ST ET, tilt steering column, custom console, left remote & right manual mirrors.			
Option Group 2, base	1304	1108	1200
Group 1 plus cruise control, intermittent wipers, lamp group.			
Option Group 3, base coupe	1609	1368	1480
Base sedan	1734	1474	1595
Group 2 plus power windows and door locks.			
Option Group 1, LE	1211	1029	1115
Air conditioning, AM/FM ST ET, cruise control, tilt steering column, intermittent wipers, lamp group, remote fuel door release, right visor mirror.			
Option Group 2, LE coupe	1853	1575	1705
LE sedan	1978	1681	1820
Group 1 plus power seat, power windows and door locks, fog lamps, remote decklid release.			
Option Group 1, SE coupe	906	770	835
SE sedan	981	834	905
Air conditioning, power windows, lamp group.			
Option Group 2, SE coupe	1135	965	1045
SE sedan	1210	1029	1115
Group 1 plus power seat, power remote mirrors, lighted right visor mirror			
Performance Value Pkg. 1, base & LE	319	271	295
Rally gauges w/tachometer, P195/70R14 tires on turbo wheels.			
Performance Value Pkg. 2, base & LE	728	619	670
Pkg. 1 plus AM/FM ST ET cassette, rear defogger.			
2.5-liter 4-cylinder engine, SE (credit)	(660)	(561)	(561)
3.0-liter V-6, base & LE	660	561	605
5-speed manual trans, SE w/2.5 (credit)	(490)	(417)	(417)
3-speed automatic trans, base & LE	490	417	450
Air conditioning	675	574	620
Rear defogger	145	123	133
Driver Enthusiast Pkg., LE	793	674	730
Courtesy and reading lamps, fog lamps, leather-wrapped steering wheel, Driver Information Center, turbo wheels, rally tuned suspension, gauge cluster w/tachometer, P215/60R14 tires.			
California emissions pkg.	99	84	91
Engine block heater	18	15	16
Rally instruments, base & LE	127	108	117
Decklid luggage carrier	115	98	106

Prices are accurate at time of printing; subject to manufacturer's change

	Retail Price	Dealer Invoice	Low Price
AM/FM ST ET, base & LE	217	184	200
AM/FM ST ET cassette, base & LE	339	288	310
SE	132	112	121
AM/FM ST ET w/cassette & EQ, base & LE .	489	416	450
SE	282	240	260
Above w/Touch Control, base & LE	529	450	485
SE	322	274	295
AM delete (credit), base & LE	(56)	(48)	(48)
AM/FM ST ET delete (credit), SE	(263)	(224)	(224)
Performance Sound System	125	106	115
Includes six speakers; requires power windows & stereo radio			
Power antenna . . . . :	70	60	64
Pallex cloth seats w/leather trim, LE & SE .	150	128	138
Articulating bucket seats, LE & SE	450	383	415
Removable glass sunroof	350	298	330
Rally tuned suspension (Y99)	50	43	46
14" turbo aluminum wheels, base & LE . .	215	183	198

Pontiac Sunbird

Pontiac Sunbird SE 2-door

Semi-hidden headlamps and new front and rear fascias are added to the Sunbird SE model, wagons are now called Safari and two new engines and a new 5-speed manual transmission are being introduced this year in the front-drive Sunbirds (part of GM's J-car family). A new overhead cam 2.0-liter 4-cylinder engine with single-point injection is standard and a turbocharged multi-point injected 2.0-liter is available in all but the wagon. In addition, GM's new Getrag-designed 5-speed manual is standard with the turbo engine. The 2.0-liter engine replaces a 1.8-liter engine (from which it was derived). The 2.0 produces 96 horsepower, 12 more than last year's 1.8, and the turbocharged engine develops 165 horsepower, 15 more than last year's. Both engines are available with a 3-speed automatic. This year's healthy horsepower increase makes Sunbird's standard engine more palatable with automatic transmission, yet our initial impressions are that it's still somewhat sluggish with the 3-speed automatic. Acceleration is livelier and throttle response more prompt with the 5-speed manual, plus you'll get better mileage. This year's larger, more powerful turbocharged four provides outstanding acceleration that comes on with a bang; the turbo boost cuts in abruptly and the difference from off-boost performance is dramatic. All Sunbirds are fairly agile subcompacts with good maneuverability, but non-turbo models come with standard P175/80R13 tires that don't have great road grip or cornering ability. The optional rally suspension and P195/70R13 tires will improve handling with little detriment to ride.

Specifications	2-door coupe	3-door coupe	2-door conv.	4-door sedan	5-door wagon
Wheelbase, in.	101.2	101.2	101.2	101.2	101.2
Overall length, in. . . .	173.7	173.7	173.7	175.7	175.9
Overall width, in.	66.6	66.0	66.0	66.3	66.3
Overall height, in. . . .	51.9	51.9	51.9	53.8	54.1
Front track, in.	55.4	55.4	55.4	55.4	55.4
Rear track, in.	55.2	55.2	55.2	55.2	55.2
Curb weight, lbs.	2353	2399	2532	2404	2466
Cargo vol., cu. ft.	12.6	43.3	10.4	13.5	64.4
Fuel capacity, gal. . . .	13.6	13.6	13.6	13.6	13.6
Seating capacity	5	5	4	5	5
Front headroom, in. . .	37.7	37.6	38.5	38.6	38.3
Front shoulder room, in.	53.7	53.7	53.7	53.7	53.7
Front legroom, max., in.	42.2	42.2	42.2	42.2	42.2
Rear headroom, in. . . .	36.7	36.4	37.4	38.0	38.8
Rear shoulder room, in.	52.5	52.5	38.0	53.7	53.7
Rear legroom, min., in.	31.8	31.8	31.1	34.3	33.7

Body/Chassis

Drivetrain layout: transverse front engine/front-wheel drive. **Front suspension:** MacPherson struts, lower control arms, coil springs, stabilizer bar. **Rear suspension:** beam axle, trailing arms, coil springs (stabilizer bar optional). **Steering:** rack and pinion, 4.0 turns lock-to-lock. **Turn diameter, ft.:** 34.7. **Front brakes:** 9.7-in. discs. **Rear brakes:** 7.9-in. drums. **Construction:** unit.

Powertrains	ohc I-4	ohc I-4T
Displacement, l/cu. in.	2.0/121	2.0/121
Compression ratio	8.8:1	8.0:1
Fuel delivery	TBI	PFI
Net bhp @ rpm	96 @ 4800	165 @ 5600
Net torque @ rpm	118 @ 5600	175 @ 4000
Availability	S	O[1]

1. SE

Final drive ratios

5-speed OD manual	3.45:1	3.61:1
3-speed automatic	3.43:1	3.18:1

KEY: bbl = barrel (carburetor); **bhp** = brake horsepower; **torque** = pounds/feet; **Cal.** = California only; **TBI** = throttle body (single-point) fuel injection; **PFI** = port (multipoint) fuel injection; **MFI** = mechanical fuel injection; **ohv** = overhead valve; **ohc** = overhead cam; **dohc** = double overhead cam; **I** = inline engine; **V** = V engine; **flat** = horizontally opposed engine; **D** = diesel; **T** = turbocharged; **OD** = overdrive transmission; **S** = standard; **O** = optional.

PRICES

PONTIAC SUNBIRD	Retail Price	Dealer Invoice	Low Price
4-door sedan	$7999	$7143	$7520
5-door wagon	8529	7616	8015
SE 2-door coupe	7979	7125	7500
SE 3-door coupe	8499	7590	7990
SE 2-door convertible	13799	12323	12970
GT 2-door coupe	10299	9197	9680
GT 4-door sedan	10349	9242	9730
GT 3-door coupe	10699	9554	10055
GT 2-door convertible	15569	13903	14635
Destination charge	370	370	370

STANDARD EQUIPMENT (included in above prices):

2.0-liter (120-cid) TBI OHC 4-cylinder engine, 5-speed manual transmission, power brakes, front air dam, rear deflector (wagon), tailgate ajar warning light, upshift indicator, reclining front bucket seats, P175/80R13 tires. **SE** adds: cargo area carpet (3-doors), fog lamps, left remote and right manual mirrors, wide bodyside moldings, power steering, rally 4-spoke steering wheel. **SE convertible** adds: console, added sound insulation, custom wheel discs, power windows, air conditioning, AM radio, tinted glass. **GT** adds to SE: turbo engine, rally suspension, 4-speed manual transmission, console,

Prices are accurate at time of printing; subject to manufacturer's change

engine block heater, rally gauges with tachometer and trip odometer, AM radio, decklid spoiler, P215/60R14 tires on turbo-cast aluminum wheels.

OPTIONAL EQUIPMENT:

Option Group 1, base	433	368	400
SE exc. conv.	383	326	350
Power steering, tinted glass, left remote and right manual mirrors, bodyside moldings.			
Option Group 2, base	1531	1301	1410
SE exc. conv.	1481	1259	1365
Group 1 plus air conditioning, AM/FM ST ET, tilt steering column, intermittent wipers, rally steering wheel.			
Option Group 3, base sedan	1895	1611	1745
Base wagon	1945	1653	1790
SE exc. conv.	1644	1397	1510
Group 2 plus power door locks, lamp group, cruise control.			
Option Group 1, SE conv.	972	826	895
Air conditioning, AM/FM ST ET, tilt steering column, intermittent wipers.			
Option Group 2, SE conv.	1135	965	1045
Group 1 plus cruise control and lamp group.			
Option Group 1, GT exc. conv.	1117	949	1030
GT conv.	1012	860	930
Air conditioning, AM/FM ST ET, tilt steering wheel, tinted glass, intermittent wipers, deluxe fog lamps.			
Option Group 2, GT 2- and 3-doors	1742	1481	1600
GT 4-door	1873	1117	1725
GT conv.	1420	1207	1305
Group 1 plus power windows, cruise control, power door locks, remote hatch/decklid release, leather-wrapped steering wheel, lamp group, right visor mirror.			
Performance Value Pkg. 1, base & SE	278	236	255
Rally gauges, P195/70R13 tires on Sportech aluminum wheels.			
Performance Value Pkg. 2, SE	410	349	375
Pkg. 1 plus P215/60R14 tires on turbo aluminum wheels.			
Performance Value Pkg. 3, SE exc. conv.	807	686	740
SE conv.	707	601	650
Pkg. 2 plus AM/FM ST ET cassette, floormats.			
Turbo engine delete, GT (credit)	(768)	(653)	(653)
Turbo pkg., SE exc. conv.	1527	1298	1405
SE conv.	1312	1115	1205
Turbo engine, WS6 Performance Pkg., rally gauges, power steering.			
3-speed automatic transmission	415	353	380
Air conditioning (tinted glass req.)	675	574	620
Front center armrest	58	49	53
Custom console	45	38	41
Rear defogger (NA conv.)	145	123	133
California emissions pkg.	99	84	91
Rally cluster w/trip odometer	49	42	45
Above w/tachometer	127	108	117
Tinted glass (A/C req.)	105	89	97
Decklid luggage carrier	115	98	106
Two-tone paint, base w/o LE trim	151	128	139
Base w/LE trim, GT exc. conv.	101	86	93

Prices are accurate at time of printing; subject to manufacturer's change

	Retail Price	Dealer Invoice	Low Price
AM radio, base & SE	122	104	112
AM/FM ST ET, base & SE exc. conv. . . .	317	269	290
SE conv., GT	217	184	200
AM/FM ST cassette, base & SE	439	373	405
SE conv., GT	339	288	310
Above w/EQ & Touch Control, base & SE .	629	535	580
SE conv., GT	529	450	485
AM delete (credit), SE conv. & GT	(56)	(48)	(48)
Cargo cover, hatchbacks	69	59	63
Ripple cloth trim, base & SE	75	64	69
4-way manual seat, GT	35	30	32
Decklid spoiler, SE	70	60	64
Glass sunroof (NA wagon, conv.)	350	298	320
Y99 rally tuned suspension, exc. GT	50	43	46
Custom Trim, SE 2-door & base w/o A/C .	270	230	250
SE 2-door & base w/A/C	315	268	290
Wagon & SE 3-door w/o A/C	320	272	295
Wagon & SE 3-door w/A/C	365	310	335
GT 2- & 4-doors w/o artic. seats	168	143	155
GT 2- & 4-doors w/artic. seats	593	504	545
GT 3-door w/o artic. seats	218	185	200
GT 3-door w/artic. seats	643	547	590
GT conv. w/artic. seats	425	361	390
Rally steering wheel, custom cloth bucket seats, custom door trim & console, color-keyed seatbelts, split folding rear seatback (3- and 5-doors).			
LE Custom Trim, base sedan w/o A/C . . .	398	338	365
w/A/C	443	377	410
Wagon w/o A/C	448	381	410
Wagon w/A/C	493	419	455
Aluminum wheels	215	183	198

Pontiac 6000

New aerodynamic composite headlamps are the most visible change on the 6000, but the most significant changes are in the powertrains. The mid-size, front-drive 6000 is available in four series for 1987—base (coupe, sedan, wagon); LE (sedan and wagon); sporty S/E (sedan and wagon); and top-line STE (sedan only). Standard in the base and LE, the 2.5-liter 4-cylinder engine is revised and called Generation II, gaining six horsepower. The fuel-injected 2.8-liter V-6 optional in the base and LE and standard in the S/E and STE gets Generation II revamping for 10 more horsepower and 35 pounds less weight. Last year's

Prices are accurate at time of printing; subject to manufacturer's change

CONSUMER GUIDE®

Pontiac 6000 S/E 4-door

carbureted V-6 has been dropped. GM's new Getrag-designed 5-speed manual transmission will appear later in the model year, available with the V-6 as a credit option on the S/E and STE. The flagship STE comes standard with a 4-speed automatic this year, replacing a 3-speed, and an anti-lock braking system. Built under the same design as the Chevrolet Celebrity, Buick Century and Olds Cutlass Ciera, 6000 is closest to the Celebrity in price and content. The STE's lengthy standard equipment list makes it quite expensive, and that makes the S/E look more attractive to us. Added last spring, the S/E sedan and wagon offer the same performance and competent road manners as the STE, but are priced lower. The 6000 lacks the futuristic styling of the Ford Taurus and Mercury Sable, but has nearly as much passenger and cargo room, competitive prices and an appealing sporty model with the S/E.

Specifications

	2-door coupe	4-door sedan	5-door wagon
Wheelbase, in.	104.9	104.9	104.9
Overall length, in.	188.8	188.8	193.2
Overall width, in.	72.0	72.0	72.0
Overall height, in.	53.3	53.7	54.1
Front track, in.	58.7	58.7	58.7
Rear track, in.	57.0	57.0	57.0
Curb weight, lbs.	2792	2755	2925
Cargo vol., cu. ft.	16.2	16.2	41.6
Fuel capacity, gal.	15.7	15.7	15.7

	2-door coupe	4-door sedan	5-door wagon
Seating capacity	6	6	6
Front headroom, in.	38.6	38.6	38.6
Front shoulder room, in.	56.2	56.2	56.2
Front legroom, max., in.	42.1	42.1	42.1
Rear headroom, in.	37.9	38.0	38.9
Rear shoulder room, in.	56.2	56.2	56.2
Rear legroom, min., in.	35.8	35.8	34.7

Body/Chassis

Drivetrain layout: transverse front engine/front-wheel drive. **Front suspension:** MacPherson struts, lower control arms, coil springs, stabilizer bar. **Rear suspension:** beam twist axle with integral stabilizer bar, trailing arms, Panhard rod, coil springs. **Steering:** rack and pinion, power assisted, 3.1 turns lock-to-lock. **Turn diameter, ft.:** 36.9. **Front brakes:** 9.7-in. discs. **Rear brakes:** 8.9-in. drums. **Construction:** unit.

Powertrains	ohv I-4	ohv V-6
Displacement, l/cu. in.	2.5/151	2.8/173
Compression ratio	9.0:1	8.9:1
Fuel delivery	TBI	PFI
Net bhp @ rpm	98 @ 4800	125 @ 4800
Net torque @ rpm	135 @ 3200	160 @ 3600
Availability	S	S[1]

1. S/E, STE; opt. on others

Final drive ratios

3-speed automatic	2.84:1	2.84:1
4-speed OD automatic		3.33:1

KEY: bbl = barrel (carburetor); **bhp** =brake horsepower; **torque** = pounds/feet; **Cal.** = California only; **TBI** = throttle body (single-point) fuel injection; **PFI** = port (multipoint) fuel injection; **MFI** = mechanical fuel injection; **ohv** = overhead valve; **ohc** = overhead cam; **dohc** = double overhead cam; **I** = inline engine; **V** = V engine; **flat** = horizontally opposed engine; **D** = diesel; **T** = turbocharged; **OD** = overdrive transmission; **S** = standard; **O** = optional.

PRICES

PONTIAC 6000	Retail Price	Dealer Invoice	Low Price
2-door coupe, 4-door sedan	$10499	$9061	$9765
5-door wagon	10899	9406	10135
LE 4-door sedan	11099	9578	10320
LE 5-door wagon	11499	9924	10695
S/E 4-door sedan	12389	10692	11520

Prices are accurate at time of printing; subject to manufacturer's change

S/E 5-door wagon	13049	11261	12135
STE 4-door sedan	18099	15619	17100
Destination charge	414	414	414

STANDARD EQUIPMENT (included in above prices):

2.5-liter (151-cid) TBI 4-cylinder engine, 3-speed automatic transmission, power steering, power brakes, AM radio, full carpeting, front air dam, bumper rub strips, cigar lighter, side window demisters, carpeted lower door panels, lockable glovebox, split folding second seat (wagon), P185/75R14 SBR tires on rally wheels. **LE** adds: locking fuel filler door, door and seatback map pockets, notchback front seat with folding center armrest, tri-port wheel covers. **S/E** adds: 2.8-liter (173-cid) PFI V-6, dual exhausts, 4-wheel disc brakes, tachometer, trip odometer, voltmeter and oil pressure gauge, luggage rack (wagon), cloth reclining bucket seats, leather-wrapped steering wheel, rally-tuned suspension, electronic ride control (wagon), P195/70R14 SBR tires on aluminum wheels. **STE** adds: anti-lock braking system, 4-speed automatic transmission, accessory kit (flare, first aid kit, raincoat), air conditioning, cruise control, power windows, mirrors and door locks, Driver Information Center, tinted glass, inflator system, lamp group, two-tone paint, intermittent wipers, electronic ride control, AM/FM ST ET cassette, fog lamps.

OPTIONAL EQUIPMENT:

Option Group 1, base	1274	1083	1170
Air conditioning, AM/FM ST ET, tilt steering column, tinted glass, left remote and right manual mirrors, color-keyed seatbelts.			
Option Group 2, base coupe	1700	1445	1565
Base sedan	1750	1488	1610
Base wagon	1781	1514	1640
Group 1 plus power door locks, cruise control, exterior group, intermittent wipers, lamp group, sport steering wheel, remote tailgate release (wagon).			
Option Group 3, base coupe	1907	1621	1755
Base sedan	2032	1727	1870
Base wagon	2013	1711	1850
Power windows, front door courtesy lamps, right visor mirror.			
Option Group 1, LE sedan	1522	1294	1400
LE wagon	1513	1286	1390
Air conditioning, AM/FM ST ET, cruise control, tilt steering column, tinted glass, left remote and right manual mirrors, lamp group.			
Option Group 2, LE sedan	1999	1699	1840
LE wagon	1980	1683	1820
Group 1 plus power windows and door locks, front door courtesy lights, remote decklid release, right visor mirror.			
Option Group 3, LE sedan	2351	1998	2165
LE wagon	2294	1950	2110
Group 2 plus power 45/45 split seat, lighted right visor mirror, trunk trim (sedan), reading lamps.			
Option Group 1, S/E sedan	1461	1242	1345
S/E wagon	1452	1234	1335
Air conditioning, AM/FM ST ET, cruise control, tilt steering column, tinted glass, intermittent wipers, lamp group.			

Prices are accurate at time of printing; subject to manufacturer's change

	Retail Price	Dealer Invoice	Low Price
Option Group 2, S/E sedan	1949	1657	1795
S/E wagon	1930	1641	1775
Group 1 plus power windows, front door courtesy lights, power door locks, remote decklid/tailgate and fuel filler releases, right visor mirror.			
Option Group 3, S/E sedan	2137	1816	1965
S/E wagon	2118	1800	1950
Group 2 plus power seat, reading lamps.			
Performance Value Pkg. 1, base & LE . . .	260	221	240
Aluminum wheels, rally gauges w/tachometer, reclining passenger seat.			
Performance Value Pkg. 2, base & LE . . .	549	467	505
Pkg. 1 plus AM/FM ST ET cassette.			
Performance Value Pkg. 3, base & LE . . .	639	543	590
Pkg. 2 plus dual reclining seats, rear defogger.			
2.8-liter V-6, base & LE	610	519	560
4-speed automatic (2.8 req.)	175	149	161
5-speed manual transmission, S/E (credit) .	(440)	(374)	(374)
Air conditioning (tinted glass req.)	775	659	715
Cargo area carpet, wagons	40	34	37
Console	110	94	101
HD cooling w/o A/C, w/2.5	70	60	64
w/2.8	96	82	88
HD cooling w/A/C, w/2.5	40	34	37
w/2.8	66	56	61
Rear deflector, base & LE wagons	40	34	37
Rear defogger	145	123	133
California emissions pkg.	99	84	91
Rally cluster w/tachometer, base & LE . . .	100	85	92
Electronic instruments, base & LE	250	213	230
S/E	150	128	138
Tinted glass (A/C req.)	120	102	110
Decklid or roof luggage carrier, base & LE .	115	98	106
AM/FM ST ET	217	184	200
AM/FM ST ET cassette	339	288	310
AM/FM ST ET w/cassette & EQ	489	416	450
AM delete (credit)	(56)	(48)	(48)
Power antenna (NA wagons)	70	60	64
Roof bicycle or ski rack, S/E wagon	70	60	64
Third seat, wagons	215	183	198
Reclining front seats (each), base & LE . .	45	38	41
Custom Trim, coupes	125	106	115
Custom cloth seats, color-keyed seatbelts, 4-spoke steering wheel.			
Ripple cloth notchback seat, base	30	26	28
45/45 seat, base & LE	133	113	122
45/45 2-pass. seat, base & LE	83	71	76
Leather & Pallex bucket seats, S/E	300	255	275
Glass sunroof, base & LE exc. wagons . . .	350	298	320
Base & LE wagons, S/E	365	310	335
Power glass sunroof, sedans	918	780	845

Prices are accurate at time of printing; subject to manufacturer's change

CONSUMER GUIDE®

Y99 suspension, base & LE exc. wagon . .	50	43	46
Landau top & wire wheel covers, base coupe	712	605	655
Aluminum wheels, base & LE	215	183	198
Locking wire wheel covers	214	182	197
Rear wiper/washer, wagons	125	106	115
Simulated woodgrain, base wagon	375	319	345
LE wagon	190	162	175
8-way power seats, STE	538	457	495
Memory seat control w/above, STE	150	128	138
Suede & Pallex seat trim, STE	545	463	500
Power glass sunroof, STE	895	761	825

Renault Alliance

Renault GTA

The Encore name has been dropped, but the 3- and 5-door models that wore that moniker are now called Alliance Hatchbacks, putting all of AMC's front-drive subcompacts under one name. AMC's marketing will center on the new Alliance GTA, a sporty model powered by a 2.0-liter 4-cylinder engine and zooted-up with aerodynamic body trim and monochromatic paint. The GTA is limited to 2-door sedan and 2-door convertible versions. The 2.0-liter engine, available only in the GTA with a 5-speed manual transmission, is fed through a single-point fuel-injection system and rated at 95 horsepower, 18 more than the 1.7-liter engine. A sport suspension package and P195/50VR15 Michelin XGT tires on aluminum wheels are part of the package. Elsewhere in the expanded Alliance line an automatic seat belt system is standard on 2-door sedans and 3-door hatchbacks in the L and DL price levels, and optional on base versions of those body styles, to comply with the federal requirement that 10 percent of 1987 cars be equipped with passive restraints. All models get new grilles and headlamps. Despite its good credentials, the GTA is a late arrival to the crowded "pocket rocket" field and the Alliance in general suffers from a poor performance and quality reputation, so the GTA may not be that big a market factor. Avoid the base 1.4-liter engine in other Alliance models since it is too weak for even adequate acceleration. The 1.7-liter engine has adequate performance with manual shift, and marginal performance with automatic. Alliance's base prices are attractively low, but you don't get much for your money. Once you start adding popular options, price is no longer an advantage here, though AMC has been offering nearly constant incentives to try to move these cars. AMC's generous warranties are one of Alliance's strong points (5 years/50,000 miles on the powertrain and rust, plus some free maintenance), but reliability and resale value unfortunately aren't.

Specifications

	2-door sedan	3-door sedan	4-door sedan	5-door sedan	2-door conv.
Wheelbase, in.	97.8	97.8	97.8	97.8	97.8
Overall length, in. . . .	163.8	160.6	163.8	160.6	163.8
Overall width, in.	65.0	65.0	65.0	65.0	65.0
Overall height, in. . . .	51.3	51.3	51.3	51.3	53.1
Front track, in.	55.2	55.2	55.2	55.2	55.2
Rear track, in.	52.8	52.8	52.8	52.8	52.8
Curb weight, lbs.	1959	2009	1997	2039	2206
Cargo vol., cu. ft.	12.8	32.0	12.8	32.4	7.5
Fuel capacity, gal. . . .	12.5	12.5	12.5	12.5	12.5
Seating capacity	5	5	5	5	4
Front headroom, in. . .	37.1	37.1	37.1	37.1	38.5
Front shoulder room, in.	52.6	52.6	52.6	52.6	52.6
Front legroom, max., in.	40.8	40.8	40.8	40.8	40.8
Rear headroom, in. . . .	37.0	36.4	37.0	36.4	38.1
Rear shoulder room, in.	51.0	51.7	51.7	51.7	38.4
Rear legroom, min., in.	38.4	38.5	38.4	38.5	40.8

Body/Chassis

Drivetrain layout: transverse front engine/front-wheel drive. **Front suspension:** MacPherson struts, lower control arms, coil springs, stabilizer bar. **Rear suspension:** independent; trailing arms, transverse torsion bars, stabilizer bar. **Steering:** rack and pinion, 4.0 turns lock-to-lock manual; 3.2 power. **Turn diameter, ft.:** 30.3. **Front brakes:** 9.4-in. discs. **Rear brakes:** 8.0-in. drums. **Construction:** unit.

Powertrains	ohv I-4	ohc I-4	ohc I-4
Displacement, l/cu. in.	1.4/85	1.7/105	2.0/120
Compression ratio	9.0:1	9.5:1	9.5:1
Fuel delivery	TBI	TBI	TBI
Net bhp @ rpm	NA	77 @ 5000	95 @ 5250
Net torque @ rpm	NA	96 @ 3000	114 @ 2750
Availability	S	O[1]	S[2]

1. std. convertible   2. GTA

Final drive ratios

4-speed OD manual	3.29:1		
5-speed OD manual	3.56:1	3.56:1	4.07:1
3-speed automatic	3.56:1	3.56:1	

KEY: bbl = barrel (carburetor); **bhp** =brake horsepower; **torque** = pounds/feet; **Cal.** = California only; **TBI** = throttle body (single-point) fuel injection; **PFI** = port (multi-point) fuel injection; **MFI** = mechanical fuel injection; **ohv** = overhead valve; **ohc** = overhead cam; **dohc** = double overhead cam; **I** = inline engine; **V** = V engine; **flat** = horizontally opposed engine; **D** = diesel; **T** = turbocharged; **OD** = overdrive transmission; **S** = standard; **O** = optional.

PRICES

RENAULT ALLIANCE	Retail Price	Dealer Invoice	Low Price
2-door sedan, 3-door sedan	$6399	$6156	$6255
4-door sedan	6599	6347	6450
L 2-door sedan	6925	6313	6510
L 4-door sedan	7200	6561	6760
L 2-door convertible	11099	10089	10290
L 3-door sedan	6975	6358	6560
L 5-door sedan	7250	6607	6805
DL 2-door sedan	7625	6946	7145
DL 4-door sedan	7900	7195	7395
DL 2-door convertible	12099	10994	11195
DL 3-door sedan	7675	6991	7190
DL 5-door sedan	7950	7240	7440
GS 3-door sedan	8499	7736	7935
GTA 2-door sedan	8999	8189	8390
GTA 2-door convertible	12899	11718	11920
Destination charge	365	365	365

Prices are accurate at time of printing; subject to manufacturer's change

STANDARD EQUIPMENT (included in above prices):

1.4-liter (85-cid) TBI 4-cylinder engine, 4-speed manual transmission, power brakes, coolant temperature gauge, halogen headlamps, carpet, console with storage area, cigar lighter, day/night mirror, vinyl bucket seats, P155/80GR13 SBR tires. **L** adds: black bodyside moldings, fabric sunvisors, bright hubcaps. **DL** adds: 3.56 axle ratio, 5-speed manual transmission, digital clock, added sound insulation, low-fuel warning light, tachometer, power steering, AM/FM ST radio, trip odometer, headlights-on chime, two rear ashtrays, full trunk trim, upgraded door panels with hockey-stick armrests and stowage bins, rocker/recliner fabric seats, P175/70R13 tires. **Convertible** adds to L: 1.7-liter (105-cid) 4-cylinder engine, 5-speed manual transmission, power top, oil level gauge, P175/70R13 tires. **GS** adds to DL: front air dam, upgraded carpet and door panels, 1.7-liter engine with tuned exhaust, fog lamps, handling package, light group, wingback luxury cloth bucket seats, soft-feel sport steering wheel, Visibility Group, P185/60R14 tires on aluminum wheels. **GTA** adds: 2.0-liter (120-cid) engine, 4.07 axle, lockable glovebox, dual remote mirrors, AM radio, sport suspension, P195/50VR15 tires on aluminum wheels.

OPTIONAL EQUIPMENT:

1.7-liter engine, L & DL	169	140	155
5-speed manual transmission, L	103	85	95
3-speed auto trans, DL, L conv., GS	380	315	350
Base & L exc. conv.	483	401	444
Metallic paint	164	136	151
Fabric seats, base & L	81	67	75
Vinyl reclining seats, base & L	73	61	67
Fabric	154	128	142
Wingback seats, DL	123	102	113
Conventional spare tire (NA 3- & 5-doors)	67	56	62
Air conditioning (power steering req. w/1.7)	705	585	650
HD alternator & cooling	110	91	101
HD battery	30	25	28
Black bodyside moldings, base	46	38	43
Digital clock, base	64	53	59
Cold Climate Group, w/o A/C	87	72	80
w/A/C	66	55	61
Cruise control (NA base)	188	156	173
Luggage rack, DL 2- & 4-door	117	97	108
Rear defogger (NA conv.)	144	120	132
Electronic instruments, L & DL (1.7 req.)	509	422	470
Added sound insulation, L	70	58	64
Fog lamps	83	69	76
Keyless entry (power locks & clock req.)	106	88	98
Light Group, L & DL	67	56	62
Passive restraint system, 2-door			

Prices are accurate at time of printing; subject to manufacturer's change

CONSUMER GUIDE®

Power door locks, 2- & 3 doors	134	111	123
4 & 5-doors	188	156	173
Power steering	234	194	215
AM radio, base	96	80	88
AM/FM mono, base	169	140	155
L & DL	73	61	67
AM/FM ST ET (NA base)	198	164	182
AM/FM ST ET cassette (NA base)	367	305	338
AM/FM cass. w/EQ & Jensen speakers (NA base)	632	525	580
Jensen speakers (stereo req.)	106	88	98
Glass sunroof (NA base)	342	284	315
Sunshine Pkg., L	557	462	510
DL	379	315	350
Sunroof, aluminum wheels, soft-feel steering wheel.			
Tachometer, L	92	76	85
Tilt steering wheel, L & DL	102	85	94
Visibility Group, L	178	148	164
DL	144	120	132
Intermittent wipers, dual remote mirrors, lighted right visor mirror.			
Rear wiper/washer, 3 & 5-doors (NA base) .	131	109	121
Aluminum wheels, L	325	270	300
DL	227	188	209

Saab 900

Saab 900 Turbo

Saab's older line of cars (the design dates to 1969) takes on a more modern look this year with new headlamps, a sloped chrome grille and wraparound, integrated bumper. The 2-door notchback that debuted a year ago and was offered only in mid-level 900S trim has been dropped. A 4-door sedan is offered in base and 900S trim, while a 3-door continues in all three price levels, base, 900S and

Prices are accurate at time of printing; subject to manufacturer's change

Turbo. The 900 Turbo convertible that arrived last spring will be in greater supply for 1987. Other changes are that a stereo radio with anti-theft circuitry is now standard on the base 900 and the heated driver's seat gains an off switch. Base 900 models have a single overhead cam 2.0-liter four with two valves per cylinder while 900S versions have a dual-cam cylinder head with four valves per cylinder, good for 15 more horsepower. Turbocharged models also have the dual-cam cylinder head. A Special Performance Group option package to be available on the Turbo later in the year will include a firmer suspension, aerodynamic body trim and slight horsepower and torque increases. The 900 is remarkably functional for its age, with ample interior space for four adults, easy entry/exit through the tall doorways on the 4-door sedans and more than adequate cargo space augmented by the folding rear seatback. The base 900 models are underpowered with only 110 horses for 2800 pounds of curb weight. Performance is uninspired, especially with automatic transmission. The 125-horsepower, twin-cam engine in the 900S provides a little relief, but is still no fireball. You'll get better performance and mileage from the 5-speed manual transmission with either engine. The 160-horsepower turbocharged engine suffers none of the performance maladies and works quite well with automatic transmission, though it's the most expensive to buy and operate. With all models you get capable handling and roadholding, high quality materials and good warranty coverage (3 years/36,000 miles on the car and six years on rust). Prices on the 900 line are quite high these days, making it hard to justify the modest performance of the base and 900S models, despite the generous amount of standard equipment.

Specifications

	3-door sedan	4-door sedan
Wheelbase, in.	99.1	99.1
Overall length, in.	184.5	184.3
Overall width, in.	66.5	66.5
Overall height, in.	56.1	56.1
Front track, in.	56.3	56.3
Rear track, in.	56.7	56.7
Curb weight, lbs.	2744	2724
Cargo vol., cu. ft.	56.5	53.0

	3-door sedan	4-door sedan
Fuel capacity, gal.	16.6	16.6
Seating capacity	5	5
Front headroom, in.	36.8	36.8
Front shoulder room, in.	52.2	53.0
Front legroom, max., in.	41.7	41.7
Rear headroom, in.	37.4	37.4
Rear shoulder room, in.	53.3	54.5
Rear legroom, min., in.	36.2	36.2

Body/Chassis

Drivetrain layout: longitudinal front engine/front-wheel drive. **Front suspension:** transverse control arms, coil springs (stabilizer bar, 900S and Turbo). **Rear suspension:** tubular beam axle, trailing arms, Panhard rod, coil springs (stabilizer bar, 900S and Turbo). **Steering:** rack and pinion, 3.6 turns lock-to-lock. **Turn diameter, ft.:** 33.8. **Front brakes:** 11.0-in. discs. **Rear brakes:** 10.6-in. discs. **Construction:** unit.

Powertrains	ohc I-4	dohc I-4	dohc I-4T
Displacement, l/cu. in.	2.0/121	2.0/121	2.0/121
Compression ratio	9.25:1	10.0:1	9.0:1
Fuel delivery	PFI	PFI	PFI
Net bhp @ rpm	110 @ 5250	125 @ 5500	160[1] @ 5500
Net torque @ rpm	119 @ 3500	123 @ 3000	188[1] @ 3000
Availability	S[2]	S[3]	S[4]

1. 165 bhp and 195 lbs/ft with SPG option.   2. base 900   3. 900S   4. 900 Turbo

Final drive ratios

	ohc I-4	dohc I-4	dohc I-4T
5-speed OD manual	3.67:1	3.67:1	3.67:1
3-speed automatic	3.67:1	3.67:1	3.67:1

KEY: bbl = barrel (carburetor); **bhp** = brake horsepower; **torque** = pounds/feet; **Cal.** = California only; **TBI** = throttle body (single-point) fuel injection; **PFI** = port (multipoint) fuel injection; **MFI** = mechanical fuel injection; **ohv** = overhead valve; **ohc** = overhead cam; **dohc** = double overhead cam; **I** = inline engine; **V** = V engine; **flat** = horizontally opposed engine; **D** = diesel; **T** = turbocharged; **OD** = overdrive transmission; **S** = standard; **O** = optional.

PRICES

SAAB 900	Retail Price	Dealer Invoice	Low Price
900 3-door sedan	$14115	$11857	$13915
900 4-door sedan	14515	12193	14315
900S 3-door sedan	17585	14683	17385
900S 4-door sedan	17985	15017	17785

Prices are accurate at time of printing; subject to manufacturer's change.

	Retail Price	Dealer Invoice	Low Price
900 Turbo 3-door sedan	20405	16936	20205
900 Turbo 2-door convertible	26580	21796	26380
Destination charge	370	370	370

These models sell at or above retail in many locations.

STANDARD EQUIPMENT (included in above prices):

2.0-liter (120-cid) 4-cylinder PFI engine, 5-speed overdrive manual transmission, power steering, power 4-wheel disc brakes, air conditioning, clock, tachometer, trip odometer, electric rear-window defroster, intermittent wipers, central locking, tinted glass, driver's seat tilt/height adjuster, full carpeting, reclining front bucket seats, fold-down rear seat. AM/FM stereo radio, halogen headlamps, electrically heated front seats. S adds: dohc 16-valve engine, 195/60R15 tires, alloy wheels, cruise control, fold-down rear center armrest, power mirrors, power windows, AM/FM ETR cassette, manual sunroof. Turbo adds: electric remote-control door mirrors, power windows, front and rear spoilers (3-door), turbocharged engine, uprated suspension and tires, sport seats, graphic equalizer.

OPTIONAL EQUIPMENT:

3-speed automatic transmission	420	349	400
Metallic & special black paint	410	328	390
Special Performance Group, Turbo	2630	2157	2500

Aerodynamic lower body fairings, light alloy wheels, power sunroof, fog lamps, 5 Pirelli P6 tires.

Saab 9000

A non-turbo 9000S model with the same 2.0-liter engine as the 900S (dual-cams, 4-valves per cylinder) arrived last fall and automatic transmissions will be readily available this year on Saab's flagship sedan. The 9000 debuted in the U.S. a year ago only with a turbocharged 2.0 and 5-speed manual transmission. A 4-speed overdrive automatic transmission became available later, but only a few hundred made it to the U.S. Saab says more automatics will be available for 1987 and will be offered on turbo and non-turbo 9000 models. Other changes are that the turbocharger gets a new water-cooling circuit for better durability, standard tires on both models are Pirelli P600s and leather upholstery is standard on the 9000 Turbo, optional

Prices are accurate at time of printing; subject to manufacturer's change.

Saab 9000 Turbo

on the 9000S. The front-drive 9000 comes only as a 5-door hatchback sedan. The 9000 Turbo impressed us as a well-designed, well-executed sport sedan with exhilarating engine performance, fine handling and road grip, and generous interior and cargo space. You'll get all those features on the less-expensive 9000S except for the exhilarating performance. We haven't driven the 9000S, but based on the modest performance of its 125-horsepower engine in the lighter 900S, we don't think it promises much excitement here, especially with automatic transmission. It should be adequate for the 3000-pound 9000S, but at these prices you expect more than adequate performance. Both 9000s come with loads of comfort and convenience features that are functional rather than gimmicky and the cars are backed by a warranty that protects the owner from mechanical disaster for 3 years/36,000 miles.

Specifications

	5-door sedan
Wheelbase, in.	105.2
Overall length, in.	181.9
Overall width, in.	69.4
Overall height, in.	55.9
Front track, in.	59.9
Rear track, in.	58.7
Curb weight, lbs.	2967[1]
Cargo vol., cu. ft.	56.5
Fuel capacity, gal.	17.9
Seating capacity	5
Front headroom, in.	38.5

	5-door sedan
Front shoulder room, in.	NA
Front legroom, max., in.	41.5
Rear headroom, in.	37.4
Rear shoulder room, in.	NA
Rear legroom, min., in.	38.7

1. 3048 lbs., Turbo

Body/Chassis

Drivetrain layout: transverse front engine/front-wheel drive. **Front suspension:** MacPherson struts, coil springs, stabilizer bar. **Rear suspension:** beam axle, panhard rod, coil springs, stabilizer bar. **Steering:** rack and pinion, power assisted, 3.2 turns lock-to-lock. **Turn diameter, ft.:** 35.8. **Front brakes:** discs. **Rear brakes:** discs. **Construction:** unit.

Powertrains	dohc I-4	dohc I-4T
Displacement, l/cu. in.	2.0/121	2.0/121
Compression ratio	10.1:1	9.0:1
Fuel delivery	PFI	PFI
Net bhp @ rpm	125 @ 5500	160 @ 5500
Net torque @ rpm	123 @ 3000	188 @ 3000
Availability	S	S

Final drive ratios

	dohc I-4	dohc I-4T
5-speed OD manual	4.45:1	4.21:1
4-speed OD automatic	4.28:1	4.28:1

KEY: bbl = barrel (carburetor); **bhp** = brake horsepower; **torque** = pounds/feet; **Cal.** = California only; **TBI** = throttle body (single-point) fuel injection; **PFI** = port (multi-point) fuel injection; **MFI** = mechanical fuel injection; **ohv** = overhead valve; **ohc** = overhead cam; **dohc** = double overhead cam; **I** = inline engine; **V** = V engine; **flat** = horizontally opposed engine; **D** = diesel; **T** = turbocharged; **OD** = overdrive transmission; **S** = standard; **O** = optional.

PRICES

SAAB 9000	Retail Price	Dealer Invoice	Low Price
5-door sedan, 5-speed	$21805	$17880	$21605
5-door sedan, automatic	22355	18331	22155
Turbo 5-door sedan, 5-speed	25515	20922	25315
Turbo 5-door sedan, automatic	26065	21373	25865
Destination charge	370	370	370

These models sell at or above retail in many locations.

Prices are accurate at time of printing; subject to manufacturer's change.

STANDARD EQUIPMENT (included in above prices):

2.0-liter (120-cid) 16-valve PFI 4-cylinder engine, 5-speed manual or 3-speed automatic transmission as above, power windows, central locking, AM/FM stereo ET cassette with graphic EQ and power antenna, locking fuel filler door, automatic climate control, analog quartz clock, halogen headlamps, front and rear reading lights, pictogram for exterior light failure & door open, sport driver's seat with adjustable height/tilt, lumbar and thigh support, emergency tensioner retractor on front seatbelts, two rear shoulder belts and center lap belt, telescopic steering wheel, 195/60R15 high-speed SBR tires. **Turbo** adds: turbocharged, intercooled engine.

OPTIONAL EQUIPMENT:

Leather pkg.	1010	808	960

Sterling 825

Sterling 825SL

Based on the same design as the Acura Legend, the Sterling 825 premium sedan is a joint venture between Britain's Austin Rover Group and Japan's Honda Motor Co. The front-drive 825 and Legend both use Honda's 2.5-liter V-6 engine and share major chassis components, though the 825 has firmer springs and shock absorbers and a self-leveling feature for the rear suspension. The 825 also wears distinct sheetmetal and has its own interior design, plus Sterling offers a Bosch anti-lock braking system (ABS) not available on Legend. The 825 comes in two trim levels: base S and top-line SL. Standard features on the S include central locking with remote control, power windows, air conditioning, power moonroof and 5-speed manual transmission. The SL adds ABS, leather upholstery, power front

Prices are accurate at time of printing; subject to manufacturer's change.

seats, heated driver's seat and 4-speed automatic transmission (the 5-speed manual is available at no cost). ABS, leather upholstery and the automatic transmission are available at extra cost on the S model. Prices weren't announced, but Austin Rover officials estimated the 825S will start at under $20,000 and the 825SL will be $4000 higher. The 825's firmer suspension gives it sportier ride and handling than Legend, with less body roll in cornering yet no loss of suppleness or bump absorption. Inside, the real wood trim gives the interior a high-bucks look, but that is contrasted by cheap-looking plastic column stalks and controls. The control layout isn't as convenient as Legend's, but otherwise the 825 matches its Japanese cousin in accommodations and performance. The availability of anti-lock brakes is a big plus for the 825 in our book. With the 825 you're getting the same basic car as the Legend, but this one is made in Britain, not a country known for consistently producing top-quality automobiles. However, since we rate the Legend highly, we think the 825 deserves a close look by those shopping in the premium sedan market.

Specifications	4-door sedan
Wheelbase, in.	108.6
Overall length, in.	188.8
Overall width, in.	76.8
Overall height, in.	54.8
Front track, in.	58.8
Rear track, in.	57.1
Curb weight, lbs.	3164[1]
Cargo vol., cu. ft.	12.1
Fuel capacity, gal.	18.0
Seating capacity	5
Front headroom, in.	37.8
Front shoulder room, in.	54.9
Front legroom, max., in.	41.2
Rear headroom, in.	36.3
Rear shoulder room, in.	54.3
Rear legroom, min., in.	36.4

1. 3252 lbs., 825 SL

Body/Chassis

Drivetrain layout: transverse front engine/front-wheel drive.
Front suspension: upper and lower control arms, MacPherson

struts, coil springs, stabilizer bar. **Rear suspension:** MacPherson struts, trailing arms, coil springs, stabilizer bar. **Steering:** rack and pinion, power assisted, 3.5 turns lock-to-lock. **Turn diameter, ft.:** 36.5. **Front brakes:** 11.2-in. discs. **Rear brakes:** 10.2-in. drums. **Construction:** unit.

Powertrains	ohc V-6
Displacement, l/cu. in.	2.5/152
Compression ratio	9.0:1
Fuel delivery	PFI
Net bhp @ rpm	151 @ 5800
Net torque @ rpm	154 @ 4500
Availability	S
Final drive ratios	
5-speed OD manual	4.20:1
4-speed OD automatic	4.20:1

KEY: bbl = barrel (carburetor); **bhp** = brake horsepower; **torque** = pounds/feet; **Cal.** = California only; **TBI** = throttle body (single-point) fuel injection; **PFI** = port (multi-point) fuel injection; **MFI** = mechanical fuel injection; **ohv** = overhead valve; **ohc** = overhead cam; **dohc** = double overhead cam; **I** = inline engine; **V** = V engine; **flat** = horizontally opposed engine; **D** = diesel; **T** = turbocharged; **OD** = overdrive transmission; **S** = standard; **O** = optional.

Prices not available at time of publication.

Subaru Hatchback & Sedan/ Wagon/3-Door Coupe

Subaru gained fame for being the first manufacturer to offer 4WD in small passenger cars, but this year a new permanent, full-time 4WD system will be available on the sedan and coupe, meaning that power is delivered to all four wheels constantly. Until now, Subaru has offered only on-demand, part-time 4WD for use on slippery surfaces, but the permanent 4WD gives its cars the same capability as the Audi Quattros and Volkswagen Quantum Syncro. Other changes are that the sedan, coupe and wagon get 5-mph bumpers (instead of 2.5-mph), the overhead-cam 1.8-liter engine is reworked internally and most models get all-season tires as standard. The sedan and wagon have

Subaru 3-Door 4WD Turbo

a new body-color grille (except DL models) and Turbo 3-door coupes gain a rear spoiler. The smaller 3-door hatch-back sedan, based on the old Subaru design, is a carryover available in Standard and GL trim, with 4WD available on GL models. It has been the entry-level "Sube," but will not be dropped in January when the smaller, cheaper Justy arrives. We have not driven the 1987 models, so we can't comment on the new full-time 4WD system, but the on-demand, part-time system still available gives these cars impressive traction in slippery conditions and it can be engaged on the fly. Engine performance is average at best, even on turbocharged models. It takes a long time for turbo boost to build up from a standing start and acceleration is only brisk once it kicks in. The 4WD models weigh 300-400 pounds more than the front-drive models, putting a greater burden on the engines, all of which have modest performance to begin with. Subaru provides only a 12-month warranty on its cars and our impressions have been that Subaru's overall quality doesn't match that of Honda or Toyota. However, Subaru has established an enviable reputation for reliability and its cars offer an impressive array of features for relatively modest prices. Snow Belt residents looking for the added traction of 4WD have flocked to Subaru as the answer to their needs and owner surveys indicate most have been happy with their decision.

Specifications	3-door coupe	3-door sedan	4-door sedan	5-door wagon
Wheelbase, in.	97.2	93.7	97.2	97.2
Overall length, in.	174.6	156.9	174.6	176.8

	3-door coupe	3-door sedan	4-door sedan	5-door wagon
Overall width, in.	65.4	63.4	65.4	65.4
Overall height, in.	51.8	53.7	52.5	53.0
Front track, in.	56.1	52.8	56.1	55.9
Rear track, in.	56.1	53.0	56.1	56.1
Curb weight, lbs.	2240	2050	2195	2330
Cargo vol., cu. ft.	39.8	33.9	14.9	70.3
Fuel capacity, gal.	15.9	13.2	15.9	15.9
Seating capacity	5	4	5	5
Front headroom, in.	37.6	38.2	37.6	37.6
Front shoulder room, in.	53.5	51.0	53.5	53.5
Front legroom, max., in.	42.2	39.3	41.7	41.7
Rear headroom, in.	35.8	36.6	36.5	37.7
Rear shoulder room, in.	52.8	52.4	53.5	53.5
Rear legroom, min., in.	32.6	30.2	35.2	35.2

Body/Chassis

Drivetrain layout: longitudinal front engine/front- or 2/4-wheel drive. **Front suspension:** MacPherson struts, lower control arms, coil springs (adjustable air springs on GL-10 4WD Turbo), stabilizer bar. **Rear suspension:** independent; semi-trailing arms, coil springs (torsion bars on Hatchback; adjustable air springs on GL-10 4WD Turbo), stabilizer bar (except Hatchback). **Steering:** rack and pinion, 3.7 turns lock-to-lock. **Turn diameter, ft.:** 30.8, Hatchback; 34.8, others. **Front brakes:** 9.5-in. discs. **Rear brakes:** 7.1-in. drums (8.9-in. discs, Turbo). **Construction:** unit.

Powertrains	ohv flat-4	ohv flat-4	ohc flat-4	ohc flat-4	ohc flat-4T
Displacement, l/cu. in. . .	1.6/97	1.8/109	1.8/109	1.8/109	1.8/109
Compression ratio	9.0:1	8.7:1	9.0:1	9.5:1	7.7:1
Fuel delivery	2 bbl.	2 bbl.	2 bbl.	TBI	PFI
	69 @	73 @	84 @	90 @	115 @
Net bhp @ rpm	4800	4400	5200	5200	5200
	86 @	94 @	101 @	101 @	134 @
Net torque @ rpm . . .	2800	2400	3200	2800	2800
Availability	S	S	S	S	S

Final drive ratios

4-speed OD manual . .	3.45:1	3.89:1			
5-speed OD manual . .	3.70:1		3.90:1	3.90:1	3.70:1
3-speed automatic		3.36:1	3.60:1	3.60:1	3.36:1

KEY: bbl = barrel (carburetor); **bhp** = brake horsepower; **torque** = pounds/feet; **Cal.** = California only; **TBI** = throttle body (single-point) fuel injection; **PFI** = port (multipoint) fuel injection; **MFI** = mechanical fuel injection; **ohv** = overhead valve; **ohc** = overhead cam; **dohc** = double overhead cam; **I** = inline engine; **V** = V engine; **flat** = horizontally opposed engine; **D** = diesel; **T** = turbocharged; **OD** = overdrive transmission; **S** = standard; **O** = optional.

PRICES

SUBARU

	Retail Price	Dealer Invoice	Low Price
Standard 3-door hatchback, 4-speed	$5398	—	—
GL 3-door sedan, 5-speed	7588	—	—
GL 3-door sedan, automatic	8093	—	—
GL 4WD 3-door sedan, 4-speed	8293	—	—
DL 4-door sedan, 5-speed	8808	—	—
DL 4-door sedan, automatic	9518	—	—
GL 4-door sedan, 5-speed	9838	—	—
GL 4-door sedan, automatic	10643	—	—
GL Turbo 4-door sedan, 5-speed	12383	—	—
GL-10 4-door sedan, automatic	12348	—	—
GL-10 Turbo 4-door sedan, 5-speed	13628	—	—
GL-10 Turbo 4-door sedan, automatic . . .	14053	—	—
GL 4WD 4-door sedan, 5-speed	10308	—	—
GL 4WD 4-door sédan, automatic	11138	—	—
RX 4WD Turbo 4-door sedan, 5-speed . . .	13833	—	—
GL-10 4WD Turbo 4-door sedan, 5-speed .	15068	—	—
GL-10 4WD Turbo 4-door sedan, automatic .	15243	—	—
DL 3-door coupe, 5-speed	9108	—	—
GL 3-door coupe, 5-speed	10138	—	—
GL 3-door coupe, automatic	10673	—	—
GL Turbo 3-door coupe, 5-speed	12593	—	—
GL 4WD 3-door coupe, 5-speed	10608	—	—
GL 4WD 3-door coupe, automatic	11143	—	—
GL 4WD Turbo 3-door coupe, 5-speed . . .	14053	—	—
DL 5-door wagon, 5-speed	9208	—	—
DL 5-door wagon, automatic	9918	—	—
GL 5-door wagon, 5-speed	10238	—	—
GL 5-door wagon, automatic	11043	—	—
GL Turbo 5-door wagon, 5-speed	12783	—	—
GL-10 5-door wagon, automatic	12748	—	—
GL-10 Turbo 5-door wagon, 5-speed	14028	—	—
GL-10 Turbo 5-door wagon, automatic . . .	14453	—	—
DL 4WD 5-door wagon, 5-speed	9598	—	—
GL 4WD 5-door wagon, 5-speed	10708	—	—
GL 4WD 5-door wagon, automatic	11538	—	—
GL 4WD Turbo 5-door wagon, 5-speed . .	13388	—	—
GL-10 4WD Turbo wagon, 5-speed	14688	—	—
GL-10 4WD Turbo 5-door wagon, automatic	15643	—	—
XT DL 2-door coupe, 5-speed	9593	—	—
XT GL 2-door coupe, 5-speed	11518	—	—
XT GL 2-door coupe, automatic	11943	—	—
XT GL-10 Turbo 2-door coupe, 5-speed . .	14573	—	—
XT GL-10 Turbo 2-door coupe, automatic .	14998	—	—

Prices are accurate at time of printing; subject to manufacturer's change.

CONSUMER GUIDE®

XT GL-10 4WD Turbo 2-door coupe, 5-speed	15648	— —
XT GL-10 4WD Turbo 2-door coupe, automatic	16098	— —

Destination charge varies by region. Dealer invoice and low price not available at time of publication.

STANDARD EQUIPMENT (included in above prices):

Standard: 1.6-liter (97-cid) 4-cylinder engine, power brakes, vinyl carpeting, side window defoggers, trip odometer, temperature gauge, graphic telltale monitor, lockable glovebox, day/night mirror, reclining front vinyl bucket seats, fold-down rear seatback, 155SR13 tires. **DL** adds: 1.8-liter (109-cid) engine, cigar lighter, carpeting, quartz digital clock, hill holder clutch, rear defogger, remote fuel filler release, tinted glass, halogen headlamps, child safety rear door locks, door map pockets, black bodyside moldings, AM/FM monaural radio, cloth reclining front seats, fold-down rear seatback (wagons), adjustable suspension height (4wd wagon), remote trunk release (sedans & XT), rear wiper/washer (wagons), 155SR13 tires (sedans), 165SR13 (4wd wagon). **DL XT** adds: center console, overhead spotlights, sport seats, tilt/telescopic steering column with memory, tachometer, intermittent wipers. **GL** adds: 1.8-liter (109-cid) ohc TBI 4-cylinder engine (exc. Hatchback), 1.6-liter engine (Hatchback), 1.8-liter PFI turbocharged engine (turbo models) console storage compartment (4- and 5-doors), rear seat heater outlets (4- and 5-doors), low fuel warning light, cargo area cover, right visor mirror, AM/FM stereo (ET on XT), 50/50 split fold-down rear seatback (3- and 5-doors), tilt steering column (with memory on 2-, 4- and 5-doors), adjustable suspension height (except Hatchback and 2wd wagon), tachometer, remote trunk release, power steering (XT), 175/70SR13 tires (2wd), 185/70SR13 all-terrain tires (4wd). **GL Turbo** models add limited-slip differential, dual range transmission. **GL-10** adds: air conditioning, front air dam (exc. turbos), 4-wheel power disc brakes (turbos), luxury carpeting, cruise control, power windows and door locks, cloth-trimmed door panels, outside temperature gauge, cloth headliner, digital instruments, front seat map pockets, dual visor mirrors, AM/FM stereo ET, power sunroof, 3-way fold-down rear seatback with trunk through, rear seat headrests and center armrest, power steering, air suspension with height adjustment (4wd turbos), high-speed tires, full wheel covers. **RX** adds: assist grips, rear door window defoggers, limited slip differential, rear spoiler, rally suspension, oil pressure gauge, voltmeter, turbo boost gauge, limited-slip differential, dual-range transmission, Bridgestone Potenza high-speed tires.

OPTIONAL EQUIPMENT:

J Pkg., GL 3-door coupe	1005	— —
Power steering, power windows, air conditioning, cruise control.		
HT Pkg., GL-10 sedans & wagons	515	— —
Power sunroof with shade.		

OTHER OPTIONS (air conditioning, sound systems, alloy wheels, etc.) are available as dealer-installed accessories; prices may vary.

Prices are accurate at time of printing; subject to manufacturer's change.

Subaru XT Coupe

Subaru XT Turbo

The 2-door notchback XT Coupe shares the 97-inch wheelbase of the Subaru sedan/wagon/3-door trio, but has its own flamboyant styling and different seating arrangements (2-seats on the base DL and 2 + 2 on the GL and GL Turbo). The sporty XT will be a carryover from 1986 until next spring, when a late-1987 model is scheduled to arrive with undisclosed changes, except that motorized automatic seat belts will become standard. DL models have front-wheel drive with a non-turbo 1.8-liter 4-cylinder engine. GLs come three ways: front-drive/non-turbo, front-drive/ turbocharged and 4-wheel drive/turbocharged. The 4WD system is an on-demand part-time system, but the XT is likely to gain Subaru's new permanent, full-time 4WD system next spring. Subaru's sporty coupe offers the same virtues as the sedan/wagon/3-door group, except for interior room. Tall drivers are crowded by the low roof and lack of rearward seat travel. Performance is mediocre with the base 94-horsepower 1.8-liter engine and nothing to rave about with the 110-horsepower turbocharged 1.8. The XT's best selling point is the available 4WD, activated by a pushbutton on the shift knob. When the roads are covered with snow and ice, other sporty coupes will be slipping and sliding, but the 4WD XT motors along with outstanding traction. As with other Subarus, the XT offers a lot of sophisticated hardware and comfort/convenience features for the money.

Specifications

	2-door coupe
Wheelbase, in.	97.1
Overall length, in.	175.2
Overall width, in.	66.5
Overall height, in.	49.4
Front track, in.	56.5
Rear track, in.	56.1
Curb weight, lbs.	2280
Cargo vol., cu. ft.	11.6
Fuel capacity, gal.	15.9
Seating capacity	4[1]
Front headroom, in.	37.4
Front shoulder room, in.	52.8
Front legroom, max., in.	43.3
Rear headroom, in.	34.5
Rear shoulder room, in.	52.0
Rear legroom, min., in.	26.2

1. 2 on DL

Body/Chassis

Drivetrain layout: longitudinal front engine/front- or 2/4-wheel drive. **Front suspension:** MacPherson struts, lower control arms, coil springs (adjustable air springs on 4WD Turbo), stabilizer bar. **Rear suspension:** independent; semi-trailing arms, coil springs (adjustable air springs on 4WD Turbo), stabilizer bar. **Steering:** rack and pinion, 3.7 turns lock-to-lock. **Turn diameter, ft.:** 35.1. **Front brakes:** 9.5-in. discs. **Rear brakes:** 7.1-in. drums (8.9-in. discs, Turbo). **Construction:** unit.

Powertrains

	ohc flat-4	ohc flat-4T
Displacement, l/cu. in.	1.8/109	1.8/109
Compression ratio	9.0:1	7.7:1
Fuel delivery	PFI	PFI
Net bhp @ rpm	94 @ 5200	110 @ 4800
Net torque @ rpm	101 @ 2800	134 @ 2800
Availability	S	S
Final drive ratios		
5-speed OD manual	3.90:1	3.70:1
3-speed automatic	3.60:1	3.22:1

KEY: bbl = barrel (carburetor); **bhp** = brake horsepower; **torque** = pounds/feet; **Cal.** = California only; **TBI** = throttle body (single-point) fuel injection; **PFI** = port (multipoint) fuel injection; **MFI** = mechanical fuel injection; **ohv** = overhead valve; **ohc** = overhead cam; **dohc** = double overhead cam; **I** = inline engine; **V** = V engine; **flat**

= horizontally opposed engine; **D** = diesel; **T** = turbocharged; **OD** = overdrive transmission; **S** = standard; **O** = optional.

Prices appear on page 344

Toyota Camry

Toyota Camry LE 4-door

Camry has been redesigned for 1987, acquiring new styling, a more powerful engine, a new station wagon model and standard automatic seat belts. The new model is 6½ inches longer and slightly wider, cargo volume is increased to 15.4 cubic feet from 14 and base curb weight is up by more than 200 pounds to 2734. The new 5-door wagon replaces a 5-door Liftback in the lineup and comes with 60/40 split rear seatbacks that fold flat to create 65.1 cubic feet of cargo space. A new 2.0-liter 4-cylinder with dual overhead cams and four valves per cylinder is standard in all models. The new engine has a horsepower rating of 115, 20 more than last year's single-cam 2.0. A 5-speed manual transmission is standard on the Deluxe sedan; the other models come only with a 4-speed overdrive automatic. New features include automatic shoulder belts that pivot around the front-seat occupants when the doors are closed and the ignition is turned on. The system is the same as the one used on the Cressida since 1981 and it requires that the lap belt be buckled manually. All 1987 Toyotas are covered by longer warranties: 3 years/36,000 miles on major powertrain, electronic, steering, brake and suspension components, and 5 years/unlimited mileage on body rust, with no deductibles. The new Camry sedan borrows several ideas from the archrival Honda Accord, such as split, folding rear seatbacks on the LE sedan, a roomier trunk that opens at bumper level and an optional power glass moonroof for the LE sedan and wagon (a moonroof is standard on the Accord LXi). The new 2.0-liter 16-valve engine gives the Camry livelier performance off the line and better highway passing compared to last year's 95-horsepower engine. This year's chassis benefits from standard 185/70R14 all-season tires (last year's were 13-inch without all-season tread) and more lateral rigidity so there's less body lean in turns, better road grip, more capable handling, and no loss of ride quality. The old Camry established an impressive reputation for reliability and durability, so if the new one matches that, it will be an even more formidable family compact.

Specifications

	4-door sedan	5-door wagon
Wheelbase, in.	102.4	102.4
Overall length, in.	182.1	183.1
Overall width, in.	67.3	67.3
Overall height, in.	54.1	54.5
Front track, in.	58.1	58.1
Rear track, in.	56.9	56.9
Curb weight, lbs.	2734	2855
Cargo vol., cu. ft.	15.4	65.1
Fuel capacity, gal.	15.9	15.9
Seating capacity	5	5
Front headroom, in.	37.9	37.9
Front shoulder room, in.	54.5	54.5
Front legroom, max., in.	42.9	42.9
Rear headroom, in.	36.6	36.6
Rear shoulder room, in.	54.5	54.5
Rear legroom, min., in.	33.9	33.9

Body/Chassis

Drivetrain layout: transverse front engine/front-wheel drive. **Front suspension:** MacPherson struts, coil springs, lower control arms, stabilizer bar. **Rear suspension:** independent, MacPherson struts, coil springs, parallel lower arms. **Steering:** rack and pinion, power assisted, turns lock-to-lock NA. **Turn diameter, ft.:** 34.8. **Front brakes:** 8.9-in. discs. **Rear brakes:** 8.5-in. drums. **Construction:** unit.

Powertrains	dohc I-4
Displacement, l/cu. in.	2.0/122
Compression ratio	9.3:1
Fuel delivery	PFI
Net bhp @ rpm	115 @ 5200
Net torque @ rpm	125 @ 4400
Availability	S

Final drive ratios

5-speed OD manual	3.74:1
4-speed OD automatic	3.74:1

KEY: bbl = barrel (carburetor); **bhp** = brake horsepower; **torque** = pounds/feet; **Cal.** = California only; **TBI** = throttle body (single-point) fuel injection; **PFI** = port (multi-point) fuel injection; **MFI** = mechanical fuel injection; **ohv** = overhead valve; **ohc** = overhead cam; **dohc** = double overhead cam; **I** = inline engine; **V** = V engine; **flat** = horizontally opposed engine; **D** = diesel; **T** = turbocharged; **OD** = overdrive transmission; **S** = standard; **O** = optional.

PRICES

TOYOTA CAMRY	Retail Price	Dealer Invoice	Low Price
Deluxe 4-door sedan, 5-speed	$10798	$9254	$10600
Deluxe 4-door sedan, automatic	11478	9837	11280
LE 4-door sedan, automatic	13398	11348	13200
Deluxe 5-door wagon, 5-speed	11488	9845	11290
Deluxe 5-door wagon, automatic	12168	10428	11970
LE 5-door wagon, automatic	14168	12000	13970

Destination charge varies by region. These models sell at or above retail in many locations.

STANDARD EQUIPMENT (included in above prices):

Deluxe: 2.0-liter (122-cid) DOHC 16-valve PFI 4-cylinder engine, 5-speed manual or 4-speed automatic transmission as above, power steering, power brakes, dual remote mirrors, composite halogen headlamps, wide bodyside moldings, coolant temperature gauge, tilt steering column, center console with storage bin, velour reclining front bucket seats with driver's side height adjustment, automatic shoulder belts, glovebox, ashtray and trunk/cargo area lights, full carpeting including trunk/cargo area, automatic-off headlamp feature, remote fuel filler and trunk/liftgate releases, rear defogger, tinted glass, split fold-down rear seatback (wagon), rear wiper/washer (wagon), P185/70SR14 all-season SBR tires on styled steel wheels. **LE** adds: dual power mirrors, tachometer, console armrest, multi-adjustable driver's seat, fold-down rear center armrest, cargo cover (wagon), illuminated entry with fadeout, upper windshield tint band, AM/FM ST ET with power antenna.

Prices are accurate at time of printing; subject to manufacturer's change.

OPTIONAL EQUIPMENT:

Air conditioning	795	636	755
Power moonroof, LE	660	528	625
Cruise control	205	164	195
Power windows & locks, LE	510	408	485
Aluminum wheels, LE	385	308	365
AM/FM ST ET, Deluxe sedan	330	264	315
Deluxe wagon	360	288	340
AM/FM ST ET cassette, Deluxe sedan	520	416	495
Deluxe wagon	550	440	525
LE	190	152	181
Above w/Acoustic Flavor EQ & diversity, LE	460	368	435
Digital instruments, LE	345	276	330
Cargo cover, Deluxe wagon	50	41	48
Two-tone paint, LE sedan	224	280	215
Full wheel covers, Deluxe	70	56	67
Tachometer	60	48	57
Two-tone paint & alloy wheels, Deluxe	635	508	605

Toyota Celica

Toyota Celica GT-S 2-door

A new 16-valve, dual overhead cam 2.0-liter 4-cylinder engine powers the Celica ST and GT models for 1987, while the Celica convertible returns after a year's absence, and all models are covered by longer warranties. The new convertible is offered in mid-level GT trim only. Celica was redesigned to front-wheel drive last year, debuting in 2-door and 3-door coupe styling with three trim levels: base ST, mid-level GT and top-line GT-S. The performance-

Prices are accurate at time of printing; subject to manufacturer's change.

oriented GT-S was the only Celica with a 16-valve engine last year, a 135-horsepower 2.0-liter four. The ST and GT join the multi-valve club this year, but with a new 2.0-liter four rated at 115 horsepower. The same engine is standard in the Camry and replaces a 97-horsepower, single-overhead cam 2.0. Toyota's warranties now cover major powertrain, steering, suspension and brake components for 3 years/36,000 miles, and body rust for 5 years/unlimited mileage. The new engine standard in the ST and GT closes the considerable performance gap that existed last year between those models and the high-performance GT-S. The new ST/GT engine gives these models much better acceleration, so the performance comes closer to matching the sporty looks. The GT-S remains the enthusiast's choice among Celicas with its higher-revving, more potent engine, firmer suspension and larger tires. As with most sporty coupes, the rear seat is a token gesture, unless you're using it for small children or friends who fold up easily. GT-S prices get pretty steep when you add a few options, so the GT may be more affordable for those who don't need as much performance.

Specifications

	2-door coupe	2-door conv.	3-door coupe
Wheelbase, in.	99.4	99.4	99.4
Overall length, in.	173.6	173.6	171.9
Overall width, in.	67.3	67.3	67.3
Overall height, in.	49.8	50.8	49.8
Front track, in.	57.9	57.9	57.9
Rear track, in.	56.5	56.5	56.5
Curb weight, lbs.	2455	2700	2555
Cargo vol., cu. ft.	NA	NA	25.2
Fuel capacity, gal.	15.9	15.9	15.9
Seating capacity	4	4	4
Front headroom, in.	37.8	37.8	37.8
Front shoulder room, in.	52.1	52.1	52.1
Front legroom, max., in.	44.4	44.4	44.4
Rear headroom, in.	34.0	34.0	34.0
Rear shoulder room, in.	50.9	36.6	50.9
Rear legroom, min., in.	27.9	27.9	27.9

Body/Chassis

Drivetrain layout: transverse front engine/front-wheel drive.
Front suspension: MacPherson struts, coil springs, lower control arms, stabilizer bar. **Rear suspension:** independent, MacPherson

struts, coil springs, dual lower links, stabilizer bar. **Steering:** rack and pinion, power assisted, turns lock-to-lock NA. **Turn diameter, ft.:** 35.4. **Front brakes:** 9.5-in. discs. **Rear brakes:** 8.9-in. drums (10.6-in. discs, GT-S). **Construction:** unit.

Powertrains	dohc I-4	dohc I-4
Displacement, l/cu. in.	2.0/122	2.0/122
Compression ratio	9.3:1	9.2:1
Fuel delivery	PFI	PFI
Net bhp @ rpm	115 @ 5200	135 @ 6000
Net torque @ rpm	124 @ 4400	125 @ 4800
Availability	S[1]	S[2]

1. std. ST and GT   2. std., GT-S

Final drive ratios

5-speed OD manual	3.74:1	4.18:1
4-speed OD automatic	3.53:1	3.28:1

KEY: bbl = barrel (carburetor); **bhp** =brake horsepower; **torque** = pounds/feet; **Cal.** = California only; **TBI** = throttle body (single-point) fuel injection; **PFI** = port (multipoint) fuel injection; **MFI** = mechanical fuel injection; **ohv** = overhead valve; **ohc** = overhead cam; **dohc** = double overhead cam; **I** = inline engine; **V** – V engine; **flat** = horizontally opposed engine; **D** = diesel; **T** = turbocharged; **OD** = overdrive transmission; **S** = standard; **O** = optional.

PRICES

TOYOTA CELICA	Retail Price	Dealer Invoice	Low Price
ST 2-door coupe, 5-speed	10598	9061	10400
ST 2-door coupe, automatic	11198	9571	11000
GT 2-door coupe, 5-speed	10238	10232	10040
GT 2-door coupe, automatic	12638	10742	12440
GT 3-door coupe, 5-speed	12288	10445	12090
GT 3-door coupe, automatic	12888	10955	12690
GT 2-door convertible, 5-speed	16798	14278	16600
GT 2-door convertible, automatic	17398	14788	17200
GT-S 2-door coupe, 5-speed	13978	11811	13780
GT-S 2-door coupe, automatic	14668	12394	14270
GT-S 3-door coupe, 5-speed	14328	12107	14130

Destination charge varies by region. These models sell at or above retail in many locations.

STANDARD EQUIPMENT (included in above prices):

2.0-liter (122-cid) PFI dohc 16-valve 4-cylinder engine, 5-speed manual or 4-speed automatic transmission as above, power steering, power brakes, 3-spoke urethane steering wheel, lockable glovebox, side defoggers, tinted

Prices are accurate at time of printing; subject to manufacturer's change.

glass with upper shaded band, full center console with padded cover and dual coin pockets, foot rest, rear defogger, remote trunk/hatch and fuel door releases, front stepless reclining seats with fabric upholstery, passenger side walk-in device, door ajar warning light, automatic headlights-off system, full instrumentation, digital clock, cigar lighter, AM/FM stereo ET, all-weather guard package, 165SR13 tires on alloy wheels with full-size spare. **GT** adds: cargo area carpet, split folding rear seats, upgraded seat trim, passenger visor mirror, push-type heater controls, ignition key light, cargo area lamp, AM & FM stereo ET, dual power mirrors, tilt steering wheel with memory, tonneau cover (3-door), 185/70SR13 tires. **Convertible** adds: power top, power rear windows. **GT-S** adds: 135-bhp engine, rear spoiler, mud guards, rear intermittent wiper/washer (3-door), variable intermittent wipers, 8-way adjustable sport seats with power lumbar and lateral support, leather shift knob (w/5-speed), tilt/telescope steering wheel with memory, single coin pocket, 205/60R14 Michelin tires on aluminum alloy wheels.

OPTIONAL EQUIPMENT:

Air conditioning, ST & GT	795	636	755
Automatic, GT-S	960	768	915
Power Pkg., GT exc. conv.	390	312	370
GT conv.	220	176	210
GT-S	365	292	345
Power windows, power door locks (exc. conv.), heated power mirrors.			
AM/FM ST ET cassette (NA ST or conv.) .	190	152	181
Above w/Acoustic Flavor EQ (NA ST) . .	420	336	400
Aluminum wheels, GT	360	288	340
Power sunroof (NA ST or conv.)	660	528	625
Cruise control (NA ST)	205	164	195
Leather Sport Seat Pkg., GT-S	800	640	760
Requires Power Pkg. & cruise control.			
Two-Tone Paint Pkg. (NA ST or conv.) . .	200	160	190
Digital instruments, GT exc. conv.	360	288	340
Rear wiper/washer, GT 3-door	125	102	119
Tilt & tel. steering col., GT exc. conv. . . .	70	60	67
All-Weather Tire Pkg., ST	130	104	124
Black cloth top, conv.	100	80	95

Toyota Corolla/FX16

Toyota fields three distinct models under the Corolla banner and this report covers the family-car 4-door sedans and 5-door Liftbacks built in Japan and the sporty FX16 built at the GM-Toyota plant in California on the same assembly line as the Chevrolet Nova. Corolla is nearly

Prices are accurate at time of printing; subject to manufacturer's change.

Toyota Corolla FX16

identical to Nova and changes are restricted to new electronically tuned stereos and dropping the LE Limited luxury mini-sedan. Front-drive Corollas are powered by a 74-horsepower, carbureted 1.6-liter 4-cylinder engine. The sporty FX16, also with front-wheel drive, will not appear as a Chevrolet under the operating agreement between the two auto giants. FX16 is powered by the twin cam, 16-valve 1.6-liter 4-cylinder engine also used in the rear-drive Corolla Sport GT-S and MR2, but in this front-drive application it's rated at four less horsepower (108). FX16 is available only as a 3-door hatchback in base and GT-S trim. There aren't many similarities between the family-variety Corolla and sport-oriented FX16, except that they're derived from the same front-drive platform and both have Toyota's generous warranties: 3 years/36,000 miles on major powertrain, steering, suspension, brakes and electronic components, and 5 years/unlimited miles on body rust. Since Corolla enjoys an excellent reliability record, this makes an extra-cost service contract even more extravagant than before. Corolla has only a few differences from the Chevy Nova, among them availability of a 4-speed overdrive automatic (Chevy offers a 3-speed only) and folding rear seatbacks on the LE. Corolla's drawbacks are the same as Nova's, namely uninspired performance with automatic transmission, too much engine and exhaust noise, and ordinary, family-car handling from the front-drive chassis. The virtues far outweigh the vices, however, and this is a fine choice in an economical, durable subcompact. The American-made FX16 is more fun to drive, and probably will be just as reliable.

Specifications

	3-door coupe	4-door sedan	5-door sedan
Wheelbase, in.	95.7	95.7	95.7
Overall length, in.	160.0	166.3	166.3
Overall width, in.	65.2	64.4	64.4
Overall height, in.	52.8	53.0	52.8
Front track, in.	56.5	56.1	56.1
Rear track, in.	55.7	55.3	55.3
Curb weight, lbs.	2141	2110	2141
Cargo vol., cu. ft.	30.0	12.7	26.0
Fuel capacity, gal.	13.2	13.2	13.2
Seating capacity	4	4	4
Front headroom, in.	38.3	38.3	37.8
Front shoulder room, in.	53.2	53.9	53.9
Front legroom, max., in.	42.4	42.4	42.4
Rear headroom, in.	36.9	36.9	35.6
Rear shoulder room, in.	52.2	53.7	53.7
Rear legroom, min., in.	32.0	32.0	32.0

Body/Chassis

Drivetrain layout: transverse front engine/front-wheel drive.
Front suspension: MacPherson struts, coil springs, lower control arms, stabilizer bar. **Rear suspension:** independent, MacPherson struts, coil springs, dual links, stabilizer bar. **Steering:** rack and pinion, 3.2 turns lock-to-lock. **Turn diameter, ft.:** 30.8. **Front brakes:** 9.6-in. discs.. **Rear brakes:** 7.9-in. drums (9.5-in. discs, FX16). **Construction:** unit.

Powertrains

	ohc I-4	dohc I-4
Displacement, l/cu. in.	1.6/97	1.6/97
Compression ratio	9.0:1	9.4:1
Fuel delivery	2 bbl.	PFI
Net bhp @ rpm	74 @ 5200	108 @ 6600
Net torque @ rpm	86 @ 2800	96 @ 4800
Availability	S[1]	S[2]

1. std., Corolla   2. std., FX16

Final drive ratios

5-speed OD manual	3.72:1	4.31:1
3-speed automatic	3.42:1	
4-speed OD automatic	2.82:1	

KEY: bbl = barrel (carburetor); **bhp** = brake horsepower; **torque** = pounds/feet; **Cal.** = California only; **TBI** = throttle body (single-point) fuel injection; **PFI** = port (multi-point) fuel injection; **MFI** = mechanical fuel injection; **ohv** = overhead valve; **ohc** = overhead cam; **dohc** = double overhead cam; **I** = inline engine; **V** = V engine; **flat** = horizontally opposed engine; **D** = diesel; **T** = turbocharged; **OD** = overdrive transmission; **S** = standard; **O** = optional.

PRICES

TOYOTA COROLLA

	Retail Price	Dealer Invoice	Low Price
Deluxe 4-door sedan, 5-speed	$8178	$7033	$7980
Deluxe 4-door sedan, automatic	8608	7403	8410
LE 4-door sedan, 5-speed	9278	7951	9080
LE 4-door sedan, automatic	9878	8465	9680
Deluxe 5-door sedan, automatic	9038	7773	8840
FX16 3-door sedan, 5-speed	9678	8323	9480
FX16 3-door sedan, automatic	10368	8916	10170
FX16 GT-S 3-door sedan, 5-speed	10668	9174	10470
FX16 3-door sedan, automatic	11358	9768	11160

Destination charge varies by region. These models sell at or above retail in many locations.

STANDARD EQUIPMENT (included in above prices):

1.6-liter (97-cid) 4-cylinder engine, 5-speed manual, 3-speed automatic (Deluxe) or 4-speed overdrive automatic transmission as above, power brakes, electric rear window defogger, reclining front bucket seats, tinted glass, remote trunk/hatch release, 155SR13 tires (sedan). **LE** adds: multi-adjustable driver's seat, split folding rear seatback, rear seat headrests on 5-doors, center console, AM/FM stereo radio, tilt steering column, remote control power mirrors, AM/FM ST ET. **FX16** has: DOHC 16-valve PFI engine, close-ratio 5-speed or 4-speed automatic transmission as above, power steering, four-wheel disc brakes, halogen headlamps, integrated front air dam, front sport seats, split folding rear seat, cut-pile carpeting, tachometer, 175/70HR13 Goodyear Eagle GT tires. **FX16 GT-S** adds: sports exterior package, leather-wrapped steering wheel and shift knob, digital clock, 185/60HR14 Eagle GT tires.

OPTIONAL EQUIPMENT:

Air conditioning	745	596	710
CQ Convenience Pkg., Deluxe	195	159	185
Tilt wheel, intermittent wipers, dual remote mirrors, digital clock.			
LQ Convenience Pkg., Deluxe	380	307	360
CQ pkg. plus cruise control.			
Power steering (std. FX16)	240	205	230
Power sunroof	500	400	475
Cruise control & intermittent wipers	205	164	195
Rear wiper/washer, 5-door & FX16	125	102	119
Aluminum wheels, LE	515	412	490
FX16 GT-S	370	296	350
Cloth seat trim, Deluxe	55	47	52
AM/FM ST ET, Deluxe & FX16	300	240	285
Above w/cassette, Deluxe & FX16	490	392	465
LE	190	152	180

Prices are accurate at time of printing; subject to manufacturer's change.

	Retail Price	Dealer Invoice	Low Price
Tilt steering col., Deluxe & LE	60	51	57
Power windows, locks & mirrors, LE . . .	560	448	532
Power windows & locks, FX16 GT-S	360	288	340
Two-Tone Paint Pkg., LE	300	240	285
7-way sport seat, FX16 GT-S	120	96	114
Digital clock, base FX16	55	44	52
185/60HR14 tires, base FX16	115	92	109

Toyota Cressida

Toyota Cressida 4-door

Toyota's rear-drive luxury line rolls into 1987 with a new grille, headlamps, front air dam and taillamps, a new automatic transmission, more standard features and longer warranties. The Cressida 4-door sedan is available with either a 5-speed manual transmission or the Supra's 4-speed overdrive automatic, while the slow-selling 5-door wagon comes only with the automatic. The lone engine remains a 2.8-liter double overhead cam in-line 6-cylinder. An automatic on/off control for the headlamps that uses light sensors is now standard and it includes a variable time feature for leaving the headlamps on after the engine has been shut off. Sport bucket seats, optional last year, are standard this year and leather or velour seats with "pillowed" upholstery are optional. Also available for the first time is a power driver's seat with 3-position memory. An "Acoustic Flavor" graphic equalizer is now standard

Prices are accurate at time of printing; subject to manufacturer's change.

and the stereo system has new controls. Warranty coverage on all 1987 Toyotas has been broadened to cover major powertrain, suspension, brake, steering and electronic components for 3 years/36,000 miles and body rust for 5 years/unlimited miles. The rear-drive Cressida's plus points include a powerful, smooth engine, refined road manners, plush appointments and a long list of standard features that help justify its high price tag. Cressida also has a fine durability record, making it a good alternative to more expensive European premium sedans and the Japanese Acura Legend.

Specifications

	4-door sedan	5-door wagon
Wheelbase, in.	104.5	104.5
Overall length, in.	187.8	187.8
Overall width, in.	66.5	66.5
Overall height, in.	54.1	54.1
Front track, in.	56.7	56.7
Rear track, in.	57.3	57.3
Curb weight, lbs.	3296	3240
Cargo vol., cu. ft.	13.0	70.2
Fuel capacity, gal.	18.5	18.5
Seating capacity	5	5
Front headroom, in.	38.8	38.8
Front shoulder room, in.	55.1	55.1
Front legroom, max., in.	43.7	43.7
Rear headroom, in.	37.6	37.6
Rear shoulder room, in.	54.9	54.9
Rear legroom, min., in.	35.2	35.2

Body/Chassis

Drivetrain layout: longitudinal front engine/rear-wheel drive. **Front suspension:** MacPherson struts, lower control arms, coil springs, stabilizer bar. **Rear suspension:** Sedan: independent; coil springs, stabilizer bar. Wagon: rigid axle, four links, coil springs, anti-roll bar. **Steering:** rack and pinion, power assisted, 3.3 turns lock-to-lock. **Turn diameter, ft.: .8. Front brakes:** 10.4-in. discs. **Rear brakes:** Sedan: 10.0-in. discs; Wagon: 9.0-in. drums. **Construction:** unit.

Powertrains

	dohc I-6
Displacement, l/cu. in.	2.8/168
Compression ratio	9.2:1
Fuel delivery	PFI
Net bhp @ rpm	156 @ 5200

	dohc I-6
	165 @
Net torque @ rpm	4400
Availability	S
Final drive ratios	
5-speed OD manual[1]	3.73:1
4-speed OD automatic	3.91:1

1. NA wagons

KEY: bbl = barrel (carburetor); **bhp** =brake horsepower; **torque** = pounds/feet; **Cal.** = California only; **TBI** = throttle body (single-point) fuel injection; **PFI** = port (multi-point) fuel injection; **MFI** = mechanical fuel injection; **ohv** = overhead valve; **ohc** = overhead cam; **dohc** = double overhead cam; **I** = inline engine; **V** = V engine; **flat** = horizontally opposed engine; **D** = diesel; **T** = turbocharged; **OD** = overdrive transmission; **S** = standard; **O** = optional.

PRICES

TOYOTA CRESSIDA	Retail Price	Dealer Invoice	Low Price
4-door sedan	$19350	$15867	$19150
5-door wagon	19410	15916	19210

Destination charge varies by region. These models sell at or above retail in many locations.

STANDARD EQUIPMENT (included in above prices):

2.8-liter (168-cid) 6-cylinder PFI engine, 5-speed overdrive manual or 4-speed overdrive automatic transmission (automatic on wagon), theft deterrent system, power steering, power brakes, cruise control, auto-temp air conditioning, sport seats, automatic headlamp control, rear-window defroster, AM/FM stereo radio w/power antenna and Acoustic Flavor EQ, intermittent wipers, aluminum alloy wheels, tinted glass, power door locks and windows, halogen high-beam headlamps, velour upholstery, remote control mirrors, tilt steering wheel, 195/70SR14 tires (wagon), 205/60R15 (sedans). Sedan with 5-speed has sport group package including electronically controlled suspension, limited slip differential, headlamp washers (package optional on automatic sedan).

OPTIONAL EQUIPMENT:

Power sunroof, sedans	790	632	750
Digital instruments, sedan w/automatic ..	300	240	285
Leather trim, sedans	850	680	810
Power Seat Pkg., sedans	1030	824	980
w/leather trim	1780	1424	1690
Trip computer/service reminder	240	192	230
Two-tone paint, sedans	200	160	190
Sports pkg., sedan w/automatic	470	376	445

Prices are accurate at time of printing; subject to manufacturer's change.

Toyota MR2

Toyota MR2

A new T-top model with removable glass roof panels is added this year and the base model loses some standard equipment to keep the price down on Toyota's mid-engine, 2-seat sports car. The base MR2 loses the leather wrapping on the steering wheel and shift knob, substitutes steel wheels for alloy and gets regular bucket seats instead of sport seats with more adjustments. Those features are standard on the T-top model. A transverse brace has been added between the front strut towers for greater rigidity in cornering, plus the rear shock absorbers and rear disc brakes are larger this year on the rear-drive MR2. Longer warranties this year cover major powertrain, suspension, brake, steering and electronic components for 3 years/ 36,000 miles and body rust for 5 years/unlimited miles. Toyota's mid-engine 2-seater matches or beats the similar Pontiac Fiero in most areas, including the key performance categories. MR2's manual steering is light and responsive, while Fiero's is heavy and numb. Mister Two is agile and athletic, while the heavier Fiero GT requires muscle and determination to point in the right direction. The Fiero GT's suspension delivers a rocky, jarring ride; MR2's is more absorbent. Toyota's free-revving, twin-cam 1.6 engine loses a lot of zest when it's hitched to the automatic transmission, so don't count on the same performance that comes with the 5-speed. Like the Fiero, MR2 is short on cargo space, making it less practical than the front-drive Honda Civic CRX 2-seater.

Specifications

	2-door coupe
Wheelbase, in.	91.3
Overall length, in.	155.5
Overall width, in.	65.6
Overall height, in.	48.6
Front track, in.	56.7
Rear track, in.	56.7
Curb weight, lbs.	2350
Cargo vol., cu. ft.	7.8
Fuel capacity, gal.	10.8
Seating capacity	2
Front headroom, in.	37.4
Front shoulder room, in.	53.2
Front legroom, max., in.	43.0
Rear headroom, in.	—
Rear shoulder room, in.	—
Rear legroom, min., in.	—

Body/Chassis

Drivetrain layout: transverse mid-engine/rear-wheel drive. **Front suspension:** MacPherson struts, lower control arms, coil springs, stabilizer bar. **Rear suspension:** independent; MacPherson struts, coil springs, dual links. **Steering:** rack and pinion, 3.2 turns lock-to-lock. **Turn diameter, ft.:** 31.5. **Front brakes:** 9.6-in. discs. **Rear brakes:** 9.5-in. discs. **Construction:** unit.

Powertrains

	dohc I-4
Displacement, l/cu. in.	1.6/97
Compression ratio	9.4:1
Fuel delivery	PFI
Net bhp @ rpm	112 @ 6600
Net torque @ rpm	97 @ 4800
Availability	S

Final drive ratios

5-speed OD manual	4.31:1
4-speed OD automatic	2.96:1

KEY: bbl = barrel (carburetor); **bhp** = brake horsepower; **torque** = pounds/feet; **Cal.** = California only; **TBI** = throttle body (single-point) fuel injection; **PFI** = port (multi-point) fuel injection; **MFI** = mechanical fuel injection; **ohv** = overhead valve; **ohc** = overhead cam; **dohc** = double overhead cam; **I** = inline engine; **V** = V engine; **flat** = horizontally opposed engine; **D** = diesel; **T** = turbocharged; **OD** = overdrive transmission; **S** = standard; **O** = optional.

PRICES

TOYOTA MR2	Retail Price	Dealer Invoice	Low Price
2-door coupe, 5-speed	$12548	$10603	$12350
2-door coupe, automatic	13238	11189	12040
2-door coupe w/T-bar roof, 5-speed	13738	11609	13540
2-door coupe w/T-bar roof, automatic . . .	14428	12195	14030

Destination charge varies by region. These models sell at or above retail in many locations.

STANDARD EQUIPMENT (included in above prices):

1.6-liter (97-cid) DOHC 16-valve 4-cylinder engine, close-ratio 5-speed manual or 4-speed automatic transmission, power 4-wheel disc brakes, front air dam, tinted glass with shaded windshield band, tungsten halogen headlamps with automatic off feature, remote hood and deck releases, full instrumentation, door map pockets, dual outside power door mirrors, AM/FM stereo, intermittent wipers, 185/60R14 speed-rated SBR tires. **T-bar roof models** add: Performance Interior Pkg. (sport seats, cut-pile carpet, leather-wrapped steering wheel and shift knob).

OPTIONAL EQUIPMENT:

Air conditioning	795	636	755
Moonroof w/sunshade, base	355	284	335
Power Pkg.	465	372	440
Power windows, locks and mirrors; requires Performance Interior Pkg.			
Performance Interior Pkg., base	340	272	325
Cruise control	220	176	210
Rear spoiler, w/o Aerodynamic Spoiler Pkg. .	210	168	200
Aerodynamic Spoiler Pkg.	475	380	450
Color-keyed rear spoiler, side skirts & rear mudguards, transparent rear sunshade.			
Alloy wheels	425	340	405
AM/FM ST ET cassette	250	200	240
Above w/Acoustic Flavor EQ, base	455	364	430
T-bar models	400	320	380

Toyota Supra

Turbocharging and an air-to-air intercooler available for 1987 will add 30 horsepower to Supra's 3.0-liter, 24-valve in-line 6-cylinder engine and anti-lock brakes will be offered as an option. Horsepower on the Supra Turbo jumps to 230, while torque takes an even greater jump, to 246

Prices are accurate at time of printing; subject to manufacturer's change.

Toyota Supra Turbo

pounds/feet from 185 on the normally aspirated engine. The new anti-lock braking system is optional on base and Supra Turbos. Supra was redesigned and released as a 1986½ model, so the base version is little changed for 1987. Supra Turbo gets several upgrades over the base model, including a turbo boost gauge, rear deck spoiler, an engine oil cooler, a new 5-speed manual transmission and beefed up 4-speed automatic designed to handle the greater torque, and a new ignition system with a 3-coil control unit that replaces the distributor. As with other Toyotas this year, Supra is covered by longer, more comprehensive warranties: 3 years/36,000 miles on major powertrain, suspension, brake, steering and electronic components, and 5 years/unlimited miles on body rust. The new turbocharged engine improves Supra's performance under all circumstances, with the turbo boost coming in quickly yet smoothly and providing a strong surge of power across a broad range of engine speeds.

Specifications

	3-door coupe
Wheelbase, in.	102.2
Overall length, in.	181.9
Overall width, in.	68.7
Overall height, in.	51.6
Front track, in.	58.5
Rear track, in.	58.5
Curb weight, lbs.	3450
Cargo vol., cu. ft.	12.8
Fuel capacity, gal.	18.5
Seating capacity	4
Front headroom, in.	37.5

	3-door coupe
Front shoulder room, in.	52.4
Front legroom, max., in.	43.6
Rear headroom, in.	33.9
Rear shoulder room, in.	50.4
Rear legroom, min., in.	24.7

Body/Chassis

Drivetrain layout: longitudinal front engine/rear-wheel drive. **Front suspension:** double wishbones, MacPherson struts, coil springs, stabilizer bar. **Rear suspension:** independent, double wishbones, MacPherson struts, coil springs, stabilizer bar. **Steering:** rack and pinion, power assisted, 3.0 turns lock-to-lock. **Turn diameter, ft.:** 35.4. **Front brakes:** 11.9-in. discs. **Rear brakes:** 10.1-in. discs. **Construction:** unit.

Powertrains	dohc I-6	dohc I-6T
Displacement, l/cu. in.	3.0/180	3.0/180
Compression ratio	9.2:1	8.4:1
Fuel delivery	PFI	PFI
Net bhp @ rpm	200 @ 6000	230 @ 5600
Net torque @ rpm	185 @ 4800	246 @ 4000
Availability	S	S
Final drive ratios		
5-speed OD manual	4.30:1	3.90:1
4-speed OD automatic	4.30:1	3.90:1

KEY: bbl = barrel (carburetor); **bhp** = brake horsepower; **torque** = pounds/feet; **Cal.** = California only; **TBI** = throttle body (single-point) fuel injection; **PFI** = port (multi-point) fuel injection; **MFI** = mechanical fuel injection; **ohv** = overhead valve; **ohc** = overhead cam; **dohc** = double overhead cam; **I** = inline engine; **V** = V engine; **flat** = horizontally opposed engine; **D** = diesel; **T** = turbocharged; **OD** = overdrive transmission; **S** = standard; **O** = optional.

PRICES

TOYOTA SUPRA	Retail Price	Dealer Invoice	Low Price
3-door coupe, 5-speed	$19990	$16392	$19790
3-door coupe, automatic	20680	16958	20480
3-door coupe w/Sport Roof, automatic	20990	17212	20790
Turbo 3-door coupe, 5-speed	22260	18253	22060
Turbo 3-door coupe, automatic	22950	18819	22750
Turbo 3-door coupe w/Sport Roof, 5-speed	23260	19073	23060

Destination charge varies by region. These models sell at or above retail in many locations.

Prices are accurate at time of printing; subject to manufacturer's change.

STANDARD EQUIPMENT (included in above prices):

3.0-liter (180-cid) PFI 24-valve 6-cylinder engine, 5-speed close ratio manual or 4-speed automatic transmission, variable-assist power steering, power 4-wheel disc brakes, pushbutton automatic climate control air conditioning, power windows and door locks, power remote mirrors with defogger, halogen fog lights, tungsten halogen headlights, theft deterrent system, transparent wide bodyside moldings, front and rear mud guards, full instrumentation including tachometer, voltmeter, coolant temperature and oil pressure gauges, trip odometer, variable intermittent wipers, full console with storage area and padded armrest, cloth sport seats with driver's side power lumbar and lateral support adjusters, split fold-down rear seatbacks, cut-pile carpeting including cargo area, illuminated visor mirrors, remote fuel filler door and hatch releases, automatic-off headlight system, illuminated entry system, tinted glass with upper shaded windshield band, rear defogger, cargo area cover, AM/FM stereo ET cassette with power amp, Acoustic Flavor equalizer and diversity-type power antenna, 225/50VR16 Goodyear Eagle GT "Gatorback" tires on seven-inch-wide alloy wheels, full-size spare on steel wheel. **Turbo** adds: turbocharged, intercooled engine, oil cooler, turbo boost gauge, Sports Pkg. (Electronically Modulated Suspension, limited-slip differential, headlamp washers).

OPTIONAL EQUIPMENT:

Leather Sport Seat Pkg. (power seat req.) .	950	760	905
Power driver's seat	210	168	200
Sports Pkg., base	700	560	665
Limited-slip differential, base	230	184	220
Trip computer/service reminder	290	232	275
Two-tone paint	200	160	190
Anti-lock braking system	900	720	855

Toyota Tercel

The front-drive Tercel hatchbacks have been redesigned so the new models are similar to the old ones in name only. The new 3- and 5-door Liftbacks sport more aerodynamic sheetmetal and a new 1.5-liter 4-cylinder engine with three valves per cylinder instead of two. The engine is mounted transversely instead of longitudinally, as it was in the old Tercel hatchbacks, and it uses a variable-venturi carburetor. Wheelbase on both Liftbacks is 93.7 inches and overall length is 157.3 inches, a couple of inches shorter than last year on both counts. Next spring, a 2-door coupe available in base and Deluxe trim will join

Toyota Tercel 5-door sedan

the new hatchbacks. The Tercel station wagons, available in front-drive and 4-wheel drive configurations, are carried over mechanically unchanged from last year, which means they come with the 62-horsepower 1.5-liter engine mounted longitudinally. The Tercel wagons get new flush-mounted halogen headlamps and new grilles. All Toyotas are covered by new warranties this year: 3 years/36,000 miles on major powertrain, electronic, brake, steering and suspension components, and 5 years/unlimited miles on body rust. The redesigned Tercel has a much friskier personality thanks to its new engine, which is more potent, smoother and quieter than last year's. With its skinny tires and family car suspension, the new Tercels have competent handling at moderate speeds, but are no threat to the MR2 sports car on a slalom course.

Specifications	3-door sedan	5-door sedan	5-door wagon
Wheelbase, in.	93.7	93.7	95.7
Overall length, in.	157.3	157.3	169.7
Overall width, in.	64.0	64.0	63.6
Overall height, in.	52.6	52.8	56.1
Front track, in.	54.3	54.3	54.5
Rear track, in.	54.1	54.1	53.8
Curb weight, lbs.	1970	2015	2145[1]
Cargo vol., cu. ft.	36.2	37.8	63.7
Fuel capacity, gal.	11.9	11.9	13.2
Seating capacity	5	5	5
Front headroom, in.	38.5	38.5	40.2
Front shoulder room, in.	51.6	51.6	52.8
Front legroom, max., in.	41.5	41.5	42.4
Rear headroom, in.	37.2	37.2	39.4

	3-door sedan	5-door sedan	5-door wagon
Rear shoulder room, in. ...	51.6	51.6	52.6
Rear legroom, min., in. ...	31.7	31.7	33.9

1. 2270 lbs., 4WD wagon

Body/Chassis

Drivetrain layout: longitudinal front engine/front- or 4-wheel drive on wagons; transverse front engine/front-wheel drive on sedans. **Front suspension:** MacPherson struts, coil springs, lower control arms (stabilizer bar, wagons). **Rear suspension:** independent; MacPherson struts, coil springs, twist beam axle and stabilizer bar on sedans (rigid axle, four trailing links on wagons). **Steering:** rack and pinion, turns lock-to-lock NA. **Turn diameter, ft.:** 31.2 sedans; 32.2 wagons. **Front brakes:** 8.5-in. discs. **Rear brakes:** 7.9-in. drums. **Construction:** unit.

Powertrains	ohc I-4	ohc I-4
Displacement, l/cu. in. ...	1.5/89	1.5/89
Compression ratio ...	9.3:1	9.0:1
Fuel delivery ...	1 bbl.[1]	2 bbl.
Net bhp @ rpm ...	76 @ 6000	62 @ 4800
Net torque @ rpm ...	85 @ 3800	76 @ 2800
Availability ...	S[2]	S[3]

1. Variable venturi.   2. std., sedans.   3. std., wagons.

Final drive ratios

4-speed OD manual ...	3.10:1	
5-speed OD manual ...	3.72:1	3.58:1
6-speed OD manual ...		4.10:1
3-speed automatic ...	3.53:1	3.73:1

KEY: bbl = barrel (carburetor); **bhp** = brake horsepower; **torque** = pounds/feet; **Cal.** = California only; **TBI** = throttle body (single-point) fuel injection; **PFI** = port (multi-point) fuel injection; **MFI** = mechanical fuel injection; **ohv** = overhead valve; **ohc** = overhead cam; **dohc** = double overhead cam; **I** = inline engine; **V** = V engine; **flat** = horizontally opposed engine; **D** = diesel; **T** = turbocharged; **OD** = overdrive transmission; **S** = standard; **O** = optional.

PRICES

TOYOTA TERCEL	Retail Price	Dealer Invoice	Low Price
3-door sedan, 4-speed ...	$5898	$5367	$5700
Deluxe 3-door sedan, automatic ...	7788	6698	7590
Deluxe 3-door sedan, 5-speed ...	7358	6328	7160
Deluxe 5-door sedan, automatic ...	7988	6870	7790

Prices are accurate at time of printing; subject to manufacturer's change.

Deluxe 5-door wagon, automatic	. . . . . .	8678	7540	8570
Deluxe 5-door wagon, 5-speed	. . . .	8398	7222	8200
Deluxe 4WD wagon, automatic	. . . . . .	9938	8557	9740
Deluxe 4WD wagon, 6-speed	. . . .	9588	8150	9390
SR5 4WD wagon, 6-speed	. . . .	10638	8989	10440

Destination charge varies by region. These models sell at or above retail in many locations.

STANDARD EQUIPMENT (included in above prices):

1.5-liter (89-cid) 12-valve 4-cylinder engine, 4-speed manual transmission, power brakes, composite halogen headlamps, locking fuel filler door, trip odometer, cup holder, easy-entry sliding passenger seat, vinyl upholstery, door map pockets, carpeting, fold-down rear seatback, 145/80SR13 tires on styled steel wheels. **Deluxe** adds: 5-speed manual or 3-speed automatic transmission as above, wide bodyside moldings, passenger visor mirror, rear defogger, tinted glass, 155SR13 all-season tries. **Wagon** adds: 8-valve engine, split fold-down rear seat. **SR5 4WD wagon** adds: rear wiper/washer, tachometer, digital clock, cloth sport seats, mud guards, cargo area cover and lamp, AM/FM ST ET, 175/70SR13 M&S SBR tires.

OPTIONAL EQUIPMENT:

All Weather Guard Pkg., Standard	. . . .	85	73	81
Deluxe 2WD	. . . .	55	46	52
Air conditioning (NA Standard)	. . . .	735	588	700
Power steering (NA Standard)	. . . .	240	205	230
Power sunroof, Deluxe 3-door	. . . .	350	280	335
Wagons	. . . .	480	384	455
Rear wiper/washer (std. SR5)	. . . .	125	102	119
Fabric interior, Standard	. . . .	40	34	38
Deluxe 3-door	. . . .	185	158	175
Deluxe 5-door	. . . .	135	115	128
Wagon	. . . .	65	56	62
AM&FM ST ET, sedans (NA Standard)	. . .	240	192	230
Wagons	. . . .	300	240	285
Above w/cassette, Deluxe	. . . .	490	392	465
SR5 wagon	. . . .	190	152	181
175SR13 M&S tires, Deluxe 4WD	. . . . .	190	152	181
Cargo area cover, 3-doors	. . . .	50	41	48
Aluminum wheels, SR5	. . . .	350	280	335
Two-tone paint, SR5	. . . .	200	160	190
Cruise control & int. wipers (NA Standard)	.	195	156	185
CQ Convenience Pkg., Deluxe 3-door	. . .	495	410	470
Deluxe 5-door	. . . .	395	326	375

Cloth seats and door trim, split folding rear seatbacks, analog clock, dual remote mirrors, intermittent wipers, tilt steering column, rear console, low fuel lamp.

LQ Convenience Pkg., Deluxe 3-door	. . . .	670	550	635
Deluxe 5-door	. . . .	570	466	540

CQ pkg. plus cruise control.

Prices are accurate at time of printing; subject to manufacturer's change.

	Retail Price	Dealer Invoice	Low Price
CX Convenience Pkg., Deluxe 3-door	985	802	935
Deluxe 5-door	885	718	840
CQ pkg. plus AM&FM ST ET cassette.			
LQ Convenience Pkg., Deluxe 3-door	1160	942	1102
Deluxe 5-door	1060	858	1005
LX pkg. plus AM&FM ST ET cassette.			

Volkswagen Fox

Volkswagen Fox 4-door

Fox is a front-drive subcompact based on the Brazilian Volkswagen Voyage sedan and Parati station wagon, but substantially revised for the U.S. market. Fox will go on sale early in 1987 as VW's new U.S. price leader with a base price under $6000, well below the Golf hatchbacks. The primary cost advantage for VW comes from lower labor and materials costs in Brazil, where Fox is built. Fox will come in three body styles: 2- and 4-door notchback sedans and, later this year, a 3-door wagon. All will use the 1.8-liter fuel-injected engine from the Golf/Jetta, though the engine is mounted longitudinally here instead of transversely. The only transmission initially is a 4-speed overdrive manual. A 5-speed manual is planned for 1988, but VW hasn't decided whether it will offer automatic. Fox sedans are about eight inches shorter than Jetta; they ride a 92.8-inch wheelbase, 4.5 inches shorter than Golf and Jetta. The 2-door is the base model, while the 4-door comes in GL trim, gaining a tachometer, digital clock, carpeted trunk and right outside mirror. Only three options are listed: air conditioning, stereo radio with cassette player and metallic paint. The 4-door handles better than the 2-door by virtue of its larger tires (175/70R13 vs. 155SR13), but even the base model is quite competent on the road and more enjoyable to drive than other cars in this price range.

Specifications

	2-door sedan	4-door sedan	3-door wagon
Wheelbase, in.	92.8	92.8	92.8
Overall length, in.	163.4	163.4	163.4
Overall width, in.	63.0	63.0	63.9
Overall height, in.	53.7	53.7	54.3
Front track, in.	53.1	53.1	53.1
Rear track, in.	53.9	53.9	53.9
Curb weight, lbs.	2150	2190	2190
Cargo vol., cu. ft.	9.9	9.9	33.4
Fuel capacity, gal.	12.4	12.4	12.4
Seating capacity	4	4	4
Front headroom, in.	NA	NA	NA
Front shoulder room, in.	NA	NA	NA
Front legroom, max., in.	NA	NA	NA
Rear headroom, in.	NA	NA	NA
Rear shoulder room, in.	NA	NA	NA
Rear legroom, min., in.	NA	NA	NA

Body/Chassis

Drivetrain layout: longitudinal front engine/front-wheel drive. **Front suspension:** MacPherson struts, lower control arms, coil springs, stabilizer bar. **Rear suspension:** semi-independent, torsion beam axle, trailing arms, coil springs. **Steering:** rack and pinion, 3.9 turns lock-to-lock. **Turn diameter, ft.:** 31.5. **Front brakes:** 7.6-in. discs. **Rear brakes:** 7.1-in. drums (7.7-in., wagon). **Construction:** unit.

Powertrains

	ohc I-4
Displacement, l/cu. in.	1.8/109
Compression ratio	9.0:1
Fuel delivery	PFI
Net bhp @ rpm	81 @ 5500
Net torque @ rpm	93 @ 3250
Availability	S
Final drive ratios	
4-speed OD manual	3.89:1

Prices not available at time of publication.

Volkswagen Golf/Jetta

Volkswagen GTI

Golf models move slightly upscale this year, while the twin-cam, 16-valve engine that debuted in the Scirocco 16V last summer will become standard in the sporty GTI in late February. Golfs now carry a GL designation and these models gain aerodynamic headlamps, velour cloth interior trim (instead of tweed) and new hub caps and wheel trim rings. VW is dressing up Golf models since the Brazilian-made Fox subcompact will become the company's new entry-level car. When the 123-horsepower 16-valve engine arrives for the GTI 16V, VW will then add a new Golf GT series, using the 102-horsepower engine, sport suspension and 14-inch wheels and tires off last year's GTI, but not its sport seats or rear disc brakes. The GT will be available as either a 3- or 5-door hatchback and automatic transmission will be an option. All Golf/GTI hatchbacks are made in the U.S., while the similar Jetta sedans previously were always imported from Germany. However, Volkswagen has started building 4-door Jettas at its Pennsylvania plant to increase supply of its most popular U.S. model. The main change on Jetta this fall is the addition of rear headrests to the GL 4-door. The 16-valve engine will become available about April in the Jetta GLI, the sporty sedan counterpart to the GTI hatchback. The German-made Cabriolet, based on the old Rabbit design, is a carryover model for 1987, except that the standard stereo system gains anti-theft coding that makes the radio inoperable if it's removed from the car. The same stereo system is optional on Golf, Jetta and GTI. Automatic front seat belts are listed as a no-cost option on Golfs, base Jettas and Jetta GLs to meet the federal government's mandate that 10 percent of each manufacturer's 1987 models be equipped with passive restraints. Diesel engines will be available on Golfs this year, but not Jettas. The Golf hatchbacks and Jetta sedans use the same front-drive chassis and share drivetrains and suspensions, differing only in exterior styling. There's plenty to recommend both models, including brisk performance from the spirited 1.8-liter gas engines, fine agility and good road grip from the front-drive chassis, comfortable driving position, roomy interiors and ample cargo space.

Specifications	Golf,GTI 3-door sedan	Golf 5-door sedan	Cabriolet 2-door conv.	Jetta 2-door sedan	Jetta 4-door sedan
Wheelbase, in.	97.3	97.3	94.5	97.3	97.3
Overall length, in.	158.0	158.0	159.3	171.7	171.7
Overall width, in.	65.5	65.5	64.2	65.5	65.5
Overall height, in.	55.7	55.7	55.6	55.7	55.7
Front track, in.	56.3	56.3	54.7	56.3	56.3
Rear track, in.	56.0	56.0	53.5	56.0	56.0
Curb weight, lbs.	2150	2194	2214	2275	2330
Cargo vol., cu. ft.	17.9	17.6	6.2	16.6	16.6
Fuel capacity, gal.	14.5	14.5	13.8	14.5	14.5
Seating capacity	5	5	4	5	5
Front headroom, in. ...	38.1	38.1	NA	38.1	38.1
Front shoulder room, in.	53.3	53.3	NA	53.3	53.3
Front legroom, max., in.	39.5	39.5	NA	39.5	39.5
Rear headroom, in. ...	37.5	37.5	NA	37.1	37.1
Rear shoulder room, in.	54.3	54.3	NA	53.3	53.3
Rear legroom, min., in.	.4	.4	NA	35.1	35.1

Body/Chassis

Drivetrain layout: transverse front engine/front-wheel drive.
Front suspension: MacPherson struts, lower control arms, coil

springs, stabilizer bar. **Rear suspension:** semi-independent; torsion beam axle, trailing arms, coil springs (stabilizer bar, Cabriolet, GLI and GTI). **Steering:** rack and pinion, 3.8 turns lock-to-lock. **Turn diameter, ft.: .4 (31.2 Cabriolet). Front brakes:** 9.4-in. discs. **Rear brakes:** 7.1-in. drums (9.4-in. discs, GTI & GLI). **Construction:** unit.

Powertrains	ohc I-4	ohc I-4	ohc I-4D	ohc I-4	dohc I-4
Displacement, l/cu. in. .	1.8/109	1.8/109	1.6/97	1.8/109	1.8/109
Compression ratio	8.5:1	8.5:1	23.0:1	10.0:1	10.0:1
Fuel delivery	PFI	PFI	MFI	PFI	PFI
Net bhp @ rpm	85 @ 5250	90 @ 5500	52 @ 4800	102 @ 5250	123 @ 5800
Net torque @ rpm	98 @ 3000	100 @ 3000	71 @ 2000	110 @ 3250	120 @ 4250
Availability	S	S[1]	O[2]	S[3]	S[4]

1. Cabriolet only   2. Golf only   3. GT, Jetta GLI   4. GTI

Final drive ratios

5-speed OD manual . . .	3.67:1	3.67:1	3.94:1	3.67:1	3.67:1
3-speed automatic	3.12:1	3.42:1		3.42:1	

KEY: bbl = barrel (carburetor); **bhp** =brake horsepower; **torque** = pounds/feet; **Cal.** = California only; **TBI** = throttle body (single-point) fuel injection; **PFI** = port (multipoint) fuel injection; **MFI** = mechanical fuel injection; **ohv** = overhead valve; **ohc** = overhead cam; **dohc** = double overhead cam; **I** = inline engine; **V** = V engine; **flat** = horizontally opposed engine; **D** = diesel; **T** = turbocharged; **OD** = overdrive transmission; **S** = standard; **O** = optional.

PRICES

VOLKSWAGEN GOLF, GTI & CABRIOLET

	Retail Price	Dealer Invoice	Low Price
GL 3-door sedan, diesel	NA	NA	NA
GL 3-door sedan, gas	8190	7201	7700
GL 5-door sedan, diesel	NA	NA	NA
GL 5-door sedan, gas	8400	7385	7895
GTI 3-door sedan	10325	8863	9705
Cabriolet 2-door convertible	13250	11496	12455
Destination charge	320	320	320

STANDARD EQUIPMENT (included in above prices):

GL: 1.6-liter (97-cid) 4-cylinder diesel or 1.8-liter (109-cid) PFI gas engine, 5-speed manual transmission, power brakes, front-door armrests, assist handles w/coat hooks, cut-pile carpeting, cigar lighter, clock (analog on diesels, digital on gas models), rear defogger, locking gas cap, tachometer and coolant temperature gauge, tinted glass, optical horn, halogen headlamps, lockable glovebox, illuminated luggage compartment w/carpet, dual remote mirrors, bodyside moldings, package trays, velour upholstery, fold-

Prices are accurate at time of printing; subject to manufacturer's change.

ing rear seatback, trip odometer, rear wiper/washer with intermittent feature, console, 155/80SR13 tires on diesels, 175/70SR13 on gas models. **GTI** adds: 1.8-liter (109-cid) 4-cylinder engine, 5-speed overdrive manual transmission, tuned exhaust, vented front disc brakes, sport suspension, alloy wheels, 185/60HR14 steel-belted radial tires, height-adjustable driver's seat, front air dam, black wheel opening flares, sport seats, special instrumentation, sport steering wheel. **Cabriolet** has GTI engine, transmission, and suspension, digital clock, center console, AM/FM stereo w/cassette player, integrated roll bar, padded convertible top w/boot, reclining front seats, tachometer, bright wheel trim rings, front vent windows, rear defogger, intermittent wipers.

OPTIONAL EQUIPMENT:

3-speed auto trans (NA GTI & diesels) . . .	460	415	435
Engine preheater, diesels	40	32	38
Heavy-duty cooling pkg. (NA w/A/C)	80	67	76
California emissions pkg., gas	90	90	90
Split folding rear seat	140	118	133
Clearcoat metallic paint, exc. Cabrio	150	126	143
Cabrio	160	134	152
Air conditioning, exc. Cabrio	740	622	705
Cabrio	795	668	755
Cruise control (NA diesels), exc. Cabrio . .	205	172	195
Cabrio	220	185	210
Height-adjustable driver's seat	80	67	76
Passive restraint (NA w/above)	NC	NC	NC
Power mirrors	170	143	162
Power Pkg., 3-doors	550	485	525
5-doors	650	575	620
Power windows, central locking, power mirrors.			
Stereo radio prep (antenna & speakers) . .	155	124	147
AM/FM ST ET	305	244	290
w/cassette	505	404	480
Power steering exc. Cabrio	250	210	240
Cabrio	280	235	265
Alloy wheels, Cabrio	330	264	315
Bestseller Pkg., Cabrio	630	580	600

Color-coordinated paint, top & boot, wheelhouse flares, cloth sport seats with leatherette bolsters, leatherette door panel trim, leather-wrapped steering wheel and shift knob, alloy wheels.

VOLKSWAGEN JETTA

2-door sedan	$9290	$8024	$8780
4-door sedan	9510	8214	8985
GL 4-door sedan, ...	9990	8626	9440
GLI 4-door sedan	11690	10088	11045
Destination charge	320	320	320

Prices are accurate at time of printing; subject to manufacturer's change.

STANDARD EQUIPMENT (included in above prices):

1.8-liter (109-cid) PFI 4-cylinder engine, 5-speed manual transmission, power brakes, cut-pile carpeting, front and rear armrests, cigar lighter, digital clock, rear defogger, cloth upholstery and door panel trim, locking gas cap, tachometer and coolant temperature gauge, tinted glass, lockable glovebox, halogen headlamps w/optical horn, hubcaps, left remote mirror, package trays, intermittent wipers, 175/70SR13 steel-belted radial tires. **GL** adds: full luggage compartment carpet, time-delay courtesy lights, rear headrests, dual remote mirrors, 4-spoke sport steering wheel. **GLI** adds: high-output engine, close-ratio 5-speed manual transmission, extra-wide lower bodyside moldings, sport seats w/driver's height adjustment, leather shift knob and boot, power steering, sport suspension, wheelhouse flares, 185/60HR14 steel-belted radial tires on alloy wheels.

OPTIONAL EQUIPMENT:

3-speed automatic transmission	460	410	435
California emissions pkg.	90	90	90
Clearcoat metallic paint	160	134	152
Air conditioning	795	668	755
Cruise control	220	185	210
Height-adjustable driver's seat	80	67	76
Passive restraint (NA w/above)	NC	NC	NC
Power mirrors	170	143	162
Power Pkg.	650	575	620
Power windows, central locking, power mirrors.			
Power steering, base & GL	280	235	265
Ski sack (NA base)	85	71	81
Manual sunroof	360	302	340
Stereo radio prep (speakers & antenna)	205	164	195
AM/FM ST ET cassette	595	476	565
Alloy wheels, base & GL	330	264	315

Volkswagen Scirocco

A 123-horsepower 16-valve engine that arrived in early summer breathed new life into VW's front-drive sport coupe. The Scirocco 16V and base Scirocco will be carried over practically unchanged this year. The base model, available with a 5-speed manual or 3-speed automatic transmission, is powered by a 90-horsepower 1.8-liter 4-cylinder engine. The Scirocco 16V comes only with a 5-speed

Prices are accurate at time of printing; subject to manufacturer's change.

Volkswagen Scirocco

manual. The current Scirocco has sold poorly in the U.S., partly because of VW's own doing. The Golf-based GTI offered better acceleration, better handling and more practicality at a lower price, so why buy a Scirocco? The 16-valve engine changes the Scirocco dramatically, giving it much livelier acceleration than the 90-horsepower engine could and a more sporting personality. The Scirocco 16V also benefits from a firmer suspension and 14-inch, low-profile tires that improve handling over the base model, plus disc brakes at the rear and larger discs at the front for better stopping ability. Inside, the Scirocco 16V has the same cramped cabin as the base model. The rear seat has little head room and almost no leg room, making this a 2-seater for all intents and purposes (not unusual for a sport coupe).

Specifications

	2-door coupe
Wheelbase, in.	94.5
Overall length, in.	165.7
Overall width, in.	64.0
Overall height, in.	51.4
Front track, in.	54.7
Rear track, in.	53.5
Curb weight, lbs.	2221
Cargo vol., cu. ft.	19.3
Fuel capacity, gal.	13.8
Seating capacity	4
Front headroom, in.	36.6
Front shoulder room, in.	53.5
Front legroom, max., in.	39.0

	2-door coupe
Rear headroom, in.	34.0
Rear shoulder room, in.	52.8
Rear legroom, min., in.	30.3

Body/Chassis

Drivetrain layout: transverse front engine/front-wheel drive. **Front suspension:** MacPherson struts, lower control arms, coil springs, stabilizer bar. **Rear suspension:** semi-independent; torsion beam axle, coil springs, stabilizer bar. **Steering:** rack and pinion, 3.8 turns lock-to-lock. **Turn diameter, ft.:** 31.2. **Front brakes:** 9.4-in. discs (10.1-in., 16V). **Rear brakes:** 7.1-in. drums (9.4-in. discs, 16V). **Construction:** unit.

Powertrains	ohc I-4	dohc I-4
Displacement, l/cu. in.	1.8/109	1.8/109
Compression ratio	8.5:1	10.0:1
Fuel delivery	PFI	PFI
Net bhp @ rpm	90 @ 5500	123 @ 5800
Net torque @ rpm	100 @ 3000	120 @ 4250
Availability	S	S
Final drive ratios		
5-speed OD manual	3.67:1	3.67:1
3-speed automatic	3.42:1	

KEY: bbl = barrel (carburetor); **bhp** = brake horsepower; **torque** = pounds/feet; **Cal.** = California only; **TBI** = throttle body (single-point) fuel injection; **PFI** = port (multipoint) fuel injection; **MFI** = mechanical fuel injection; **ohv** = overhead valve; **ohc** = overhead cam; **dohc** = double overhead cam; **I** = inline engine; **V** = V engine; **flat** = horizontally opposed engine; **D** = diesel; **T** = turbocharged; **OD** = overdrive transmission; **S** = standard; **O** = optional.

PRICES

VOLKSWAGEN SCIROCCO	Retail Price	Dealer Invoice	Low Price
3-door coupe	$10680	$9220	$9985
16 Valve 3-door coupe	12980	11198	12135
Destination charge	320	320	320

STANDARD EQUIPMENT (included in above prices):

1.8-liter (109-cid) PFI 4-cylinder engine, 5-speed manual transmission, power brakes, carpeting, digital clock, center console, rear defogger, tinted glass, halogen headlamps, dual electric outside heated mirrors, reclining front bucket seats w/driver's height adjustment, split fold-down rear seatbacks, 4-spoke leather sport steering wheel, tachometer, trip odometer,

Prices are accurate at time of printing; subject to manufacturer's change.

alloy wheels, 175/70HR13 steel-belted radial tires. **16 Valve** adds: DOHC engine, sport seats, power steering, rear wiper/washer, 185/60HR14 tires on alloy wheels.

OPTIONAL EQUIPMENT:

3-speed auto trans (NA 16 Valve)	460	410	435
California emissions pkg.	90	90	90
Leather upholstery, 16 Valve	650	546	620
Clearcoat metallic paint	160	134	152
Air conditioning	795	668	755
Cruise control	220	185	315
Power Pkg., base	570	479	540
16 Valve	470	395	445
Power windows and door locks, power antenna (base).			
Power steering, base	280	235	265
Rear wiper/washer, base	165	139	156
Manual sunroof	475	399	450
AM/FM ST ET cassette	410	328	390

Volvo 240

Volvo 240 GL wagon

A 5-speed manual transmission becomes standard on the 240 sedans and wagons for 1987, replacing a 4-speed manual that included an overdrive gear engaged electrically by a button on the top of the shift lever. The new transmission simply moves the overdrive top gear to the regular shift pattern; gear ratios are the same as before. A 4-speed overdrive automatic transmission is available at extra cost. The 240 continues in DL and GL trim levels, with only minor equipment changes and a longer rust warranty that extends coverage of structural components to eight years. GL models are available only with automatic transmission this year. A new feature on the wagons allows the rear seat to be removed for additional cargo space, with no tools required for removal. No diesel engines are available for the second year in a row due to lack of interest by U.S buyers. The only engine available in the 240s is the 2.3-liter gas 4-cylinder engine, rated at 114 horsepower. The On Call service instituted during 1986, giving Volvo owners 24-hour road-assistance, will be continued for 1987. Volvo's older line of sedans and wagons still offers plenty of virtues, including a functional design that provides room for up to five adults, competent handling from the rear-drive chassis, a steady, comfortable ride and good workmanship. Acceleration is adequate, but you don't get premium performance despite the premium price tags.

Specifications

	4-door sedan	5-door wagon
Wheelbase, in.	104.3	104.3
Overall length, in.	189.9	190.7
Overall width, in.	67.3	67.3
Overall height, in.	56.2	57.5
Front track, in.	56.3	56.3
Rear track, in.	53.5	53.5
Curb weight, lbs.	2957	3079
Cargo vol., cu. ft.	14.0	76.0
Fuel capacity, gal.	15.8	15.8
Seating capacity	5	5
Front headroom, in.	37.4	37.4
Front shoulder room, in.	55.3	55.3
Front legroom, max., in.	39.8	39.8
Rear headroom, in.	36.3	36.8
Rear shoulder room, in.	54.1	54.1
Rear legroom, min., in.	36.6	36.8

Body/Chassis

Drivetrain layout: longitudinal front engine/rear-wheel drive. **Front suspension:** MacPherson struts, lower control arms, coil springs, stabilizer bar. **Rear suspension:** rigid axle, four links, Panhard rod, coil springs, stabilizer bar. **Steering:** rack and pinion, power assisted, 3.5 turns lock-to-lock. **Turn diameter, ft.:** 32.2. **Front brakes:** 10.3-in. discs. **Rear brakes:** 11.0-in. discs. **Construction:** unit.

Powertrains	ohc I-4
Displacement, l/cu. in.	2.3/141
Compression ratio	9.8:1
Fuel delivery	PFI
Net bhp @ rpm	114 @ 5400
Net torque @ rpm	136 @ 2750
Availability	S
Final drive ratios	
5-speed OD manual	3.31:1
4-speed OD automatic	3.73:1

KEY: bbl = barrel (carburetor); **bhp** = brake horsepower; **torque** = pounds/feet; **Cal.** = California only; **TBI** = throttle body (single-point) fuel injection; **PFI** = port (multi-point) fuel injection; **MFI** = mechanical fuel injection; **ohv** = overhead valve; **ohc** = overhead cam; **dohc** = double overhead cam; **I** = inline engine; **V** = V engine; **flat** = horizontally opposed engine; **D** = diesel; **T** = turbocharged; **OD** = overdrive transmission; **S** = standard; **O** = optional.

PRICES

VOLVO 240 SERIES	Retail Price	Dealer Invoice	Low Price
DL 4-door sedan, 5-speed	$15400	—	—
DL 4-door sedan, automatic	15945	—	—
DL 5-door wagon, 5-speed	15890	—	—
DL 5-door wagon, automatic	16435	—	—
GL 4-door sedan, automatic	18095	—	—
GL 5-door wagon, automatic	18745	—	—
Destination charge	320	320	320

Dealer invoice and low price not available at time of publication. These models sell at or above retail in many locations.

STANDARD EQUIPMENT (included in above prices):

DL: 2.3-liter (141-cid) 4-cylinder PFI engine, transmission as above, power steering, air conditioning, rear fog lights, 4-wheel power disc brakes, clock, electric rear window defroster, tinted glass, halogen headlamps, remote control left side mirror, reclining front seats, cloth/vinyl upholstery, trip odometer, intermittent wipers, full carpeting, central door locks, 185/70R14 tires. **DL wagon** adds: rear window wiper and remote control right side mirror. **GL** adds: sliding steel sunroof (sedans), electrically heated driver's seat, power windows, tachometer, remote control right side mirror, metallic paint, velour upholstery (leather on wagon).

OPTIONAL EQUIPMENT:

Metallic paint, DL	380	320	360
Leather upholstery, GL sedan	695	580	660

Prices are accurate at time of printing; subject to manufacturer's change.

Volvo 740/760

Volvo 740 Turbo 4-door

Anti-lock brakes are now standard on 760 sedans, a driver-side air bag will become standard on all 760s and the 760 GLE gets a reworked V-6 engine with more horsepower. The 760 sedans are the first Volvos to be sold in North America with anti-lock brakes, a feature that later in the model year will become available as an option on 740 sedans. The driver-side air bag and padded knee bolsters will be standard on 760 sedans and wagons produced after Jan. 1, when prices will likely be raised to reflect the cost of the new safety equipment. The air bag will be optional on some 740 models produced after Jan. 1. Only a few diesel-powered 740s were sold last year, and none will be sold for 1987 as Volvo withdraws diesel models from the U.S. at least temporarily. The 2.8-liter V-6 engine offered only in the 760 GLE has been extensively revamped and now produces 145 horsepower, 11 more than last year. Other changes are that all 740s now have padded head restraints front and rear and all models are covered by an eight-year rust warranty on structural components (a year longer than last year). The 740s and 760s share the same design, but differ in equipment, engine availability and price. The 740s come with a 2.3-liter 4-cylinder in turbo or non-turbo form, while the 760s come with either the turbo 2.3 or the V-6. If you want a turbocharged Volvo, the 740/760 line is the only place you'll find one these days since the turbo 2.3-liter engine was withdrawn from the 240 Series at the end of 1985.

Specifications

	4-door sedan	5-door wagon
Wheelbase, in.	109.1	109.1
Overall length, in.	188.4	188.4
Overall width, in.	69.3	69.3
Overall height, in.	55.5	56.5
Front track, in.	57.9	57.5
Rear track, in.	57.5	57.5
Curb weight, lbs.	2928	3049
Cargo vol., cu. ft.	16.8	76.0
Fuel capacity, gal.	15.8	15.8
Seating capacity	5	5
Front headroom, in.	38.6	38.6
Front shoulder room, in.	55.9	55.9
Front legroom, max., in.	41.0	41.0
Rear headroom, in.	37.1	37.6
Rear shoulder room, in.	55.9	55.9
Rear legroom, min., in.	34.7	34.7

Body/Chassis

Drivetrain layout: longitudinal front engine/rear-wheel drive.
Front suspension: MacPherson struts, lower control arms, coil springs, stabilizer bar. **Rear suspension:** rigid axle, trailing arms, Panhard rod, self-leveling gas-filled shock absorbers, stabilizer bar. **Steering:** rack and pinion, 3.5 turns lock-to-lock. **Turn diameter, ft.:** 32.2. **Front brakes:** 10.2-in. discs. **Rear brakes:** 11.1-in. discs. **Construction:** unit.

Powertrains

	ohc I-4	ohc I-4T	ohc V-6
Displacement, l/cu. in.	2.3/141	2.3/141	2.8/174
Compression ratio	9.8:1	8.7:1	8.8:1
Fuel delivery	PFI	PFI	PFI
Net bhp @ rpm	114 @ 5400	160 @ 5300	145 @ 5100
Net torque @ rpm	136 @ 2750	187 @ 2900	173 @ 3750
Availability	S[1]	S[2]	S[3]

1. 740 GLE   2. 740 Turbo and 760 Turbo   3. 760 GLE

Final drive ratios

4-speed manual + OD	3.31:1	3.54:1	
4-speed OD automatic	3.91:1	3.73:1	3.73:1

KEY: bbl = barrel (carburetor); **bhp** = brake horsepower; **torque** = pounds/feet; **Cal.** = California only; **TBI** = throttle body (single-point) fuel injection; **PFI** = port (multipoint) fuel injection; **MFI** = mechanical fuel injection; **ohv** = overhead valve; **ohc** = overhead cam; **dohc** = double overhead cam; **I** = inline engine; **V** = V engine; **flat** = horizontally opposed engine; **D** = diesel; **T** = turbocharged; **OD** = overdrive transmission; **S** = standard; **O** = optional.

PRICES

VOLVO 740/760	Retail Price	Dealer Invoice	Low Price
740			
GLE 4-door sedan, 4-speed	$20155	—	—
GLE 4-door sedan, automatic	20610	—	—
GLE 5-door wagon, 4-speed	21565	—	—
GLE 5-door wagon, automatic	22020	—	—
Turbo 4-door sedan, 4-speed	22135	—	—
Turbo 4-door sedan, automatic	22590	—	—
Turbo 5-door wagon, 4-speed	22735	—	—
Turbo 5-door wagon, automatic	23190	—	—
760			
GLE 4-door sedan, automatic	27160	—	—
Turbo 4-door sedan, automatic	28060	—	—
Turbo 5-door wagon, automatic	27485	—	—
Destination charge	320	320	320

Dealer invoice and low price not available at time of publication. These models sell at or above retail in many locations.

STANDARD EQUIPMENT (included in above prices):

740 GLE: 2.3-liter (141-cid) PFI 4-cylinder, 4-speed manual with overdrive or 4-speed automatic transmission as above, power steering, power 4-wheel disc brakes, air conditioning, center armrest w/storage compartment, quartz clock, electric rear window defogger, tachometer, coolant temperature & oil pressure gauges, tinted glass, halogen headlamps, heated front seat, engine compartment and delayed courtesy lights, locking glovebox, central locking, floor mats, remote control door mirrors, AM/FM stereo cassette w/amplifier, audio package, front & rear speakers and power antenna, front velour bucket seats w/adjustable lumbar support (leather upholstery, wagon), sunroof, trip odometer, power windows, intermittent wipers, 185/70R14 steel-belted radial tires. **740 Turbo** adds: 2.3-liter (141-cid) turbocharged 4-cylinder engine w/intercooler, turbo boost gauge, velour and leather upholstery, 195/60R15 tires. **760** adds: 2.8-liter (174-cid) PFI V-6 or 2.3-liter turbocharged 4-cylinder PFI engine as above, 4-speed automatic transmission, anti-lock brakes (sedans), dual heated front seats, illuminated visor vanity mirrors, heated power door mirrors, leather upholstery.

OPTIONAL EQUIPMENT:

Anti-lock brakes, 740 GLE sedans	1400	1170	1330
740 Turbo sedans	1175	945	1115
Leather upholstery, 740 GLE sedans	810	665	770

Prices are accurate at time of printing; subject to manufacturer's change.

CONSUMER GUIDE®